DATE DUE

Further Essays in Monetary Economics

BOOKS BY HARRY G. JOHNSON

The Overloaded Economy
International Trade and Economic Growth
Money, Trade and Economic Growth
Canada in a Changing World Economy
The Canadian Quandary
The World Economy at the Crossroads
Economic Policies towards Less Developed Countries
Essays in Monetary Economics
Aspects of the Theory of Tariffs
The Two-Sector Model of General Equilibrium
Macroeconomics and Monetary Theory
Inflation and the Monetarist Controversy

Further Essays in Monetary Economics

HARRY G. JOHNSON

HARVARD UNIVERSITY PRESS

CAMBRIDGE, MASSACHUSETTS

1973

Library of Congress Catalog Card Number 72-95183

SBN 674-33525-2

Printed in the United States of America

To Liz

Contents

CONTENTS

Introduction

This book is intended as a sequel to and a complement of my *Essays in Monetary Economics* of 1967. It incorporates the bulk, intellectually if not in terms of total pages published, of my subsequent work on domestic and international monetary theory and my sustained fascination with the problems of the international monetary system. I make no apologies for either my concern with the international aspects of money, or the inclusion in this book of so much international monetary material; for I have become increasingly impressed in recent years with the conviction that the traditional division between closed-economy and open-economy monetary theory is a barrier to clear thought, and that domestic monetary phenomena for most of the countries with which most economists are concerned can only be understood in an international monetary context.

Part I begins with an extensive survey, written seven years after my last effort in this direction, of the current state and central problems of monetary theory. The second essay, in a quite different *genre*, is an exercise in the history of economic thought, focused on the Keynesian revolution and the monetarist counter-revolution, and aimed at explaining how and why revolutionary movements in monetary theory are successful. I have appended two related shorter essays dealing in greater detail with specific aspects of this problem.

The third essay contains an extensive analysis of problems of efficiency in monetary management. It is an academic expression of more informal activities in which I became engaged on my return to the United Kingdom in 1966, concerned with the question of competition in banking and with arguing for the dismantling of the direct methods of monetary and credit-market intervention developed by the Bank of England in the post-Radcliffe Report period. These activities have I hope had some influence in producing the Bank's 1971 decision to re-establish a relatively competitive system of banking and credit control, though I am still not reassured that the Bank has shaken itself free of the Radcliffe Committee's concern with liquidity control rather than control of the supply of money.[1]

The fourth essay was evoked by Pesek and Saving's provocative but I think fundamentally mistaken work on the fundamentals of monetary theory. The fifth is a short and I hope clarificatory essay on the related topic, the subject of much recent monetary theorizing, of the optimal money supply and how to attain it. Readers will, I hope, appreciate the close connection both between this essay and the preceding two, and the later essays on seigniorage and the problems of the international monetary system (later in the book, but actually earlier in time).

Part II deals with international monetary theory. It begins with an earlier piece of mine which despite its rather obscure Italian publication excited some interest from my specialist colleagues in international monetary theory, inasmuch as it extended Robert A. Mundell's earlier analysis of the effects of capital mobility on economic policy problems by assuming that international capital flows could be sensitive to movements of national income as well as to interest-rate differentials. I now think that the game of extending Keynesian international economic policy models by introducing further differentiation of the variables is both far too easy for the mathematically competent theorist and not very illuminating for the policy-makers, but considered that the essay should be made available to students interested in the development of this particular line of analysis.

There follows what is essentially a survey of the literature on the theoretical problems of the international monetary system as it stood at the time of the famous 1966 University of Chicago conference on the problems of the international monetary system, organized by Mundell with some assistance from myself.[2] Then comes an essay on the case for flexible exchange rates as it stood

[1] Harry G. Johnson, 'Harking Back to Radcliffe', *The Bankers Magazine*, Vol. CCXII, No. 1530 (September 1971), pp. 115–20.

[2] See R. A. Mundell and A. K. Swoboda, *Monetary Problems of the International Economy* (Chicago: University of Chicago Press, 1969).

early in 1969, which incorporates the main development in the theory of exchange rates that has occurred since Milton Friedman's classic argument of the case for flexible rates nearly twenty years before, the theory of optimum currency areas, developed by R. A. Mundell and R. I. McKinnon. That theory also underlies much of the analysis of the current problems of the international monetary system in Part III. To illustrate that I and other 'flexible rate men' are not as dogmatic on the subject as we are often made out to be, I append a short piece on the monetary system of Panama, a country which I am quite prepared to agree with Mundell certainly ought not to go for monetary independence.

Since the occurrence of the Chicago conference mentioned above, Mundell has been leading, and we and our students and junior colleagues at Chicago, the London School of Economics and the Graduate Institute of International Studies in Geneva, have been elaborating, an alternative to the Keynesian approach to balance-of-payments theory pioneered by Joan Robinson, A. J. Brown, Fritz Machlup and Lloyd Metzler, and synthesized in James Meade's famous volume on *The Balance of Payments*,[1] which has had a tremendous and worldwide influence, notably in familiarizing the concepts of internal and external balance. The new approach goes back beyond the seeds of the dominant contemporary theory in the work of Keynes and others immediately after the First World War to David Hume's invention of the price-specie-flow mechanism, and views the balance of payments as a monetary phenomenon governed by monetary forces and monetary policy rather than as a real phenomenon governed by real incomes and relative prices operating through spending propensities and price elasticities of demand for exports and imports. I find the new approach very congenial intellectually – in some ways it is merely the logical elaboration of an aspect of my own earlier work on balance-of-payments theory[2] that concentrates attention on the long-run monetary implications of balance-of-payments disequilibrium that I then ignored in order to

[1] J. E. Meade, *The Theory of International Economic Policy*, Vol. I, *The Balance of Payments* (London: Oxford University Press, 1951).

[2] Harry G. Johnson, 'Vers une Théorie Générale de la balance des paiements', *Cahiers de l'Institut de Science Economique Appliquée*, No. 81 (May 1959), pp. 1–12; reprinted in English in Harry G. Johnson, *International Trade and Economic Growth* (London: Allen & Unwin, 1958), Ch. VI, pp. 153–68.

concentrate on the problems of short-run international adjustment – but much remains to be done in developing it to the point of practical usefulness.

In particular, the analysis is concerned with the long run in which competition can be assumed to produce full employment of factors of production and an equilibrium relationship among commodity and factor prices in the various countries of the system; and there is a natural tendency of theorists to go for elaboration of the implications of these assumptions in the context of a growing world economy – where analysis can be greatly facilitated by use of the 'small-country assumption' that world prices and interest rates are fixed and the individual country must adjust to them. But the real practical problem – with which theorists and empirical workers have been struggling for some years in the area of domestic monetary theory – is how to marry the monetarist and the Keynesian analysis in a way relevant to the short-run context (albeit a run of several calendar years) with which the policy-makers are concerned, and which is characterized both by variations in production and employment as well as in money prices, and by variations in the relations among export, import and non-traded goods prices which are assumed away in the long-run equilibrium analysis of the monetarist approach. Chapter 9 presents only the bare monetarist bones of the new approach and does not attempt to arrive at any such synthesis; but the achievement of such a synthesis is, to my mind, the really challenging task facing international monetary theory in its next stage of development, and I hope that some readers will be stimulated to attack it.

The next chapter is a compendium of notes and short pieces of analysis only remotely related to one another. It contains a reworking of a highly original but neglected article by John C. Hause on the welfare costs of exchange rate stabilization (his original treatment neglected the existing literature on the transfer problem aspects of the income transfer involved in surpluses and deficits; mine tackles these and attempts to overcome some of the defects of the calculus in this context); an extensive note on the problem of seigniorage and its distribution in the issuance of domestic and international money, prepared for the Chicago conference referred to above, and related as mentioned to the more general issue of optimizing the money supply; a shorter related piece on efficiency in international money supply; and an analysis written with Mel Krauss on the balance-of-payments and efficiency aspects of border tax adjustments, which have been a subject of lively concern in the United States for at least a decade.

The final piece in this chapter, 'Are you Worth Your Weight In Gold?', is obviously not international monetary economics at all. I include it only because I had a great deal of intellectual fun working it out at the proper level of mock academic seriousness. I suppose its inclusion could be defended as raising indirectly the question of the adequacy of gold as a basis for the international monetary system, by pointing out that gold has been losing real purchasing power quite rapidly; but if one took it seriously, one would have not only to perform many more computations to take account of subsequent developments,[1] but also venture into the outer reaches of basic monetary philosophy at the risk of being regarded as an eccentric methodologist.

Part III, devoted to the international monetary crisis, contains a group of very recent essays, generally written at a far more popular level than those contained in the preceding two parts of the book. International monetary crises may be socially costly, but they are privately beneficial to academic experts who receive in consequence both immaterial and material rewards from a puzzled public seeking understanding, reassurance, and guidance from the Solons of the subject. I have responded, in good company or so I feel, to the popular demand for commentary on the international monetary crisis as it has evolved over recent years. But in winnowing the crops for this book, I have attempted to confine myself to those pieces that I hope have either some lasting value as interpretations, or some current interest as contributions to the understanding of problems that are still unresolved.

The first, and longest, item is an evaluation of the problems of the international monetary system as they looked during the transitory

[1] All figures on the U.S. dollar value of the gold equivalent of human capital should now be increased by 8·5 per cent; but if one allows for the interim world inflation, and assumes that it has been generally reflected in increases in money earnings, one should write down the 1965 dollar value of the gold equivalent of human capital by at least that percentage to determine whether a typical person is not worth his weight in gold.

calm of 1969, when it appeared that these problems could be solved by intelligent officials sobered by recent experience of standing on the brink of disaster. But that experience led the bureaucrats of Brussels, not into wisdom and responsibility, but into the effort to symbolize a non-existent unity and strengthen their power within the existing international monetary system by attempting to create a common European currency in rivalry to the U.S. dollar. The problems involved in this endeavour are discussed in Chapter 12. The effort turned out to be unavailing, at least for the immediate future, as reflected in the fact that the Germans were forced to let the mark float while the other members of the European economic communities could not make up their minds between the two alternatives of a common set of exchange controls and a common-currency flotation.

The basic source of the problem, as argued in Chapter 13, was a worldwide inflation emanating from the United States. The view that the recent inflation has been a worldwide – and monetary – phenomenon is to be contrasted with the view of both the OECD secretariat and many of my eminent British colleagues that recent inflation is the result of a concatenation of individual national accidents, requiring a retreat from economics into sociology (not a subject basic to any past or present course in formal economics) for its explanation. Given a world inflation, countries on a fixed exchange rate have to conform to it; their only alternative is to let their currencies' values float upwards, individually or collectively. This view is developed in Chapter 14, in the context of the stabilization problem facing an individual country in the system, a paper written for a German conference held as a sort of inquest on the May 1971 decision to float the mark.

If the peripheral countries in the system refuse to recognize the nature of the problem of inflation in a fixed exchange-rate system, and attempt to maintain their fixed rates while arguing that someone else should stop the inflation, the centre country responsible for the inflation may become exasperated enough with their ignorance and foot-dragging to take actions designed to force them to see what the problem really is. This happened in August 1971, when the United States took a package of actions designed to force the other leading countries to revalue their currencies against the dollar. The meaning and implications of this move are discussed in Chapter 15 in two sections: the first was written shortly after the action was taken, the second in January 1972 when, contrary to intervening expectations, the American initiative proved by-and-large to be successful – though, as recorded in the second part of that chapter, the international monetary system is by no means out of the woods yet. The history of that period, incidentally, testifies both to the American capacity for bold if not altogether rationally considered world leadership, and to European, and especially British, incapacity for it. Faced with an American challenge to devise a solution to the international monetary crisis under the gun of the import surcharge and deprived of the moral advantage of the crippling of American policy by dependence on the crutch of a fixed dollar price of gold, the Europeans were unable to agree among themselves and dithered and dallied away an opportunity to take decisive action of a kind that they have long regarded themselves as culturally far more qualified than the Americans to take. The British government has been particularly culpable in this respect; having led its public into voting for joining the Common Market as a means of at last achieving the influence on world affairs that the British feel themselves innately qualified to exercise, the government immediately allied itself with the French and Italian demand for an irrelevant increase in the dollar price of gold as a *quid pro quo* for solution of the real problem of revaluation of the European currencies relative to the dollar, and arranged for the pound to be revalued less than the other currently strong currencies as a means of disguising from the British public the real costs of joining the Common Market, which up till that point most observers had expected would require a devaluation of the pound. Undervaluation now avoids devaluation later; opportunism always wins over leadership in intellectually bankrupt countries, and domestic politics over international statesmanship.

I am grateful to the editors of *Encounter*, *Euromoney*, *The Journal of Money, Credit and Banking*, *The Pakistan Development Review*, *The Journal of Finance*, *Money Management*, *The Canadian Journal of Economics*, *Revista Internazionale di Scienze Economiche e Commerciali*, the *Quarterly Review* of Rowe, Rudd & Co., *The American Economic Review*; to the Oxford University Press, The University of Chicago Press, and the Institute of Economic Affairs; and to Alexander Swoboda, Robert Mundell, Richard Snape and Herbert

Giersch for permissions to reprint articles contained in this volume. In the course of my life, in response to critics of previous works of mine and my own scholarly training, I have actually written two real books; but one was financed by a foundation[1] and the other could find no official publication by the government that paid for it, let alone a commercial publisher.[2] I have therefore become used to, though still not entirely happy with, the idea that no book-length work of mine, and least of all one that contains what for me is real work and not just ideas directed at an audience intelligent enough to understand them, can be published without pre-testing on a small sample of the market. On the other hand, I challenge anyone, to the extent of offering a prize of $100 (or the equivalent in Europas if they ever get established), to prove that he subscribes personally to and has in his library all the publications in which the contents of this book were first published.

This book is dedicated to my wife. Most authors hedge themselves against familial problems by dedicating their books in succession to the members of their family most likely to disappear from their consciousness, either by natural biological processes or by equally natural irritation with the long-sustained and relatively costly process of building an academic career out of a limited input of original resources and an unlimited input of scarce labour-time. In such a list of parties injured by the choice of an academic career the wife is likely to stand second, if not first, to the parents, and well ahead of the innocent children and the understanding academic friends. I am grateful to Liz for having the confidence in me and in herself to know that she could afford to wait it out, and to let others enjoy the tributes for the work she has enabled me to do.

[1] Harry G. Johnson, *Economic Policies Towards Less Developed Countries* (Washington, D.C.: The Brookings Institution, 1967; London: Allen & Unwin, 1968).
[2] Harry G. Johnson and J. W. L. Winder, *Lags in the Effects of Monetary Policy in Canada* (Ottawa, Royal Commission on Banking and Finance: The Queen's Printer, 1964, long out of mimeograph).

18

Part 1

GENERAL MONETARY THEORY

Chapter 1

Recent Developments in Monetary Theory— a Commentary*

I. INTRODUCTION

The Radcliffe Committee initiated its investigations into the working of the British monetary system at a time when the intellectual environment could be characterized as the high tide of Keynesian scepticism about the importance of monetary policy and the relevance of monetary theory. By the time its Report was published, however, that tide had begun markedly to ebb, a fact which accounts for the unexpectedly harsh reception the Report received even from what might have been expected to be intellectually sympathetic quarters. In the ensuing ten years, the tide has set markedly in the opposite direction, towards emphasis on the importance of monetary policy and concern with the theory of money (as distinct from the theory of income and employment), to the point where contemporary controversy centres on the so-called 'rise of monetarism'.

The purpose of this chapter is to survey developments in monetary theory since the Radcliffe Report, with particular emphasis on developments subsequent to two previous surveys of mine, written in 1961–62 and 1963.[1] The first of those surveys, designed to provide a comprehensive overview of the field for graduate students and non-specialist professional economists, organized the material presented within the broad analytical framework of demand for and supply of money. The second, an essay in personal interpretation unrestricted

* Reprinted from David R. Croome and Harry G. Johnson (eds), *Money in Britain, 1959–1969* (Oxford: Oxford University Press, 1970), Ch. III pp. 83–114.
[1] Harry G. Johnson, 'Monetary Theory and Policy', *The American Economic Review*, Vol. LII, No. 3 (June 1962), pp. 335–84, and 'Recent Developments in Monetary Theory', *The Indian Economic Review*, Vol. VI, No. 4 (August 1963), pp. 1–28; reprinted in H. G. Johnson, *Essays in Monetary Economics* (London: Allen & Unwin, 1969), Ch. I and II.

21

by the obligation of representation by population, took as its organizational focus six problems originating in Keynes's *General Theory*, and emphasized the two themes of the application of capital theory to monetary theory and the trend towards dynamic analysis.

For the purposes of this chapter, the type of approach of the second survey referred to seems the more suitable. Accordingly, I will discuss recent developments under a series of topical headings chosen to represent themes considered to be of general interest to monetary economists. However, in comparison with the 1963 survey, emphasis is placed rather less on unifying strands of thought and rather more on current controversy. Also, certain themes are treated in exceptional detail, in view of their presumed interest to British readers – particularly the first two, the revival of monetarism and the rehabilitation of Keynes. The remaining topics are the fundamentals of monetary theory, the problems associated with financial intermediation, money in growth models, and the theory of inflation and economic policy.

II. THE REVIVAL OF THE QUANTITY THEORY AND THE RISE OF 'MONETARISM'

As already remarked, the dominant feature of the post-Radcliffe era, in the American if not quite yet the British literature, has been the revival of the quantity theory of money and the rise of the associated 'monetarist' approach to economic policy – an approach which stresses the explanatory and controlling power of changes in the quantity of money, in contrast to the Keynesian emphasis on fiscal policy, and as regards monetary policy on credit and interest-rate policies. It may be useful, though it risks the accusation of putting an unwarranted motivational construction on a process of scientific development, to trace the stages in the intellectual revival of the quantity theory, which has been almost exclusively the work of Milton Friedman.

The Keynesian revolution left the quantity theory thoroughly discredited, on the grounds either that it was a mere tautology (the quantity equation), or that it 'assumed full employment' and that the velocity factor it emphasized was in fact highly unstable. The revival of a quantity theory that could claim to rival the Keynesian theory required a restatement of it that would free it from these objections and give it an empirical content. Such a restatement was provided by Milton Friedman's classic article,[1] which redefined the quantity theory as a theory of the demand for money (or velocity) and not a theory of prices or output, and made the essence of the theory the existence of a stable functional relation between the quantity of real balances demanded and a limited number of independent variables, a relation deduced from capital theory. This version of the quantity theory, Friedman asserted, had been handed down through the 'oral tradition' of the University of Chicago. In fact, as Don Patinkin has recently shown conclusively,[2] it is to be found neither in the written tradition of Chicago – which on the contrary stressed the quantity equation and the cumulative instability of velocity – nor in the oral tradition of Chicago as Patinkin himself experienced it: 'What Friedman has actually presented is an elegant exposition of the modern portfolio approach to the demand for money which . . . can only be seen as a continuation of the Keynesian theory of liquidity preference' (p. 47). In recent writings, Friedman has ceased to refer to the Chicago oral tradition, and has admitted that his reformulation of the quantity theory was 'much influenced by the Keynesian liquidity analysis'.[3]

Redefinition of the quantity theory as hypothesizing a stable demand function for money not only gave it an empirical content subject to testing,[4] but facilitated the interpretation by researchers

[1] Milton Friedman, 'The Quantity Theory of Money: A Restatement', in Milton Friedman (ed.), *Studies in the Quantity Theory of Money* (Chicago: The University of Chicago Press, 1956); reprinted in Milton Friedman, *The Optimum Quantity of Money* (Chicago: Aldine Publishing Co., 1969).

[2] Don Patinkin, 'The Chicago Tradition, the Quantity Theory, and Friedman', *Journal of Money, Credit and Banking*, Vol. I, No. 1 (February 1969), pp. 46–70.

[3] M. Friedman, *The Optimum Quantity of Money*, p. 73. (My personal hypothesis is that, as a result of his studies of the Marshallian demand curve and his year as a visitor in Cambridge, Friedman became enamoured of the 'Cambridge oral tradition' as a concept permitting the attribution to an institution of a wisdom exceeding that displayed in its published work, and unconsciously stole a leaf from Cambridge's book for the benefit of his own institution.)

[4] For a review of the relevant empirical studies, see David Laidler, *The Demand for Money* (London: The International Textbook Co., 1969); and Laurence Harris, 'Regularities and Irregularities in Monetary Economics', in C. R. Whittlesey and J. S. G. Wilson (eds), *Essays in Money and Banking in Honour of R. S. Sayers* (Oxford: The Clarendon Press, 1968), Ch. 5, pp. 85–112.

of good statistical results as evidence in favour of the quantity theory and against the rival 'income–expenditure' theory (the Chicago term for the prevalent version of Keynesian economics). The next stage was to devise a set of tests of the rival theories against one another; this was the subject of the Friedman–Meiselman study for the Commission on Money and Credit of 'The Relative Stability of Monetary Velocity and the Investment Multiplier in the United States, 1898–1958'.[1]

The tests in question rested on some fundamental – and debatable – methodological principles; and the failure of the critics to understand these principles, as well as to appreciate the depth of the intellectual effort put into the tests, made their criticisms and attempted refutations less powerful and persuasive than they might have been. The crucial principle is that the test of good theory is its ability to predict something large from something small, by means of a simple and stable theoretical relationship; hence the essence of the quantity theory was specified to be the velocity function relating income to money, and the essence of the income–expenditure theory was specified to be the multiplier relationship relating income to autonomous expenditure (for the purposes of the tests, these relationships were redefined in terms of consumption rather than income, to avoid pseudo-correlation). This principle is in sharp contrast to the more common view that the purpose of theory in this context is to lay out the full structure of a general-equilibrium model in the detail necessary to produce an adequately good statistical 'fit'. A second principle is that behavioural relationships should be invariant to institutional and historical change; hence the Friedman–Meiselman emphasis on a long run of data. A third principle, whose practical application has given rise to legitimate criticism, is that since Keynesian theory does not specify exactly what is to be treated as 'autonomous' and what as 'induced' in an economy with governmental and foreign trade sectors, the classification must be effected by statistical tests of independence and interdependence.

According to the Friedman–Meiselman tests, the quantity theory consistently out-performed the Keynesian theory, with the exception of the 1930s sub-period. A conscientious, or nonchalant, Keynesian

[1] 'Commission on Money and Credit', *Stabilization Policies* (New Jersey: Prentice-Hall, 1963), pp. 165–268.

might well have interpreted these results as confirming the master's insight, insofar as the tests could be considered relevant at all. Instead a number were provoked into attempting to disprove the findings; and, as mentioned, their efforts were generally vitiated in their impact by violation of one or another of the rules of the game as laid down by Friedman and Meiselman.[1]

As restated by Friedman, the quantity theory still laboured under the handicap of two potentially powerful criticisms. The first was the long-standing traditional criticism of the quantity theory, that the theory is irrelevant because the quantity of money supplied responds passively to the demand for it – the 'Banking School' position which remains strong in popular thinking on monetary policy. This criticism was quelled by the publication of the long-awaited, monumental volume by Friedman and Schwartz on the monetary history of the United States,[2] and the companion volume by Cagan on the supply of money in the United States.[3] These works demonstrated both the independent determination of the supply of money, and the significant influence of monetary changes on U.S. economic history. The second criticism stemmed from the strongly-held belief that the great depression of 1929 and after was the consequence of the collapse of the willingness to invest and proved conclusively the inability of monetary policy to remedy mass unemployment. The Friedman–Schwartz volume demonstrated as conclusively as possible the causal role played by rapid and substantial monetary contraction in

[1] Donald D. Hester, 'Keynes and the Quantity Theory: A comment on the Friedman–Meiselman CMC Paper', and M. Friedman and D. Meiselman, 'Reply to Donald Hester', *Review of Economics and Statistics*, Vol. 46, No. 4 (November 1964), pp. 364–8 and 369–76; Albert Ando and Franco Modigliani, 'Velocity and the Investment Multiplier', Michael de Prano and Thomas Mayer, 'Autonomous Expenditure and Money', Milton Friedman and David Meiselman 'Reply', and 'Rejoinders', *The American Economic Review*, Vol. LV, No. 4 (September 1965), pp. 693–728, 729–52, 753–85, 786–90, 791–2. For a commentary on the issues, see Stephanie K. Edge, 'The Relative Stability of Monetary Velocity and the Investment Multiplier', *Australian Economic Papers*, Vol. 6, No. 9 (December 1967), pp. 192–207.

[2] Milton Friedman and Anna J. Schwartz, *A Monetary History of the United States, 1867–1960* (Princeton, N.J.: Princeton University Press for the National Bureau of Economic Research, 1963).

[3] Phillip C. Cagan, *Determinants and Effects of Changes in the Stock of Money, 1867–1960* (New York: Columbia University Press for the National Bureau of Economic Research, 1965).

the depression of the 1930s, and thus paved the way for a dismissal of the Keynesian analysis as based on a misinterpretation of the facts of experience.[1] There remains, however, acute controversy over the interpretation of the emergence of large holdings of excess reserves by the American banking system in the latter part of the 1930s.

While, as already mentioned, Friedman's restatement of the quantity theory of money should probably be interpreted as an appropriation of portfolio-balance analysis on Keynesian lines for use against those Keynesians who have neglected the monetary side of Keynes's theory in favour of the income–expenditure side, there is one important difference between the Friedman (quantity-theory) approach and the Keynesian approach to that analysis which is of considerable importance both theoretically and practically. This difference is that the restated quantity theory introduces explicitly, and emphasizes, expected changes in the price level as an element in the cost of holding money and other assets fixed as to both capital value and yield in money terms, whereas Keynesian portfolio-balance theory almost invariably starts from the assumption of an actual or expected stable price level (though this asumption may subsequently be modified).[2] The assumption in question has the great theoretical advantage of endowing money with an absolutely certain yield of zero per cent, and hence making it a fixed point of reference for portfolio choices; but this advantage is bought at the cost of giving money in the portfolio attributes of safety which in general it does not possess. Moreover, from the standpoint of application of monetary theory to the interpretation of actual events and policies, the assumption is likely to be consistently misleading, because it encourages practitioners of the approach to interpret changes in market interest rates on monetary assets as indicators of changes in monetary ease or tightness, without proper allowance for the effects on the relation between money and real rates of interest of changes in expected rates of inflation or deflation.

This difference is in an important sense the essence of the differentiation between the 'monetarist' and the alternative 'Keynesian'

[1] See Milton Friedman, 'The Monetary Theory and Policy of Henry Simons', *The Journal of Law and Economics*, Vol. 10 (October 1967), pp. 1–13; reprinted in M. Friedman, *The Optimum Quantity of Money*, Ch. 4, pp. 81–93.

[2] See, for example, James Tobin, 'Money and Economic Growth', *Econometrica*, Vol. 33, No. 4 (October 1965), pp. 671–84.

approach to problems of economic policy. The monetarist approach stresses the unreliability of money interest rate changes as economic indicators, owing to the influence on them of price expectations, and concentrates instead on changes in the money supply as a variable over which the monetary authority has control and whose meaning is theoretically clear. In addition, and more fundamentally, the monetarist approach rests on the assumption that velocity rather than the multiplier is the key relationship in the understanding of macro-economic developments in the economy. This was the point of the Friedman–Meiselman test already discussed. Subsequently, the focus of the controversy has shifted from autonomous expenditure versus money supply to fiscal policy versus monetary policy as the subject of empirical testing. In this connection, tests performed at the Federal Reserve Bank of St Louis at the initiative of the Bank's staff have been advanced in support of the monetarist as against the Keynesian approach; but these tests too have been the subject of considerable criticism.[1]

As mentioned above, Friedman's restatement of the quantity theory obtained the immediate tactical advantage of freeing it from the Keynesian criticism of assuming an automatic tendency towards full employment in the economy, by making it a theory of the demand for money without commitment to the analysis of prices and employment. This advantage, however, has proved something of an embarrassment subsequently, given the success of the quantity-theory counter-attack on Keynesianism and the rise of the monetarist approach to economic policy, since it apparently leaves the quantity theorist with nothing to say about the relative impact of short-run variations in the money supply, and hence in aggregate demand, on money prices on the one hand and physical output on the other. (It may be noted that a similar problem arises for the Keynesian theory, under conditions of near full employment, which the Phillips curve analysis seeks to resolve but which it resolves rather unsatisfactorily – see below.) The obvious answer to this problem, in neo-quantity terms, lies in an application of expectations theory to the determina-

---

[1] Leonall C. Andersen and Jerry L. Jordan, 'Monetary and Fiscal Actions: A Test of Their Relative Importance in Economic Stabilization', *Federal Reserve Bank of St. Louis Review*, Vol. 50, No. 11 (November 1968), pp. 11–23; further discussion may be found in the April 1969 and August 1969 issues of the *Review*.

tion of the division of an increase in monetary demand between changes in money wages and prices and changes in employment and output; but thus far no satisfactory theory along these lines has been produced.[1]

In concluding this section, a brief reference should be made to recent extensions of the monetarist approach to problems of balance-of-payments analysis and policy. As regards individual countries, prevailing theory emphasizes the balance of aggregate demand and aggregate supply capacity on the one hand, and the relation between domestic and foreign price levels on the other, as the key determinants of the balance of payments. A monetarist approach, on the other hand, as reflected in the new IMF-inspired emphasis of British economic policy on 'Domestic Credit Expansion', emphasizes the relation between the growth of domestic demand for money and the growth of supply intended by the monetary authority as the key determinant of international reserve gains or losses. As regards the international monetary system as a whole, the monetarist approach emphasizes the relation between the growth of total desired reserves and the growth of overall reserve supplies as determining the need for some countries to have deficits, and the relation between national growth of desired money balances and national expansion of domestic credit as determining which countries will have the necessary deficits.[2]

III. THE REHABILITATION OF KEYNES

The quantity-theory counter-revolution discussed in section II has been directed against the so-called 'income–expenditure' school, by which is meant those economists in the Keynesian tradition who have concentrated their analysis and policy prescriptions on the income–expenditure side of the Keynesian general-equilibrium apparatus. (This focus has been the dominant impact of the Keynesian revolution on governmental and other practical thinking on economic fore-

---

[1] The issue is discussed in Milton Friedman, 'A Theoretical Framework for Monetary Analysis', *Journal of Political Economy*, Vol. 78, No. 2 (March/April 1970), pp. 193–238.

[2] For an example of the monetary approach to balance-of-payments theory, see R. A. Mundell, 'Real Gold, Dollars and Paper Gold', *The American Economic Review, Papers and Proceedings*, Vol. 59, No. 2 (May 1969), pp. 324–31.

casting and policy-making.) There is, it should be remarked, nothing to prevent the absorption of the empirical evidence of a stable demand function for money into the corpus of the Keynesian general-equilibrium model – a stable demand function for money is in fact implicit in the liquidity-preference component of the standard Hicksian *IS–LM* diagram – other than the conditioned Keynesian reflex against the 'quantity-theory' label and the conditioned Keynesian belief that 'money does not matter' (or, at least, 'does not matter much').

'Keynesian economics' came very rapidly to be epitomized by the *IS–LM* diagram of the textbooks, in terms of which Keynesian underemployment equilibrium depends either on the rigidity of money wages or on the special case of the 'liquidity trap' (a perfectly interest-elastic liquidity-preference function) keeping the rate of interest above that consistent with full-employment equilibrium between saving and investment; and this special case was disposed of by the critics through the introduction of the 'Pigou effect' of a falling price level on the real value of money balances and hence on real wealth and consumption. As a result, Keynes has become 'the greatest economist of modern times' (an obituary remark indicating that his contribution was so indisputable as to require no explanation) and the *General Theory* has been shelved as a 'classic' (meaning an acknowledged great book that no one reads, for fear of discovering that the author was himself not clear about the message his disciples derived from his work). Put differently, Keynes has been assigned to the shadow regions, as one who had a tremendous influence on popular (i.e. undergraduate-level) economic theory and on the thinking of the makers of public policy, but whose theoretical contribution considered at the highest scientific level was shamefully amateurish, if not downright clownish, and is best passed over with a curt but fulsome general acknowledgement.

The position thus assigned to Keynes in contemporary economic folklore has been challenged in a recently-published, monumentally scholarly work of exegesis and interpretation of the *General Theory* by Axel Leijonhufvud.[1] Leijonhufvud distinguishes sharply between

---

[1] Axel Leijonhufvud, *On Keynesian Economics and the Economics of Keynes* (London: Oxford University Press, 1968); see also his *Keynes and the Classics* (London: The Institute of Economic Affairs, Occasional Paper 30, 1969).

'Keynesian economics' – essentially the *IS–LM* analysis summarized above – and 'the economics of Keynes', as represented by the *General Theory* and the *Treatise on Money*, on which the *General Theory* built to a greater extent than Keynes's followers have appreciated; and he seeks to show that the latter economics is both quite different from, and far more subtle and profound than, the former. In this endeavour he draws heavily on some very recent work unfamiliar to most monetary economists, notably R. W. Clower's attack on the extension of the Walrasian general-equilibrium apparatus to a monetary economy by Patinkin and others (to be discussed subsequently), and the work of Alchian and others on the economic theory of market information and search; and the structure of his argument rests importantly on one proposition that readers who think they have understood Keynes may have difficulty in accepting as essential to Keynes's thought, namely the assertion of a 'second psychological law of consumption', according to which a fall in the rate of interest increases consumption by increasing the 'perceived wealth' of the community (described as Keynes's 'windfall effect').

Leijonhufvud's re-interpretation of Keynes's economics, and differentiation of it from 'Keynesian economics', can be briefly but crudely summarized in the following propositions. First, what Keynes was challenging, and what he found most difficult to escape from, was the concentration of received economic theory on a dynamic adjustment process in which prices moved instantaneously to equilibrate markets. His dynamic adjustment process focused on quantity adjustments; and quantity adjustments by producers give rise to destabilizing feedback processes, epitomized in the multiplier analysis. If Walras's Law held in reality, any excess supply of one commodity (or labour or money) would imply an excess demand for others, and produce an adjustment process consistent with full employment. But in a monetary economy, Walras's Law refers to potential and not to 'effective' demands, because goods and labour are exchanged proximately for money and only ultimately for labour and goods; there is an 'income-constrained process' by which an excess supply of labour ('involuntary unemployment') appears not as an excess demand for goods signalling to producers the need to increase output and demand for labour, but as an equilibrium position in which the excess demands of the unemployed either proximately for money or ultimately for goods are not 'effective' and hence do not work to restore full-employment equilibrium.

Second, the core of Keynes's analysis is 'liquidity preference', the unwillingness of asset holders to allow an equilibrating fall in the rate of interest, motivated by inelastic expectations about future rates of interest based on past experience. The cause of underemployment equilibrium is neither interest inelasticity of investment demand – because Keynes aggregated bonds and real assets, and a fall in the rate of interest means a rise in the demand price for real capital – nor interest inelasticity of saving – because while Keynes discounted the pure intertemporal substitution effect of interest-rate changes, he attached (or so Leijonhufvud asserts) considerable importance to the 'windfall effect' described above – but the prevention by liquidity preference of the equilibrating fall in interest rates necessary to counteract a decline in the inducement to invest. For economic policy it follows that, for an economy in the neighbourhood of full-employment equilibrium, stabilization policy should rely primarily on monetary policy, to keep market rates of interest in line with the 'natural rate'. But for an economy in deep depression, interest rates may well be low enough for consistency with full-employment equilibrium, and the problem may instead be depression of entrepreneurial expectations requiring fiscal policy of a pump-priming nature to restore a full-employment level of activity. For a near-full-employment economy, however, Leijonhufvud reasons that the logic of the 'income-constrained process' implies that fiscal policy will not be a powerful tool, because, short of a general liquidity crisis, the public will be able to maintain its normal consumption levels by drawing on its financial assets.[1] Leijonhufvud, incidentally, argues that Keynes in fact recognized the real balance effect of a reduction in wages and prices, but attached predominant importance to the interest-rate effect precisely because he believed that both investment and saving were highly sensitive to the influence of lower interest rates in raising the values of real assets.

Leijonhufvud's rehabilitation of Keynes is virtually certain to be widely acclaimed by economists of most persuasions, not merely on the scientific account of its scholarly grasp and range, but also for the

---

[1] Leijonhufvud, *Keynes and the Classics*, pp. 40–5.

broadly political reason that it writes 'Keynesian economics' as it has been developed by mathematical economists, primarily in America, out of the 'true' Keynesian tradition, and that it does so by the application of concepts and approaches either developed by or congenial to contemporary quantity theorists – especially, the application of the 'human capital' approach to labour and wage determination and of expectations theory to the determination of wages and interest rates. Hence it provides common ground of an intellectually appealing kind on which both 'old-line' Keynesian revolutionaries (such as Joan Robinson) and neoquantity-theory counter-revolutionaries (such as Milton Friedman) can unite in condemnation of their common enemy, the dominant school of orthodox macro-economic theory based on the *IS–LM* model. From the point of view of scientific progress in the understanding of macro-economics and monetary theory, Leijonhufvud's work provides an extremely useful assemblage and conspectus of emerging concepts and approaches on which further theoretical work is required, and also clears the air of a number of prevailing myths about the true nature of the Keynesian revolution. In a very broad sense, his work carries forwards the process of transformation of monetary theory by the application of capital-theory concepts and the analysis of dynamic processes discussed in my 1963 survey.

IV. FUNDAMENTAL ISSUES IN MONETARY THEORY

As recorded in my 1962 survey, one of the major contributions to the development of monetary theory consequent on the Keynesian revolution was Patinkin's integration of monetary and value theory within the framework of Hicksian general-equilibrium analysis.[1] That integration rested on the conception of money as 'outside money' – an asset of the community matched by no corresponding debt of the community to a monetary institution – and the mechanics of the analysis depended heavily on the real-balance (real-wealth) effect of a change in the money price level. Subsequently, Gurley and Shaw developed an alternative 'inside-money' model, in which the mechanics of the analysis rested instead on the substitution effect of a

[1] H. G. Johnson, *Essays in Monetary Economics*, pp. 17–21.

change in the ratio of privately-held money to privately-held assets of other kinds. The 'neutrality of money' issue on which the Patinkin–Gurley and Shaw controversy focused need not detain us here, since the essential rules of the game are clear enough in retrospect. What is more relevant from the contemporary perspective is the distinction introduced by the debate between 'inside' and 'outside' money, and the ensuing proclivity of monetary theorists to distinguish between models built on the two alternative assumptions about the institutional nature of money, one involving both a wealth and a substitution effect and the other involving only a substitution effect.

The validity of the distinction between 'inside' and 'outside' money has been successfully challenged in a recent book by Boris Pesek and Thomas Saving,[1] distinguished on the one hand by its insight into relevant questions and on the other by analytical confusions into which it stumbles. Put very briefly, Pesek and Saving have shown that, for purposes of model-building, the relevant distinction is not between 'inside' and 'outside' money, but between money bearing a zero rate of interest (or more generally money bearing a rate of interest fixed in nominal terms, of which zero interest is a special case), and money bearing an interest rate competitive with rates of return on other available assets. In the former case the services of money, being 'monopolized' in a sense, have a scarcity value for the community and hence a wealth value for the community as a whole; in the latter case the services of money become a free good and hence have no wealth value, though the fact that they are a free good maximizes community welfare. Unfortunately Pesek and Saving fail to understand the distinction between a zero alternative opportunity cost of money services to money holders, and a zero purchasing power of money itself in terms of goods and services: the former involves the payment of competitive interest on real balances, the latter will result from the absence of any restriction on the freedom of the banking system to expand its issue of (assumedly costless) paper credit.[2] Hence the initial insight, which has important implica-

[1] Boris P. Pesek and Thomas R. Saving, *Money, Wealth, and Economic Theory* (New York: Macmillan, 1967).

[2] On these issues see my 'Inside Money, Outside Money, Income, Wealth, and Welfare in Monetary Theory', *Journal of Money, Credit and Banking*, Vol. I, No. 1 (February 1969), pp. 30–45; also my 'Comment', *op. cit.*, No. 3 (August 1969), pp. 535–7. Reprinted as Ch. 4 and Appendix below.

tions for the efficiency of monetary arrangements and for various monetary-theoretic problems such as optimal monetary growth (see below), is vitiated by illogical analysis and absurd conclusions.

The main purpose of the Pesek and Saving analysis, however, was to establish an *a priori* theoretical definition of what should and what should not be counted in practice as part of the money stock for purposes of monetary analysis, and in particular to establish the medium-of-exchange function as decisive (i.e. to validate the conventional definition of money as currency in circulation plus deposits subject to cheque). A parallel attempt has been made by Newlyn,[1] and subsequently by Yeager,[2] to arrive at an *a priori* definition of money in terms of 'neutrality', by which is meant that the use of the monetary item can affect aggregate expenditure on goods and services without affecting the market for loans, rather than in terms of non-interest-bearingness. Friedman and Schwartz[3] have recenty shown that both efforts rest on special sets of assumptions – about the banking system in the former case and about the nature of relevant monetary transactions in the latter – and that properly interpreted both lead back to the identification of money with the cash base provided by the central bank. The definition of money for purposes of empirical application of monetary theory therefore remains an empirical question.

Patinkin's integration of monetary and value theory rested on a particular way of incorporating money into the general-equilibrium framework, namely through the attribution of 'utility' to the services provided by real money balances. As has long been recognized, money can be incorporated into a general-equilibrium system in an alternative way, as part of the budget restraint that conditions the maximization of utility from the consumption of real goods and services. This alternative approach is represented by the inventory-theoretic analysis of transactions demand for cash developed by Baumol and Tobin. It has significant implications for the national

[1] W. T. Newlyn, 'Definitions and Classifications', *Theory of Money* (Oxford: The Clarendon Press, 1962), Ch. 1, pp. 1–11.

[2] Leland B. Yeager, 'Essential Properties of the Medium of Exchange', *Kyklos*, Vol. XXI (1968), Fasc. 1, pp. 45–69.

[3] Milton Friedman and Anna J. Schwartz, 'The Definition of Money: Net Wealth and Neutrality as Criteria', *Journal of Money, Credit and Banking*, Vol. I, No. 1 (February 1969), pp. 1–14.

income accounting aspects of monetary theory,[1] important in some theoretical contexts (see below on money in growth models). Though the concept of money as a producers' good (as well as a consumer's good), which incorporates the essence of the inventory approach, has long been a part of the neo-quantity-theory conceptual approach to monetary theory,[2] the lines of battle between contemporary quantity theorists and Keynesians have gradually been drawing up on the issue of the 'utility approach' versus the 'transactions-cost approach' to monetary theory.[3] This line of division is unlikely to prove fruitful in the advancement of knowledge in the field. On the one hand, the utility approach is to be interpreted as an 'as if' or 'revealed preference' means of introducing the notion that the demand for money is subject to the ordinary analytics of choice among rival assets; it is thus unspecific enough to absorb any more specific theory based on the precise circumstances of choice. On the other hand, insofar as there is an empirically resolvable conflict between the two approaches, it must imply either a prediction as to which of alternative empirical variables will produce the better econometric results (e.g. measured current income as a proxy for transactions versus 'permanent' income as a proxy for wealth), or a prediction of the empirical magnitude of a statistical elasticity co-efficient (e.g. the transactions approach predicts interest and scale elasticities of the demand for real balances significantly below unity); and the empirical studies of demand for money available so far provide little clear support for the transactions-cost approach.[4] In addition, the inventory approach is open to the general theoretical objection that it takes the patterns of payments and receipts as given, whereas these patterns can be construed instead as an optimizing response to the social usefulness of money as a medium of exchange and store of value.

[1] See Don Patinkin, *Money, Interest, and Prices: An Integration of Monetary and Value Theory*, 2nd edn (New York: Harper and Row, 1965), Ch. VII.

[2] Milton Friedman, 'The Quantity Theory of Money: A Restatement' and 'The Optimum Quantity of Money', in *The Optimum Quantity of Money*, Ch. 2 and 1, respectively.

[3] See, for example, James Tobin, 'Notes on Optimal Monetary Growth', *Journal of Political Economy*, Vol. 76, No. 4, Part II (July/August 1968), pp. 833–59.

[4] See, for example, David W. Laidler, *The Demand for Money, op. cit.* n., 4, p. 23.

The integration of monetary and value theory that has ensued on the Keynesian revolution, the work of Lange, Patinkin, and many others, has built on the Hicksian formulation of general-equilibrium theory. As applied by these writers, the approach treats money as parallel to any other good that is the object of utility-maximizing choice. In my 1962 survey, I called attention to certain difficulties that arise in treating money – as a capital good with a service flow – on a par with current flows of perishable consumption goods in a utility-maximization process subject to a budget constraint involving both current income and inherited money capital.[1] More recently, Robert Clower has attacked this type of formulation of the economic theory of a monetary economy, as making money just like any other good and therefore omitting from the analysis the essence of the difference between a monetary and a barter economy, which is precisely that in a barter economy goods exchange for other goods without differentiation of the goods, whereas in a monetary economy money plays a unique role distinct from that of goods, because goods have to be exchanged for money and money for goods. In consequence of this difference, economic actors have to be considered as constrained in their choices, not by the potential worth of their initial endowments of goods and money, but as purchasers by their initial cash balances (the 'expenditure constraint') and as sellers by the value of desired intra-period receipts of money income (the 'income constraint').[2] The outcome is a drastic reformulation of the general-equilibrium theory of a monetary economy, some of the implications of which have been discussed above in connection with Leijonhufvud's rehabilitation of Keynes. It may be remarked that in its own way Hicks's recent re-examination of the transactions demand for money,[3] intended indirectly to support the Radcliffe Report position, has attempted to cope with the same problem, though Hicks has been justly criticized for failing to realize that the transactions demand for money is conditional on and inseparable from its characteristics as a store of value, and that the pattern of use of money for transac-

---

[1] *Ibid.*, p. 20, text and fn. 1.

[2] R. W. Clower, 'A Reconsideration of the Microfoundations of Monetary Theory', *Western Economic Journal*, Vol. VI, No. 1 (December 1967), pp. 1–8.

[3] Sir John Hicks, *Critical Essays in Monetary Theory* (Oxford: The Clarendon Press, 1967), Ch. 1.

tions is, in anything longer than the very short run, the resultant of acts of choice and therefore not 'involuntary'.[1] Similar questions can be raised about Clower's sharp distinction between purchasers and sellers and between the budget constraints to which they are subject.

V. FINANCIAL INTERMEDIARIES AND THE 'NEW VIEW' OF MONETARY THEORY AND POLICY[2]

As mentioned in section I, the Radcliffe Committee's emphasis on 'the liquidity of the economy' as the key variable for monetary analysis and policy represented the high tide of Keynesian disbelief in the practical relevance and theoretical importance of money as formulated in traditional monetary theory, and as such met a harsh critical reception from the spokesmen of resurgent monetarism. In my 1962 survey I remarked that one important group working in the Keynesian liquidity-preference tradition had yet to be heard from: those pursuing the Markowitz 'portfolio-balance' approach to monetary analysis under the leadership of James Tobin at Yale University.[3] The collective works of this group have recently been published in three Cowles Commission monographs,[4] which constitute something of a delayed Yale counter-blast against the Chicago School's famous *Studies in the Quantity Theory of Money*.[5] These monographs, and especially Monograph 21, *Financial Markets and*

[1] N. J. Gibson, 'Foundations of Monetary Theory: A Review Article', *The Manchester School of Economic and Social Studies*, Vol. XXXVII, No. 1 (March 1969), pp. 59–75; and Laurence Harris, 'Professor Hicks and the Foundations of Monetary Economics', *Economica*, Vol. 36, No. 142 (May 1969), pp. 196–208.

[2] For an extended treatment of the subject matter of this and the following section, see Allan H. Meltzer, 'Money, Intermediation, and Growth', *Journal of Economic Literature*, Vol. VII, No. 1 (March 1969), pp. 27–56.

[3] H. G. Johnson, *Essays in Monetary Economics*, p. 30.

[4] Donald D. Hester and James Tobin (eds), *Risk Aversion and Portfolio Choice*, Cowles Foundation Monograph 19; *Studies of Portfolio Behavior*, Cowles Foundation Monograph 20; *Financial Markets and Economic Activity*, Cowles Foundation Monograph 21: (New York: John Wiley and Sons, 1967). For a textbook presentation of the Yale approach, see Basil J. Moore, *An Introduction to the Theory of Finance: Assetholder Behaviour Under Uncertainty* (London: Collier-Macmillan, 1968).

[5] M. Friedman (ed), *Studies in the Quantity Theory of Money* (Chicago: University of Chicago Press, 1956).

Economic Activity,[1] may be interpreted as providing belatedly the intellectual foundations of the Radcliffe Committee's position on monetary theory and policy – what has come to be described in the American literature, following a phrase in Tobin's important essay on 'Commercial Banks as Creators of "Money" ',[2] as the 'new view' of money.

In the general approach of the Yale School, 'monetary theory broadly conceived is simply the theory of portfolio management by economic units: households, businesses, financial institutions, and governments. It takes as its subject matter stocks of assets and debts (including money proper) and their values and yields; its accounting framework is the balance sheet. It can be distinguished from branches of economic theory which take the income statement as their accounting framework and flows of income, saving, expenditure, and production as their subject matter.' This distinction is admitted to be artificial, but useful because 'the processes which determine why one balance sheet or portfolio is chosen in preference to another are just beginning to be studied and understood'.[3] One of the major implications of this approach is the necessity 'to regard the structure of interest rates, asset yields, and credit availabilities rather than the quantity of money as the linkage between monetary and financial institutions on the one hand and the real economy on the other'[4] – hence the relevance to Radcliffe.

The crucial distinction for the Yale School, then (as for the Radcliffe Committee), is between the financial sector and the real sector (or between stock and flow analysis) rather than between the banking system and the rest of the economy (as various versions of the contemporary quantity theory would have it) or between liquid and illiquid assets (which Leijonhufvud interprets to be the essential distinction drawn in Keynes's own theory). Their central contribution is an elaborate analysis of the competition between banks and non-bank financial intermediaries – acknowledged to stem from the

[1] Monographs 19 and 20 are concerned with the applications of the portfolio-balance approach to the micro-economics of investor and of institutional behaviour, and hence fall outside the field of interest of this chapter.

[2] Deane Carson (ed), *Banking and Monetary Studies* (Homewood, Ill.: Richard D. Irwin, 1963), pp. 408–19; Ch. 1, pp. 1–11 in Monograph 21.

[3] Quotations from 'Foreword' (to the series), Monograph 21, pp. v–vi.

[4] J. Tobin, 'Commercial Banks as Creators of "Money" ', Monograph 21, p. 3.

earlier work of Gurley and Shaw[1] – from which emerges the conclusions that 'the quantity of money as conventionally defined is not an autonomous variable controlled by governmental authority but an endogenous or 'inside' quantity reflecting the economic behaviour of banks and other private economic units'; that 'commercial banks differ . . . from other financial units less basically in the nature of their liabilities than in the controls over reserves and interest rates to which they are legally subject';[2] and that controls over non-bank financial intermediaries may increase the effectiveness of monetary policy in influencing the real sector.[3]

As its authors acknowledge, this last proposition is not particularly impressive or useful, since there is no obvious economic gain discernible in enabling the monetary authority to operate on the economy by smaller rather than larger monetary-policy operations. The main argument for controls on financial intermediaries is in fact the rather disreputable one of shielding the interest cost of the public debt from the impact of general economic policy, and so forcing the burden of adjustment to changes in general economic policy on to the private sector; and the practice of such controls raises the question of the effects on the efficiency of the economic system as a whole. It is the first two propositions that raise fundamental issues in monetary theory.

Both of these propositions are rendered difficult to deal with by the strict separation of the monetary and the real sectors assumed by the basic approach, and particularly by the assumption of prices of real goods and services fixed autonomously in terms of money, on which the analysis rests, and which precludes consideration of many of the aspects of the problem that would naturally occur to a

[1] In connection with the discussion of the work of Gurley and Shaw in my 1962 survey (*Essays in Monetary Economics*, pp. 36–7), it may be remarked that the empirical volume that was to have validated their theoretical work on financial intermediation has not yet appeared.

[2] Quotations from 'Foreword', Monograph 21, p. viii; these two propositions are developed in Tobin, *op. cit.*

[3] James Tobin and William C. Brainard, 'Financial Intermediaries and the Effectiveness of Monetary Controls', *The American Economic Review*, Vol. LII, No. 2 (May 1963), pp. 383–400, reprinted as Ch. 3, pp. 55–93, of Monograph 21; see also William C. Brainard, 'Financial Intermediaries and a Theory of Monetary Control', *Yale Economic Essays*, Vol. 4, No. 1 (Autumn 1964), pp. 431–82, reprinted as Ch. 4, pp. 94–141, of Monograph 21.

quantity theorist. The second proposition on its positive side is essentially that controls on banks place the latter in the position of making a 'monopoly' profit on marginal business, so that an increase in reserves will automatically induce them to expand the scale of their operations, whereas other institutions are marginally in equilibrium so that their response to changes effected by monetary policy or otherwise will involve a general-equilibrium adjustment in asset values and yields. This is certainly a possibility. But it fits easily into the general framework of analysis of the efficiency effects of controls mentioned in the previous paragraph (and also into the Pesek–Saving analysis of the wealth effect of an expansion of 'inside' money discussed in section IV); and it does not suffice to equate banks in the really relevant respects with non-bank financial intermediaries, the negative side of the proposition. Further, what it implies is only that on impact an increase in bank reserves will have a wealth effect on the economy; when all the repercussions of an increase in the cash base are taken into account (including the repercussions on prices) there should be no change in the relative size of the banking sector, in spite of the marginal excess profitability of banking.

The crux of the matter is the first proposition, that the quantity of money as conventionally defined is an endogenous variable. This proposition derives its force by contrast with a straw man, the 'textbook' old view that the quantity of bank deposits is determined by a mechanical multiplier process operating on bank reserves, in which the preferences of the public play no part. Even in theoretical analyses of the determination of the money supply long pre-dating the Keynesian revolution, the preferences of the public, in the form of the desired ratio of currency to deposits, played an essential part in the determination of the volume of bank deposits erectable on a given cash base provided by the monetary authority.[1] The contemporary theory of money supply, which has developed very rapidly since my 1962 survey, has incorporated all the relevant influences of the choices of the public among competing monetary and near-

---

[1] See, for example, J. E. Meade, 'The Amount of Money and the Banking System', *Economic Journal*, Vol. 44 (1934), pp. 77–83; reprinted as Ch. 5, pp. 54–62, in American Economic Association, *Readings in Monetary Theory* (Homewood, Ill.: Richard D. Irwin, 1951).

monetary liabilities and of the financial institutions (both bank and non-bank) among reserves and other assets in the theory of the relation of the conventionally-measured money supply to the cash base provided by the central bank.[1] The crucial issue is whether the interrelationships (deduced from rational maximizing behaviour on the part of all economic actors) in the financial sector are stable enough to permit changes in the monetary base (or, more proximately, changes in the conventionally-measured quantity of money) to be used to analyse and predict changes in the real sector (including both output and price level changes), or whether detailed understanding of the financial sector and the effects of monetary changes on the 'structure of interest rates, asset yields, and credit availabilities' is a necessary prerequisite of this endeavour. In this connection, the 'new view' is long on elegant analysis of theoretical possibilities, but remarkably short on testable or tested theoretical propositions about the way the economy works, and specifically how it responds to monetary impulses, when the interaction of the monetary and the real sectors is taken into account.

VI. MONEY IN GROWTH MODELS AND MONETARY EFFICIENCY

In concluding my 1962 survey, I remarked that 'almost nothing has yet been done to break monetary theory loose from the mould of short-run equilibrium analysis . . . and to integrate it with the rapidly developing literature on economic growth.'[2] The period since has seen a rapid development of theorizing in this direction, to the point where a whole issue of the new *Journal of Money, Credit and Banking* has been devoted to publication of the proceedings of a conference held of this precise subject.[3] This literature has raised in a fresh form many of the fundamental problems of monetary theory, notably those of the role and functions of money in the economy; as yet, however, it has barely approached the question of quantification

---

[1] For discussion see Allan H. Metzler, 'Money, Intermediation and Growth', *Journal of Economic Literature*, Vol. VII, No. 1 (March 1969), pp. 27–56, and Karl Brunner, 'Yale and Money', *Journal of Finance*, Vol. XXVI, No. 1 (March 1971), pp. 165–75.

[2] H. G. Johnson, *Essays in Monetary Economics*, p. 66.

[3] *Journal of Money, Credit and Banking*, Vol. I, No. 2 (May 1969).

of the influence of money and monetary policy on economic growth. It does, however, overlap with an emerging body of analysis dealing with the requirements of efficiency in the organization of the monetary and financial sector, of considerably more relevance to practical economic policy.

The starting point of the latter body of analysis is the proposition that money, as an instrument of exchange and an item of wealth, is socially virtually costless to create (though not necessarily socially costless to use) and hence that the stock of it should be maintained at the satiety level for society. In the context of the problem of monetary efficiency, this proposition implies that taxes on the use of money, such as are involved in the imposition of required reserves in the form of non-interest-bearing currency and deposits at the central bank and other restrictions on commercial banking, as well as restrictions on the freedom of competition among financial intermediaries, restrict the use of money and money substitutes to suboptimal levels and hence reduce the efficiency of the economy. (If restrictions are applied to commercial banks only, there may be an extra-optimal resort to non-bank intermediary services.[1]) This proposition refers to optimization of the holding of real balances; if banks are left free to compete without restriction in providing nominal money, the gains from using costless paper as a medium of exchange and store of value will be dissipated through inflation. The proposition also abstracts from the practical point that the payment of interest on currency holdings is infeasible.[2] If this last point is taken as being of predominating importance, monetary efficiency requires the establishment of a zero money rate of interest on other financial claims to parallel the assumedly inherently institutionally necessary zero money rate of return on currency. To analyse the condition for accomplishing this, the analysis must move from a static to a dynamic framework, and appeal to the Fisherian distinction between the real and the money rate of interest, as separated by the expected

[1] Recognition of these points motivated, at least in part, the *Report on Bank Charges* of the National Board for Prices and Incomes, which argued against traditional methods of monetary control in the United Kingdom and in favour of more competition in banking.

[2] On these issues see my 'Problems of Efficiency in Monetary Management', *Journal of Political Economy*, Vol. 76, No. 5 (September/October 1968), pp. 971–90; reprinted as Ch. 3 below.

rate of inflation or deflation. The conclusion then emerges that monetary efficiency and the optimization of social welfare require management of the growth of the money supply so as to cause the price level to fall at a rate equal to the real rate of return on capital.[1]

Recent work on the problem of introducing money and monetary policy into models of economic growth, however, has started from a quite different analytical framework, namely the artificial conventions of 'real' growth models. These models postulate a constant ratio of savings to income (real output), and proceed to determine (i) the conditions under which the model will converge on a steady-state growth path, the rate of growth being determined by the exogenously-given rates of growth of the population and of technological efficiency, and (ii) that savings ratio which will maximize consumption per head along the steady-state growth path. The problem of introducing money into such a model presents itself as the problem of incorporating money and monetary growth into the concept of 'income' to which the assumed fixed savings ratio is to be applied, and deducing the influence of variation in the rate of monetary expansion (or proximately the trend rate of change of prices) on the proportion of physical output available for investment in additions to the physical capital stock. It has been recognized that this problem has a close affinity to Metzler's classic article on the neutrality of money in a short-run Keynesian system.[2] A subsidiary problem has been the interpretation of the welfare implications of the consumption-maximizing savings ratio, epitomized in 'the golden

[1] For a recent analysis leading to this conclusion, couched in quantity theory terms and rich in the application of relevant capital theory, see M. Friedman, *The Optimum Quantity of Money.* Besides being misleadingly titled, since the analysis refers to a growing and not a static economy, this essay is rather distracting in its pursuit of theoretical side issues suggested by past controversies and its intrusive concern for a quantification of potential welfare gains which is provided only fragmentarily and inconclusively; the need for the rather embarrassing 'final schizophrenic note' could have been avoided by presenting the argument more frankly as a logical exercise. It may be recalled that the pre-Keynesian quantity theorists recognized the problem of the optimal trend of the price level, but tended to interpret it as a problem of social justice in the division of the gains from technical progress between the active and the retired population, because they failed to understand the link between the money and the real rate of interest provided by the expected rate of inflation.

[2] L. A. Metzler, 'Wealth, Saving and the Rate of Interest', *Journal of Political Economy*, Vol. 59, No. 2 (April 1951), pp. 93–116.

rule of accumulation'.[1] So long as the actual savings ratio is above the consumption-maximizing ratio, no problem results, because by reducing the savings ratio society can increase its consumption level at all points of time, present, and future, which must be accounted an indisputable welfare gain; but if the actual ratio falls short of the consumption-maximizing ratio, the welfare implications of a movement towards the latter are ambiguous, because the move involves a sacrifice of present consumption for the sake of future consumption, and the model contains no specification of the terms on which such an intertemporal substitution between present and future consumption can be analysed.

Subtleties of welfare analysis apart, the problem is how to introduce money and monetary growth into the 'real' model of accumulation described above. For this purpose, 'money' has been generally defined as an asset bearing interest at a rate fixed in monetary terms – usually taken as zero by convention – so that its real rate of return is determined by the (assumed to be fully expected) rate of inflation or deflation determined by monetary policy. The original analysis of the problem by Tobin[2] treated money as an asset pure and simple, contributing nothing to real income and welfare; hence monetary growth entered the model purely as a capital gain additional to current production, which added to perceived income but subtracted from the saving available for real investment, and hence reduced real output per head. Thus inflation appeared to be 'a good thing', if the savings ratio fell short of the consumption-maximizing ratio and the intertemporal choice problem was ignored.

My own analysis of the problem[3] stressed the necessity of allowing money a function in a monetary economy, and therefore of attributing to the presence of money an increase in economic welfare and so in the base to which the assumed constant savings ratio was applied, thus introducing two conflicting terms in the effect of the

[1] E. S. Phelps, 'The Golden Rule of Accumulation: A Fable for Growthmen', *The American Economic Review*, Vol. 51, No. 4 (September 1961), pp. 638–48.

[2] James Tobin, 'Money and Economic Growth', *Econometrica*, Vol. 33, No. 4 (October 1965), pp. 671–84.

[3] Harry G. Johnson, 'Money in a Neo-Classical One-Sector Growth Model', in *Essays in Monetary Economics*, Ch. IV, pp. 143–78. See also my 'Inside Money, Outside Money . . .', *Journal of Money, Credit and Banking;* reprinted in Ch. 4 below.

presence of money and the exercise of monetary policy – the Tobin capital-gains effect of real monetarý growth reducing the real savings ratio and the Johnson consumption-of-cash-balance-services effect raising it – with an ambiguous result for the specification of optimal monetary policy. My contribution violated some of the canons of sound national income accounting in attempting to capture intra-marginal consumers' surplus in the representation of the income-augmenting effect of cash-balance services. Levhari and Patinkin[1] have subsequently explored the implications of a more conventional valuation of the services of cash balances (at their marginal value) for income and consumption accounting, with the predictable conse-quence of making their conclusions depend on the elasticity or inelasticity of demand for cash-balance services.

Other writers, especially the late Miguel Sidrauski,[2] have departed from the confining influence of the Metzler assumption that saving is inversely related to wealth, and placed their analytical emphasis on time preference, i.e. on some minimum acceptable rate of interest as the ultimate determinant of the accumulation of material capital per head. In such a theoretical framework, or in one in which the savings ratio is regarded as amenable to influence by fiscal policy, the analysis must return to regarding the optimization of the quantity of money at any point of time as a separable problem from that of maximizing consumption of real goods and services per head, in which case its solution (again assuming the infeasibility of paying explicit interest on currency) must be management of the money supply so as to produce a rate of price decline equal to the real rate of interest – as pointed out above in connection with the static problem of monetary efficiency. In this connection, it should be noted, the same conclusions follow whether money is regarded as 'productive', and/or yielding utility, or whether it is treated on transactions-demand theory lines as the cheapest means of reconciling different temporal patterns of receipts and payments – in which latter case money balance holdings affect economic welfare via the observable flow of goods and services rather than via the 'utility' yielded by money services.

[1] D. Levhari and D. Patinkin, 'The Role of Money in a Simple Growth Model', *The American Economic Review*, Vol. 58, No. 4 (September 1968), pp. 713–53.

[2] Miguel Sidrauski, 'Inflation and Economic Growth', *Journal of Political Economy*, Vol. 75, No. 6 (December 1967), pp. 796–810.

VII. THE THEORY OF INFLATION AND OF ECONOMIC POLICY

The objectives of macro-economic policy for the government of a contemporary 'mixed-capitalist' country have come to be formulated as the maintenance of high employment without inflation, consistently with the achievement of an adequate rate of economic growth and the preservation of balance-of-payments equilibrium. In this context a major contribution to the theory of economic policy – in my judgement the only significant contribution to emerge from post-Keynesian theorizing – has been the 'Phillips curve'.[1] The Phillips curve is an empirical relationship between the rate of unemployment (taken as an index of demand conditions in the labour market) and other variables on the one hand, and the rate of increase of money wages on the other. From it can be deduced, through the assumption that the trend of prices is determined by the trend of wages via the deduction of the rate of increase of productivity, a 'trade-off function' between the rate of inflation and the rate of unemployment; and the policy-makers can either be assumed to choose a point on this function according to their or the community's preferences, or advised to choose a point on it that maximizes social welfare (minimizes social loss).[2]

Much work has been done on the econometric refinement and testing of the Phillips curve. Recently there has been a recurrence of the initial doubts about the concept, namely about whether the assumed rounded-L shape of the curve does not represent an arbitrary and illegitimate linkage of the behaviour of the labour market under conditions of approximately full employment and of mass unemployment.[3] More fundamentally, the concept of the curve has been

[1] A. W. Phillips, 'The Relation Between Unemployment and the Rate of Change of Money Wages in the United Kingdom, 1862–1957', *Economica*, Vol. 25, No. 100 (December 1958), pp. 283–99.

[2] See, for example, G. L. Reuber, 'The Objectives of Canadian Monetary Policy, 1949–61: Empirical "Trade-offs" and the Reaction Function of the Authorities', *Journal of Political Economy*, Vol. 72, No. 2 (April 1964), pp. 109–32.

[3] See, for example, Bernard Corry and David Laidler, 'The Phillips Relation: A Theoretical Explanation', *Economica*, Vol. XXXIV, No. 134 (May 1967), pp. 189–97; also A. G. Hines, 'Unemployment and the Rate of Change of Money Wages in the United Kingdom 1862–1963: A Reappraisal', *Review of Economics and Statistics*, Vol. L, No. 1 (February 1968), pp. 60–7.

attacked as being logically inconsistent in ignoring the influence on the wage-fixing process of expectations about the rate of wage and price inflation, which expectations themselves are derived by a learning process from past experience of the rate of inflation chosen by the policy-makers. On the assumption that inflation eventually becomes fully expected and translated into wage- and price-fixing behaviour, the trade-off for the policy-makers is not between a 'permanent' rate of unemployment and a 'permanent' rate of inflation, but between the gains from less unemployment now and the losses from more inflation later.[1] The most elegant statement of this position is to be found in Milton Friedman's Presidential Address to the 1967 Meetings of the American Economic Association,[2] which argues forcefully that in the long run monetary policy cannot control real variables – notably the real rate of interest and the level of unemployment – but can only control nominal money variables – the behaviour of the price level and of the money rate of interest.

The Friedman argument from the quantity theory of money raises the empirical question of the effects of introducing the expected rate of inflation into the estimation of the Phillips curve. If the coefficient of the expected rate of inflation is unity, the Phillips curve vanishes, and only one rate of unemployment – 'the natural rate of unemployment', in Friedman's terminology – is consistent with a constant rate of inflation (which may – and may as well – be zero) in the long run. While various recent writers have attempted to investigate this empirical question, the most thorough examination of it is to be found in a rather obscure source, a symposium held at New York University on January 31, 1968.[3] Empirical evidence produced by Robert M. Solow strongly supports, and evidence produced by Phillip Cagan (on a somewhat different methodological approach) does not effectively refute, a coefficient for expected inflation signifi-

[1] E. S. Phelps, 'Phillips Curves, Expectations of Inflation and Optimal Unemployment Over Time', *Economica*, Vol. XXXIV, No. 135 (August 1967), pp. 254–81.

[2] Milton Friedman, 'The Role of Monetary Policy', *The American Economic Review*, Vol. 58, No. 1 (March 1968), pp. 1–17; reprinted in M. Friedman, *The Optimum Quantity of Money*, Ch. 5, pp. 95–110.

[3] Stephen W. Rousseas (ed.), *Proceedings of a Symposium on Inflation: Its Causes, Consequences and Control* (Wilton, Conn.: The Calvin K. Kazanjian Economics Foundation, Inc., 1969). Tobin's comment (pp. 48–54) is especially apposite.

cantly below unity (in the neighbourhood of one-half). The outcome is a 'sophisticated' Phillips curve, based on a dynamic version of 'money illusion', which still offers a trade-off to the policy-makers, though its slope is steeper than that implied by the 'naive' Phillips curve.

Recognition of the Phillips curve relationship has prompted governments, particularly in the United Kingdom, to resort to 'incomes policy' as a way to alter the Phillips curve and permit the achievement of fuller employment consistently with the maintenance of price stability. The Phillips curve approach has suggested an obvious test of the effectiveness of incomes policy as practised on past occasions, namely its effectiveness in shifting the Phillips curve to the left in the standard diagram. Such tests have almost invariably shown incomes policy to have been of negligible effectiveness in terms of the relevant policy objective.[1] Very recently, R. G. Lipsey has argued that this formulation of the problem is wrong, and that the purpose of incomes policy is to change the slope of the Phillips curve (specifically, to flatten it) rather than to change the constant term that determines its location. The empirical work on the British data by Lipsey and Parkin[2] shows that incomes policy, interpreted this way, has in fact been successful; but that because the policy-makers have reduced the level of employment simultaneously with the introduction of incomes policy, they have in fact achieved the pessimum result of increasing both the level of unemployment and the rate of inflation.

VIII. CONCLUDING COMMENTS

Since the Radcliffe Committee was appointed, and even more since it reported, there has been a tremendous surge of interest in and research into the general field of monetary economics. This chapter has attempted to survey the major topics of probable interest to British readers. One topic important for the development of British monetary economics has been deliberately omitted as not yet lending

[1] See for example David C. Smith, 'Incomes policy', Ch. III, pp. 104–44, in R. E. Caves and Associates, *Britain's Economic Prospects* (Washington: The Brookings Institution, London: Allen & Unwin, 1968).

[2] R. G. Lipsey and J. M. Parkin, 'Incomes Policy: A Reappraisal', *Economica*, N.S., Vol. XXXVII, No. 146 (May 1970), pp. 115–38.

itself to generalization: the long and frequently confused debate over the theory of the money-supply process in the United Kingdom and the role and objectives of the Bank of England, a debate sparked by the Radcliffe Report itself and strongly influenced by the development of theory and research in the United States. Of the topics surveyed, the one probably of greatest current interest is the rise of monetarism and particularly the implications of monetarism for the theory of the balance of payments. Perhaps the greatest disservice that Keynes rendered to the development of economics in Britain was to develop the theory of macro-economics and money on the assumption of a closed economy. The extension of Keynesian theory to an open economy – which has been largely the work of economists in other countries, though the classic contribution of James Meade must be recognized[1] – has been built on the manifestly unsatisfactory assumption of money illusion on the part of the wage-earners, which assumption is necessary to permit exchange rate changes to be treated as producing changes in real-price relationships. Much work remains to be done in developing a monetary economics appropriate to the analytical and policy problems of the British economy.

[1] J. E. Meade, *The Theory of International Economic Policy*, Vol. I: *The Balance of Payments*; Vol. II: *Trade and Welfare* (London: Oxford University Press, 1951 and 1955).

Chapter 2

The Keynesian Revolution and the Monetarist Counter-Revolution*

As is well known from the field of economic history, the concept of revolution is difficult to transfer from its origins in politics to other fields of social science. Its essence is unexpected speed of change, and this requires a judgement of speed in the context of a longer perspective of historical change, the choice of which is likely to be debatable in the extreme. Leaving the judgemental issue aside for the moment, one could characterize the history of our subject in terms of a series of 'revolutions', very broadly defined, as follows. Economics as we know it began with what might be called the 'Smithian revolution' against the established body of doctrines generically described as 'mercantilism', a revolution which changed ideas on the nature and sources of the wealth of nations and the policies required to promote the growth of what we now call 'affluence'. The Ricardian revolution turned the attention of economists from concern with national wealth and its growth to the distribution of income among social classes and the interactions of growth and income distribution. The marginalist revolution of the 1870s essentially introduced a new and superior analytical technology for dealing with Ricardo's distribution problem, in the process gradually depriving Ricardian economics of its social content; hence, the results of that revolution have been described as neo-Ricardian or more commonly neo-classical economics.

Contemporary economics is based on this development and on at least four discernible 'revolutions' that occurred in the late 1920s and in the 1930s. One was the imperfect-monopolistic competition revolution, which challenged the validity of the assumption of perfect

* The Richard T. Ely Lecture at the 1970 Meetings of The American Economic Association, *The American Economic Review*, Vol. LXI, No. 2 (May 1971), pp. 1–14.

competition on which value theory had come to be built following the marginalist revolution, and particularly the conclusions about the welfare effects of competition to which that theory led. This revolution has more or less fizzled out, though its fossilized remnants continue to plague both students and their instructors in elementary courses. Another was the empirical or econometric revolution, with its insistence initially on the measurement of economic relationships and, subsequently and more ambitiously, on the testing of economic hypotheses – though the 'testing of hypotheses' is frequently merely a euphemism for obtaining plausible numbers to provide ceremonial adequacy for a theory chosen and defended on *a priori* grounds. The third was the general-equilibrium revolution, based on the introduction by Hicks and Allen of the continental Walrasian–Paretoan approach into the Anglo-Saxon tradition in replacement of the then-dominant Marshallian partial-equilibrium approach. Finally, and most sweeping in its effects, there was the Keynesian revolution in monetary theory.

By contrast with the abundance of revolutions, counter-revolutions are hard to find in the development of economic thought. About the closest one can come to a counter-revolution in the history of economic thought is to interpret the development of the Austrian theory of value as a counter-revolution against the socialist, and especially the Marxist, tradition of economic theorizing; and that aspect of the work of the Austrian school was a side issue in the marginalist revolution. The monetarist counter-revolution of contemporary times is probably the first significant counter-revolution in the development of our subject. In venturing this judgement, however, I should note that the disrepute into which the theories of imperfect and monopolistic competition have fallen, as theories of contemporary industrial competition, in the period since the Second World War could be described as the result of an intellectual counter-revolution, based on a combination of faith in the pre-existing theory of competition and devotion to the empirical revolution; and also that, if one is prepared to disregard the political labels that people choose to attach to themselves, the left-wing student and faculty demand for a politically and socially relevant 'radical' economics and protest against emphasis on mathematical and econometric quantification can be classed as counter-revolutionary, inasmuch as it seeks to revert to the pre-marginalist-revolution concern with the economic system as a system of relationships among social classes.

As already mentioned, the chief problem in identifying revolutions and counter-revolutions and distinguishing them from slower and more comprehensible and rational processes of change in economic thought is to arrive at a judgement of the relative speed of change and the degree to which the speed is justifiable. From this point of view, some of what I have described above as revolutions were not really revolutionary – notably the Smithian and marginalist revolutions, the imperfect-monopolistic competition revolution, and the general-equilibrium and empirical revolutions. The Smithian and marginalist revolutions spread relatively slowly, through the force of their scientific superiority and intellectual appeal and the process of natural wastage of their opponents. The imperfect-monopolistic competition revolution was the end result of puzzling by many minds over a problem that Marshall had stated but had been unable to solve satisfactorily – the existence of downward-sloping cost curves for individual firms. The general-equilibrium revolution was a result of the delayed appreciation by economists of the need for a better command of mathematical techniques, the delay being occasioned by the long association of the subject with philosophy in the English academic tradition and its continuing association with law in the continental tradition. And the empirical revolution depended on the development of the techniques of statistical inference – most of the historically great economists were quantitatively oriented, or at least paid lip service to the need for quantitative work, but lacked the requisite tools to carry out such work themselves. For real intellectual revolutions, we are left with three major examples: the Ricardian revolution, the reasons for whose rapid propagation were examined some twenty years ago by S. G. Checkland [1], the Keynesian revolution, and the monetarist counter-revolution. These last two are the subject of this chapter.

My concern, specifically, is with the reasons for the speed of propagation of the monetarist counter-revolution; but I cannot approach this subject without reference to the reasons for the speed of propagation of the Keynesian revolution, since the two are inter-related. Indeed, I find it useful in posing and treating the problem to adopt the 'as if' approach of positive economics, as expounded by the chief protagonist of the monetarist counter-revolution, Milton Friedman, and to ask: suppose I wished to start a counter-revolution against the Keynesian revolution in monetary theory, how would I go about it – and specifically, what could I learn about the technique from the revolution itself? To pose the question in this way is, of course, to fly in the face of currently accepted professional ethics, according to which purely scientific considerations and not political considerations are presumed to motivate scientific work; but I can claim the protection of the 'as if' methodology against any implication of a slur on individual character or a denigration of scientific work.

From this point of view, obviously, the first problem is to identify the elements in the situation at the time of the *General Theory* that accounted for its rapid acceptance and propagation among professional economists. Such elements are of two types, one relating to the objective social situation in which the new theory was produced, the other relating to the scientific characteristics of the new theory itself.

As regards the objective social situation, by far the most helpful circumstance for the rapid propagation of a new and revolutionary theory is the existence of an established orthodoxy which is clearly inconsistent with the most salient facts of reality, and yet is sufficiently confident of its intellectual power to attempt to explain those facts, and in its efforts to do so exposes its incompetence in a ludicrous fashion (on this see Appendix B [6]). Orthodoxy is, of course, always vulnerable to radical challenge: the essence of an orthodoxy of any kind is to reduce the subtle and sophisticated thoughts of great men to a set of simple principles and straightforward slogans that more mediocre brains can think they understand well enough to live by – but for that very reason orthodoxy is most vulnerable to challenge when its principles and slogans are demonstrably in conflict with the facts of everyday experience.

So it was in the 1930s, and particularly in the 1930s in Britain, which had already experienced a decade of mass unemployment associated with industrial senescence and an overvalued exchange rate, mass unemployment which the prevailing orthodoxy could neither explain nor cope with. This, it may be noted, was in large part the fault of the economists themselves. There existed already a body of monetary analysis that was quite capable of explaining both Britain's and the industrial world's unemployment problems as a consequence of monetary mismanagement. But, hypnotized by the notion that money is merely a veil cast over real phenomena – the homogeneity postulate of contemporary monetary theory – the economists of the time attempted to explain what were essentially monetary phenomena by real causes. Eminent British economists sought to explain mass unemployment as a consequence of the satiation of real human wants, a satiation that should have produced a general reduction in working hours but unfortunately and inexplicably operated instead differentially to reduce the working hours of a substantial part of the population to absolute zero. Other economists viewed the depression as a punishment justly visited upon enterprises and individuals for past sins of speculation and erroneous micro-economic decision-taking. The concern for micro-economic explanations diverted attention from what the available macro-economic analysis could have said about the problem; it also led to the recommendation of *ad hoc* remedies such as public works that lacked any firm grounding in theory as generally understood.

In this situation of general confusion and obvious irrelevance of orthodox economics to real problems, the way was open for a new theory that offered a convincing explanation of the nature of the problem and a set of policy prescriptions based on that explanation. Such a theory, however, would have to possess certain characteristics if it were to win intellectual acceptance and political success. In particular, it would have to come from within yet offer liberation from the established orthodoxy – for one must remember that orthodoxy includes both an established conservative orthodoxy and an established self-termed 'radical' orthodoxy, and, since each recognizes and accommodates the other's arguments, there is no real hope of progress being achieved by a switch from one position to the other.

To be more specific, a revolutionary theory had to depend for its success on five main characteristics – here I must admit that I am conducting my analysis in the blinding light of hindsight. First, it had to attack the central proposition of conservative orthodoxy – the assumed or inferred tendency of the economy to full employment – with a new but academically acceptable analysis that reversed the proposition. This Keynes did with the help of Kahn's concept of the multiplier and his own invention of the propensity to consume.

Second, the theory had to appear to be new, yet absorb as much as possible of the valid or at least not readily disputable components of existing orthodox theory. In this process, it helps greatly to give old concepts new and confusing names, and to emphasize as crucial analytical steps that have previously been taken as platitudinous; hence, in the *General Theory*, the marginal productivity of capital became the marginal efficiency of capital; the desired ratio of money to income, the k of the Cambridge tradition, became a minor constituent of the new theory of 'liquidity preference'; and the *ex post* identity of savings and investment, which previous theorists including Keynes himself had rightly recognized as unhelpful to dynamic analysis, became the *sine qua non* of right reasoning.

Third, the new theory had to have the appropriate degree of difficulty to understand. This is a complex problem in the design of new theories. The new theory had to be so difficult to understand that senior academic colleagues would find it neither easy nor worth while to study, so that they would waste their efforts on peripheral theoretical issues, and so offer themselves as easy marks for criticism and dismissal by their younger and hungrier colleagues. At the same time, the new theory had to appear both difficult enough to challenge the intellectual interest of younger colleagues and students, but actually easy enough for them to master adequately with a sufficient investment of intellectual endeavour. These objectives Keynes's *General Theory* managed to achieve: it neatly shelved the old and established scholars, like Pigou and Robertson, enabled the more enterprising middle- and lower-middle-aged like Hansen, Hicks and Joan Robinson to jump on and drive the bandwaggon, and permitted a whole generation of students (as Samuelson has recorded) to escape from the slow and soul-destroying process of acquiring wisdom by osmosis from their elders and the literature into an intellectual realm in which youthful iconoclasm could quickly earn its just reward (in its own eyes at least) by the demolition of the intellectual pretensions of its academic seniors and predecessors. Economics, delightfully, could be reconstructed from scratch on the basis of a little Keynesian understanding and a lofty contempt for the existing literature – and so it was.

Fourth, the new theory had to offer to the more gifted and less opportunistic scholars a new methodology more appealing than those currently available. In this respect, Keynes was lucky both in having a receptive audience available, and to hit somewhere conveniently between the old and the newly emerging styles of economic theorizing. The prevailing methodological orthodoxy was that of Marshall – a partial-equilibrium approach set within a clear appreciation of the two complex problems of general equilibrium and of historical change, and hence both unsatisfactory at the simple level of partial-equilibrium analysis taken by itself, and extremely difficult to apply skilfully in a broader analytical and social context. The new methodological challenge was coming from the explicitly mathematical general-equilibrium approach of Hicks and Allen, an approach whose empirically and historically almost empty generality was of little general appeal. The *General Theory* found a middle ground in an aggregated general-equilibrium system which was not too difficult or complicated to work with – though it demanded a substantial step forwards in mathematical competence – and which offered a high degree of apparent empirical relevance to those who took the trouble to understand it.

Finally, the *General Theory* offered an important empirical relationship for the emerging tribe of econometricians to measure – the consumption function, a far more challenging relationship than the demand for sugar, a relationship for which the development of national income statistics provided the raw material needed for estimation, and which could be estimated with surprising success given the limitation of the available data to approximately a single business cycle.

In my judgement, these factors accounted for the success of the Keynesian revolution: on the one hand, the existence of an important social and economic problem with which the prevailing orthodoxy was unable to cope; on the other hand, a variety of characteristics that appealed to the younger generation of that period – notably the claim of the new theory to superior social relevance and intellectual distinction, its incorporation in a novel and confusing fashion of the valid elements of traditional theory, the opportunity it offered to bypass the system of academic seniority by challenging senior colleagues with a new and self-announcedly superior scientific approach, the presentation of a new methodology that made general-equilibrium theory both manageable and socially relevant, and the advancement of a new empirical relationship challenging for econometricians to estimate.

The very success of the Keynesian revolution, however, ensured that it would in its turn become the established orthodoxy, and as such be as vulnerable as the old to revolutionary attack – which would necessarily have to be a counter-revolutionary attack. Keynes himself, as Leijonhufvud's monumental re-interpretation of his thought [7] has reminded us, had a seasoned and subtle mind, conscious both of the flow of economic history and of the role of theory as an adjunct to policy-making in a given set of historical circumstances. His followers – which means the profession at large – elaborated his history-bound analysis into a timeless and spaceless set of universal principles, sacrificing in the process much of his subtlety, and so established Keynesianism as an orthodoxy ripe for counter-attack.

There are several factors in this transmogrification worthy of note. The first, and probably most important, has been the conviction of Keynesians that the mass unemployment of the 1930s represents the normal state of capitalist society – more accurately, of capitalist society unaided by Keynesian management – and that unemployment is always the most urgent social problem. This view was elevated into a dogma in the United States under the leadership of Alvin Hansen, whose theory of secular stagnation was the subject of his Presidential Adress to the American Economic Association [4]. While that theory has been quietly forgotten, or frugally converted into a theory applicable to the underdeveloped countries, vestiges of it linger on in the thinking of American Keynesians. The view that unemployment is the overriding social problem also lingers on among British Keynesians such as Joan Robinson, Roy Harrod and Thomas Balogh, though I should note that Nicholas Kaldor has for many years taken a much more optimistic view of the resilience of capitalism. The corollary of the Keynesian view of the primacy of the unemployment problem has been a pronounced tendency to play down the adverse economic consequences of inflation, and to assume that, if only the unemployment consequences of anti-inflationary policies were properly understood, society would cheerfully agree to adopt and implement an incomes policy instead.

A second factor in the transformation of Keynesianism into an orthodoxy has been that people who made their academic reputations and earned their present status on the basis of an early and enthusiastic conversion to Keynesianism in the late 1930s and early 1940s have continued to trade on their foresight, to the academic detriment of their juniors, who have never had the same chance to jump onto the front – and not the rear – of an academic bandwaggon. This factor has been far more effective in paving the way for a monetarist counter-revolution in the United States, where institutional competition prevents centralized control of professional advancement, than in the United Kingdom, where Oxbridge continues to dominate the academic scene.

A third factor has been that, while the Keynesian revolution in its time offered a tremendous liberation to the energies of young economists in the fields of pure theorizing about concepts, the construction of macro-economic general-equilibrium models, and the estimation of econometric models of the economy, these activities have run into diminishing returns so rapidly that they have ceased to be appealing to young and ambitious economists.

The result has been that – beginning perhaps sometime in the mid-1950s – Keynesianism has become itself an established orthodoxy, ripe for attack in exactly the same way as what Keynes chose to call 'classical economics' and to attack in the 1930s. It has had the same two vulnerable characteristics: inability to prescribe for what has come to be considered a major social problem – inflation, in contrast to the unemployment of Keynes's time – and a dependence on the authority and prestige of senior scholars which is oppressive to the young. Also, ironically enough in view of Keynes's own long concern with the influence of money on the economy, it has suffered from the same major defect as the orthodoxy Keynes attacked – the attempt to explain essentially monetary phenomena in terms of a mixture of real theory and *ad-hoc*-ery, and specifically to explain inflation in terms of real effective demand and the Phillips curve. The fact that Keynesian economics has stumbled into the same pitfall as the 'classical' orthodoxy it succeeded is, perhaps, an indication of the difficulty of monetary theory as contrasted with value theory, as well as of the perils of abandoning monetary theory in favour of what appears seductively to be more reasonable common sense.

If, in accordance with the 'as if' methodology of positive economics that I adopted earlier in this chapter one posed the question of how to mount a counter-revolution against Keynesian orthodoxy, and considered the question in the light of the factors that contributed to the success of the Keynesian revolution, one would, I think, be driven inescapably to two sets of conclusions.

The first would be the need to find an important social problem that the established orthodoxy is incapable of dealing with, even though it tries its best and claims to be successful. The second would be the need to develop a counter-revolutionary theory that had the requisite characteristics to be academically and professionally successful in replacing the previous revolutionary theory.

The obvious answer to the first problem – finding an important social problem that orthodox theory cannot solve – is to concentrate on the issue of inflation, the issue that Keynesian theory was least well designed to deal with. The trouble with that answer has been that, under the influence of both experienced inflation and Keynesian theory, the public has for the most part not been much concerned about the economic evils of inflation, and so has not regarded inflation as an important test of the intellectual strength of Keynesian orthodoxy. The history of the monetarist counter-revolution has, in fact, been characterized by a series of mostly vain efforts to convince the profession and the public (i) that inflation is an important question and (b) that monetarism can provide an explanation and a policy whereas Keynesianism cannot. Proposition (ii) is eminently plausible; but it can only get a hearing if proposition (i) is accepted first; and, aside from a brief interlude in the late 1950s, the public has become convinced of proposition (i) only very recently. It is no accident that the appearance of monetarism as a strong intellectual movement has had to wait until the aftermath of the escalation of the war in Vietnam in 1965. It is even less of an accident that its current success has depended on a prior Keynesian claim to, and acceptance of, responsibility for efforts to stop inflation by Keynesian fiscal means, under the auspices of the 'New Economics'. Monetarism has until the past few years been in the position of investing a great deal of intellectual ability in analysing problems and producing solutions that no one else has considered worth the effort involved. It has eventually become a public force less by its own efforts than as a consequence of the 'New Economics' over-reaching itself when it was riding high in the formation of national economic policy. The 'New Economics' was favoured by the opportunity to sell Keynesian policies to meet a Keynesian problem; it encountered disaster when it tried to sell reverse Keynesian policies to meet a non-Keynesian problem. And the monetarist counter-revolution has been cashing in on that mistake of intellectual strategy.

Nevertheless, on this score of social relevance, the monetarist counter-revolution has had certain factors working in its favour which have enabled it to survive and prosper despite the absence of an overwhelmingly obvious inadequacy of the established Keynesian orthodoxy, for most of the postwar period. One has been that, with the growing professionalization of economics and the expansion of academic support of interest in it, it has become increasingly possible for an issue to be deemed scientifically interesting and worthy of investigation even if the general public displays no visible interest in it. Another has been the rise of the United States to the position of a world power, which has made the exploration of issues of no direct relevance to the economic interests of the United States nevertheless worth pursuing as potentially matters of the national interest in the world economy. Both the hyper-inflations in Europe and elsewhere that followed the two world wars, and the strong inflations that have characterized Latin American economic history, have lent themselves to investigation with the aid of the quantity theory as matters of potential relevance to U.S. economic policy. But, as already mentioned, while these foreign experiences have provided fodder for monetarism, and in the course of time support for the contention that monetarism rests on a far wider base of empirical investigation than Keynesianism, the real counter-revolutionary thrust of monetarism has only developed since inflation became a major problem for the United States itself. Further, it is only since that event – which, given the world importance of the United States, has meant the emergence of inflation as a worldwide problem – that monetarism has been taken seriously by academic and public opinion in other countries.

Practical social relevance apart, the question of success for a new theory, whether revolutionary or counter-revolutionary, depends on its fitting appropriately into the intellectual climate of its time. Here we may apply what has already been said about the reasons for the successful rapid propagation of the Keynesian revolution to the 'as if' question of how to proceed to mount a quantity-theory counter-revolution. There were, as I have explained above, five elements in the success of the Keynesian revolution, and I shall take them in turn.

The first was a central attack, on theoretically persuasive grounds, on the central proposition of the orthodoxy of the time. In the case of the Keynesian revolution, that proposition was the automatic tendency of the economy to full employment. In the case of the counter-revolution, the obvious point of attack, in a world characterized by high employment and inflationary tendencies, was the vulgar Keynesian orthodox position that 'money does not matter'. As James Tobin has pointed out, there is a world of difference between two alternatives to this proposition, namely, (i) 'money does too matter' and (ii) 'money is all that matters'. But this difference was easily and conveniently blurred, to the benefit of the counter-revolution, by seizing on the extreme Keynesian position that money does not matter at all as the essence of the prevailing orthodoxy.

The second aspect of Keynesian success was the production of an apparently new theory that nevertheless absorbed all that was valid in the existing theory while so far as possible giving these valid concepts confusing new names. This was the technique followed – again I would emphasize the 'as if' character of my interpretation – in Friedman's classic restatement of the quantity theory of money [2]. The restated quantity theory is, as Patinkin has recently pointed out, essentially a generalization of Keynes's theory of liquidity preference on the basis of a more sophisticated analysis of the nature of wealth and the relation of wealth to income. Novelty and the requisite intellectual confusion were provided by the substitution of the concept of 'permanent income' for that of wealth, and the dragging across the trail of the red herring of human capital that was emerging from other work being conducted at Chicago at that time. Nevertheless, the restatement of the quantity theory of money did include one important and genuinely novel element, drawn not from Keynes but from his predecessors in monetary theory, which was highly relevant to the problem of inflation and which continues to distinguish quantity theorists from Keynesians;

this consisted in its emphasis on the Fisherian distinction between the real and the money rate of interest and on the expected rate of price inflation or deflation as determining the difference between the two.

For the reasons just given, the restatement of the quantity theory provided a new theory meeting the third criterion for success, a degree of difficulty of understanding just sufficient to deter the old and to challenge and reward the young, and hence to re-open the avenues of professional opportunity for the ambitious.

The fourth criterion for success was a new and appealing methodology. Here the counter-revolutionary theory could appeal against the tendency of Keynesian economics to proliferate into larger and yet larger models of the economic system, a tendency which sacrificed theoretical insights to the cause of descriptive realism and which had the incidental but important detractions of demanding large sums of scarce research money available only to senior economists and of turning young economists into intellectual mechanics whose function was to tighten one bolt only on a vast statistical assembly line, the end product of which would contain nothing that could be visibly identified as their own work. In place of this approach, the counter-revolution set up the methodology of positive economics, the essence of which is not to pursue descriptive realism as represented by the largest possible system of general-equilibrium equations, but to select the crucial relationships that permit one to predict something large from something small, regardless of the intervening chain of causation. This methodology obviously offered liberation to the small-scale intellectual, since it freed his mind from dependence on the large-scale research team and the large and expensive computer programme.

The fifth criterion for success was the advancement of a new and important empirical relationship, suitable for determined estimation by the budding econometrician. That relationship was found in the demand function for money, the stability of which was claimed to be the essence of the traditional quantity theory of money. Presentation of the stable demand function for money as the essence of the quantity theory offered a close parallel to the Keynesian consumption function of the 1930s – a statistical relationship simple to understand theoretically and not too hard to estimate statistically, which promised, nonetheless, to contribute importantly to the resolution of central theoretical issues. Moreover, since intelligent and gifted young men and women will persevere until they succeed in finding statistical validation of an allegedly important theoretical relationship, and will then interpret their results as evidence in favour of the theory that originally suggested the relationship, their efforts will inevitably be extremely favourable to the theory in question. And so it has proved. A stable demand function for money is by no means inconsistent with the Keynesian macro-economic general-equilibrium model, and indeed is presumed to exist in the construction of the standard *IS–LM* diagram. But the empirical finding of the existence of such a function has been widely adduced in support of the quantity theory as against the rival Keynesian theory, a procedure justified only by the identification of the Keynesian orthodoxy with the proposition that money does not matter and that velocity is either highly unstable or infinitely interest-elastic.

The quantity-theory counter-revolution could therefore make use of the same factors as facilitated the rapid propagation of Keynesian economics – the attack on a central and widely held theoretical proposition, the development of a new theory that absorbed and rechristened the best of the old, the formulation of that theory in terms that challenged the young and enabled them to leapfrog over the old, the presentation of a new methodology that made more immediate sense than the prevailing methodology, especially in terms of accessibility to the young and to those outside the established centres of academic excellence, and a new and presumptively crucial empirical relationship suitable for relatively small-scale econometric testing.

A counter-revolution, however, has to cope somehow with a problem that a revolution by definition can ignore – though it can trade on it in its propaganda – the problem of establishing some sort of continuity with the orthodoxy of the past. Specifically, the monetarist counter-revolutionaries were burdened with the task of somehow escaping from the valid criticisms of the traditional quantity theory, which the Keynesian revolution had elevated into articles of dogma and self-justification. These criticisms were, first, that the quantity theory had assumed an automatic tendency to full employment, which was manifestly in conflict with the facts of experience; and, second, that velocity was a highly unstable variable, useful, if at all, only for the *ex post* description of historical events. The restatement of the quantity theory met these criticisms by two counter-contentions: that the question of whether the economy responds to monetary impulses by price-level or by output changes is an empirical question falling outside the domain of monetary theory properly defined, because the quantity theory is a theory of the demand for money and not a theory of aggregate response to monetary change; and that the essence of the quantity theory as a theory of the demand for money is not presumptive constancy of velocity but the stable functional dependence of velocity on a few major variables. The former counter-contention freed the quantity theory from the charge that it was too silly to be worth considering, and opened the way for fruitful scientific controversy and development in monetary theory – though, as explained, the abnegation of responsibility for explaining the division of the effects of monetary change between price and quantity movements has subsequently proved a serious shortcoming of the counter-revolution, now that the counter-revolution has come to be taken seriously. The latter counter-contention, involving emphasis on the existence of a stable demand function for money, permitted the absorption of the best of Keynesian ideas into the quantity-theory cause, without any recognized need for acknowledgement of their source. The problem in the case of both counter-contentions was to establish a plausible linkage with pre-Keynesian orthodoxy.

The solution to this problem was found along two lines. The first was the invention of a University of Chicago oral tradition that was alleged to have preserved understanding of the fundamental truth among a small band of the initiated through the dark years of the Keynesian despotism. The second was a careful combing of the *obiter dicta* of the great neo-classical quantity theorists for any bits of evidence that showed recognition (or could be interpreted to show recognition) of the fact that the decision to hold money involves a choice between holding money and holding wealth in other forms, and is conditioned by the rates of return available on other assets.

Don Patinkin has very recently – and over-belatedly, from the standpoint of the history of economic thought – exploded these efforts to provide bridges between the pre-Keynesian orthodoxy and the monetarist counter-revolution [8]. He demonstrates conclusively that in their theorizing the neo-classical theorists did assume a tendency to automatic full employment, and that in their analyses of practical policy problems they regarded the inherent instability of velocity as a major disturbing element and made no use whatever of the functional relationship between velocity and other aggregate variables implied by their own *obiter dicta*. And he shows specifically that the Chicago quantity theorists – Simons and Mints – were no different from their quantity theory colleagues elsewhere in these respects. There was no lonely light constantly burning in a secret shrine on the Midway, encouraging the faithful to assemble in waiting for the day when the truth could safely be revealed to the masses; that candle was made, and not merely lit, only when its light had a chance of penetrating far and wide and attracting new converts to the old-time religion.

Nevertheless, one should not be too fastidious in condemnation of the techniques of scholarly chicanery used to promote a revolution or a counter-revolution in economic theory. The Keynesian revolution derived a large part of its intellectual appeal from the deliberate caricaturing and denigration of honest and humble scholars, whose only real crime was that they happened to exist and stand in the way of the success of the revolution. The counter-revolution had to endow these scholars, or at least their intellectual successors, with a wisdom vastly superior to what their opponents had credited them with. *Obiter dicta* and an oral tradition are at least semi-legitimate scholarly means to this polemical end. Moreover, as time has passed and the counter-revolution has acquired increasing academic respectability, it has become increasingly possible to admit, and even to brag, that the useful ideas have been drawn from the revolution and not from the pre-existing orthodoxy. Indeed, this is a necessary element in a successful counter-revolution, an element for which a previously successful revolution inevitably provides the foundations – because it ultimately becomes possible to draw an intellectually acceptable distinction between the sophisticated ideas of the revolutionary leader and the unsophisticated ideas of the revolutionary followers and executors, and to absorb the former into the counter-revolutionary ideology while discarding the latter as beneath intellectual contempt. The service of drawing this distinction in intellectually acceptable terms has been performed for the monetarist counter-revolution with great scholarly distinction by Axel Leijonhufvud's book on Keynesian economics and the economics of Keynes.

I have in this chapter been concerned primarily with the intellectual and social factors that make it possible to launch a successful revolution or counter-revolution in economic theory. However, I would judge that the key determinant of success or failure lies, not in the academic sphere, but in the realm of policy. New ideas win a public and a professional hearing, not on their scientific merits, but on whether or not they promise a solution to important problems that the established orthodoxy has proved itself incapable of solving. Keynes, and many other economists in Britain and elsewhere, spent much time in the 1920s and 1930s advocating public works as a cure for unemployment – a cure that, because it conflicted with prevailing orthodoxy, was unacceptable. The *General Theory* was successful, precisely because, by providing an alternative theory to the prevailing orthodoxy, it rationalized a sensible policy that had hitherto been resisted on purely dogmatic grounds. Similarly, the monetarist counter-revolution has ultimately been successful because it has encountered a policy problem – inflation – for which the prevailing Keynesian orthodoxy has been able to prescribe only policies of proven or presumptive incompetence, in the form of incomes or guidelines policy, but for which the monetarist counter-revolution has both a theory and a policy solution.

No particular point would be served in an essay of this kind by recounting the stages of accomplishment in the monetarist counter-revolution (see [5]). The advance from strength to strength is summarizable in a few key phrases: the restatement of the quantity theory, a statistical illusion in the judging of Keynesian models, velocity versus the multipler in U.S. monetary history, monetarism versus fiscalism, and 'the new new economics'. The question of interest is whether the monetarist counter-revolution will sweep the board and become the orthodoxy of the future, itself ripe for attack by a new revolution, or whether it will gradually peter out.

Personally, I expect it to peter out, for two reasons. The first, and most important, is that I believe the Keynesians are right in their view that inflation is a far less serious social problem than mass unemployment. Either we will vanquish inflation at relatively little cost, or we will get used to it. The odds at present are that we will accept it as a necessary price of solving other pressing domestic issues – this seems to be the current view of the present Administration – and in that case monetarism will again be reduced to attempting to convince the public of the importance of the problem it is equipped to solve before it can start arguing about the scientific superiority of its proposed solution to the problem. The second reason is that monetarism is seriously inadequate as an approach to monetary theory, judged by prevailing standards of academic economics, and in the course of repairing its intellectual fences and achieving full scientific respectability it will have to compromise irretrievably with its Keynesian opposition.

The most serious defects of the monetarist counter-revolution from the academic point of view are, on the one hand, the abnegation of the restated quantity theory of money from the responsibility of providing a theory of the determination of prices and of output, and, on the other hand, its continuing reliance on the methodology of positive economics. Abnegation of responsibility for analysing the supply response of the economy to monetary impulses, and particularly the disclaiming of the need for an analysis of whether monetary changes affected prices or quantities, was, as I have explained above, necessary to the restoration of the quantity theory to a position of academic respectability. But this need was transitory: once the quantity theory regained academic respectability, it was obliged to resume responsibility for the short-run forecasting of aggregate movements of prices and quantities (see [3]). This it has begun to do, most importantly through the research work of the Federal Reserve Bank of St Louis, and with appreciable success; but it has been lured into playing in a new ball-park, and playing according to a different set of rules than it initially established for itself.

In similar fashion, the methodology of positive economics was an ideal methodology for justifying work that produced apparently surprising results without feeling obliged to explain just why they occurred, and in so doing mystifying and exciting the interest of non-committed economists and wavering Keynesians. But the general-equilibrium and empirical revolutions of the recent past have taught economists to ask for explicit specification of the full general-equilibrium system with which the theorist or empiricist is working, and to distrust results that appear like rabbits out of a conjurer's hat – and an old-fashioned top-hat at that. The demand for clarification of the mechanism by which results can be explained is contrary to the methodology of positive economics, with its reliance on the 'as if' approach. But it will have to be answered satisfactorily if the monetarist counter-revolution is to win general acceptance among the profession; and the attempt to answer it will necessarily involve the counter-revolutionaries in the opposing methodology of general-equilibrium systems and multi-equation econometric models. The quantity theorists have already begun to extend their efforts into simultaneous-equation formulations and estimations of economic relationships. In so doing, they have been making important methodological compromises with the Keynesian opposition – or, to put it another way, reaching out for a synthesis between the revolution and the counter-revolution.

In summary, it seems to me that the monetarist counter-revolution has served a useful scientific purpose, in challenging and disposing of a great deal of the intellectual nonsense that accumulates after a successful ideological revolution. But its own success is likely to be transitory, precisely because it has relied on the same mechanisms of intellectual conquest as the revolution itself, but has been forced by the nature of the case to choose a less important political issue – inflation – to stand on than the unemployment that provided the Keynesian revolution with its political talking point, and has also espoused a methodology that has put it in conflict with long-run trends in the development of the subject. If we are lucky, we shall be forced as a result of the counter-revolution to be both more conscious of monetary influences on the economy and more careful in our assessment of their importance. If we are unlucky (those of us who are not good at jumping on bandwaggons) we shall have to go through a post-counter-revolution revolution as the price of further progress on the monetary side of our science.

REFERENCES

1. S. G. Checkland 'The Propagation of Ricardian Economics in England', *Economica*, N.S., Vol. 16, No. 61 (February 1949), pp. 40–52.
2. Milton Friedman 'The Quantity Theory of Money – A Restatement', in M. Friedman (ed.), *Studies in the Quantity Theory of Money* (Chicago: The University of Chicago Press, 1956), pp. 3–21.

3. Milton Friedman 'A Theoretical Framework for Monetary Analysis', *Journal of Political Economy*, Vol. 78, No. 2 (March/April 1970), pp. 193–238.
4. Alvin Hansen, 'Economic Progress and Declining Population Growth', *The American Economic Review*, Vol. 29 (March 1939), pp. 1–15.
5. Harry G. Johnson, 'Recent Developments in Monetary Theory – A Commentary', in David R. Croome and Harry G. Johnson (eds), *Money in Britain, 1959–1969* (Oxford: Oxford University Press, 1970), pp. 83–114; reprinted as Ch. 1 in this book.
6. 'Monetary Theory and Monetary Policy', *Euromoney,* Vol. 2, No. 7 (December 1970), pp. 16–20; reprinted as Appendix B to this chapter.
7. Axel Leijonhufvud, *On Keynesian Economics and the Economics of Keynes* (London: Oxford University Press, 1968); my review of this book is reprinted as Appendix A to this chapter.
8. Don Patinkin, 'The Chicago Tradition, The Quantity Theory, and Friedman', *Journal of Money, Credit and Banking*, Vol. 1, No. 1 (February 1969), pp. 46–70.

Appendix A

Keynes and the Keynesians[*]

For the first fifteen years after the publication of Keynes's *General Theory of Employment, Interest and Money* (1936), controversy raged in the pages of the learned economic journals over the meaning and validity of virtually every concept and proposition contained in the book. Thereafter there emerged very rapidly an orthodox consensus on what Keynes's contribution to economic theory and policy had been, and controversy virtually ceased – with the exception of an interchange in the pages of *Encounter* some years ago,[1] on the question of whether 'we are all Keynesians now' in our ideas on economic policy, which interchange eventuated in the production of a rather pedestrian book by Robert Lekachman affirming and up-dating the orthodox consensus.[2] Thus Keynes became 'the greatest economist of our time' (meaning that his contribution was so indisputable that no one need concern himself over precisely what it was) and the *General Theory* an 'acknowledged classic' (meaning that no active economist reads it, for fear of discovering that the master was himself confused about the message he had to impart to posterity). Meanwhile 'Keynesian economics' has become the staple fare offered by the textbooks and 'Keynesian' ideas about the economic system have become the foundation of popular and governmental understanding of economic policy issues and policy formation.

The Keynesian approach to economic policy stresses the key importance of the national budget ('fiscal policy' in America) as an

[*] Reprinted from *Encounter*, Vol. XXXIV, No. 1 (January 1970), pp. 70–3.

[1] Robert Lekachman, 'John Maynard Keynes' (December 1963) and Roy Harrod, 'Are We Really All Keynesians Now?' (January 1964). See also the articles by Michael M. Postan, Harry Johnson and Michael Stewart in *Encounter* (January, May and September 1968).

[2] Robert Lekachman, *The Age of Keynes* (London: Allen Lane The Penguin Press, 1967).

instrument of overall economic control. It tends to belittle the relevance and effectiveness of monetary policy (bank rate and all that) as traditionally practised. This approach has been coming increasingly under fire from the resurgent exponents of the quantity-theory approach to monetary matters (dubbed 'monetarists' in the United States), a school of thought that Keynesians had believed vanquished forever by the 'Keynesian revolution'. In Britain ,the Keynesian approach has been severely discredited by the failure of Keynesian policies to make the devaluation of 1967 the predicted success in the year following it, to the point where the Treasury has been obliged to convert to a 'monetarist' approach to the handling of monetary policy. In the United States Keynesianism has been discredited, though to a lesser extent, by the failure of the tax surcharge recommended by the 'New Economics' of the Keynesians (led by Walter Heller) to control the inflation associated with the war in Vietnam.

In these politically exciting circumstances, the question of what Keynes was really driving at, and specifically whether orthodox 'Keynesian economics' represents the essence of Keynes's contribution to the development of economic theory, itself becomes a live and exciting intellectual issue, and not merely a subject for arid scholarly debate among the downtrodden historians of economic thought. The publication of Axel Leijonhufvud's monumentally scholarly – but at the same time enjoyably readable – study of Keynes's economics[1] is therefore most appositely timed, from the point of view not only of the author's reputation but (as it turns out) of the repute of all other interested parties except the beleaguered Keynesians themselves – who in this context are to be identified with an American-led group of economists oriented towards mathematical and econometric model-building. For Leijonhufvud draws a sharp distinction between 'Keynesian economics' and 'the economics of Keynes'. He shows that (on the one hand) the conventional beliefs of the Keynesians find virtually no support in the economics of Keynes,

[1] Axel Leijonhufvud, *On Keynesian Economics and the Economics of Keynes* (London: Oxford University Press, 1968). The main propositions of the book, and a perspective on its contribution, may be found in its author's subsequent pair of lectures at the London School of Economics, *Keynes and the Classics* (London: The Institute of Economic Affairs, Occasional Paper 30, 1969).

and that (on the other hand) Keynes was wrestling with basic theoretical problems of a kind which have attracted in recent times the attention of the neo-quantity theorists rather than the Keynesian model-builders, while his views on economic policy questions broadly accord with the emphasis of the monetarists on the import-ance of money and of monetary policy.

Thus Keynes himself re-emerges as a brilliantly insightful student of the problems of a capitalist economy, whose ideas are directly relevant to ongoing scientific research at the frontiers of contemporary economics and not merely the fossilized relics of the intellectual evolutionary process. The neo-quantity theorists can dispute the credentials of the contemporary Keynesians, and claim the master's blessing for their own endeavours. At the same time, those Keynesians who followed Keynes for what they took to be his social message about capitalism – and have been both resentful and scornful of the way in which the mathematicians and econometricians have whisked Keynes the social critic beyond their (pre-eminently literary) in-tellectual competence and transformed his economics into an arcane quantitative expertise – can take comfort from the thought that those who snatched up and ran with the ball that Keynes put into play were after all heading for the wrong goal-posts and playing by the wrong rules. The only losers are those who have invested heavily of their time and intellect in perfecting the rules and the practice of a game in which Keynes himself was never interested. To put the point in terms of personalities: both Milton Friedman as the leading quantity-theoretic critic of Keynesian economics and Joan Robinson as the leading custodian of the true Keynesian tradition can with a clear conscience commend Leijonhufvud's book to their students; Paul Samuelson, leader of the American Keynesian tradition, will find it embarrassing to do so.

While the general interest in Leijonhufvud's re-interpretation of Keynes lies in its implications for economic policy, the concern of the work is with Keynes's contribution to economic theory. As its author points out (in *Keynes and the Classics*), Keynes cannot really be accorded greatness on the basis of his contributions to thought on economic policy, since these ideas were very much in the air in the 1920s and his policy recommendations were by no means original.

As a background to the understanding of Keynes's real contribution to theory, as Leijonhufvud reconstructs it, it is necessary to describe briefly the standard 'income–expenditure' model of the economy which is the conventional representation of that contribution.

In this model there is one relation between the level of output and the rate of interest which will ensure equilibrium between demand and supply in the market for goods and services, and another relation between the same two variables which will ensure equilibrium between the demand for and supply of money. The two together determine a general equilibrium of the interest rate, output, and employment that will generally not be a full-employment equilibrium. The evolution of the orthodox interpretation of Keynes's contribution proceeded in two stages of counter-revolution.

First, the critics asserted that the Keynesian under-employment equilibrium depended on the assumption that wages were rigid in terms of money, because otherwise wage deflation would increase the quantity of money in real terms, hence lower interest rates and increase output and employment. To this the Keynesians replied that the expected result might not occur, either because investment and consumption were insensitive to interest-rate changes, or because 'liquidity preference' (the willingness to hold more money as interest rates fall) might become absolute, preventing the postulated fall in interest rates. The critics then brought in the 'Pigou effect' – the effect of a rise in the purchasing power of money due to falling prices in increasing wealth and hence consumption, independently of any change in the interest rate. There the matter rested. The critics were content to have proved that Keynesian under-employment equilibrium was a special case of a more general 'classical' economic model, resting either on wage rigidity or neglect of the 'Pigou effect'; and the Keynesians were content to regard the special case as the practically relevant one, on the grounds of the observable reality of wage rigidity. Moreover, the Keynesians belittled the potential effectiveness of monetary expansion as a way of achieving by policy the effect that would follow automatically from wage flexibility if it existed. This was based on the grounds established in defence of Keynes against the first counter-attack, that both investment and consumption expenditure were in practice very insensitive to changes in interest rates. Instead, they placed their faith in fiscal policy, i.e. direct operation on spending through the budget.

Leijonhufvud's interpretation of the economics of Keynes attacks the conventional income-expenditure model of Keynesian economics on two fronts.

First, Leijonhufvud contests the relevance of the framework for assessment of Keynes's contribution provided by a model of the economic system in which wages and prices are assumed to be perfectly flexible. The essence of Keynes's long struggle to escape from the classical tradition of economic theory, he argues, was precisely that Keynes had a vision of the dynamics of the economic process in which the economy responds to disturbances, not by adjusting prices in order to clear markets at unchanged output levels, but by adjusting quantities of goods produced and labour employed in order to adjust output to prices regarded as 'normal'. This procedure is perfectly rational in view of uncertainty about whether changes in demand are temporary or permanent, and in the light of the contemporary theory of information in the market, according to which it is worth while within limits to hold supplies off the market in the hope of ascertaining whether a better price than that immediately available can be obtained by waiting. But the implication of the switch from the assumption of a price-adjusting to that of a quantity-adjusting market-clearing process is precisely the cumulation of disequilibrium through the famous Keynesian multiplier process. This is a concept which contemporary Keynesian theory has tended to abandon as an unnecessary fifth wheel on the elegant coach of general-equilibrium theory.

Second, Leijonhufvud contests the interpretation of Keynes's economics as 'the economics of the [Keynesian] special case'. This requires him to marshal a great deal of complex modern economic theory to set the stage for making his point; and he has to depend heavily on exegetical analysis of some brief and ambiguous passages in the *General Theory*, as well as to draw on aspects of Keynes's *A Treatise on Money*, which he regards as having been subsumed in (whereas many Keynesians have regarded them as replaced by) the analysis of the *General Theory*. Very briefly, Leijonhufvud argues that the essential distinction drawn in the model construction of the

General Theory is between short-lived and long-lived assets, the latter including both bonds and real capital assets. The real capital assets in Keynes's approach must be distinguished from consumption goods, the former having a rising marginal cost of production in terms of the latter. Hence, in Keynes's view, a fall in the money rate of interest must have a substantial stimulative effect on investment, by raising the present value of income streams from long-lived capital assets; hence the demand price offered for newly produced real assets of this kind; and hence the current rate of production of capital goods.

Leijonhufvud further argues that, in sharp and admittedly very controversial contrast with the accepted reading of Keynes's concept of the 'propensity to consume' as a relation between current income and current consumption expenditure, Keynes placed great store on the effect of a fall in the interest rate in increasing the perceived wealth of owners of long-lived assets, and so increasing their consumption expenditure. This argument gets him into the very deep theoretical water of how to rationalize this 'second psychological law of consumption' – since a change in the rate of interest does nothing immediate to alter society's stock of real capital, future flow of output, and consequently objective wealth. His answer is that, because of the limitation of human life expectancy and the nature of capital, the typical wealth-owner has a flow of expected income outlasting his expected needs; so that a fall in the interest rate increases the present value of future income more than that of future needs and makes him feel subjectively wealthier than before. This point Leijonhufvud takes to be the essence of Keynes's concept of 'liquidity preference', the preference for holding wealth in immediately realizable form.

Since, according to Leijonhufvud, Keynes believed that a fall in the interest rate would powerfully affect spending on investment and consumption, the essence of his theory of under-employment equilibrium must lie in those forces in the money economy that prevent the interest rate from falling automatically sufficiently to prevent the multiplier process from doing its fell work of propagating unemployment. Here Leijonhufvud appeals to Keynes's emphasis on expectations about the future rate of interest as an influence on the current interest rate, and the inelasticity of these expectations in response to downward pressures on the currently prevailing rate. But,

Leijonhufvud argues, Keynes did not believe in the power of the speculators to frustrate the use of monetary policy to maintain employment, except during a deep depression. In these circumstances, as Leijonhufvud interprets him, he thought that the problem might be a collapse of the confidence of entrepreneurs in the profitability of investment, rather than too high a market rate of interest. In that case, the appropriate policy would be public investment of a pump-priming nature, rather than monetary expansion aimed at reducing interest rates.

On this interpretation, Keynes appears as both far more perceptive as an economic theorist – and far less devoted to the superiority of fiscal over monetary policy as an economic policy adviser – than contemporary Keynesians would like to believe.

As with any re-interpretation of a classic writer in the light of subsequent scientific progress, there must be a residual doubt as to how far Leijonhufvud's re-reading of Keynes is snatching at straws in order to prevent the breaking of the camel's back and to retain the beast as a working member of the caravan of progress. But there can be no doubt that this work has cleared the air of a stultifying ideological controversy, and paved the way for further advance in the understanding of the workings of a monetary economy.

Appendix B

Monetary Theory and Monetary Policy*

My purpose is to discuss the relation between monetary theory and policy in a broad and general way intended to put current issues of monetary theory and policy in a more general perspective.

In the nature of the case, there is inevitably an evolutionary interaction between monetary theory and monetary policy; and this is a two-way interaction. On the one hand, monetary theorists, like many other academics, have a pronounced tendency towards intellectual laziness. This reflects itself in a tendency to direct theories at current policy problems, and to over-generalize theories which contain large elements of the *ad hoc*. This is one reason why the field of monetary economics is generally more controversial than other areas of economics. On the other hand, the policy-makers tend to become interested in theories only when they know they have made serious mistakes, or have been floundering and everyone knows it, and when a new theory on offer appears to promise a better understanding of the policy problem and a better basis for future policy-making. In between times, the policy-makers tend to take a superior attitude towards theory, and while they use its language, they do so only for the sake of better rationalization of policy decisions taken for their own reasons. On neither side is there a continuing pure-minded search for fundamental truth – which is one reason why claims to have discovered truth, when made, are usually made in exceptionally strident terms.

I should like to begin by sketching briefly the broad outlines of this interaction between theory and policy in contemporary times – by which term I mean to include not merely our own lifetimes, but the relevant historical past.

* Reprinted from *Euromoney*, Vol. 2, No. 7 (December 1970), pp. 16–20.

We may begin with Keynes's *General Theory*. This book rapidly attained the status of a classic – meaning a book whose message everyone thinks he understands too well to need to read it – but its message has recently been re-interpreted in a brilliant book by Axel Leijonhufvud (*Of Keynesian Economics and the Economics of Keynes*). From this re-interpretation emerges, among other things, that the so-called *General Theory* was strongly influenced by Keynes's long concern with British economic policy – which at the time meant monetary policy – in the 1920s, and especially his service on the Macmillan Committee. Put very briefly, as Leijonhufvud interprets him, Keynes believed firmly in the power of monetary policy to control the economy, because he believed that expenditure was responsive to changes in interest rates, *and* that the central bank could control interest rates in spite of the presence of speculators exercising liquidity preference. His concern was not that monetary policy could not work, but that central bankers would not have the courage to use it boldly enough. He also believed, though, according to Leijonhufvud, that in the circumstances of a deep depression the appropriate policy might be, not further reduction of interest rates, but fiscal pump-priming directed at reviving the optimism of private (real) investors.

This, however, was not the message drawn from the *General Theory* by Keynes's fellow economists and, ultimately, by the policy-makers. In part this was due to the fact that Keynes's main theoretical message concerned the proposition that a capitalist system would not automatically produce full employment, but on the contrary some degree of 'involuntary' unemployment would be the general case. In part it was due to the fact that the book appeared at the end of an exceptionally deep depression. The depression was widely interpreted as demonstrating the incapacity of monetary policy, since interest rates everywhere had fallen to exceptionally low levels. In fact, re-examination of the historical evidence (especially in the *Monetary History of the United States* by Friedman and Schwartz) strongly suggests that the deepness of the depression can be accounted for by a twofold failure or perversity of monetary policy: the failure of Federal Reserve policy to prevent a violent contraction of the money supply in the United States, accompanied by widespread bank failures and a loss of confidence in bank deposits, and a failure at the international level to prevent the collapse of world liquidity. Finally, the Keynesian model suggested two special cases in which monetary policy could not work, and in which fiscal policy alone could stimulate economic activity. The first was absolute liquidity preference – a situation in which monetary expansion could not reduce interest rates – and this seemed to be either an actuality or a strong empirical possibility on contemporary interpretations of experience with 'cheap money'. The other case involved inelasticity of spending with respect to interest rates. Keynes himself had argued, with respect to the responsiveness of savings to changes in interest rates, that the effect might go either way, and this was accepted, wrongly, as proving that this effect could be neglected. Everything then turned on the responsiveness of private investment to interest rates; and empirical work through survey research of a kind now regarded as hopelessly superficial, conducted by the Oxford Institute of Statistics, appeared to demonstrate conclusively that private investment was completely insensitive to interest rate changes. Hence monetary policy, which Keynes had regarded as normally a powerful tool of policy, became virtually completely discredited, and fiscal policy, which he had regarded as a tool that might be necessary only in a deep depression, became established as the central and only reliable tool of economic policy.

Central bankers might note that in this way the evolution of Keynesian economics put the seal of intellectual approval on a political event that had already occurred as a result of the great depression and the collapse of the international monetary system, the demotion of central banks as a policy-making force and the rise to prominence of treasuries as the most important policy-making branch of government. This demotion was symbolized, in the history of the Bank of England, by the fact that Montagu Norman at last felt free to marry. Along with the demotion went both great popular hostility to and suspicion of central bankers – in this country accentuated by the political circumstances of the suspension of the gold standard – and more important hostility and suspicion on the part of academic monetary experts. This is still a strong element in the British cultural heritage, and one with which the Bank of England still has to cope. One might regard the abasement of central banks in the 1930s as no more than just retribution for their stupidity and gutlessness in allowing the depression and the collapse of the international monetary system; but the continuing legacy of hostility and suspicion, and especially its concentration on the desirability of low nominal interest rates and hostility to high interest rates on the basis of a variety of completely fallacious economic arguments, is a serious obstacle to efficient policy-making in an era when the chronic problem is to restrain an ebullient and inflation-prone economy.

The particular interpretation of Keynes's theory to which I have referred proved highly useful to treasuries, especially during the Second World War, because it implied that if interest rates had little or no influence on economic activity via aggregate demand, they might as well be kept as low as possible. Further, the expansion of money supply and liquid asset holdings by the public was regarded as harmless and even quite desirable, because on the basis of Keynesian analysis – elaborated by American Keynesians, and especially Alvin Hansen of Harvard, into a general theory of the tendency of capitalism to wallow in secular stagnation – it was believed almost universally that there would be a tremendous depression as soon as the war ended, and that the accumulation of paper wealth in the hands of the public would help to maintain purchasing power. In fact – as a little reference to history would have made perfectly obvious – wars are typically followed by a period of inflation, though the period of inflation may be made very short by a deliberate policy of monetary deflation, such as followed the Napoleonic Wars or the First World War in Britain (in each case induced by a desire to return to the pre-war exchange value of gold). The Second World War was no exception, and both the super-abundance of liquidity and the continued pursuit of cheap money policies after the war contributed greatly to the inflationary experience, the final straw of which was the inflationary impact of the war in Korea.

It was the inflationary period that followed the Second World War combined with the longer-run implications of the return to an international system of fixed exchange rates with currency convertibility, that set in train the process of revival of the powers and prestige of central bankers from the low state of disrepute established in the 1930s. The policy of cheap money had to be abandoned, and the central bank had to cease being merely the government's agent in the twin tasks of minimizing the interest costs of the public debt and attempting to prevent or mitigate the inflationary consequences of such a policy by imposing restrictions of various kinds on commercial-bank lending to the private sector. The process has, however, proceeded at a far slower rate in Britain than in the United States, and – this is probably an important explanatory factor – has been accompanied by far less theoretical controversy, at least until the past few years. The reasons for this difference, I think, are interesting to go into, though in doing so I shall be speculating on matters that require more expert study than I can bring to them. There are, in my view, two fundamental reasons for the difference.

The first stems from the difference between the systems of government in the two countries. The most important difference is that between the parliamentary and the presidential–congressional systems of enacting legislation, with respect to the capacity to use fiscal policy swiftly and flexibly. Under the parliamentary system, the Cabinet can make fiscal policy and implement it, whether its party members understand and accept the theories involved or not. Under the presidential–congressional system, the Administration can design a fiscal policy, but it has to persuade Congress to legislate it – and congressmen are independent, apt to be suspicious of new theories that do not fit their own understandings of common sense, and slow to take action in response to currently apparent needs. The result has been that, until the mid-1960s, the United States did not have a deliberate fiscal policy, and indeed its fiscal legislation was, at times, strongly destabilizing from a Keynesian point of view.

Moreover, though since then the efforts of Walter Heller and the 'New Economics' have succeeded in popularizing the principles of stabilization by fiscal policy, the actual legislation required has been long delayed beyond the need for it, and has had either a destabilizing effect or an insufficiently stabilizing effect. Specifically, the much-heralded tax reduction of 1964 should have been effected in 1960 or 1961, and arrived just in time to contribute to the inflationary boom associated with the escalation of the war in Vietnam. Similarly, the tax surcharge of 1968 arrived two years late, and not soon enough to contribute much to damping the Vietnam war boom. As a consequence, monetary policy has had to bear most of the burden of stabilization policy in the United States – whether it has performed well or badly is another question, the answer to which depends on one's evaluation of the political constraints on the Federal Reserve's actions.

This brings me to a second major difference, that the Federal Reserve is a truly autonomous body, in contrast to the Bank of England, which is nominally, at least, the Treasury's agent. However, though autonomous, the Federal Reserve has to be political, because it is a creation of Congress, and must retain broad support to survive – and it has powerful enemies among both populists, like Wright Patman, who believe in low interest rates as a matter of natural right, and sophisticated left-wing Keynesians, who believe in low interest rates as the key to full employment and economic growth. But it has room for manoeuvre, and has had to use it in the pursuit of unpopular policies. In the course of doing so, its actions have been subjected to a great deal of criticism and analysis from professional economists; and this, in turn, has forced it to take considerable interest both in academic monetary theories and in their application to the formation and evaluation of monetary policy. There are now, if I am correct, three Ph.D.s in economics on the Board of Governors of the Federal Reserve System, including the chairman, and, of course, countless economists working for the System in the various reserve banks; but whether these facts indicate any great reliance on economic science in the formation of monetary policy is an open question.

The second major reason for the difference in experience between the two countries stems from the difference between their academic establishments – the British highly centralized, the American extremely decentralized – and the implications of this difference for the extent of the intellectual conquest of the academic world by the Keynesian revolution. In Britain, Keynesianism was successful in virtually sweeping the intellectual board, and becoming the dominant orthodoxy. Those of the older generation who did not accept the new Keynesian orthodoxy had either to shut up and divert their intellectual efforts to another field of economics, or become pitiful and pitied voices crying in the wilderness. Intellectual support of a politically powerful kind was always forthcoming for the Keynesian (and Treasury) view of how monetary policy fitted into the totality of economic policy, the Radcliffe Report marking the high tide of Keynesianism in this respect. Fundamental doubts about and criticisms of the

Keynesian orthodoxies have begun to appear – and be accorded attention – only recently. This has been due to three factors, in my view.

The first has been the influence of the 'generation gap', which is a powerful force in academic life; a new generation grows up that confronts the prospect of simply perpetuating an established orthodoxy of knowledge, or possibly adding a little at the margins by dint of a great deal of hard work. Some are content and comfortable with this prospect – it is a low-return but low-risk enterprise. Others, however, are not content with defending their elders' orthodoxy and are keen to make a breakthrough in their own right. To do so they need a new set of ideas – and the second factor has been the availability of a ready-made set of concepts and research techniques developed by Milton Friedman and others in the United States, material academically respectable both in its own right and because it comes from the country with leadership in the field as it now stands, yet challenging to apply to U.K. conditions, and promising to permit defeat of the older generation. The third factor, essential to success in this endeavour, is that both the 1967 devaluation and the subsequent failure of devaluation to succeed in improving the balance of payments as soon as promised by the policy-makers, created an intellectual and social environment in which politicians and policy-makers were anxious for new ideas that would redeem the recorded failures. As already hinted, I am cynical enough to think that new ideas get a hearing not on their own merits (which may be virtually completely untested), but because old ideas have become painfully obviously bankrupt.

In the United States, on the other hand, the diversity and competition of the academic world meant that Keynesianism never succeeded in sweeping the academic board. It conquered Harvard and the eastern establishment, and secured its outposts in the west; and this enabled it to dominate so long as the Democrats were in power. But it could not prevent the academic survival of the pre-Keynesian tradition; and indeed its dominance in the eastern establishment fostered a counter-reaction in the hinterlands to the west. Moreover, in the United States, in contrast to Britain, it is possible to be both intellectually and academically respectable and, at the same time, a conservative with significant political influence. Hence an anti-Keynesian school, basing itself on a modernized quantity theory of money, could flourish; and it could be (and inevitably would be) based on institutional and geographical rivalries between men in the same age group rather than on the mechanics of the generation gap as has been necessary in Britain. The intellectual rivalry between Paul Samuelson, as leader of the Keynesians, and Milton Friedman, as leader of the quantity theorists, is a rivalry between generational, intellectual and institutional equals, a very different kind of rivalry than the conflict in Britain between the older generation in command of Oxford and Cambridge and the younger generation in the provincial universities (which term now includes the London School of Economics). Further, given the difference between the roles of intellectuals on the conservative side of politics in the two countries, it was predictable that a shift from a Democratic to a Republican Administration would be accompanied by a rise in prestige for the quantity theorists and a decline in the prestige of the Keynesians – especially as, under the Kennedy Administration, the Keynesian school had achieved political power and influence never achieved before in American political history by a school of economic thought. (Roosevelt's brain trust in comparison was a very mixed bag of indifferently qualified economists.)

Nevertheless, the difference between the two countries in academic organization, and politics in the broad sense of the word, does not really explain the rise to prominence of the monetarist school of thought on American economic policy. Rather, as in Britain, the growth of its popularity has been due to the demonstrated failure of the policy-makers to make policy effectively, and the consequent problem of inflation and balance-of-payments deficit. Here the dishonours are about equally distributed between fiscal policy and monetary policy. The Administration and its economists failed to realize that the escalation of the war in Vietnam would be strongly inflationary unless the Administration introduced large tax increases to finance it – and by the time they realized it, public opinion was unprepared to pay the bill. Monetary policy, on its part, for political reasons, was strongly inflationary when it ought to have been severely deflationary. The result, so far as policy debate has been concerned, has been an ultimately inconclusive wrangle over whether fiscal policy or monetary policy should bear the blame for the inflation, and over which of the two policy instruments is the really powerful one. As in the British case, the interest is monetarism and the quantity theory is to be explained more by the fact that policy based on Keynesian theory, and concentrating on fiscal policy, has been an evident failure, and that monetarism is a new idea that promises to do better, than on full-scale scientific testing of the relative strengths of the two approaches.

Thus far, I have been concerned with the interaction of policy and theory, without much reference to the logical validity of the theory and its empirical reliability. In conclusion, however, I should like to remark that the monetarist counter-revolution has produced some important ideas – new or old – that it is important for policy-makers to integrate into their thinking. This does not, however, mean that I think that policy-makers should go all the way to acceptance of the two key ideas of the monetarist counter-revolution – that the money supply should be expanded at a constant rate based on the normal rate of real economic growth of the economy, and that the economy should adopt a floating exchange rate in order to make this kind of monetary management possible.

There are three ideas that seem to me to emerge from the monetarist controversy that are particularly important. The first is the notion that people get used to the fact of inflation, and that the expected rate of inflation gets incorporated into the level of money interest rates. Hence money interest rates are a very poor guide indeed to whether monetary policy is being inflationary or contractionary, and the policy-makers are better advised to look at the behaviour of the money supply or of domestic credit than at money interest rates as their method of guiding and evaluating their policy decisions. This point is not, of course, new – it is to be found in the works of such classic monetary theorists as Irving Fisher – but the monetarist counter-revolution has emphasized its importance. Quantity theorists, in contrast to Keynesian theorists, have consistently emphasized the importance for monetary developments of expectations about the course of prices. Keynesian theorists, by contrast, have tended to base their theories on the assumption that prices are stable and expected to remain so – a quite unrealistic assumption for the contemporary world.

Second, Keynesian theory has tended to base itself on the assumption that consumption expenditure is a simple function of disposable income, a proposition that supports the belief that change in fiscal policy – especially taxes on income or on expenditure – are extremely effective in altering real demands for goods and services, from a given level of income. The assumption has two major defects, both associated with the influence of expectations on consumer behaviour. First, consumers are influenced in their consumption behaviour by expectations about the future course of prices, and may delay or accelerate purchases in this light. Second, consumption decisions should naturally be influenced by whether tax changes are expected to be permanent or temporary – as well as by expectations about future tax changes themselves. Both these elements were ignored in the formation of British economic policy at the time of the devaluation of the pound in 1967. The public quite rightly expected inflation to follow devaluation. It also knew that political considerations ruled out increases in income taxation, so that the deflationary policies necessitated by devaluation would have to employ excise taxes. And for both reasons it went on a spending spree.

The third idea of importance is that there may be significant connections between monetary policy and the operation of the economy that are not explained by the Keynesian apparatus. That apparatus stresses the influence of changes in investment on consumption through the multiplier, and the feedback of multiplier changes in income on investment through the accelerator. Work on the quantity theory in the United States suggests an alternative mechanism of cyclical propagation – the influence of monetary changes on the level of consumption expenditure, and the feedback effects of changes in consumption on investment expenditures through the accelerator. It may be that consumption expenditure changes induced by monetary-policy changes are more important in generating the business cycle than changes in investment induced by changes in the optimism etc. of the investors.

A second important possibility of monetary policy influence connects the behaviour of the overall balance of payments with the relation between the rate of expansion of domestic credit and the rate of increase of demand for money. The assumed mechanism is a simple one: attempts to expand the money supply too rapidly in relation to the growth of demand for money spill outside the economy into balance-of-payments deficits, and vice versa. This mechanism is to be contrasted with the Keynesian mechanism according to which what matters is the relation of domestic to foreign prices, a relation that can be altered by domestic aggregate demand policies or, in the last resort, by devaluation. The Keynesian 'elasticity' approach to the determination of the foreign balance has not stood up well to the facts of balance-of-payments experience in the past few years. The monetarist approach provides a more plausible explanation of what has happened over the period.

Chapter 3

Problems of Efficiency in Monetary Management[*]

I. INTRODUCTION

Monetary management as generally understood means the management of the money supply and monetary and credit-market conditions by the monetary authority (the central bank) in the pursuit of certain general social objectives. These objectives may either be assigned to the central bank by the national government or be left to the central bank to establish for itself, depending on whether the central bank is a subordinate instrumentality of national economic policy or is allowed a substantial measure of independence. In the past, economists specializing in the study of monetary management have been predominantly either institutionalists concerned with the detailed structure of the financial system and the precise institutional ways in which the central bank operates on that system in pursuit of its objectives, or economic historians concerned with the evolution of the financial organization of a particular country or countries, the theories of monetary management advocated by historically influential personages, and the influence of these theories on legislation affecting the structure of the financial system and the central bank's concept of its role and functions. (There have, of course, always been non-specialist critics of financial organization and monetary management, some of whom have in due course achieved the status of historically influential personages.) With the professionalization of economics, the accompanying increase in confidence in the scientific approach to economic problems, and the resulting tendency to apply the scientific approach increasingly to problems of

* Reprinted from *Journal of Political Economy*, Vol. 76, No. 5 (September/October 1968), pp. 971–90. Copyright 1968 by University of Chicago Press, all rights reserved.

economic policy – problems in normative rather than positive economic science – that has occurred since the 1930s and especially since the Second World War, economists concerned with monetary management have become decreasingly concerned with institutional and historical questions *per se* and increasingly concerned with normative problems – i.e. with problems of efficiency in monetary management. This approach requires the application of economic theory – and in some cases of econometrics – more intensively to the processes and practices of monetary management than has generally been the case in the past.

The purpose of this chapter is to survey some of the problems of efficiency in monetary management, as they have emerged from recent theorizing and research. For this purpose, three aspects of the problem of efficiency are distinguished: (i) structural efficiency, by which is meant efficiency in the ordinary economic sense of the banking system considered as an industry whose primary function from the monetary point of view is to provide the means of payment (currency and deposits subject to check) for the economy, though from a broader point of view it also plays an important part in the capital market as a medium for saving and an allocator of capital among competing borrowers; (ii) efficiency in stabilization policy, i.e. policy directed at keeping the economy on a desired course and correcting deviations from that course; and (iii) efficiency in secular economic policy, i.e. efficiency with respect to the choice of the desired level and trend over time of the major macro-economic variables that reflect the economy's performance. It should be emphasized that these last two problems are, generally speaking, not problems of monetary management alone, if monetary management is identified with central bank policy, but are rather problems in the joint use of monetary, fiscal and possibly exchange rate policy for the purpose of economic stabilization and the fulfilment of the general objectives of full employment, price stability, economic growth and balance-of-payments equilibrium. In some cases, it is possible to indicate theoretical solutions to the problems of efficiency; in other cases, it is only possible to indicate the considerations that must enter into an efficient solution. Where the analysis depends upon assumptions about institutional practices, it should be understood that the reference is to the monetary and banking institutions of the

United States, United Kingdom, and other countries in the British tradition of banking, so that the conclusions may not be directly applicable to other countries, particularly those of Continental Europe.

II. PROBLEMS OF STRUCTURAL EFFICIENCY

As already mentioned, the banking system can be regarded as an industry that, on the one hand, provides a payments mechanism for the economy and, on the other hand, through its payments-mechanism operations and the acceptance of interest-bearing non-checkable deposits, assembles capital for investment in various forms of assets, thereby playing an important part in the capital market.

There is at the foundation of normative (welfare) economics a presumption that free competition will promote the efficient performance of economic activities; and this presumption would seem to apply to the banking industry, with important qualifications deriving from the special characteristics of money to be noted below. Free competition in the banking industry would lead banks to compete for checkable deposits by offering interest and charging competitive rates related to costs for the provision of the services of the payments mechanism, in order to obtain funds for investment. It would also lead banks in their lending operations to provide those loan facilities and invest in those marketable assets that the banks could manage with an efficiency superior to that of other financial institutions. The result, assuming that the banking system remained competitive, would be to maximize efficiency in the provision of a payments mechanism and in the allocation of capital, with one potentially important qualification.

Efficiency in the allocation of capital would follow from the usual arguments for free competition among rival business firms; the achievement of efficiency in the provision of the payments mechanism, however, requires some explanation since it involves an application of monetary theory. Briefly, the payment of competitive interest rates on checkable deposits means that holding assets in monetary form would entail no alternative opportunity cost for wealth-owners other than the real social costs – operating expenses and a normal rate of return on the capital employed – of maintaining the system of checking accounts, so that the public would be encouraged to satiate its desire for liquidity. At the abstract level of pure theory, the costs of maintaining a system of bank accounts – as distinct from the costs of using these accounts to make payments – can be regarded as negligible: in theoretical terms, money can be provided at zero social cost. Maximization of welfare requires that a good that can be provided at zero marginal social cost should be provided in the quantity that yields zero marginal utility, i.e. that satiates demand, and this result would be insured by the payment of competitive interest rates on checkable deposits. Similarly, the charging of competitive costs for the use of the services of the payments mechanism would induce the deposit-holding public to make optimal use of that mechanism: in other words, to arrange its monetary transactions so as to use the bank account payments mechanism only for transactions that are privately worth their social cost. In short, a competitive banking system would encourage the public to hold the socially optimum quantity of money and make socially optimum use of the payments mechanism.

This conclusion, however, is subject to a qualification that arises from the availability of currency – coin, but especially notes – as an alternative means of making payments. This alternative medium of exchange is non-interest-bearing, and it would be extremely difficult, though not necessarily impossible, to arrange for the issue of an interest-bearing currency. On the other hand, the issuing authority (the treasury or the central bank) bears the real resource costs of providing currency. In the case of the coinage, the direct costs are the capital cost of the metal and the running costs of coining and recoining and the loss of metal through abrasion. In the case of paper money, there is the cost of the special paper and of design, printing and reprinting. In addition, in both cases there is the additional direct cost of security precautions and the indirect cost of policing against forgery. The coinage is known to be directly profitable, as a general rule: when it ceases to be so because of a rise in the value of the metal used, steps are taken fairly quickly to restore its profitability by substitution of cheaper metals. The issue of paper money also is generally assumed to be directly profitable, in the sense that the interest earned by the issuing authority on assets bought with paper money exceeds the running cost of providing the paper money; though there are limits to the validity of this assumption, as evidenced by the fact that the Bank of England some years ago found it necessary to curb a vogue for making payments in newly printed money by requesting the customers of banks to make do with already-used Bank of England notes. Whether coinage and the issue of paper money are socially profitable when the indirect costs of policing against forgery are taken into account is an unresolved question. But on the assumption that the issue of notes and coin is socially profitable, in the sense of yielding a surplus above the cost of production and policing, it follows that the private cost of holding currency exceeds the social cost, or that the private return from holding currency falls short of the social return. On the other hand, the private cost of using currency for making payments falls short of the social cost, insofar as the circulation of currency leads to its deterioration; but this aspect of the use of currency can probably be safely disregarded as of trivial importance, since the social cost of individual exchanges of currency, in the form of physical depreciation of the medium of exchange, must be negligible. The substantive point therefore is that, because the private cost of holding currency (the interest foregone) substantially exceeds the social cost (raw material, value added and policing), free competition in banking, by making the private and social cost of deposit-holding coincide, would tend to produce a socially non-optimum overallocation of resources to the provision of deposit money and underallocation of resources to the provision of currency for holding. The charging of full cost for the use of the deposit payments mechanism would similarly promote over-use of currency and under-use of deposits in making payments, though this source of inefficiency can be regarded as negligible for the reasons already given. The social loss resulting from the stimulus to excessive deposit-holding relative to currency-holding would depend on the elasticity of substitution between the two forms of money in the demand of users of money. On the assumption that currency cannot be issued other than as a non-interest-bearing asset, achievement of the 'second-best' welfare optimum would require a tax on the holding of deposit money at a rate somewhere between zero and the competitive interest rate on deposits, the precise tax rate depending on the relative strength of the effects of the tax in discouraging the holding of checkable bank deposits as compared with untaxed non-monetary assets and encouraging the holding of currency as compared with checkable bank deposits. This qualification of the argument for free competition in banking is disregarded in the remainder of the analysis.

The case just presented for free competition in commercial banking depends crucially on the assumption that a banking system in which competition among banks was unregulated by legislation or central bank supervision would remain competitive. Historical experience strongly suggests, however, that unrestricted competition among banks tends to lead to concentration of the industry through expansion of the larger units and through mergers. The reason presumably is that there are significant economies of scale – both in the operation of the deposit payments mechanism and in the operation of the lending and investment side of the banking business – which give a profit incentive to concentration and, on the payments side at least, may indicate the social desirability of operating the banking business as a public utility. In the United States, the tendency to concentration has been held in check at a relatively early stage of concentration by public fears of a banking monopoly given expression through banking legislation, which falls to the responsibility of the individual states in the federal system of American government; but the trend to concentration has nevertheless been persistent. The U.S. banking system therefore can probably be fairly described as competitive and efficient within the framework of legislation governing it, but possibly socially inefficient in providing a payments mechanism in the sense that a national 'giro' system of some sort might reduce substantially the cost of making payments. In the United Kingdom, control over bank mergers of an 'informal' but nevertheless effective sort, designed to prevent bank mergers in restraint of competition, was introduced after the wave of mergers that occurred towards the end of the First World War. The result has been to consolidate and perpetuate a situation of oligopolistic competition in British banking, which appears socially inefficient from a variety of points of view, but which has been tolerated and even encouraged by the monetary authorities since it lends itself readily to control by persuasion and directive in subservience to the objectives of economic policy. Britain, incidentally, to improve the efficiency of her payments mechanism, is in the process of introducing a 'giro' system with which the banks will have to compete.

In general, the presence of economies of scale in the banking business forces social policy concerned with efficiency to contemplate the familiar choice between (i) designing a regulatory system that will enable private competitive organizations to obtain the economies of scale while preventing them from exercising monopoly power, and (ii) replacing private enterprise by a public utility that will obtain the efficiency of a monopoly while operating in the public interest. With the rapid development of the electronic computer as an instrument of efficient large-scale bookkeeping, the feasibility of a single national, or even international, credit payments system that would be less expensive than traditional commercial bank payments operations is more likely; and it is possible that in the long run such systems will replace the checking facilities provided at present by the commercial banks, which would presumably revert to institutions primarily occupied in lending out savings deposits intrusted to them. In the meantime, however, to the extent that society values the preservation of a private enterprise, non-monopolized commercial banking system, the case for free competition remains relevant.

The analysis thus far has been concerned with the efficiency of the banking system, considered as an industry like any other industry. The banking system cannot, however, in strict logic, be so treated, because of the special characteristics that distinguish its product – money, the means of payment – from the products of other private enterprises – real goods and services. The crucial difference between the banking industry and other industries is that whereas other industries provide real goods and services that the public demands, so that a stable equilibrium of demand and supply will be attained under competition, the banking industry provides nominal money – money denominated in marks, pounds, dollars or other monetary units of account – while the public demands real balances – stocks of purchasing power. The public can adjust the real value of any given quantity of nominal money balances supplied by the banking system to that quantity of real balances it desires to hold by changing the price level through its efforts to substitute goods for real balances when real balances are excessive at the current price level, and to substitute real balances for goods when real balances are insufficient at the current price level. In the alternative Keynesian framework of analysis, excess real balances lower the rate of interest, increase

investment and possibly consumption demand, and so raise prices –
and conversely for deficient real balances. Thus, in terms of static
theory, the quantity of nominal balances supplied will be in neutral
equilibrium; any other quantity could be made the equilibrium
quantity through appropriate changes in the price level. Less
abstractly, a competitive banking system would be under constant
incentive to expand the nominal money supply and thereby initiate
price inflation. With random economic variations, uncertainty, and
'money illusion' on the part of the banks (defined as confidence in the
stability of the value of money), the price level would be inherently
unstable; variations in it would produce changes in bank lending
and the quantity of money that would reinforce the initial change.

Stability in the trend of prices (a special case of which is price
stability) and in the trend of expectations about the future course of
prices – which are generally agreed to be important to the social
welfare – requires social control over the total quantity of money
supplied by the banking system. By tradition, this control is exercised by the central bank. According to the general-equilibrium
theory of a monetary economy, central bank control presupposes the
power to determine one nominal monetary magnitude in the system
and one interest rate. In traditional central banking practice, this
requirement is fulfilled by the central bank's control over the quantity of cash reserves available to the commercial banking system, its
reserves being its own note and deposit liabilities (less currency in
circulation among the public), and by the convention that its notes
and deposits bear zero interest for the holder.

For the same reasons that economic efficiency requires the payment of interest on deposit money held by the public, optimal resource allocation requires the payment of interest by the central bank
on its liabilities held as reserves by the commercial banks, at a rate
determined by the yield on its assets less operating costs. This
principle by itself is somewhat ambiguous, since as a government-
sponsored monopoly the central bank is under no pressure to practise
efficiency in its staffing and other management policies and is under
considerable pressure to use its resources to lend to government at
subsidized rates; and it should be extended by a stipulation of central
bank efficiency in both office and portfolio management. The
principle also raises the practical problem of implementation with

respect to commercial bank holdings of reserves of currency, which as already mentioned conventionally bears no interest. Payment of interest on commercial bank holdings of central bank deposits but not on their holdings of currency would create an incentive for the banks to hold an excessive ratio of deposits to currency in their reserves. This incentive could possibly be removed by the central bank's paying interest on the reported average currency holdings of the commercial banks. The convention of non-payment of interest by the central bank on commercial bank reserves constitutes in effect a tax on the creation and use of deposit money, which militates against the efficient provision of a payments mechanism. The incidence of this tax falls entirely on the deposit-holding public if the banking system is competitive and banking services can be provided at constant cost; it is shared between the public and the banks if the banking industry is subject to rising costs as scale increases or if the banking industry is monopolized or oligopolistic.

As just mentioned, the central bank can control the price level if it fixes the yield on its liabilities and controls the quantity thereof through open-market operations, quite consistently with free competition in the banking industry. It will, of course, have to acquire from experience an accurate knowledge of the factors determining the ratios of reserves to deposits the commercial banks will choose in their own self-interest to hold under varying circumstances; but this is a legitimate part of the task of central bank management. In the actual practice of central banking, however, reliance is placed on additional instruments and techniques of control over the commercial banks. From the point of view of the theory of monetary control, these additional controls are unnecessary, if not positively mischievous; and their effect for the most part is to impose taxation on the commercial banks and ultimately on the users of deposit money, additional to what is imposed by the non-payment of interest on bank reserves, to the detriment of efficiency in the long-run allocation of the economy's resources between the provision of the payments mechanism and other uses.

In the grand tradition of central banking, and especially in the practice of the Bank of England, great emphasis is placed on the use of rediscount policy, especially changes in the rediscount rate, as an instrument of monetary policy – in British practice, the primary instrument. The availability of the rediscount facility in fact, however, constitutes a breach in the central bank's control of the volume of its liabilities, permitting the commercial banks to offset the central bank's open-market operations by temporary or renewed borrowing; and this breach has to be plugged by the establishment of conventions against continued or 'excessive' use of the facility, supported ultimately by the threat of central bank denial of the facility to a transgressor, a situation undesirable because it entrusts the central bank with the exercise of arbitrary and ill-defined authority. At least in the presence of a well-developed capital market, and on the assumption of intelligent and responsible monetary management by the central bank, the commercial banks should be able to manage their reserve positions without the need for the central bank to function as 'lender of last resort'. Apart from this consideration, it is questionable whether changes in the rediscount rate perform very efficiently as signals of the central bank's intentions with respect to monetary policy – if communication of this kind is desirable, there are other ways of providing it. And at a deeper level of analysis it is questionable whether the central bank is well advised to aim at exercising monetary control through the fixing of the level of short-term interest rates rather than through the determination of the reserve base of the monetary system. Finally, the fact that in British practice changes in bank rate derive much of their leverage from the conventional fixing of interest rates on clearing bank deposits, advances, and other accounts by a percentage margin below or above bank rate raises the question whether a cartelized pricing policy of this type serves the interests of economic efficiency.

As already mentioned, the conventional non-payment of interest on commercial bank reserve holdings of central bank liabilities constitutes an implicit tax on the provision of deposit money through the commercial banking system. The burden of this tax is increased by the stipulation of minimum or average cash reserve ratios, to the extent that such stipulation obliges the banks to hold a larger volume of non-interest-earning reserves than they would voluntarily choose to hold for the efficient conduct of their business. By comparison with conventional average reserve ratio requirements, legal minimum requirements impose an additional burden, since the banks must guard against violation of the requirement by holding excess cash reserves or by keeping their non-cash assets sufficiently liquid to be able to meet unexpected reserve drains. In addition to this implicit tax imposed through the central bank's monopoly of the provision of cash reserves and the government's power to impose reserve requirements, the commercial banks, and ultimately the deposit-holding public, are taxed indirectly in a variety of other ways through regulations adopted either to control the banks' commercial operations, to facilitate central bank control, or to cushion the market for government debt against the impact of monetary policy. Thus, prohibiting the banks from undertaking certain kinds of lending or restricting the amount of such lending they can undertake, either permanently or in times of restrictive monetary policy, reduces the commercial profitability of banking; so does the fixing of liquid asset ratios, which obliges the banks to hold a larger proportion of lower-yielding assets than they would voluntarily choose and may also reduce the yield on these assets below what it would otherwise be. In similar fashion, the fixing of maximum interest rates on certain kinds of bank lending, such as consumer loans and mortgage lending, acts as an implicit tax by confining banks to those loans in these categories for which the credit risk is low enough to justify lending at the permitted rate.

The rule or convention against the payment of interest on checking accounts which exist in some countries is a special kind of tax, since it is levied on the depositors for the benefit of the banks rather than the government. The main argument for not paying interest on checking accounts, that it prevents reckless competition for deposits among banks, has been shown to be unsupported by the empirical evidence in the country where the argument is most fashionable (the United States) and is inconsistent also with the broad range of historical evidence. In any case the rule is impossible to enforce, since banks can get around it in part by crediting notional interest earnings against charges for deposit operation until charges are reduced to zero (as in Britain), or by offering free checking and other services proportioned to the size of the customer's account, and by competing via other attractions, such as gifts of merchandise (in the United States) or a plethora of conveniently located branches (as in Britain). To the extent that the ban on paying interest is effective, the result is a socially inefficient restriction on the holding of checking deposits; to the extent that interest can only be received by making free use of the payments mechanism, the result is the encouragement of socially excessive use of that mechanism; and to the extent that implicit interest earnings are returned to the customer in banking services and convenience that he would not freely choose if offered the alternative of cash payments, the result is a partial waste of resources.

From the point of view of the monetary authority, the various interferences with the commercial banks' freedom to choose the composition of their asset portfolios to maximize profits, discussed above, have the advantages (apparent or real) of increasing the predictability of commercial bank response to monetary policy action and of improving the short-run effectiveness of monetary control of economic activity. The latter is particularly the case where directives can strike at borrowers who have no other source of credit than the commercial banks (such as many consumers and small businesses), or where maximum lending rates imposed on certain types of bank lending lead the banks to discontinue such lending when interest rates rise. Even from the point of view of effectiveness of control, however, such selectivity has corresponding disadvantages: credit discrimination against particular classes of borrower or of loan-financed activity may involve short-run disruption of established financial relations and in the longer run distort the growth of the economy and reduce its efficiency. From the point of view of structural efficiency considered here, the most relevant consideration is that by imposing an implicit tax on commercial banking, these techniques of control restrict the scale of the cheque-payment system provided by the commercial banks to something below the social optimum. They also encourage the growth, in competition with the commercial banks, of rival financial institutions which offer money substitutes to asset holders and conduct lending operations similar to those of the banks, more or less free of the burden of implicit taxation imposed by monetary management proximately on the banks and ultimately on their depositors.

Furthermore, in this connection it is important to note that the burden of implicit taxation on the commercial banking system and its depositors is in general an increasing function of the level of interest rates. This is obviously so with respect to the taxation implicit in the compulsory holding of non-interest-bearing reserves, and also with respect to interest ceilings on particular categories of bank lending. As regards depositors, the burden of the ban on interest payments for checking deposits obviously increases as the general level of interest rates increases – with a consequent tendency for depositors to shift out of such deposits into substitutes bearing a more flexible rate of interest. The banks, by contrast, derive from this ban in the short-run additional earnings which may compensate or more than compensate them for the greater loss of interest on their reserve holdings; but in the longer run, the effect must be to reduce the relative scale of the banking industry by reducing the relative attractiveness of its product.

The general effect of these various implicit taxes on commercial banking, in the context of the general trend towards rising interest rates since the Second World War, has undoubtedly been to contribute to the development of competing financial intermediaries and a relative loss of business to them by the banks. The spokesmen for the banking community have generally reacted to this development by arguing for the application to their competitors of the same sort of reserve requirements and control by directives as those to which the banks are subjected. This is an argument, however, for what is technically known as a 'second-best' solution, which might or might not produce an improvement from the social point of view. That is, while the equalization of conditions of competitition between banks and rival financial intermediaries would improve the allocation of a given amount of resources between the two types of institutions, the imposition of comparable taxation on all intermediaries would involve a socially non-optimal restriction of all financial intermediation as compared with alternative economic activities, and the social loss on this account might outweigh the gain from improved allocation of resources among financial intermediaries. Improvement from the social point of view is far more likely to be attained by mitigation of the special implicit tax burden which existing techniques of monetary control impose on the commercial banking system.

III. PROBLEMS OF EFFICIENCY IN STABILIZATION POLICY

Stabilization policy, as defined above, comprises the use of the government's instruments of economic control – monetary policy, fiscal policy and possibly exchange rate policy, as well as more direct and selective controls – to keep the economy on a desired path of evolution in the face of spontaneous destabilizing developments in the economic system. The general nature of the corrective actions that may need to be taken is familiar from the Keynesian theory of income determination and the associated theories of fiscal and monetary policy. These theories are, however, couched in terms of static-equilibrium analysis, whereas the stabilization problem in practice requires the use of policy instruments which operate with a varying ('distributed') lag on an economic system that responds to both spontaneous and policy-induced changes according to its own distributed lag pattern. This fact creates a problem of efficiency in the design and operation of stabilization policy, quite apart from the problem of efficiency in the selection of the desired path of evolution of the economy, to be considered in section IV.

Ideally, those responsible for stabilization policy should be armed both with full knowledge of the distributed lag structures according to which the economy reacts to spontaneous and policy-induced changes, and with the means of forecasting accurately the spontaneous changes that it is the responsibility of stabilization policy to offset. Near-perfect or perfect stabilization would then be possible. In practice, however, forecasting ability is limited, and the authorities have to rely to a large extent on responding in their policy actions to deviations of the current or immediately past performance of the economy from the desired path of evolution. Moreover, knowledge of the pattern and time distribution of lags in the response of the economy to spontaneous and policy-induced changes is also limited. This situation raises problems of efficiency in the design of policy responses to deviations in actual from desired performance; questions about the efficiency of stabilization policies as traditionally practised, especially by central banks, in achieving a significant improvement in the stability of the economy; and the general problem of improving the stabilization operations of the central banks by founding them more securely on economic analysis of and empirical research on the stabilization problem.

The problem of efficient policy-response design in a system in which policy responds to deviations of actual from desired performance ('errors') is very similar to the engineering problem of designing efficient automatic control mechanisms and has been explored most thoroughly by electrical engineers interested in economic policy problems, notably by A. W. Phillips. An obvious point that emerges from this exploration is the importance of rapid reaction of policy to the observation of errors: the longer the lag in policy response, the lower the degree of improvement in stability that can be achieved, and the more likely is a policy response of a given magnitude to destabilize rather than stabilize the system. Less obvious, but in some respects more important, is the fact that an efficient system of economic control (stabilization) requires some mixture of three types of control reaction – the mixture and magnitudes of the control reactions depending on the general characteristics of the economic system being controlled, the lengths of the time lags in the reaction of the system to change, and the structures or time profiles of the various lags.

The three types of control reaction can be characterized as different ways of formulating the error in the performance of the system for the purposes of taking corrective policy action. Control may be based on three mathematical expressions of the error – its current level (*proportional control*), its cumulative value (*integral control*), and its rate of change (*derivative control*). Each has its advantages and disadvantages from the viewpoint of efficient stabilization. Proportional control has the advantage of pulling the economy in the right direction so long as it is off-target, but for that very reason it must fall short of the goal of stabilization; in addition, a sufficiently strong control response operating with a sufficiently long lag will introduce fluctuations. Integral control will keep the economy on target if it is already there and will tend to return it to the desired path in case of errors, but it involves a strong tendency towards overshooting especially if it operates with a long lag. Derivative control tends to stabilize the economy at its current level of operation – whatever that level may be – and may also induce fluctuations about that level if applied forcefully but with a long lag. Thus, for efficient stabilization, the three must be used in combination, both the relative and the absolute dependence on each having to be determined from the characteristics of the economy mentioned above.

The engineering approach to the requirements of an efficient

102

stabilization policy leaves something to be desired from the economic point of view, since it formulates the problem in mechanical terms of achieving approximation to a desired stable path without reference either to the social costs of deviating from that path, or to the economy's reactions to the control operation itself. Further, this approach assumes somewhat inconsistently that disturbances cannot be forecast and that lags in policy response to errors cannot be altered, but that the requisite information on the lag structures of the economy's response to changes can be obtained. Nevertheless, the analysis does raise questions about the likely efficiency in stabilization policy of traditional central bank policy formation procedures, and it points to the need for scientific study of lag structures in the economy and in policy responses to change and for the use of the results of such study in the design of appropriate policy responses.

The prevalence of lags in the response of the policy-makers to changes in the economy, and in the response of the economy to changes in economic policy, together with the variability of these lags, has led a number of monetary experts to question whether traditional central banking operations can contribute much to the stabilization of the economy. Some – notably Milton Friedman – have become convinced by theoretical and empirical analysis that efforts at short-run stabilization given the present state of knowledge and with present institutional practices are likely to do more harm than good, and they have consequently argued that such efforts should be abandoned in favour of a 'monetary rule' according to which the monetary authority would be obliged to expand the money supply at a steady rate proportional to the normal rate of growth of the demand for money as the economy expands with stable prices. The argument for this proposal is partly that while a rule of this kind would not do as well as an ideal stabilization policy, it would produce better results than stabilization policy as actually practised. More fundamentally, the proposal rests on the belief that arbitrary changes in monetary policy have been a more important source of economic disturbance than spontaneous changes arising in the private sector of the economy and that the primary problem of stabilization policy is to create a stable monetary environment within which the private sector can calculate rationally.

A number of economists have been concerned recently with the alternative possibility of improving the central bank's methods of management of stabilization policy to make it more effective in achieving its objectives. Formally, the central bank (and, more generally, the economic policy authorities) can be conceived of as making policy decisions on the basis of certain 'indicator' variables, which are taken to reflect the current state and direction of the economy, and adjusting the 'instrument' variables of policy to alter the levels of 'target' variables which are assumed to govern the operations of the economy. (The same variable may serve in more than one capacity.) The problem of maximizing effectiveness then becomes a series of sub-problems in the choice of the most reliable indicator variable or variables, and the choice of target variables at once amenable to control by the central bank by use of its policy instruments and potent in governing the economy, these choices requiring an empirically validated knowledge of the structure of the economy and the time lags of its responses. One of the chief issues in this area is whether the central bank should seek to control the economy by controlling the level of interest rates, or the level of some monetary magnitude such as total money supply, bank cash reserves, the 'free' reserves of the banking system, or the cash base of the entire monetary system. There is a theoretical presumption in favour of control of a monetary magnitude rather than interest rates (and, among the monetary magnitudes, in favour of the cash base) on the grounds of directness of control and clarity of theoretical significance of what is being controlled, but the issue can only be resolved by empirical exploration.

Like the application of control-system engineering to the design of monetary policy responses, work on these lines has tended to suffer somewhat from taking stabilization *per se* as the objective of policy and the measure of success. Even on this mechanical basis, a generally acceptable measure of performance with respect to stabilization of the economy is not easy to devise. In the broader context of economic theory, however, the purpose of short-run stabilization is to increase the economic welfare of the community, and an economic measure of the success of stabilization policy would have to specify what welfare is presumed to be in this context and how it is affected by stabilization policy operations. A major implication of the concept of 'stability' as an objective of policy is that stability will improve the accuracy of the calculations and predictions on the basis of which resources are allocated among current uses and between current consumption and investment for the satisfaction of future needs. This suggests that both the formulation of policy and the evaluation of its success require a formal definition of the economic costs of instability more sophisticated than some mechanical measure of the deviations of indicator variables from a trend or norm. It also suggests that there may arise internal contradictions between the objective of stabilization policy and the means employed to implement it, in the sense that stabilization operations, by disturbing public expectations derived from previous experience, may cause more distortions of private economic calculations than they prevent. The proponents of a 'monetary rule' believe that stability would be improved by removing the possibility of arbitrary discretionary policy changes by the central bank. Whether that belief is justified or not, it is clear that knowledge of the mechanisms by which the expectations of the public are formed, and the influence on these expectations of policy actions, is of great importance to the design of short-run stabilization policy, and these mechanisms cannot be fully satisfactorily dealt with by compressing them into the distributed lag structure of the economy.

IV. PROBLEMS OF EFFICIENCY IN SECULAR ECONOMIC POLICY

Short-run stabilization policy is concerned with minimizing deviations of the economy from its desired trend path of evolution. Secular economic policy is concerned with the selection of the desired trend path of evolution itself. While the objectives relevant to this social choice comprise at least the standard four of full employment, price stability, economic growth at a satisfactory rate, and balance-of-payments equilibrium, with possibly the addition of a fifth in the form of an equitable distribution of income, the analysis of the choice as its affects the use of the macro-economic instruments of stabilization policy (monetary and fiscal policy) has concentrated on the first two, and specifically on the conflict or possible trade-off between full employment and price stability.

The possibility of a conflict between the objectives of full employment and price stability was discerned by writers on economic policy very soon after Keynes's *General Theory* had demonstrated that full employment was legitimately an objective of economic policy. (Previously, when the concern of policy was limited to the achievement of price stability, a similar conflict had been discerned between internal and external stability in a fixed exchange-rate system, a conflict which is still urgent but lies outside the scope of this chapter.) Analysis of this conflict and the social choice it made necessary was, however, confined to elaboration of the problem and exploration of the possibility of mitigating it by institutional reforms designed to increase the perfection of competition in the goods and labour markets of the economy, until the nature of the choice involved was formalized in the concept of the 'Phillips curve'.

The Phillips curve in its simplest form hypothesizes a relation between the percentage of unemployment in the economy and the rate of increase in wages or prices (the rate of price increase being lower than the rate of wage increase by the rate of increase of productivity), such that the rate of inflation increases more than proportionately as the percentage of unemployment falls and decreases less than proportionately as the percentage of unemployment increases. (In idealized geometrical textbook representations, the rate of inflation asymptotically approaches infinity as the unemployment percentage approaches zero; as the percentage of unemployment increases, inflation turns into deflation, and the rate of deflation asymptotically approaches a constant as unemployment increases.) This hypothesis derived great appeal from the fact that early empirical work, based on British data, appeared to confirm the presence of a surprisingly stable econometric relationship of this type; subsequent research, however, has called into question both the theoretical foundations and the statistical reliability of the curve.

Assuming the reality of the Phillips curve, society can be envisaged as choosing the socially optimum combination of unemployment and inflation available to it on its Phillips curve as the target which fiscal and monetary policy should be directed towards achieving. Additionally, society would seek to use its control over the institutions of competition to shift the Phillips curve as far as possible in the favourable direction of less inflation with a given rate of unemployment and vice versa. The choice of position on a given Phillips curve can be formalized in the notion of a social preference system, attributing greater social welfare to less unemployment and less inflation, the optimal choice being represented by the tangency of an indifference curve of the preference system with the Phillips curve.

This formalization, while popular, is unfortunately rather empty of economic content, since it simply postulates that society is able to weigh more unemployment against more inflation in some unspecified manner to arrive at a preferred position. Yet the rate of inflation and the rate of unemployment, unlike the nuts and apples of conventional individual preference theory, are not strictly comparable objects of choice which can be rationally evaluated according to this theoretical schema. From one important point of view, indeed, the avoidance of inflation and the maintenance of full employment can be most usefully regarded as conflicting class interests of the bourgeoisie and the proletariat, respectively, the conflict being resolvable only by the test of relative political power in the society and its resolution involving no reference to an overriding concept of the social welfare.

If some concept of the general welfare is to be applied, it would seem necessary to go beyond the mere postulation of a social preference function comprising inflation and unemployment rates as arguments, into an analysis of the relative social costs of inflation and unemployment. The formation of these costs turns out to be more difficult than may appear at first sight.

With respect to unemployment, it would seem natural to measure the social cost by the loss of potential output it causes; and this method has in fact been followed by the U.S. Council of Economic Advisers, among others. But this measure tends to overstate the social cost, for several reasons. One of the most important is that an expansion of employment is secured partly by a reduction in unemployment and partly by an expansion of the labour force through increased participation in it by housewives, older people and youths, and by the working of more hours by the existing labour force. To the extent that the people or hours added to the labour supply are drawn from activities that contribute to economic welfare but are not included in the conventional measures of national income or output – such as the services of housewives in the home, or merely the enjoyment of leisure – the apparent expansion of output associated with increased employment is largely fictitious. Conversely, the reduction of output associated with an increased unemployment rate will be largely fictitious, to the extent that those who retire from the active labour force, or cut down their working hours, have been in the margin of indifference between paid employment and other, unpaid activities. The problem becomes even more serious when the activities which are close substitutes for paid employment are of the nature of an investment in increasing future earning power, as when the state of demand for labour influences the choices of youth between taking immediate employment or remaining in school for a longer period, or when overtime hours compete with self-education. Another relevant consideration is that, where workers become unemployed, the idle time is usually of some value to the unemployed individual, either as leisure time, or as time for self-employment in the improvement of the individual's housing facilities, or as time to be used for searching the labour market for better employment opportunities. The value of these uses of 'idle' time should be subtracted from the value of the output lost by unemployment to arrive at the true social cost of the latter.

With respect to inflation, the appropriate formulation of the social cost depends on the assumption made about whether the inflation is expected by the public or not. If inflation is assumed not to be expected, in the sense that in spite of actual inflation people continue to make their economic decisions on the basis of an assumed stability in the value of money, inflation entails no true social cost (waste of real resources) but only a redistribution of resources from the holders of assets whose value is fixed in terms of money to those whose liabilities are fixed in terms of money. It might, however, be possible to assign a social cost – or possibly a social benefit – to such redistributions according to whether the redistribution were judged to be undesirable or desirable. If on the other hand inflation is assumed to be expected, in the sense that the calculations underlying people's decisions incorporate the rate of increase in prices that is actually occurring, market rates of interest on securities and loans fixed in monetary terms will rise to include compensation for the rate of fall in the value of money, and there will be no redistribution of resources from creditors to debtors in the market for debt instruments contracted in monetary terms. There will, however, be a redistribution of real resources from creditors to debtors on monetary assets the rate of return on which is not fixed in a competitive market; specifically, if by convention or law, currency (and possibly bank deposits subject to check) bears no interest, holders of money will suffer a loss of real resources to the issuers of money (the monetary authority, and possibly the commercial banks). Since this loss will by assumption be expected, it will create a tendency for the holders of money to economize on their holdings of it by using real resources in various ways to substitute for it (e.g. by increasing the frequency of income receipts or planning a closer matching of current receipts and payments); and this substitution will involve a waste of resources which, together with whatever social cost or value is attached to the redistribution of resources from holders to issuers of money, will constitute the social cost of inflation in this case.

The formulation of the costs and benefits of different combinations of inflation and unemployment in this way, and the determination of the optimum position on the Phillips curve by a cost-minimization criterion of social choice, rests, however, on the crucial assumption that the position of the Phillips curve is given independently of the expected rate of inflation, so that society can choose to move along the Phillips curve by an appropriate choice of fiscal and monetary policy. It has recently been argued by Friedman and Phelps that this assumption does not make economic sense and, consequently, that the Phillips curve cannot be used as a basis for secular policy-making. Their contention is that the statistical Phillips curve is derived from historical experience characterized by considerable variability of price movements and by consequent uncertainty about what rate of inflation or deflation to expect, and so incorporates the average expectation about prospective price movements during the period (which may be assumed to be an average expectation of price stability). If the monetary authority, instead of allowing variability of unemployment and inflation rates, attempted to pin the economy down to a particular position on the Phillips curve which involved a non-zero rate of price change, the public would come to expect this rate of price change and attempt to incorporate it in wage bargains and price-determination decisions. Consequently, in diagrammatic terms, the Phillips curve would shift upwards. The unemployment rate initially associated with price stability would gradually come to require the rate of inflation the authorities had selected as their target, so that the benefit of lower unemployment would gradually disappear leaving no offset to the costs of inflation; or, conversely, unemployment could only be held at a level lower than that consistent with price stability by ever-accelerating inflation and the associated rising social cost.

On this analysis, society does not in fact face a choice between alternative combinations of rates of inflation and rates of unemployment. Instead, the choices facing it involve securing transitional benefits from less unemployment currently and in the near future, at the expense of greater costs of inflation in the more remote future. The socially optimal choice will depend on the time lag in the adjustment of the economy's expectations to experience, and on the social rate of time preference used to discount the present benefits from increased employment and the future cost of more rapid inflation.

If the social rate of time preference is assumed to be zero, or attention is focused on the long-run equilibrium growth path of the economy, the problem of efficient economic policy becomes that of choosing the optimal rate of price inflation or deflation. This problem raises some extremely complex theoretical issues if the influence of monetary policy on growth, as mediated by the target rate of price change, is assumed to be the only instrument for affecting economic growth available to the policy-makers, and if (as is customary in contemporary models of growth in a monetary economy) the rate of saving is assumed to be influenced by the rate of inflation. If, on the other hand, the policy-makers are assumed to have sufficient other policy instruments at their disposal for the analyst to be able to isolate the influence of the chosen price trend on monetary behaviour from its influence on the 'real' side of the economic system, the solution becomes much simpler. If the distinguishing characteristic of money, as contrasted with other assets, is taken to be the non-payment of explicit interest on it, it follows from welfare-maximizing principles of the type analysed in section II of this chapter that the optimal monetary policy entails deflation of prices at a rate equal to the rate of return on non-monetary assets. This would provide an implicit rate of return on money sufficient to encourage optimal holdings of it, that is, to reduce the marginal private cost of money-holding to equality with its (approximately zero) marginal social cost. If, on the other hand, the system of provision of money were made to conform to the requirements of the social optimum, on the lines suggested in that section, the public's holdings of money would be optimal regardless of the rate of inflation or deflation chosen by the authorities, since the real rate of return on money holdings would be the same as the real rate of return on alternative assets, and the chosen rate of price change would be neutral with respect to the social welfare achieved. That being the case, it could be argued that the authorities should aim at the achievement of price stability rather than at any non-zero rate of price change, inflationary or deflationary, on the consideration not so far introduced into the analysis that the costs of rational economic calculations will be less with price stability than when prices are expected to change at some rate, even though those expectations are held with certainty.

REFERENCES

Section I

Milton Friedman, *A Program for Monetary Stability* (New York: Fordham University Press, 1959).

Harry G. Johnson, 'Monetary Theory and Policy', *The American Economic Review*, Vol. LII, No. 3 (June 1962), pp. 335–84; reprinted in his *Essays in Monetary Economics* (London: Allen & Unwin, 1967).

Alternative Guiding Principles for the Use of Monetary Policy in Canada (Princeton International Finance Series No. 44, November 1963). Reprinted in his *Essays in Monetary Economics* (London: Allen & Unwin, 1967).

Section II

Harry G. Johnson, 'The Report on Bank Charges', *Banker's Magazine*, Vol. CCIV (August 1967), pp. 64–8.

Allan Metzler, 'Major Issues in the Regulation of Financial Institutions', *Journal of Political Economy* (Suppl.), Vol. LXXV, No. 4, Pt II (August 1967), pp. 482–501; and comments by M. A. Adelman, A. L. Marty, James Tobin and Charles E. Walker.

Section III

A. W. Phillips, 'Stabilization Policy in a Closed Economy', *Economic Journal*, Vol. LIX, No. 254 (June 1954), pp. 290–323.

T. R. Saving, 'Monetary-Policy Targets and Indicators', *Journal of Political Economy* (Suppl.), Vol. LXXV, No. 4, Pt II (August 1967), pp. 446–56; and comments by George Horwich and William C. Hood.

Section IV

Harry G. Johnson, 'Money in a Neo-Classical One-Sector Growth Model', in *Essays in Monetary Economics* (London: Allen & Unwin, 1967), Ch. IV.

E. S. Phelps, 'Phillips Curves, Expectations of Inflation and Optimal Unemployment over Time', *Economica*, Vol. XXXIV, No. 135 (August 1967), pp. 254–81.

A. W. Phillips, 'The Relation between Unemployment and the Rate of Change of Money Wages in the United Kingdom, 1862–1957', *Economica*, Vol. XXV, No. 100 (November 1968), pp. 283–99.

G. L. Reuber, 'The Objectives of Canadian Monetary Policy, 1949–61: Empirical "Trade-Offs" and the Reaction Function of the Authorities', *Journal of Political Economy*, Vol. LXXII, No. 2 (August 1964), pp. 109–32.

Chapter 4

Inside Money, Outside Money, Income, Wealth and Welfare in Monetary Theory*

Monetary theorists have for many years been accustomed to proceed on the assumption that the fundamental nature and properties of money can be assumed to be known and agreed from the facts of experience, and to construct on this basis theoretical models which pay scant if any attention to the rationale for the incorporation of money and the theoretically correct way of incorporating it. Recently, however, monetary economists working in different areas have come to appreciate that the role of money in the economy is theoretically more complicated than appears at first sight, and have been grappling with the problem of formulating this role in a theoretically satisfactory fashion. Specifically, the new interest in the fundamental nature of money has appeared in three contexts. First, controversy has arisen over my suggestion that the utility yield on money balances should be included, in addition to the capital gains created by the growth of the real money stock, in the concept of income employed in the construction of growth models incorporating money and designed to investigate the influence of alternative monetary policies on the characteristics of the long-run equilibrium growth path.[1] Second, international monetary economists have encountered the problem of

* Read to the 1968 Conference of the Association of University Teachers of Economics, York, United Kingdom and published in the *Journal of Money, Credit and Banking*, Vol. I, No. 1 (February 1969), pp. 30–45. Copyright by The Ohio State University Press, 1969, all rights reserved. Since it was submitted for publication, I came across Milton Friedman's long essay on 'The Optimum Quantity of Money' which covers much of the same ground.

[1] Harry G. Johnson, 'Money in a Neo-Classical One-Sector Growth Model', in his *Essays in Monetary Economics* (London: Allen & Unwin, 1967) Ch. IV. A. L. Marty, 'The Optimal Rate of Growth of Money', and comment by M. J. Bailey, Proceedings of the 1967 Conference of University Professors of Monetary Economics, in the *Journal of Political Economy*, Vol. 76 (July/August 1965), pp. 860–76.

the social saving accruing from the use of credit rather than commodity money, and the problem of optimal distribution of the 'seigniorage' earned by the creation of new international credit money, in connection with the analysis of alternative plans for international monetary reform.[1] Third, Boris Pesek and Thomas Saving, in an important new book[2] have argued – correctly as will be shown below – that the distinction introduced by Gurley and Shaw[3] between 'inside' money and the 'outside' money employed in Patinkin's analysis,[4] the former in contrast to the latter involving no net wealth for the community as a whole, is incorrect, and that, provided that money is defined to be non-interest-bearing, both types of money will constitute net wealth for the community. Unfortunately, however, the Pesek and Saving analysis of the role of money as wealth is seriously flawed by a propensity to reason by analogy from current production and consumption flows problems to problems of stock equilibrium, and contains serious analytical errors deriving from their mistaken belief that wealth must be identified with the capitalized value of an income stream objectively measurable by a price-quantity product observable in the market, and their failure to appreciate and apply to the problem the relevant theory of free goods.

The purpose of this chapter is to state the essentials of a theory of the role of money in the economy, making use of the contribution of Pesek and Saving but correcting their errors. Section I develops the theory of the role of money in a static economy. Section II develops the implications of the theory for monetary growth models. In both Sections, money is interpreted as a form of wealth the yield on which is a stream of utility. Section III sketches an alternative approach in which money does not provide services entering directly into the

[1] H. G. Grubel, 'The Distribution of Seigniorage from International Liquidity Creation', and H. G. Johnson, 'A Note on Seigniorage and the Social Saving from Substituting Credit for Commodity Money', in R. A. Mundell (ed.), *Monetary Problems of the International Economy* (Chicago: University of Chicago Press, 1969); reprinted as Ch. 10(1) below. See also Harry G. Johnson, 'Theoretical Problems of the International Monetary System', *Pakistan Development Review*, Vol. 7 (Spring 1967) pp. 1–28, esp. Pt II, reprinted as Ch. 7 below.

[2] B. P. Pesek and T. R. Saving, *Money, Wealth and Economic Theory* (New York: Macmillan, 1967).

[3] J. G. Gurley and E. S. Shaw, *Money in a Theory of Finance* (Washington: The Brookings Institution, 1960).

[4] Don Patinkin, *Money, Interest and Prices*, 1st edn (Evanston, Ill.: Row Peterson, 1956).

utility function, but instead economizes on the cost of producing a flow of utility derived from the consumption of real goods and services.

I. MONEY IN A STATIC ECONOMY

We begin by assuming a barter economy in static equilibrium. To make the problem interesting it must be assumed that the economy produces a variety of goods and services, which must be exchanged among the population. These goods and services, it is assumed, are produced by labour co-operating with capital equipment, the capital equipment being assumed for simplicity to be infinitely durable and perfectly malleable, so that the rate of return on capital invested in equipment will always be equalized among all uses. It is also assumed, again for simplicity, that the rate of return on capital is unaffected by variations in the ratio of capital to labour in the production of goods and services of the magnitude entailed by the invention of money to be analysed below.

In these circumstances the community will have an income measured by its flow of production and consumption of goods and services, which will be composed of the interest on its capital, the physical stock of which is assumed to be given, and the wages of its labour. The wages of labour will, by the last assumption made above, be constant and hence can conveniently be ignored in the following analysis, which concentrates on the effects of the introduction of money in various forms on the community's real wealth and income from capital ('income' for short, since labour income is being ignored).

For analytical purposes, the invention of money can be conceived of as the invention of a new form of capital equipment yielding no observable flow of output but instead a return in the form of a utility yield. This conception can be justified on the 'as if' or revealed preference basis that if people choose to forgo the holding of capital equipment that yields a positive and observable flow of output, in order to hold non-interest-bearing money, they are behaving as if they derived satisfaction from their money stocks equivalent at the margin to that derived from the goods and services produced by more conventional forms of capital equipment, whether they so conceive of themselves or not. (Alternatively, if the idea of money yielding direct utility does not appeal, the 'utility yield' can be considered as the value of the additional leisure made possible by the replacement of barter by money.)

Following an approach used previously by others,[1] the innovation process can be conceived of in terms of the utility function including the new utility-yielding good as an argument, but the price of the new good prior to the innovation being infinitely high so that none of it is consumed, the innovation consisting in reducing the price of the good to the point where some of it is purchased. For the purpose of simplifying the economic welfare analysis, it is convenient though by no means necessary to assume that the marginal utility of real goods and services is constant and unaffected by the introduction of the utility-yielding money, and that the demand for money is independent of the quantity of real goods and services consumed.[2]

On these assumptions, the effect of the introduction of a non-interest-bearing commodity money may be illustrated as in Figure 4.1. Under barter conditions, represented by the left-hand side of the figure, the given stock of material wealth OW_0 is allocated entirely to the production of real goods and services, yielding an income $r_0 W_0$. The curve DD' on the right-hand side of the diagram represents the demand curve for the new good, money services. The introduction of commodity money, which may be identified most simply with the use of one type of productive capital equipment as a medium of exchange and store of value instead of as an input into the production process, causes the community's stock of wealth to be reallocated, $W_0 W_1 = OM_1$ of it being transferred from the stock of productive wealth to the monetary stock.

In physical terms the stock of capital is unchanged. What has happened to the income of the community, derived from that stock of capital? According to conventional accounting definitions of income, which would confine income to goods and services transacted through the market, the income of the community has fallen

---

[1] E. G. Dan Usher, 'The Welfare Economics of Invention', *Economica*, Vol. 31 (August 1964), pp. 279–87.

[2] These extremely artificial assumptions are necessary to justify the use of the simple diagrammatic technique employed here; they could be dispensed with by the adoption instead of a comparatively simple exercise in the use of indifference curves, but the gain in generality does not seem worth the added complexity. The requisite analysis would parallel that of section III.

by $r_0(W_0 - W_1) = r_0 M_1$. This result is clearly paradoxical and un-acceptable, since it shows income as falling in consequence of the introduction of a new product which people prefer over the previously available products. According to a more sophisticated concept of income, a return should be imputed to the wealth embodied in the commodity money stock, equal to the return on wealth used in

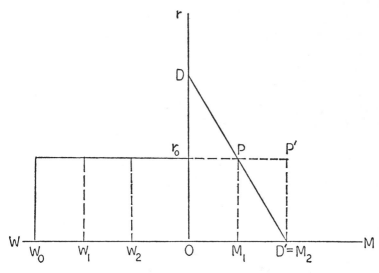

Figure 4.1. Material Wealth Used in Producing Real Goods and Services. Effect of Introduction of Non-Interest-Bearing Commodity Money Generating a Utility Yield.

production. On this concept, income is unchanged: it is $r_0 W_1 + r_0 M_1 = r_0 W_0$. But this concept fails to capture the increase in real income and welfare that results from the introduction of money. On the simplifying assumptions made earlier, this gain is the triangular con-sumers' surplus area Dr_0P; alternatively, the community can be considered as gaining consumers' surplus from the use of money equal to $ODPM_1$, at the cost of a loss of consumers' surplus $r(W_0 - W_1)$ on its consumption of real goods and services.

Now suppose that the non-interest-bearing commodity money is replaced by non-interest-bearing money created by a credit opera-tion, this being assumed to be effected in such a way as not to change the purchasing power of money. This substitution could conceivably occur in two ways. First, the state could issue certificates, assumed to be costless, in return for the commodity money, the use of the certificates in place of the commodity money resting on trust in the state reinforced if necessary by the power of legal tender. In this case, to the extent that it did not need to hold reserves of commodity money to assure confidence in its certificates, the state could reallocate the physical resources embodied in the commodity money back to the production of real goods and services. Second, a banking organization could issue non-interest-bearing deposits, assumed to be costless to administer, in return for the commodity money, the use of these deposits in place of commodity money resting on trust in the solvency of the bank. In this case, to the extent that the bank did not need to hold reserves of commodity money to ensure confidence in its solvency, it could reallocate the physical resources embodied in the commodity money it bought with its deposits back into the production of goods and services either directly, by carrying on production itself, or indirectly, by means of lending to enterprises managed by others at the going rate of return on capital.

The first way of replacing commodity by credit money establishes a fiat money or 'outside' money system, and adds to the wealth of the community the resources previously embodied in the commodity money now replaced by credit money,[1] this wealth being owned by and contributing an income source to the state. The second way of replacing commodity by credit money establishes a banking or 'inside' money system, and equally adds to the wealth of the community the resources previously embodied in the commodity money now replaced by credit money, this wealth being owned by and contributing an income source to the banking enterprise, and consequently being reflected (through discounting of the income stream) in the capital value of that enterprise.

The two ways are therefore exactly equivalent in their effects on society's wealth. That the distinction drawn in the literature between

---

[1] Commodity money held as reserves, either by the state or by the banking enterprise, is replaced by credit money so far as holders of money are concerned, but not so far as society as a whole is concerned. Hence to the extent that commodity money moves into reserves rather than into production of goods and services there is no increase in society's wealth.

inside and outside money asserts the contrary is to be attributed to one or both of two errors. The first is failure to account properly for the wealth equivalent of the income earned by a banking enterprise which can finance interest-bearing loans by interest-free borrowing made possible by the utility yielded its depositors by the holding of money.[1] While the depositors in and borrowers from a bank as a group obtain no net increment of wealth from the existence of the bank, to assume that this conclusion holds for the economy as a whole is incorrect, because it overlooks the resultant creation of wealth for the bank-owners. This is the major error in current monetary theory detected by Pesek and Saving. The second error, which Pesek and Saving also fall into, is to neglect intra-marginal gains from consumption of utility from money. While, as just maintained, there is no net wealth effect for depositors and borrowers from the existence of the bank, there is a welfare or real income effect, consisting in the consumer's surplus obtained on holdings of money.[2] This point becomes particularly relevant in the case soon to be considered, where competition among banks leads to the payment of competitive interest on deposits and the disappearance of the monopoly bank profit and corresponding bank equity value, so that financial intermediation by banks creates no net wealth and appears therefore to have no economic effects. This case, which appears to have been dimly in the back of the minds of some of the proponents of the distinction between 'outside' and 'inside' money, really involves a quite different distinction, between non-interest-bearing and competitive-interest-bearing money of either type; and, as will be seen, the implications of this distinction are different for wealth from what they are for income.

[1] My own effort to analyse the problem (*op cit.*, fn. 1) attempted to evade the accounting problem and hence blundered into identifying the analytically relevant distinction between non-interest-bearing and competitive-interest-bearing money with the institutional distinction between 'outside' and 'inside' money; on this point see below.

[2] The argument for simplicity neglects the possibility of a similar gain of producers' surplus on the borrower's side. In reality, the main importance of the development of banks and other financial intermediaries to the process of economic development may well lie in the gains in efficiency reflected in these surpluses, rather than in the implications of the presence of money for the possibility of influencing the growth process by monetary policy. This argument has been cogently put by James Tobin in 'Notes on Optimal Monetary Growth', *Journal of Political Economy*, Vol. 76 (July/August, 1968), pp. 833–59.

In the extreme case in which commodity money is entirely replaced by credit money, the state or the banking system respectively being able to command public confidence without holding any commodity money reserves, the whole of the resources previously embodied in commodity money is reallocated to the production of goods and services, and the community's real income rises by the product of the rate of interest and the quantity of money held. This case may be illustrated by reference again to Figure 4.1. The introduction of pure credit money increases production of goods and services from $r_0 W_1$ to $r_0 W_0$, i.e. by $r_0 M_1$. Income in the strictly conventional accounting sense returns to the barter economy level $r_0 W_0$; income in the more sophisticated accounting sense, imputing an alternative opportunity cost return to holdings of money, is higher than the barter and commodity money level of $r_0 W_0$ by $r_0 M_1$; and income in the real income or welfare sense is higher than in the barter economy by $DPM_1 O$ and than in the commodity money economy by $r_0 M_1$.

The analysis thus far has assumed that money is defined to be non-interest-bearing, so that its holder foregoes the ruling rate of return on productive uses of wealth. But by assumption, credit money costs nothing to create, and so should for maximum social welfare be provided up to satiety level, i.e. where the marginal utility of holding it is reduced to zero. The imposition of a cost of holding it, by making it non-interest-bearing, at the same time as it enables the replacement of commodity money by credit money to create new social wealth appropriated by the state or the banking enterprise, also gives rise to a social loss by comparison with an ideal system of money provision, represented by the loss of potential consumers' surplus $PM_1 D'$ in Figure 4.1. The ideal result could be achieved if the state in the one case, and the banking enterprise in the other, as monopolists of the money supply,[1] were to pay the

---

[1] The notion of monopolization is taken from Pesek and Saving, and reflects the proposition that for money creatible at zero cost some restriction on quantity outstanding is necessary to preserve a positive purchasing power of money. But the notion is otherwise unhelpful, and indeed misleading, because the payment of zero interest on deposits is only accidentally a monopoly-profit-maximizing policy. In terms of Figure 4.1, define r' as the net return obtained by the state from its fiat money issue or by the bank from its deposits, r' being equal to r_0 plus charges on the users of money or minus interest paid to money-holders; a mono-

holders of money a rate of return on it equal to the rate of return on real investment. This result would occur automatically if private enterprise banks were allowed to and could compete effectively with the monopoly money supplier, though such competition could only be kept consistent with stability in the purchasing power of money by some kind of central control over the total money supply. In either case, the earnings of the material wealth directly or indirectly held by the supplier of money would have all to be transferred to money-holders, so that the wealth value of the state or bank enterprise monopoly would fall to zero. This situation is illustrated again by Figure 4.1. With receipt of interest, the quantity of money held expands to OD', and the holders receive interest r_0M_2 which is equal to the output produced by W_0W_2 of productive capital held by the state or, directly or indirectly, by the bank. Paradoxically, it appears that $M_2 = W_0 - W_2$ of wealth has disappeared, and the community is no wealthier than it was under barter conditions. This is indeed the case, given the concept of wealth employed, which rests on private appropriability, because the private wealth in question was created by monopolistic restriction of the supply of money, a socially costless form of wealth to create, through the non-interest-bearing requirement, and disappears with the disappearance of the restriction. It also appears, by the strict income accounting convention, that the community's income is the same as under barter conditions; and the more sophisticated income accounting convention implies that the community's income has been reduced to the barter-economy level along with its wealth, because the marginal utility value to be imputed to the quality of 'moneyness' – which has now to be distinguished as one component only of the yield on money, the other being the interest paid on money holdings – is now reduced to zero.[1] But in reality the community is made better off in

polist would fix r' so as to maximize r' M, a rectangle within a triangle OOD'; and, as is well known, with a straight line demand curve DD' the profit-maximizing r' would be equal to $1/2$ OD, which would only by chance be equal to r_0.

[1] Pesek and Saving thoroughly confuse the issue by failing to draw this distinction, and wrongly assert that this case is a nonsense because money of zero value must have zero purchasing power. The assertion confuses two notions of 'the purchasing power of money' which must be clearly distinguished: a money asset may have zero purchasing power *as an asset*, in the sense that it cannot be exchanged for another asset yielding a larger income stream because its superior liquidity commands no premium in the market for assets, yet have a positive

terms of real income or welfare, for in addition to $r_0 W_0$ of real goods and services – its income under barter – the community now has for its enjoyment the satiation level of consumers' surplus DOD' on its holdings of money balances. Since its real income is now higher than it was under the non-payment of interest on credit money, it must in a relevant sense be wealthier than before. The paradoxical result noted above, that wealth has apparently on the contrary been reduced, must be attributed to a defect in the concept of wealth, and correspondingly in the concept of income, when these concepts are applied to an asset the demand for whose services can be satiated, so that these services become a free good having no privately appropriable value. The defect, as already mentioned, stems from the failure to take account of the superior value of intra-marginal units of consumption as a component of social income not included in the market measure of income. This is not a serious flaw when, as in most economic problems, all goods remain scarce and hence valuable, and all wealth remains productive of marketable or imputable output value. But it leads to paradox and confusion in monetary theory.[1]

II. MONEY IN GROWTH MODELS

Contemporary growth models have for the most part been built on the assumption that saving is a constant proportion of income. This is an assumption of a naiveté amounting to deliberate stupidity, in sharp contrast to the sophistication of the theory of production in

purchasing power in terms of commodities because it is an asset yielding a stream of income. In the case under discussion, the purchasing power of money assets over the income streams yielded by other assets declines to zero precisely because the setting of the yield or money assets equal to that on real assets satiates the desire for 'moneyness' of assets, or 'liquidity': but this has no implications whatsoever for the purchasing power of money over commodities, which would on the assumption used here be entirely unchanged. This is one of the more serious errors into which Pesek and Saving are led by their propensity to confuse flow-equilibrium analysis and stock-equilibrium analysis.

[1] A solution to this problem, employed in my own work cited above (fn. 1) is to define the utility yield of real balances as $\Sigma_0^m r(M)\, dM$, where $r(M)$ is the marginal alternative opportunity cost at which M is held; a symmetrical definition of the wealth equivalent of the utility yield of money balances would be $1/r_0 \Sigma_0^m r(M)\, dM$, where r_0 is the rate of return on real investment.

such models, which originated with Keynes's failure to reinforce the concept of the propensity to consume with any explicit utility-maximizing rationale, and has been perpetuated by his followers' acceptance of Kuznets's empirical finding of constancy in the long-run savings ratio and their realization of the convenience of the assumption for mathematical analysis of the growth process. In a fully rational growth model built on contemporary economic theory, the average stock of capital held by the individual over his lifetime would be deduced from a maximization exercise involving the life-time profiles of earnings and consumption desired and the rate of interest governing intertemporal substitution of consumption possi-bilities, and the rate of saving would be a consequence and not an exogenous determinant of the growth process.[1] Nevertheless, the assumption is so widely used and accepted that it must constitute a starting point for the consideration of the implications of the presence of money in growth models.

The assumption of a fixed savings ratio renders crucial to the analysis of the influence of the presence of money, and of the policy adopted by the monetary authorities, on the growth process, the definition of the concept of income to which the assumed fixed savings ratio is to be applied. The analysis of this problem initiated by James Tobin[2] focused attention on two relevant factors: the influence on accumulation through income and the savings ratio of the capital gains resulting from the growth of the real money stock demanded by a growing economy – implemented either through the creation of new nominal money or through price deflation – and the influence on the size of these gains, through the influence of the expected rate of inflation or deflation on the desired ratio of money to income, of the monetary policy pursued by the monetary authori-ties. This approach, however, neglected the consequences of the differences between a monetary and a barter economy adumbrated

---

[1] The rational individual would plan to save nothing over his lifetime, or perhaps to hand on to his heirs a somewhat larger stock of wealth than he had himself inherited. Consequently, the rate of saving for society as a whole would depend on the rate of growth of national income, determined by the assumedly exogenous forces of population growth and technical progress.

[2] James Tobin, 'Money and Economic Growth', *Econometrica*, Vol. 33 (Octo-ber 1965), pp. 671–84; see also his 'A Dynamic Aggregative Model', *Journal of Political Economy*, Vol. 63 (April 1955), pp. 103–15.

in the preceding section, and as a result arrived at the conclusion that inflation, by increasing the amount of real saving available for investment in the accumulation of real capital,[1] would increase the output per head on the steady-state equilibrium growth path of the economy, and hence in normal cases[2] would tend to increase the real income *per capita* of the economy, identified as consumption of real goods and services.

As section I of this chapter has shown, an analysis of the influence of monetary policy on growth which confines the influence of the presence of money on real income or welfare to the influence of the capital gains resulting from the expansion of real balances associated with economic growth is theoretically inadequate. Even in a completely static economy, the presence of money (in contrast to a barter economy), increases real income properly conceived; and the gain in real income from the presence of money is higher if the money is credit money than if it is commodity money, and higher again if the money pays a competitive return on holding it than if the nominal rate of return is arbitrarily fixed at zero. These propositions must be incorporated in the analysis of monetary growth models.

The simplest case which proves this necessity is a model in which no interest is paid on money, money is fiat money and the quantity of money is expanded at the rate required to keep the price level and the purchasing power of money constant. In this case, it is obvious that the concept of income should include both the utility yield of existing real balances, and the capital gain resulting from the expansion of the supply of real balances.

The matter becomes more complicated when there is an upward or downward price trend induced by monetary policy. Taking a downward trend induced by a deflationary monetary policy as a test case,

---

[1] Because inflation would reduce income, defined to include the capital gains mentioned, by less than it would reduce the amount of savings required to be devoted to the accumulation of real balances.

[2] I.e. cases in which the savings ratio falls short of the 'golden rule' condition for maximizing real consumption of goods and services *per capita*. A more careful statement of the implications of the 'golden rule', which recognizes that saving more than the golden rule implies involves social sub-optimization but that saving less raises a problem of intertemporal utility maximization not adequately dealt with by the golden rule analysis, may be found in J. Tobin, *op. cit.*, 10.

holders of money are offered an asset which as a result of policy bears a positive yield in real terms additional to the utility yield. The results are twofold. First, holders of money are induced to hold larger quantities than they would hold at a constant price level, and this increases the utility yield they enjoy. Second, since the capital gain on money from falling prices is conditional upon the desire of people in general to hold larger real balances, as growth occurs the increase in purchasing power so created will not in the aggregate ever be exercised, and so constitutes a genuine increase in aggregate income. In other words, it is quite legitimate, and appropriate, to add together the utility yield on real balances and the capital gains from the increase in real balances resulting from deflation as constituents of the real income concept to which the constant savings ratio applies. And it is not correct to argue that, since the holders of real balances obtain a return in the form of capital gains from deflation, these gains measure and exhaust the income obtained from the holding of real balances. Both elements – utility yield and capital gains – must be included in the concept of the income gain from the holding of real balances.

It follows that the treatment of the presence of money proposed in my essay on the subject[1] is correct, and that the influence of the rate of inflation adopted by the monetary authority is a compound of two influences on real income working in opposite directions. On the one hand, the influence of a lower rate of return on holdings of real balances is to lower the utility yield derived from money balance holdings, thereby lowering the proportion of national income available for investment in the accumulation of real capital; on the other hand, the lowering of the rate of return on real balances lowers the ratio of desired real balances to income, and hence lowers the proportion of any given amount of savings that has to be invested in the accumulation of real balances as contrasted with the accumulation of real capital equipment. In consequence, the implications of a more or less rapid rate of inflation implemented by the monetary authorities for the level of consumption of real goods and services *per capita* on the steady-state growth path of the economy are ambiguous, and so are the implications of differences in the rate of inflation for

---

[1] Johnson, *op. cit.*, fn. 1.

the *per capita* level of consumption, defined to include both consumption of real goods and services and the consumption of the utility yield of money balances.

This conclusion is significant for the analysis of the influence of monetary policy in monetary growth models. But the conclusion is of strictly limited significance from the point of view of a broader understanding of economic growth, for three reasons. First, the savings ratio, which is taken as given in the analysis, may be altered by fiscal policy, so that an analysis that assumes that monetary policy alone is available for influencing growth is of limited interest. Given the capacity to influence the savings ratio by fiscal policy, the role of monetary policy becomes the narrower and simpler one of optimizing the use of money. If it is assumed that money must be non-interest-bearing, the analysis indicates the necessity of deflation at the rate required to make money-holding costless; but monetary policy (conceived of in a broad sense) could alternatively aim at institutional changes designed to make money bear interest at the appropriate rate, in which case price stability might be adopted as a more reasonable objective of policy. Second, and more fundamental, the improvement of efficiency made possible by the introduction of money, and perhaps even more so the social saving made possible by the introduction of credit money in replacement of commodity money, may be a far more important component of the process of economic growth than the marginal contribution available to monetary policy as analysed in growth models, especially when the introduction of 'money' is broadened in conception to include the influence of financial intermediation in general. Third, a related point, the growth of banking and other intermediary institutions may exercise a more important determining influence on the proportion of output saved and invested in the accumulation of material capital than that of monetary policy as analysed in these models.

III. MONEY AS A FACTOR OF PRODUCTION

In the preceding two sections, money has been treated as a form of 'consumer capital good' yielding a flow of utility services. In this section, money is treated alternatively as a form of producers' capital, rendering a direct service in the production process, its

126

contribution to economic welfare consisting of an increase in the flow of final goods available for consumption.

For this purpose, we assume that production in the barter economy requires, in addition to labour, both capital in the form of productive equipment and capital in the form of inventories of various commodities. For theoretical simplicity, equipment is assumed to last forever and inventories not to deteriorate between acquisition and disposal, and for diagrammatical simplicity the ratio of the two to one another is assumed to be independent of total capital per head.

The production equilibrium of the barter economy, with a given total stock of capital per head, is depicted in Figure 4.2. In the figure, the isoquants initially represent fixed levels of output per head with varying combinations of fixed capital and inventories; the total quantity of capital per head is $OC_0 = OC_0'$, the 45° slope representing the condition of equal rates of return on the two types of capital (the rate of return on capital, and the wage rate, are not shown on the diagram but are implicit in the indices of the isoquants); and P_0 is the output-maximizing equilibrium combination of the two types of output per head under barter being X_0.

Now suppose that money is invented, in the sense that one of the commodities (assumed to be infinitely durable) acquires general acceptability as purchasing power and the productive enterprise is able to substitute the holding of a smaller value of it for the various individual inventories of commodities it previously held. Suppose further, for diagrammatic simplicity rather than realism, that the introduction of money is a Hicks-neutral innovation as regards the two types of capital, so that it can be represented simply by re-indexing the isoquants in the diagram. The old output *per capita* represented by the isoquant X_0' can now be produced with $OC_{-1} = OC_{-1}'$ of capital, $C_0' - C_{-1}'$ being one measure of the social gain from the invention of (commodity) money; another measure, which would be larger on the assumption of diminishing returns to increasing capital-intensity of production, would be $C_1 - C_0$ (not shown on the diagram), the increase in the quantity of capital per head necessary to produce the output per capita X_1' made possible by the innovation of money using the initial quantity of capital, under the technology of the barter economy.

It should be remarked that, for this three-factor problem, it is most convenient to use a fixed quantity of material capital as the standard of reference for analysing the influence of monetary innovation, though this requires ignoring or assuming away changes in the

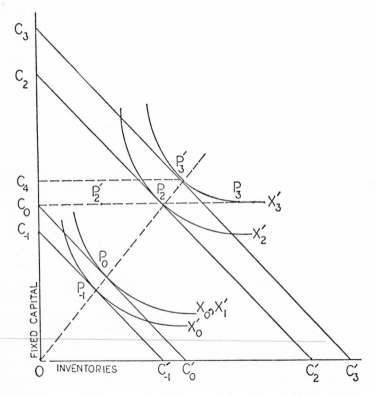

Figure. 4.2. Production Equilibrium of Economy with Inventories.

rate of return on capital and the wage rate, as was done explicitly in the utility-yield model of the previous two sections.

Now suppose that commodity money is replaced by a costless-to-create, non-interest-bearing credit money. All of the stock of material capital will now be available for embodiment in fixed capital, which would imply, if the real value of money remained constant at its initial value, production at P_2'. But this point would involve a relative scarcity of money as compared with real capital, equilibrium in production requiring real-money inventories of $C_0 P_2$, and the additional real balances required would have to be supplied either by the issue of additional nominal money or by an increase in the value of money through a fall in the general price level. The resulting social gain is equivalent to an increase of $C_2 - C_0$ in the stock of real capital in the commodity money economy. (A similar equivalent-variation measure of social gain could be constructed for comparison with the original barter economy.)

Production at P_2, however, is socially sub-optimal, since it involves producers' choosing between real and monetary capital on the assumption that they have equal real cost, whereas by assumption money has a zero social cost. If interest is paid on money at the rate of return produced by real capital, producers will treat the productive services of money as a free good, and production will move to the capital factor-combination P_3, entailing an increase in output from X_2' to X_3'. The resulting social gain is equivalent to an increase of $C_3 - C_0$ in the stock of real capital in the commodity-money economy, and to an increase of $C_4 - C_0$ in the stock of real capital in the non-interest-bearing credit-money economy. (A similar equivalent-variation measure of social gain could be constructed with reference to the barter economy.)

Note, however, that if capital in the form of credit money is valued according to standard accounting conventions, the substitution of non-interest-bearing credit money for commodity money will increase measured wealth from C_0 to C_2 while the payment of interest on credit money at the going rate will reduce measured wealth from C_2 to C_0 again. This is the Pesek–Saving paradox discussed and explained in section I.

When this formulation of the role of money in the economy is used as the basis for an analysis of the influence of a more or less inflationary or deflationary monetary policy on the characteristics of the long-run equilibrium growth path of an economy using non-interest-bearing credit money, the results show the same ambiguity in the influence of monetary policy as was revealed by the model in which money is assumed to yield a utility flow of services to consumers.

The ambiguity is illustrated diagrammatically in Figure 4.3, a version of a diagram I have employed in previous work on the subject.[1] In the figure, real capital per head (k) is measured on the horizontal axis, and output per head (y) on the vertical axis. For

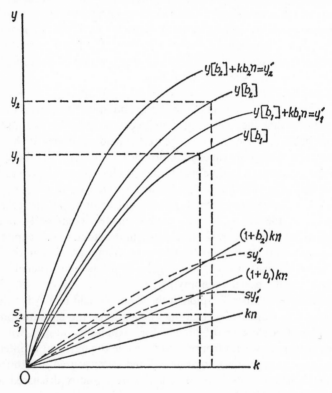

Figure 4.3. Long-Run Equilibrium Growth Path.

each level of capital per head there is a family of curves representing output per head, corresponding to different ratios of real balances to real capital employed in production. In an economy on its long-

130

run equilibrium growth path, income per head will be composed of the sum of output per head and the capital gain bkn of the additional real balances associated with growth at rate n, exogenously determined by population growth. Similarly, for each ratio of real balances to real capital there will be a capital requirements curve $(1+b)kn$ representing the investment required to keep capital per head intact. Saving is assumed as usual to be a constant fraction of income per head, and the characteristics of the long-run equilibrium growth path will be determined by the intersection of the savings curve and the capital requirements curve for the relevant real-balance-to-real-capital ratio b. The relevant b is determined by monetary policy, since production equilibrium requires that the rate of return on real balances exceed that on real capital by the rate of inflation, or conversely fall below it by the rate of deflation, set by monetary policy.

Figure 4.3 depicts the long-run equilibria of real capital, real balances, output, real saving, and consumption *per capita* for a higher and a lower rate of inflation and a correspondingly lower and higher ratio of real balances to real capital (b_1 and b_2 respectively). It illustrates that a higher rate of inflation may lower rather than raise real output per head, and therefore (provided the economy does not overshoot the golden rule position) lower consumption *per capita*.

A reduction in the inflation rate that produces a unit increase in the real-balance-to-real-capital ratio at a given level of real capital per head raises the capital requirement curve by kn, and increases saving by $s(r+\pi+n)k$, where the first two terms within parentheses represent the marginal product of real balances (the sum of the rate of return on real capital and the inflation rate) and the third the increase in the capital gain from additional real balances associated with equilibrium growth. Real capital per head will therefore increase or decrease according as $r+\pi \gtrless (1/s-1)n$.[1] If real capital per head increases, real output per head increases both for this reason and because real balances per unit of real capital have increased; and consumption per head will increase so long as the economy's saving ratio initially fell short of achieving the golden rule condition ($r = n$) with the given ratio of real balances of real capital. If real capital per

---

[1] This same condition can be deduced from the utility yield approach to the analysis of the role of money in growth models (Johnson, *op. cit.*, fn. 1), since the marginal utility of real balance holdings is also $r+\pi$.

head decreases, output per head may nevertheless increase, through the increase in the ratio of real balances to real capital offsetting the effects on output of lower real capital per head; and if output per head increases while real capital per head falls, consumption per head must increase regardless of whether or not the economy's saving ratio involved overshooting the golden rule condition with the given ratio of real balances to real capital.

Appendix

A Comment on Pesek and Saving's Theory of Money and Wealth *

This comment is intended to clarify a confusion which, in my judgement, runs through the work of Pesek and Saving on the theory of money and wealth [3]. The confusion in question wrongly identifies the price of money, in the classical sense of its purchasing power, with the alternative opportunity cost of holding real balances, in the neoclassical and Keynesian sense of the rate of interest on alternative investments foregone; and in consequence leads to the erroneous conclusion that if the latter opportunity cost is reduced to zero by payment of interest on money in order to optimize its use, the real purchasing power of money must fall to zero (the price level becomes infinitely high).

The conclusion is erroneous for the simple reason that the demand for real balances is a function of the alternative opportunity cost, while the purchasing power of nominal balances is determined by the nominal quantity of money in conjunction with the demand for real balances.

Clarification of the issue may be achieved by combining two familiar diagrams, as in Figure 4.4.[1] The top part of the diagram relates the demand for real balances, *ceteris paribus*, to the opportunity cost of holding real cash balances. If no interest is paid on money holdings, and the rate of return on real capital investment is r_0, desired real balances will be OB_0. The bottom part of the diagram relates the price level to desired real balances through rectangular hyperbolas corresponding to different nominal stocks of money;

* Reprinted from the *Journal of Money, Credit and Banking*, Vol. I, No. 3 (August 1969), pp. 535–7. Copyright 1969 by The Ohio State University Press, all rights reserved.
[1] The top part of the figure is so familiar as to need no reference, but may be found in Ch. 4 above; the bottom part of the diagram is a version of a diagram used by Patinkin [4, p. 28].

with the money stock M_0, desired real balances B_0 determine the price level P_0.

On the assumption that the cost of creating money is zero – a defensible assumption if the cost of maintaining a money stock is

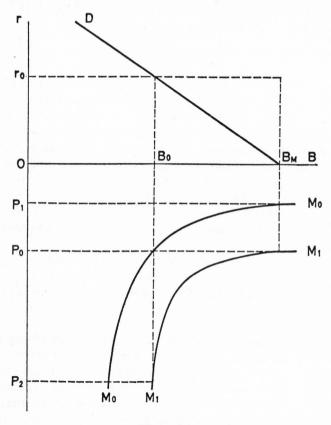

Figure 4.4

distinguished from that of operating a money payments system and the latter is disregarded at this level of abstraction[1] – real balances should be held up to the point of satiety, represented by B_M in the diagram. This can be achieved by paying interest at the rate r_0 on nominal

[1] For a fuller discussion of this distinction see my [2].

(and real) balances. With the given stock of nominal money M_0, the price level will fall from P_0 to P_1; alternatively, the nominal money supply could be increased from M_0 to M_1, consistently with the maintenance of a constant price level. Control of the nominal stock of money would permit optimization without the price level's becoming infinitely high.

It is not, however, possible to achieve satiation of demand for real balances by expanding the nominal money supply, while maintaining the non-payment of interest on money. If the price level remained constant, increasing the nominal money supply from M_0 to M_1 would increase real balances from B_0 to the satiation level B_M; but since the demand for real balances would remain at B_0, not rise to B_M, the price level would be bid up to P_2 to restore the actual real balances to the desired level B_0. In the limit under this policy the price level would approach infinity and the real value of a unit of nominal money would approximate to zero.

This analysis shows that reduction of the alternative opportunity cost of holding money to zero and reduction of the purchasing power of money to zero are two extremely different things involving different policies. The confusion between them has probably been fostered by an ambiguity in the concept of 'competition' among banks as providers of the money supply. If deposits cost nothing to create and yet the assets held against them yield a positive return, banks subject to no restraint on the nominal quantity of money they can create in the aggregate will be under competitive pressure to expand the nominal money supply until its purchasing power is reduced to zero: at best, the money supply so determined will be in neutral equilibrium.

On the other hand, if banks are competitive but subject either to a quantitative restraint on the aggregate money supply they can create or to a policy of stabilization of the aggregate price level mediated through control of the aggregate money supply, competition among them will force them to pay interest to their depositors and so optimize the supply of real balances without reducing the real value of money to zero. There is, incidentally, an interesting question, as yet unanalysed, about the competitive conditions under which an uncontrolled competitive banking system would produce a stable equilibrium nominal quantity of money, and the welfare implications of that equilibrium; I conjecture that Chamberlinian product differentiation would be required. Another problem, whose import-ance is exemplified by the pressure for and practice of currency reforms after the experience of substantial inflation, is that of optimiz-ing the price level in the lower half of the figure, on the realistic assumption that there is some real social cost of providing and main-taining the stock of money.[1]

In conclusion, it may be noted that Figure 4.4 can be used to establish in a simple way the proposition, which emerged from Patinkin's critique of Gurley and Shaw's work [5] that the monetary authority needs to control both a nominal magnitude and an interest rate to control the price level. In the figure, to stabilize the price level P the authority must control both the amount of nominal money M and the alternative opportunity cost of holding real balances, r_0.

REFERENCES

1. Harry G. Johnson, 'Inside Money, Outside Money, Income, Wealth and Welfare in Monetary Theory', *Journal of Money, Credit and Banking*, Vol. 1 (1969), pp. 30–45; reprinted in Ch. 4 above.
2. 'Problems of Efficiency in Monetary Management', *Journal of Political Economy*, Vol. 76, No. 5 (September/October 1968), pp. 971–90; reprinted in Ch. 3 above.
3. Boris Pesek and Thomas R. Saving, *Money, Wealth and Economic Theory* (New York: Macmillan, 1967).
4. Don Patinkin, *Money, Interest and Prices: An Integration of Monetary and Value Theory* (Evanston, Ill.: Row Peterson, 1956).
5. 'Financial Intermediaries and the Logical Structure of Monetary Theory', *The American Economic Review*, Vol. 51 (1961), pp. 95–116.

[1] In principle, the real social cost of providing money should be a function of the real and not the nominal stock provided. However, as currency reforms, decimalization, and so forth indicate, there are private and social costs associated with changes in the real purchasing power of the nominal monetary unit, and therefore there is a question of determining the optimal purchasing power of the standard unit of account.

Chapter 5

Is There an Optimal Money Supply?*

The title question of this chapter is provocative and interesting, inasmuch as it encapsulates a whole area of rapid recent development in monetary theory in an apparently simple question. Yet it is really a trick question, the answer to which must be 'yes' if the terms are properly defined, and the difficulty of which inheres in such proper definition of the terms. Since the question has confused some theorists, I make no apology for spending much of this chapter on clarification of the issues, even though this requires restatement of some elementary theoretical points.

To begin with – in case anyone is under any illusions on this point – the question has nothing to do with the optimal conduct of short-run stabilization policy. Instead it belongs to the pure theorists' world of continuous full employment of resources; as such, its policy relevance is to the framework of monetary organization and the long-run environmental objectives of monetary policy.

Within this frame of reference, the first point to be noticed is the elementary one that while the monetary authority fixes the nominal quantity of money, the public determines the quantity of real balances by driving the price level up or down until the real value of the given nominal money stock is what the public is content to hold. Since any nominal stock can provide any desired real stock through appropriate price-level adjustment, it obviously makes no sense to ask whether there is an optimal money supply, if 'money supply' is interpreted as it should be in terms of the nominal money supply that the authorities in fact control. The question has to be posed in terms of the real money supply. In fact there are two questions. First, is there an optimal real quantity of money generally different from

* Reprinted from *Journal of Finance*, Vol. XXV, No. 2 (May 1970), pp. 435–42.

what will be established by the actions of the public? Second, given that the monetary authorities cannot alter the real quantity of money directly by altering the nominal quantity of it, how can they alter it indirectly and what policy should they follow to establish the optimum quantity of real balances? To comprehend these two issues, the title question would better have been phrased 'Is there an optimal money supply *policy*?'

This compound question can be approached from two different angles: by the construction and exploration of a model of a monetary economy, and by a welfare analysis of the existing monetary arrangements of actual economies. I begin with the former.

The simplest type of monetary model to construct is one that employs a non-interest-bearing fiat money – assumed costless to create – as a medium of exchange and store of value. The use of money, as contrasted with barter, must be motivated somehow – a point on which Tobin's important writings in this area can be faulted. Writers in the Chicago tradition of monetary theory – Friedman, Levhari–Patinkin and myself, among others – have recognized but bypassed this issue (the transition from a barter to a monetary economy) by treating money as both a consumer's good yielding a flow of services contributing to utility and a producers' good (an inventory) contributing to output.

Any problem of sub-optimality in the working of a competitive system can be put in terms of a divergence of private from social cost, or of the presence of externalities. In the fiat money model, sub-optimality of the stock of real balances arises from the fact that while by assumption money can be created at zero social cost, to the holder it has an alternative opportunity cost given by the yield on capital; hence less of it will be held than the socially optimal quantity, which would equate the marginal utility yield of money to consumers and the marginal productivity yield to producers to zero. Friedman has recently produced a suggestive supplementary explanation in terms of externalities: in order to accumulate extra cash balances the individual must forgo real resources; but these resources accrue to his fellow citizens through a (negligible) temporary fall in the price level, and do not constitute a social cost.

To attain optimality, it is necessary to provide a yield on real balances equal to the yield on real capital, in order to equate the marginal utility and productivity yields of money to zero and thus 'satiate the demand for real balances'. One way of doing this would be to pay interest on money equal to the real rate of return on real capital, financed by the usual hypothetical non-distorting lump-sum taxes. (As will be apparent immediately, this policy would have to be accompanied by a policy of monetary growth ensuring stability of prices over time.) An alternative possibility arises from the fact that, apart from their explicit zero nominal yield, in an economy in which inflation or deflation is going on *and is fully anticipated*, holders of cash balances knowingly bear a cost or enjoy a return from holding them equal to the expected (and actual) rate of inflation or deflation respectively. Hence, by providing a rate of monetary growth (or contraction) that will produce a rate of price deflation equal to the rate of return on real assets, the monetary authority can achieve the optimum stock of real balances. An alternative way of putting this point, for an economy containing bonds bearing a monetary rate of interest, is that formulated by Friedman, that monetary policy should aim at making the monetary rate of interest zero. In a growth model in which government simultaneously establishes a savings ratio consistent with the golden rule, as Patinkin and Levhari have shown, the appropriate monetary policy simplifies to keeping the money supply constant (since the rate of interest is equal to the rate of growth of output in golden-rule conditions).

Both the payment of explicit interest on money, and the control of the behaviour of the nominal money stock over time, can and should be regarded as monetary policies. Hence there are two alternative policies available for achieving the optimum stock of real balances at every point in time – and of course these can be mixed in any desired proportion. In fact they are the extremes of the menu of possible mixtures: no deflation and an explicit rate of interest on money equal to the return on real capital, and no interest on money and deflation at a rate equal to the return on real capital. The possibility of achieving optimality of the money stock through interest payments as well as through deflation has generally been recognized as an afterthought in the literature, but put in the context of the difference between a competitive inside-money system and an outside-money system. As Pesek and Saving and I have shown, however, the difference essential for monetary theory is not between inside and outside money, but between non-interest-bearing and competitive interest-bearing money. There is, though, a serious practical problem about how to arrange interest payments on currency, a problem to which I shall return.

The alternative approach to the question of optimal money supply is through the welfare analysis of existing national monetary arrangements. These can be thought of, if we set aside the conventional conception of the government as something apart from its electorate that has been developed to justify the treatment of government liabilities to the public as 'outside money' and hence to give empirical relevance to the Pigou effect, as an inside-money system with certain distortions from the conditions of competitive optimality. Specifically, through its monopoly of legal tender, the government is able to force holders of currency to make it interest-free loans; similarly, through its monopoly of central banking, the government is able to force commercial bank holders of central bank deposits to make an interest-free loan directly to the central bank and indirectly to itself. Alternatively, the government is able through monopoly to impose a tax on the holding of these assets. To the extent that the prohibition of explicit interest on demand deposits is effective (which is doubtful), the government also levies a tax on deposit-holders for the benefit of the banks. It also taxes deposit-holders indirectly through other regulations and restrictions falling on banks and on bank entry. All these taxes imply sub-optimization of the stock of real balances held, by comparison with a situation in which commercial banks were free to compete for deposits (and obliged to do so by freedom of entry) and in which government paid commercial rates of interest on currency and on commercial bank deposits at the Federal Reserve. (The Federal Reserve could still control the nominal money supply in these circumstances.)

Elimination of restrictions and regulations and the payment of competitive interest rates on government and central bank obligations would achieve optimality of the real-money stock, as in the fiat-money model. The practical difficulty, which in this context is obviously practical and not introduced by extraneous assumption, is how to arrange payment of interest on government-issued currency. Presumably interest could be paid on the banks' vault cash, on the basis of average or daily figures; the problem is to devise a method of paying interest on the public's holdings of currency. Friedman man has suggested giving banks permission to compete in the issuance of notes – as they used to do before the Bank Charter Act of 1844 in the United Kingdom and the National Banking Act of 1863 in the United States – and leaving them to figure out the technicalities of how to pay interest on such notes.

The alternative, as in the theoretical model, would be to manage the money supply so as to deflate prices at the rate required to make the money rate of interest zero, thus eliminating the monopoly profits now accruing to government, the central bank and (possibly) the commercial banks. This is the policy recently recommended by Friedman, even though he has both to recognize the political and economic difficulties entailed in such a potentially major change from the present situation of price inflation ('potentially major' because he presents alternative calculations involving quite different rates of price deflation) and to admit to some embarrassment in reconciling this recommendation with his long-standing record of recommending pursuit of a monetary policy (adoption of a monetary rule) that would guarantee price stability. I would agree with Friedman that the step from monetary policy as presently conducted to a policy ensuring price stability is more potentially beneficial than the further step to a policy of price deflation at the appropriate rate; but I would argue further, against his general thesis, that if the steps that could feasibly be taken towards the establishment of competitive interest payments on money were in fact taken, there would probably be little further gain to be had from instituting the appropriate rate of price deflation.

It seems to me irrational to accept institutional arrangements that lead to economic inefficiency on the one hand, and on the other hand to try to persuade government to manipulate the growth of the money supply so as to offset the inefficiencies that result. Either government is unaware of the inefficiencies its practices cause, in which case it should be possible to persuade it to change those practices, specifically to terminate the prohibition of interest payments on demand deposits, to pay interest on reserve deposits of commercial banks at the Federal Reserve and on vault cash, and possibly to seek means of paying interest on the public's currency holdings. Or government is quite aware that it makes a profit out of these practices, and is determined to hold onto it, in which case, as controller of the behaviour of the money supply, it will certainly not act so as to deprive itself of those profits.

Assuming that government could be persuaded to eliminate the obviously and easily remediable institutional sources of inefficiency in the money supply – prohibition of interest on commercial bank demand deposits, non-payment of interest on commercial bank deposits at the Federal Reserve and on commercial bank cash – the remaining source of inefficiency in the provision of money (assuming for the moment the maintenance of price stability) would be the non-payment of interest on currency. Here there would be a double source of inefficiency: under present arrangements the holder of currency receives no interest but bears none of the costs of printing and minting required to create and to maintain the currency stock, whereas under efficient arrangements he would receive competitive interest on his bank deposit but pay charges for using bank money for payments. There would thus be incentives to economize on currency holding but to use currency rather than cheques for making payments.

Would the resulting welfare losses be sufficient to justify the adoption of a policy of deflating prices at the current rate of return on capital in order to avoid them? It seems very doubtful, though it may be worth someone's while to quantify. (With currency in circulation among the public running at about 5 per cent of GNP, and the elasticity of substitution between currency and interest-bearing bank deposits probably rather low, the welfare loss calculated on Friedman's lines would probably be a negligible fraction of national income.) The answer would be even more doubtful if, following Friedman's suggestion, commercial banks were allowed to experiment with the issue of interest-bearing notes.

As a digression on the question of interest-bearing currency, it should not be too difficult to devise it – any more than it has been difficult for the banks to develop new instruments such as certificates of deposit permitting them to pay higher interest on large savings deposits than on the ordinary savings deposits. In the early nineteenth century, after all, bills of exchange used to circulate in the north of England in place of money. Presumably banks would offer interest only on the higher denominations of notes, choose face values so that interest could be expressed as a gain in value of so many cents per week, and affix a maturity date so that if they over-estimated the interest rate they could pay the holder could not extract indefinite ransom. (Actually, a return of so many cents per week would be a declining rate of weekly interest, so that this problem would take care of itself if the cents offered per week were constant.)

The payment of competitive interest on money, then, is one way of achieving the optimal money supply. Yet this proposition has recently encountered considerable opposition from monetary theorists. This opposition I believe to be mistaken.

One source of criticism is to be found in Pesek and Saving's book on *Money, Wealth, and Economic Theory*, wherein it is argued that the essential characteristic of money is its non-interest-bearingness, and that if money were to bear interest it would cease to be used as money. One basis of this argument is a confusion between the two notions (i) that if banks were permitted to compete with each other in supplying socially costless money, they would expand the nominal money supply until its purchasing power fell to zero, and (ii) that if they were allowed to compete with each other in supplying money within some overall constraint on the total quantity supplied, they would drive the rate of interest paid on deposits up to a level competitive with other yields, thereby reducing the value of the marginal liquidity services of money to zero. Another is the idea that if money had a yield people would not forgo that yield for the sake of purchasing goods and services – an obvious fallacy since the function of all asset-holding is to carry purchasing power forwards through time, and this implies no desire to hold forever an asset once acquired.

Another line of criticism focuses on the vagueness of the explanation of the function of money in a monetary economy, already mentioned in connection with writers in the Chicago tradition and perhaps even more characteristic of writers in the Keynesian tradition, and specifically on the possibility that the holding of a larger (optimum) quantity of real balances induced by the payment of interest on money may introduce an offsetting waste of resources through efforts to economize on the use of money in effecting transactions. This criticism was raised vehemently by Robert Clower, in connection with an effort by Paul Samuelson to state 'What Classical and Neoclassical Monetary Theory Really Was'. Samuelson's restatement was admittedly faulty; but Clower has apparently recanted on his belief that there is something seriously wrong with the argument outlined above.

The issue can be put most clearly in terms of the Baumol–Tobin model of transactions demand for cash. That model assumes that transactions from money into goods occur in an even flow over time, and are costless. Holding all one's income in the form of money for the purposes of effecting this flow of transactions, however, means losing interest; money can be converted into interest-bearing assets and back again, but there is both a fixed and a proportional cost per such transaction; because of the fixed cost, there will be an optimum frequency of conversions of assets into cash and an optimum proportional cash balance holding varying inversely with income and the rate of interest on earning assets. Optimality would be achieved by paying interest on cash balances and so eliminating the real costs of conversions between cash and securities.

Now assume instead that there is no interest on cash, and that conversion of money into goods has both a fixed and a proportional cost. That is, there is an overhead time and real resource cost of going to the supermarket, and a time cost per item of shopping. These would indicate one trip per pay period; but there is also a storage cost proportional to their value on the holding of stocks of goods, which can be reduced by making more trips to market and holding a lower average stock of goods. Hence there is a total-cost-minimizing stock of goods in storage and of cash in hand.

It would appear that the payment of interest on money, by raising the alternative opportunity cost of holding stocks of goods, would reduce average stocks and so increase the real resources used in making trips to the supermarket, thereby wasting resources by comparison with the zero-interest-money situation. Hence the 'optimum quantity of money' achieved by paying interest on money would appear to be socially sub-optimal when the transactions costs of extra marketing induced by the payment of interest on money are taken into account.

But this conclusion would be correct only if the true social and private alternative opportunity cost of storing goods included only the real resources employed in storage, and not the interest on the resources invested in the stock itself. This is clearly not the case. Both society and the stockholding individual could convert the stocks into explicitly productive capital goods. Hence the storage cost of consumers' inventories already includes the interest rate, and is not increased by the payment of interest on money; and the payment of interest on money serves as before to eliminate the costs of converting cash into earning assets and vice versa (these costs may

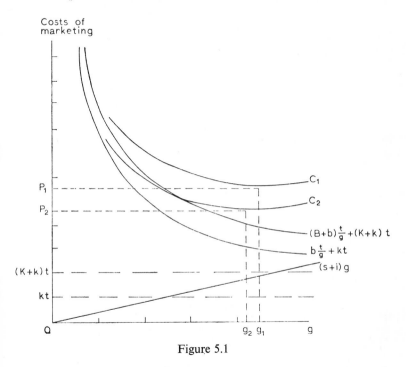

Figure 5.1

be thought of, following Samuelson, as the cost of shoe leather wasted on trips to the bank).

This point is illustrated by Figure 5.1, based on the Baumol-Tobin analysis of transactions demand for money. For the purposes of the diagram it is assumed that the individual receives an income per period of $2t$, which he receives either in interest-bearing assets or in money; that if he receives assets he earns an interest rate i per period on his average asset holding but he has an overhead charge per withdrawal of B and a proportional charge of $\frac{1}{2}K$ per unit of money withdrawn; that shopping involves an overhead cost b per shopping

145

trip and a proportional cost of $\frac{1}{2}k$ per unit monetary value purchased; and that storage of goods (in amount g on the average) involves a proportional real cost of s per period and the interest charge i. If he receives no interest on money, it is assumed that he will choose to be paid in assets; it is also assumed for simplicity, at the cost of full generality, that he will combine trips to convert assets into money with trips to the market to convert money into goods, to avoid interest loss on idle money. His cost curve as a function of his average stock of goods will be C_1, and his cost-minimizing average goods stock g_1. If, on the other hand, he received interest on money at the same rate as on earning assets, so that he could avoid conversions, his cost-minimizing stock of goods would be g_2, smaller than g_1. If, incorrectly, the rate of interest were not regarded as a proper social cost of stockholding, and comparison were made between interest-paying and non-interest-paying money, there would be a third curve C_3 representing costs of holding stocks of goods excluding any interest-rate cost of stockholding, with a minimum point below and to the right of C_2, incorrectly suggesting a social waste from the payment of interest on money.

A final line of criticism contends that payment of competitive interest on money would lead to money's replacing all other financial assets, and banks replacing all other financial intermediaries. This criticism seems to me quite unconvincing, unless the proposal is misinterpreted to mean that not only is interest to be paid on money, but that the rate is to be uncompetitively high and that no charges are to be made for the use of money in making payments. The recommendation to pay interest on money equal to the rate of return on real capital is to be understood as a shorthand phrase that abstracts from various kinds of transactions and intermediation costs that would be taken account of in a fully competitive banking system.

REFERENCES

R. W. Clower, 'What Traditional Monetary Theory really Wasn't', *Canadian Journal of Economics*, Vol. 2, No. 2 (May, 1969), pp. 299–302.

'On the Technology of Monetary Exchange' (Mimeograph for the Southern Economic Association, 1969).

M. Friedman, 'The Optimum Quantity of Money', in his *The Optimum*

Quantity of Money and Other Essays (Chicago: Aldine Publishing Co., 1969), Ch. 1, pp. 1–50.

H. G. Johnson, 'Money in a Neo-classical One-sector Growth Model', in his *Essays in Monetary Economics* (London: Allen & Unwin, 1967), Ch. IV, pp. 143–78.

'Problems of Efficiency in Monetary Management', *Journal of Political Economy*, Vol. 76, No. 5 (September/October, 1968), pp. 971–90; Ch. 3 above.

'Inside Money, Outside Money, Income, Wealth and Welfare in Contemporary Monetary Theory', *Journal of Money, Credit, and Banking*, Vol. 1, No. 1 (February, 1969), pp. 30–45; Ch. 4 above.

'Pesek and Saving's Theory of Money and Wealth: a comment', *op. cit.* Vol. 1, No. 3 (August, 1969), pp. 535–7; Appendix to Ch. 4 above.

D. Levhari and D. Patinkin, 'The Role of Money in a Simple Growth Model', *American Economic Review*, Vol. 58, No. 4 (September, 1968), pp. 713–53.

M. Perlman, 'The Roles of Money in an Economy and the Optimum Quantity of Money' (Mimeograph, 1969), subsequently published in *Economics*.

B. P. Pesek and T. R. Saving, *Money, Wealth, and Economic Theory* (New York: Macmillan, 1967).

P. A. Samuelson, 'What Classical and Neoclassical Monetary Theory really Was', *Canadian Journal of Economics*, Vol. 1, No. 1 (February, 1968), pp. 1–15.

'Nonoptimality of Money Holdings under *Laissez faire*', *op. cit.*, Vol. 2, No. 2 (May, 1969), pp. 303–8.

J. Tobin, 'Money and Economic Growth', *Econometrica*, Vol. 33, No. 4 (October, 1965), pp. 671–84.

'Notes on Optimal Monetary Growth', *Journal of Political Economy*, Vol. 76, No. 4, Pt III (July/August, 1968), 833–59.

Part II

INTERNATIONAL MONETARY THEORY

Chapter 6

Some Aspects of the Theory of Economic Policy in a World of Capital Mobility[*]

Professor Marco Fanno's best-known contribution to the English literature of economics is his monograph on *Normal and Abnormal International Capital Transfers*.[1] That monograph brought contemporary economic theory to bear on the economic effects of and policy problems raised by the abnormal capital movements – both intergovernmental and private – that plagued the interwar years and ultimately destroyed the international economic system that had evolved during the long period of peace before the First World War. Since Professor Fanno wrote, the international economic system has been reconstructed on lines in many respects parallel to those of the period with which he was concerned, and many of the same problems have returned to plague the governments and monetary authorities of the major countries. In particular, the national economic policy-makers have had to contend both with the international mobility of capital in response to interest rate movements, and with speculative capital movements. Moreover, their difficulties have been aggravated by the modern acceptance of explicit governmental responsibility for the maintenance of a high level of employment, a commitment which sharpens the conflict between external and internal equilibrium familiar to international monetary theorists since the period just after the First World War.

In the face of this conflict, practical policy-makers and international economic theorists alike have been driven to consideration of more sophisticated methods of managing economic policy so as to reconcile the objectives of internal and external balance. Specifically, attention has concentrated on the use of fiscal policy and monetary

[*] Reprinted from Tullio Bagiotti (ed.), *Essays in Honour of Marco Fanno* (Padova: CEDAM, 1966), pp. 345–59, with corrections.
[1] Minneapolis: The University of Minnesota Press, November 1939.

151

policy in combinations designed to produce the required reconcilia-tion, and on the limitations imposed on the use of either policy instrument for one or the other objective by the international mobility of capital. The experience of Canada with a floating exchange rate – at first a success and then a dismal failure – has extended theoretical interest in these problems to the contrast between the situations of countries on fixed and on floating exchange rates.[1]

The purpose of this chapter is to bring together some of the analysis relating to the design and conduct of economic policy motivated by the objectives of internal and external stability, in an environment of responsiveness of capital movements to interest rate changes, and under regimes of either fixed or floating exchange rates. The analysis proceeds through the construction of a formal model of economic policy; the model is a shortrun Keynesian model, and static. Some of its limitations are discussed after the completion of the analysis. The main contribution of this chapter lies in the exploration of a distinction between two types of mobility of capital: mobility in response to changes in income and the associated changes in the profitability of real investment (income mobility) and mobility in response to changes in relative interest rates (interest mobility).

THE MODEL

The model consists of a set of identities and behaviour relations designed to concentrate attention on the policy instruments – fiscal policy and monetary policy – and objectives of policy – income and the balance of payments.

These identities are:

$$Y \equiv E + T + G \tag{1}$$

where Y is national income, E is domestic expenditure, T is the trade surplus, and G is net government expenditure – for simplicity,

[1] The most important theoretical developments are: R. A. Mundell, 'The Monetary Dynamics of International Adjustment under Fixed and Flexible Exchange Rates', *Quarterly Journal of Economics* (May 1960); 'The Appropriate Use of Monetary and Fiscal Policy for Internal and External Stability', *IMF Staff Papers* (March 1962); 'Capital Mobility and Stabilization Policy under Fixed and Flexible Exchange Rates', *Canadian Journal of Economics and Political Science* (November 1963); and M. J. Fleming, 'Domestic Financial Policies under Fixed and under Floating Exchange Rates', *IMF Staff Papers* (November 1962).

the role of government is assumed to be confined to expenditure, G being taken as the fiscal policy variable;

$$B \equiv T + K \qquad (2)$$

where B is the balance of payments on current and capital account (excluding compensatory financing via reserve movements when the exchange rate is fixed) and K is the net capital inflow;

$$M \equiv L \qquad (3)$$

where M is the stock of money supplied by the monetary authority, taken as the monetary policy variable,[1] and L is the stock of money held by the public.

The assumed behaviour relationships are as follows (i and r represent respectively the interest rate and the domestic price of foreign exchange; in each case the third independent variable is dropped in the subsequent analysis, it being introduced at this stage to indicate possible extensions of the model; subscripts denote differentiation of the behaviour function with respect to the indicated variable):

$$E = E(Y, i, r) \qquad (4)$$

$1 > E_y > 0$

$E_i < 0$

$E_r > 0$ (according to the standard assumption that a rise in the domestic price of imports will reduce real income and therefore saving);

$$T = T(Y, r, i) \qquad (5)$$

$-E_y < T_y < 0$ (the expansion of domestic income increases imports, and may also reduce exports);

$T_r > 0$ (this assumes that the familiar elasticity conditions are satisfied);

$T_i > 0$ (this assumes a country dependent on imports for investment goods, so that a rise in the interest rate has a direct impact reducing imports in addition to its indirect 'multiplier' effect);

$$K = K(i, Y, r) \qquad (6)$$

[1] This implies that the monetary authority neutralizes the consequences of reserve movements for the balance of payments, under the fixed exchange-rate system. This constitutes a significant departure from that contained in Mundell's 1963 article.

$K_i > 0$

$K_y > 0$ (this assumes that an increase in economic activity attracts international capital, and neglects the possibility that an expansion of activity may disturb confidence);

$K_r \lessgtr 0$ (depending on the effect of the exchange rate on the domestic value of capital imports, and possibly including speculative effects of exchange rate changes);

$$L = L(Y, i, r) \tag{7}$$

$L_y > 0$

$L_i < 0$

$L_r > 0$ (assuming that the demand for money is in part a demand for purchasing power over imports).

Total differentiation of equations (1)–(3) yields the equations of change of the model, which can be arranged as follows:

$$(1 - E_y - T_y)dY - E_i\,di - (E_r + T_r)dr - dG = 0 \tag{8}$$

$$dB - (T_y + K_y)dY - K_i\,di - T_r\,dr = 0 \tag{9}$$

$$L_y\,dY + L_i\,di - dM = 0. \tag{10}$$

These three equations contain two exogenous (policy-determined) variables, dM and dG, and four dependent variables, dY, di, dr and dB. It is therefore over-determined. To render it determinate it is necessary to fix one of the dependent variables. This is accomplished through the assumption made about the international monetary system: in a fixed exchange-rate system $dr = 0$ by the pegging of the exchange rate; in a floating exchange-rate system $dB = 0$ by virtue of the automatic clearing of the exchange market through variation in the exchange rate.

THE FIXED EXCHANGE-RATE SYSTEM

The equations of change of the fixed exchange-rate system ($dr = 0$, dB a dependent variable) are:

$$(1 - E_y - T_y)dY - E_i\,di = dG \tag{8'}$$

$$dB - (T_y + K_y)dY - K_i\,di = 0 \tag{9'}$$

$$L_y\,dY + L_i\,di = dM. \tag{10'}$$

The determinant of the system is

$$\Delta = -L_i(1 - E_y - T_y) - E_i L_y. \tag{11}$$

By the assumptions about the signs and magnitudes of the partial derivatives of the behaviour functions previously listed, Δ must be positive.

By solving the system for the effects of an increase in government expenditure, and referring to the behaviour assumptions of the model, we obtain the results:

$$\frac{dY}{dG} = \frac{-L_i}{\Delta} > 0 \tag{12a}$$

$$\frac{di}{dG} = \frac{L_y}{\Delta} > 0 \tag{12b}$$

$$\frac{dB}{dG} = \frac{K_i L_y - (T_y + K_y) L_i}{\Delta} \lessgtr 0. \tag{12c}$$

In words, an increase in government expenditure (the quantity of money remaining unchanged) will raise income and the rate of interest. It may improve or worsen the balance of payments, because the latter is subject to opposing forces: both the increase in interest rates and the increase in income attract international capital flows and so tend to improve the capital account, while the increase in income worsens the current account.

Similarly, the results for an expansion of the money supply (government expenditure remaining unchanged) are:

$$\frac{dY}{dM} = \frac{-E_i}{\Delta} > 0 \tag{13a}$$

$$\frac{di}{dM} = \frac{-(1 - E_y - T_y)}{\Delta} < 0 \tag{13b}$$

$$\frac{dB}{dM} = \frac{-K_i(1 - E_y - T_y) - E_i(T_y + K_y)}{\Delta} \lessgtr 0 \tag{13c}$$

An increase in the money supply will raise income and lower the rate of interest. Again, the balance of payments is subject to conflicting forces: the increase in income worsens the current account, and the reduction of interest rates checks the inflow or encourages the outflow of international capital, thus worsening the capital account; but the expansion of income tends to attract foreign capital, and if this effect is strong enough it might outweigh the adverse effects.

The ambiguity of the result just derived with respect to the effect of monetary expansion on the balance of payments, conflicts with the commonly held view that monetary expansion must worsen the balance of payments. The difference arises from the assumption of the view in question that interest rates are the only factor influencing international capital movements, an assumption that lumps all international capital movements together in the class of portfolio investment, ignoring the important categories of equity and direct investment, which are likely to be governed more by profit prospects associated with the level of income than by the interest rates available on financial claims. Portfolio and equity capital flows may be influenced in opposite directions by monetary expansion in a country, the former being repelled by low interest rates and the latter attracted by more favourable profit prospects produced by the resulting increase in economic activity; and the latter effect may outweigh the former.

It may be noted in passing that a sufficient condition for monetary expansion to worsen the balance of payments is $(T_y + K_y) < 0$, i.e. that an expansion of income improves the capital account by less than it worsens the current account; also that the opposite of this condition, $(T_y + K_y) > 0$, is sufficient to guarantee that fiscal expansion will improve the balance of payments.

The argument just presented indicates that both fiscal and monetary expansion policies are more likely to be able to increase employment without a serious worsening of the balance of payments, or even with a favourable concomitant effect on the balance of payments, the more responsive are international capital flows to changes in profit prospects associated with changes in economic activity or the higher is income mobility of capital. It is now appropriate to consider the influence on the effects of the two policy instruments of the responsiveness of international capital flows to changes in interest rates. The responsiveness of international capital flows to interest rates is embodied in the magnitude of the parameter K_i. It is evident from equation (12c) that the greater the interest mobility of capital, the more likely is it that fiscal expansion will improve the balance of payments at the same time as it raises income. Similarly, it is evident from equation (13c) that the greater the interest mobility of capital the larger will be the balance-of-payments deficit (or possibly the smaller will be the surplus) that will result from the effort to increase employment by monetary expansion. Thus, in a system of fixed exchange rates, interest mobility of capital militates in favour of the use of fiscal expansion, and against the use of monetary expansion, by countries that desire to increase their economic activity and employment without worsening, or along with improving, their balances of payments. Similarly, interest mobility of capital militates in favour of fiscal rather than monetary contraction for countries that desire to reduce inflationary pressure without improving, or along with worsening, their balances of payments.

The analysis so far has been concerned with the effects of the separate use of fiscal and monetary policy on the targets of economic policy, the level of income and the balance of payments. We now turn to the analysis of the problem of using the fiscal and monetary policy instruments simultaneously to achieve the fulfilment of desired objectives with respect to income and the balance of payments. For this purpose it is necessary to transform the previously endogenous economic variables (income and the balance of payments) into exogenous variables, and the previously exogenous policy variables (government expenditure and the quantity of money) into endogenous variables, the values of which must be such as to produce the desired levels of the target variables.

The equations of change of the system now become:

$$dG + E_i di = (1 - E_y - T_y)dY \tag{14}$$

$$K_i di = dB - (T_y + K_y)dY \tag{15}$$

$$dM - L_i di = L_y dY \tag{16}$$

where dY and dB are now to be interpreted as target changes in the level of income and the balance of payments, and dG and dM as the changes in the policy instruments required to obtain them. The determinant of the system is

$$\Delta = K_i > 0 \tag{17}$$

and the solutions for the dependent variables are:

$$dG = \frac{(1-E_y-T_y)K_i+(T_y+K_y)E_i}{\Delta} dY - \frac{E_i}{\Delta} dB \qquad (18a)$$

$$di = \frac{I}{\Delta} dB - \frac{T_y+K_y}{\Delta} dY \qquad (18b)$$

$$dM = \frac{L_i}{\Delta} dB + \frac{K_iL_y-L_i(T_y+K_y)}{\Delta} dY. \qquad (18c)$$

The coefficients of dY and dB respectively in equations (18a) and (18c) can be read as indicating the relative change that must occur in the policy variable on the left-hand side of each equation if the target change in the one variable is to be attained with no change in the other. (Equation (18b) merely expresses the change in the interest rate that will occur when G and M are adjusted to produce the target changes in Y and B.[1]) For simplicity, the ensuing argument assumes that both dY and dB are positive, i.e. the policy-makers are seeking to bring about an increase in income and an improvement in the balance of payments.

The coefficients of dB in equations (18a) and (18c) show that to improve the balance of payments without altering the level of employment the authorities must increase government expenditure and simultaneously reduce the quantity of money; this combination of policies will be accompanied by an increase in the interest rate. It is not necessarily true, however, that to increase the level of income without altering the balance of payments the authorities must adopt the same combination of policies, with the same effect on the interest rate. In equation (18a), the first term in the numerator of the coefficient of dY is positive, while the second term is positive or negative according as $(T_y+K_y)\lessgtr0$, so that the sign of the entire coefficient is ambiguous unless $(T_y+K_y)<0$, in which case the coefficient is positive. Similarly, in equation (18c), the first term in the numerator of the coefficient of dY is positive, while the second

[1] If a third policy objective, economic growth, is introduced into the analysis, the change in the rate of interest can be interpreted as indicating the effects of economic policy on the achievement of that objective by assuming that an increase in the interest rate reduces growth and vice versa. The pursuit of three objectives simultaneously would of course require the introduction of a third policy instrument.

term is positive or negative according as $(T_y + K_y) \lessgtr 0$, so that the sign is again ambiguous unless $(T_y + K_y) > 0$, in which case the co-efficient is positive. Finally, in equation (18b) the sign of the co-efficient of dY will be positive or negative according as $(T_y + K_y) \lessgtr 0$. Thus, if $(T_y + K_y) < 0$, implying that the adverse effect of an increase in income on the current account is greater than its favourable effect on the capital account, it follows that to raise income without worsening the balance of payments the authorities must increase government expenditure and manage the money supply so as to raise the interest rate, though such management may involve either expanding or contracting the money supply. Conversely, if $(T_y + K_y)$ > 0, the money supply must be expanded and the interest rate must fall; but the requisite fiscal policy may be either an increase or a decrease in government expenditure.

Before concluding this section, it is appropriate to revert to the question of the influence of capital mobility on the results. Clearly, since the sign of $(T_y + K_y)$ is crucial to the character of the policies required to raise income, and since the larger is K_y the more likely is that sign to be positive, the greater is capital mobility in response to income changes, the more likely is it that the appropriate policy will involve monetary expansion and a reduction in interest rates, rather than fiscal expansion and an increase in interest rates. With respect to capital mobility in response to interest rate differences, since $\Delta = K_i$, the greater is capital mobility of this kind the smaller will be the increase in government spending and reduction in the money supply required to produce a given improvement in the balance of payments, and the less the accompanying change in the interest rate. As the interest mobility of capital approaches infinite sensitivity to interest rate changes, the changes in government expenditure, money supply, and the interest rate required to produce a given improvement in the balance of payments will approximate to zero. If the objective is to produce a given increase in employment rather than a given improvement in the balance of payments, the fact that K_i appears in both numerator and denominator of the coefficients of dY in equations (18a) and (18c) implies that the influence of $(T_y + K_y)$ will decrease as K_i increases, so that with sufficient interest mobility of capital government expenditure must be increased and the quantity of money decreased to increase the level of income. Moreover, as capital mobility of this type approaches infinite sensitivity to interest rate changes, the relationship of the increase in government expenditure to the required increase in income will approximate to the inverse of the simple Keynesian multiplier relationship $dG/dY \approx 1 - E_y - T_y$. The relationship of the increase in the quantity of money, to the increase in income, on the other hand, will approximate to the inverse of the simple velocity relationship of the quantity theory, $dM/dY \approx L_y$. These results mean that with sufficiently high interest mobility of capital, the policy problem of maintaining a full employment income under fixed exchange rates reduces to governing fiscal policy according to the simplest kind of Keynesian multiplier analysis, and using monetary policy to provide the money demanded at the full employment level of income on simple quantity theory lines.

THE FLOATING EXCHANGE-RATE SYSTEM

The equations of change in the floating exchange-rate system ($dB = 0$, dr a dependent variable) are:

$$(1 - E_y - T_y)dY - E_i di - T_r dr = dG \tag{8''}$$

$$(T_y + K_y)dY + K_i di + T_r dr = 0 \tag{9''}$$

$$L_y dY + L_i di = dM. \tag{10''}$$

The determinant of the system is

$$\Delta = T_r[L_y(K_i - E_i) - (1 - E_y + K_y)L_i]. \tag{19}$$

By the behaviour assumptions of the model, Δ must be positive.

The solutions for the effects of an increase in government expenditure are:

$$\frac{dY}{dG} = \frac{-T_r L_i}{\Delta} > 0 \tag{20a}$$

$$\frac{di}{dG} = \frac{T_r L_y}{\Delta} > 0 \tag{20b}$$

$$\frac{dr}{dG} = \frac{L_i(T_y + K_y) - K_i L_y}{\Delta} \lessgtr 0. \tag{20c}$$

An increase in government expenditure (the quantity of money remaining unchanged) will raise income and the rate of interest. The effect on the rate of exchange is uncèrtain, because the latter is subject to opposing influences: the increases in the interest rate and in income attract capital inflows and tend to appreciate the currency, while the increase in income worsens the current account and tends to depreciate the currency.

Similarly, the solutions for an expansion of the money supply (government expenditure remaining unchanged) are:

$$\frac{dY}{dM} = \frac{-E_i T_r + K_i T_r}{\Delta} > 0 \tag{21a}$$

$$\frac{di}{dM} = \frac{-T_r(1 - E_y + K_y)}{\Delta} < 0 \tag{21b}$$

$$\frac{dr}{dM} = \frac{K_i(1 - E_y - T_y) + E_i(T_y + K_y)}{\Delta} \lessgtr 0. \tag{21c}$$

Monetary expansion increases income and lowers interest rates. It may either raise or lower the price of foreign exchange: the reduction of interest rates encourages capital outflows and through its effects in raising income worsens the current account, thus tending to produce depreciation of the currency, but the increase in income attracts capital and tends to produce currency appreciation.

Again, the ambiguity of the result with respect to the effect of monetary expansion on the exchange rate conflicts with widely held doctrine, and again the explanation is the latter's neglect of the effect of changes in the level of income, as contrasted with changes in the rate of interest, in motivating international capital movements. In analogy with the fixed rate case, it may be noted that a sufficient condition for monetary expansion to lead to currency depreciation is $(T_y + K_y) < 0$, and that the opposite of this condition, $(T_y + K_y) > 0$, is sufficient to guarantee that fiscal expansion will lead to appreciation of the exchange rate.

As in the fixed exchange-rate case, we may now consider the influence of international mobility of capital on the effectiveness of fiscal and monetary expansion. In the floating rate case, it is generally assumed that there is only one objective of policy that need be considered, the maintenance of full employment, equilibrium in the balance of payments being secured automatically by movements in the exchange rate. Since countries on a floating exchange rate are, however, frequently concerned about the stability of the rate, in the sense of desiring to avoid either changes in both directions or depreciation alone, the implications of capital mobility for the objective of avoiding changes in the exchange rate will also be considered.

The problem is more complex than in the previous case, since the coefficients representing the two kinds of capital mobility – mobility in response to profit opportunities associated with income and mobility in response to interest rate differentials – appear in the determinant of the system as well as in the numerators of various coefficients of change.

With regard to the effects of fiscal and monetary policy on income, since K_y appears with a positive sign in the determinant but not in the numerators of equations (20a) and (21a), the effect of income mobility of capital is to reduce the effectiveness of both monetary and fiscal expansion in raising income. (The economic reason for this is that the capital inflow prompted by an increase in income tends to appreciate the exchange rate, worsening the current account and so cancelling out part of the expansionary effect.) Mobility of capital in response to interest-rate changes, on the other hand, has differential effects on the effectiveness of the two methods of promoting expansion. Since K_i appears in the denominator of equation (20a) with a positive sign, but not in the numerator, it follows that the greater is K_i (the more mobile is capital in response to interest rate changes) the less is the increase in income produced by increased government expenditure; in the extreme, if capital were infinitely mobile, the right-hand side of equation (20a) would be zero and fiscal policy would be powerless to influence income. But K_i appears in both the numerator and the denominator of equation (21a), and it can readily be shown by differentiation with respect to K_i that dY/dM increases as K_i increases. As K_i approaches infinity, in fact, dM/dY approaches $1/L_y$, the (marginal) income velocity of circulation, so that with high mobility of capital in response to interest rates the working of the system approximates to the quantity theory of money.

The conclusions that emerge with respect to mobility of capital are therefore: first, that mobility of capital in response to income variations reduces the effectiveness of both monetary and fiscal policy in raising employment (and therefore that the greater is income mobility

162

of capital, the less are the attractions of the floating rate system); second, that capital mobility in response to interest-rate differences reduces the leverage of fiscal policy and increases the leverage of monetary policy in controlling the level of employment.

With regard to the effects of fiscal and monetary policy on the exchange rate, it can readily be shown by differentiating equations (20c) and (21c) that dr/dG and dr/dM both decline as K_y increases – capital mobility in response to income changes stabilizes the exchange rate in the face of changes in both monetary and fiscal policy. But capital mobility with respect to interest-rate changes has a differential influence on the effects of fiscal and monetary policy: dr/dG declines as K_i increases, but dr/dM increases as K_i increases. Thus the higher the degree of interest mobility of capital, the less destabilizing is the effect of fiscal-policy changes and the more destabilizing is the effect of monetary policy on the market rate of exchange. These results are of course merely the obverse side of the results with respect to the effects of monetary and fiscal policy on income and employment: because demand for output has been assumed to be directly related to the exchange rate ($T_r > 0$), a larger change in the exchange rate is a concomitant of a larger change in income.

Following the procedure of the previous section, we now turn to consideration of the combined use of monetary and fiscal policy to achieve simultaneously the fulfilment of desired objectives with respect to income and (in this case) the exchange rate.

The equations of change of the system now become:

$$dG + E_i di = (1 - E_y - T_y)dY - T_r dr \tag{22}$$

$$K_i di = -(T_y + K_y)dY - T_r dr \tag{23}$$

$$dM - L_i di = L_y dY. \tag{24}$$

As in the fixed rate case, the determinant of the system is

$$\Delta = K_i > 0 \tag{25}$$

and the solutions for the dependent variables are:

$$dG = \frac{[E_i(T_y + K_y) + K_i(1 - E_y - T_y)]}{\Delta}dY + \frac{(E_i - K_i)}{\Delta}T_r dr \tag{26a}$$

$$di = -\frac{(T_y+K_y)}{\Delta}dY - \frac{T_r}{\Delta}dr \qquad (26b)$$

$$dM = \frac{[K_iL_y-L_i(T_y+K_y)]}{\Delta}dY - \frac{T_rL_i}{\Delta}dr. \qquad (26c)$$

From these equations, it follows that, to produce a depreciation of the exchange rate without altering the level of income, the authorities must expand the quantity of money and simultaneously decrease government expenditure, the rate of interest falling in consequence. The policy required to increase the level of income without altering the exchange rate, however, depends on the magnitudes of the relevant parameters. If $(T_y+K_y)>0$ (an increase in income improves the capital account by more than it worsens the current account) the quantity of money must be increased, and the rate of interest must fall; but government expenditure may have either to rise or to fall. If on the other hand $(T_y+K_y)<0$ the level of government expenditure and interest rates must rise, but either an increase or a decrease in the quantity of money may be called for.

Again it is appropriate, in concluding the section, to revert to the question of the influence of capital mobility on the results. Mobility of capital in response to income changes increases the likelihood that (T_y+K_y) will be positive, and therefore that the policy required to achieve an increase in employment at a given exchange rate will involve an increase in the quantity of money and a reduction of interest rates; it also increases the likelihood that an increase in employment will require a decrease in government expenditure.

As regards mobility of capital with respect to interest-rate changes, the greater is this mobility the smaller is the increase in the money supply (and the associated reduction in interest rates), and the decrease in government expenditure, required to achieve a given depreciation of the exchange rate holding income constant. Likewise, the greater the interest mobility of capital, the more likely it is that both an increase in the quantity of money and an increase in government expenditure will be required to achieve a given increase in income. As capital movements approach infinite sensitivity to interest-rate changes, the change in the interest rate will approach zero. The relationship between the change in the quantity of money and the change in income will approach the inverse of the income-velocity relationship of the quantity theory $(dM/dY \approx L_y)$, and the relationship between the change in government expenditure and the change in income will approach the inverse of the Keynesian multiplier relationship $(dG/dY \approx 1 - E_y - T_y)$. These results imply that with high interest mobility of capital, the problem of maintaining a full-employment level of income under a regime of floating exchange rates, which exchange rates are actually stabilized by policy, reduces to governing fiscal policy by the simplest type of Keynesian multiplier model and monetary policy by the simplest type of velocity model. This is the same result, naturally, as was obtained in the fixed exchange-rate case previously analysed, where the objectives of policy were full employment income and a balanced balance of payments.

CONCLUDING COMMENTS

This chapter has outlined some aspects of the theory of economic policy under fixed and floating exchange rates in an environment of international mobility of capital. A distinction has been drawn between income mobility and interest mobility of capital. It has been shown that income mobility of capital facilitates the task of increasing income and employment without adverse effects on the balance of payments in a fixed exchange-rate system, using either fiscal or monetary expansion, but reduces the leverage of both fiscal and monetary policy over income and employment in a floating rate system. It has also been shown that interest mobility of capital increases the advantages of fiscal policy over monetary policy in a fixed exchange-rate system, and increases the advantages of monetary policy over fiscal policy in a floating exchange-rate system. Finally, high interest mobility reduces the pursuit of full-employment income and a balanced balance of payments in a fixed rate system, or of full-employment income and a stable exchange rate under a floating rate system, to the combination of a Keynesian fiscal policy operation with a quantity-theory monetary policy operation.

The model employed has, of course, serious limitations, especially inasmuch as it treats international capital movements as flow variables dependent on income levels and interest rates, and does not allow them either to enter into the determination of aggregate expenditure or to affect the domestic money supply. More important from the viewpoint of practical application, by treating international capital movements in this fashion the model disguises the fact that balance-of payments adjustment based on the inducement of capital flows is only a temporary form of adjustment: the model contains no longer-run mechanism adjusting the level of domestic wages and prices to an equilibrium level consistent with maintenance of the value of the currency without the support of policy-induced capital flows. This defect is also a feature of the present international monetary system, which contains no automatic adjustment mechanism of this kind, and is therefore obliged to depend on policies of what has recently been termed 'systematic *ad hoc*-ery'[1] in the management of international capital movements and commercial transactions to deal with international disequilibria. A more comprehensive long-run analysis would have to introduce a long-run adjustment mechanism, and integrate it with a treatment of international capital movements as rearrangements of asset portfolios and recognition of the influence of reserve changes on monetary policy.

[1] By Robert V. Roosa.

Chapter 7

Theoretical Problems of the International Monetary System[*]

INTRODUCTION

Since 1958, international economists have been greatly concerned with the problem of international monetary reform. Research and writing on this problem has taken one or other of two broad forms. Those economists most concerned with policy have concerned themselves with emphasizing the need for international monetary reform and propounding workable (negotiable) schemes for achieving it. International monetary theorists, on the other hand, have been concerned with the theoretical policy problems of achieving and maintaining balance-of-payments equilibrium in the present international monetary system of fixed exchange rates. They have also become concerned with the problems of the system as a monetary system.

This chapter belongs to the latter category. It seeks to outline the main propositions of the analysis of international economic policy and policy problems that has been developed by economists working in this field in recent years. Section I is concerned with the economic policy problems of maintaining both full employment and balance-of-payments equilibrium, first for a single country on a fixed exchange rate, then for two or more countries linked in a multi-country international monetary system. Section II is concerned with certain features of the present international monetary system, viewed as a monetary system. The analysis of section I is Keynesian, that of section II classical, in approach. Both sections draw heavily on papers presented at the University of Chicago Conference on

[*] Reprinted from *The Pakistan Development Review*, Vol. VII, No. 1 (Spring 1967), pp. 1–28; also *Journal of Economic Studies*, Vol. II, No. 2 (January 1968), pp. 3–35.

International Monetary Problems organized by R. A. Mundell, held at Chicago in September 1966.

I. PROBLEMS OF ECONOMIC POLICY IN A SYSTEM OF FIXED EXCHANGE RATES

1. *The single economy in a world system*

It is convenient to begin the analysis with the theory of economic policy in a closed economy, in which there is assumed to be price stability around the point of full employment, and on either side of full employment a rate of change of wages and prices that can be neglected for purposes of the present analysis. Left to itself, such an economy would come into equilibrium, as is well understood, at the interest rate and level of money (and real) output indicated by the intersection of the *IS* and *LM* curves, according to the familiar Hansen–Hicks diagrammatic analysis of the Keynesian system. If the government wishes to shift the economy to the equilibrium level of output corresponding to full employment, it has two alternative instruments at its disposal. First, it could alter the money supply, shifting the *LM* curve so that its intersection with the *IS* curve yields a full-employment level of income. As is well known, this policy will fail if the liquidity preference curve becomes perfectly interest-elastic at a rate of interest above the rate at which the *IS* curve *indicates* full employment.[1] Second, it could lower taxes or raise government expenditure, thereby – on the usual assumptions that lower taxes go only partly into saving and higher expenditure is only partly financed by additional saving – shifting the *IS* curve to the right and raising both output and employment and the rate of interest. For this analysis, the *IS* curve needs to be redefined as an $I+G$, $S+T$ curve, where G represents government expenditure and T total tax receipts, reflecting the conditions for equilibrium in the goods

---

[1] As is also well known, the perfect interest-elasticity in question cannot be inferred from the speculative motive Keynes analysed, since in the long run expectations must yield to the experience of sustained low levels of interest rates; also, the monetary authority could always absorb all the bonds held by the community, and extend its lending into direct finance of material investment, so lowering rates of interest regardless of the 'liquidity trap'. The exception therefore has to be regarded as the result of time and institutional limitations on central bank operations.

market that autonomous injections of demand from new investment and government expenditure must be equal to leakages from the circular flow of income in the form of private saving and taxation, the curve lying farther to the right the higher is government expenditure and the lower is taxation. The choice between the two alternative ways of achieving the single objective of full employment will presumably be made in the light of other objectives of economic policy, such as the desired rate of economic growth and the influence on it of the full-employment interest rate, acting through its influence on the level of private investment.

Now consider an open economy, trading with the rest of the world at a fixed exchange rate. Given the exchange rate, the trade surplus (or deficit) of the country will be a decreasing (increasing) function of its level of national income and employment; and whichever choice of combination of policy instruments – fiscal policy and monetary policy – it makes to maintain full employment, the trade surplus (or deficit) will be the same. In consequence, it appears that a country on a fixed exchange rate that would have a deficit at full employment is faced with a conflict of objectives which it cannot surmount – either it must have full employment and a deficit, or it must have international balance and excessive unemployment.

To represent the policy problem of such a country, the IS–LM diagram must be revised, insofar as the IS curve is concerned, to transform the IS curve into an $I+G+X$, $S+T+M$ curve, where X represents exports and M imports at the assumed given exchange rate, X being assumed either constant or a decreasing function of national income (the latter on the assumption that a rise in income diverts production from the export to the home market), and imports being assumed to rise as national income rises. The trade balance must also be shown, in a separate quadrant, as a function of national income.

As mentioned, the situation of a country on a fixed exchange rate with a potential deficit in the trade account at full employment, appears to pose a dilemma between full employment and a deficit, or international balance and abnormal unemployment. The solution provided in the immediate postwar period by James Meade[1] and

[1] J. E. Meade, *The Theory of International Economic Policy*, Vol. I, *The Balance of Payments* (London: Oxford University Press, 1951).

other writers was to introduce the possibility of changes in the exchange rate. At a lower exchange rate (price of domestic currency in terms of foreign), given the satisfaction of certain elasticity or stability conditions, the trade deficit (surplus) associated with any particular level of income would be lower (higher). Hence the country would achieve both objectives – full employment and a balanced balance of trade, or for short internal and external balance – by a proper combination of exchange rate adjustment and fiscal- or monetary-policy change. It should be noted that, if attention is concentrated on the fiscal and monetary policies required to maintain full employment of domestic resources, a devaluation designed to shift the relation between national income and the trade balance in a favourable direction would shift the $I+G+X$, $S+T+M$ curve upwards. Consequently, to preserve exact full employment, a country seeking to correct an unfavourable trade balance by devaluation would have to counteract this shift in the trade-balance–national-income relation either by a more restrictive monetary policy designed to shift the LM curve leftwards to offset the rightward shift of the $I+G+X$, $S+T+M$ curve, or to correct the rightward shift of the $I+G+X$, $S+T+M$ curve by raising taxes or reducing government expenditure. In other words, such a country would have to accompany devaluation by a more restrictive fiscal or monetary policy. If it did not do so, the effect of its devaluation on its trade balance would be offset sooner or later by the inflationary consequences of the resulting excess demand for national output on domestic prices and therefore on the relative prices of the country's exports relative to its imports.

In the international monetary system as it has developed since the early postwar work on the theory of international economic policy, exchange rates have become for practical purposes virtually rigid, so that a country faced with the choice between balance-of-trade deficit and excess unemployment cannot resolve the dilemma by resorting to devaluation combined with some mixture of fiscal- and monetary-policy change. At the same time, the alternative to devaluation examined by the writers in question, the use of controls to foster exports and restrict imports has been ruled out – at least in large part – by the growing aversion to using variations in controls to correct balance-of-payments disequilibria. As a result, it again appears that countries will be faced by a dilemma between balance-of-payments deficits and abnormal unemployment.

This dilemma has been dispelled by recognition that the balance of payments comprises two elements, the current account and the capital account, and that while the current account balance can be taken as a function of the level of national income and employment, the flow of funds on international capital account is a function of the level of domestic interest rates relative to foreign interest rates and that this interest rate level is a function of the 'mix' of fiscal and monetary policy adopted to maintain full employment. Thus, while (in principle) the current account is determined by the exchange rate and the level of domestic activity, the capital account of the balance of payments can be adjusted to match the current account deficit or surplus by a proper choice of the fiscal–monetary policy mix. A country that would have a current account deficit at full employment greater than its normal capital inflow, or surplus less than its normal capital outflow, can adjust the latter to the former by adopting a more restrictive monetary policy and a less restrictive fiscal policy; and vice versa. Thus the two objectives of policy – full employment and a balanced balance of payments – can be secured, despite the adherence to a fixed exchange rate, by a proper choice of the fiscal–monetary policy mix.

The problem and its solution are illustrated in Figure 7.1, which is drawn to depict the policy problem facing the United States in the early 1960s, of a capital outflow greater than the current account surplus generated at the current exchange rate under full employment. In the figure, LM_1 and IS_1 (actually $I_1 + G_1 + X_1, S_1 + T_1 + M_1$) represent the curves corresponding to an initial fiscal–monetary policy mix designed to secure full employment. At that level of income and employment, the current account surplus is T_1, less than the capital outflow K_1 generated by the equilibrium domestic interest rate i_1; the country therefore has an overall deficit of $K_1 - T_1$. By lowering taxes, or raising expenditure, or both, the government can raise the IS curve to IS_2 ($I_2 + G_2 + X_1, S_2 + T_2 + M_1, X$ and M being fixed by the full-employment level of income); and by restricting the quantity of money it can raise the LM curve to LM_2; with this combination of policy changes, the interest rate i_2 corresponding to full employment is just such as to generate a lower capital outflow K_2 just equal to the current account surplus T_1, and the country achieves its two objectives of internal and external balance.

It is necessary to observe, however, that to continue to achieve these two objectives the country must continue to apply the fiscal and

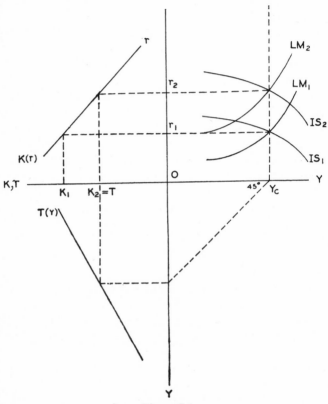

Figure 7.1

monetary policies represented by LM_2 and IS_2; by assumption, there is nothing in the situation to eventually restore a relationship between the domestic price level and foreign prices that will relieve the nation's policy-makers of the necessity of adopting this particular fiscal–monetary policy mix, regardless of any other policy objectives they may have. This is one of the major problems of the present international monetary system: it is possible to 'finance' international deficit and surplus positions by the choice of an appropriate fiscal–monetary policy mix, but this fact does not mean that there is any mechanism of adjustment present in the system. On the contrary, there may be the opposite of an adjustment mechanism, for two reasons. First, presumably a country that would be in deficit at full employment gets that way because in fact at full employment its prices and wages rise faster than those of its competitors; hence if it succeeds by proper fiscal–monetary mix policy in maintaining full employment, its current account will tend to worsen over time and therefore it will be driven still further into mixing expansion and monetary contraction, thereby piling up international debts (if it is a capital importer) or restraining its capital outflow at an increasing rate. Second, insofar as economic growth promotes international competitiveness, the higher level of interest rates it must maintain to keep its international accounts in balance will militate against a longer-run improvement in its competitiveness. (These propositions, however, obviously oversimplify the problem of restoring international balance.)

In the actual working of the international monetary system, however, there is a mechanism of adjustment at work, of the classical gold-standard kind involving deflation in the deficit countries and inflation in the surplus countries. This is so because neither deficit nor surplus countries have been able, for various reasons, to operate the fiscal–monetary policy mix technique anywhere near perfectly. The deficit countries have in practice had to undergo more unemployment that they would like, and the surplus countries have been unable to prevent their surpluses from having inflationary consequences for their domestic price levels. Since the deficit countries have been unwilling to push deflationary policies beyond the point of preventing prices from rising, the resulting system of 'reluctant adjustment'[1] operates via differences between deficit and surplus countries' average tendency to inflation. Such an adjustment mechanism is bound to operate slowly, and to be vulnerable to temporary reverses associated with surges of inflationary pressure in the deficit countries such as have occurred in the United Kingdom and the United States in the 1960s.

[1] On this concept see my *The World Economy at the Crossroads* (Oxford: The Clarendon Press, 1965), Ch. 3.

The account of the problem of reconciling internal and external balance just outlined abstracts from two rather different aspects of the policy problem, which have figured in early-1960s literature. These may be termed 'the assignment problem' (following the work of R. A. Mundell), and 'the welfare problem' (a problem which has been given birth, but not christened, by several writers).

The assignment problem follows from the observation that governments typically assign responsibility for the pursuit of policy objectives separately to separate governmental institutions which control particular instruments of economic policy – typically the central bank, controlling monetary policy, is given responsibility for external balance, and the treasury, controlling fiscal policy, is given responsibility for full employment. The assignment problem is, which objective should be assigned to which agency, to assure the most efficient operation of policy. This problem raises some complex issues in economic dynamics, arising from what may be termed 'the feedback problem'.

That problem is that the pursuit of its assigned objective by each policy agency may disrupt the pursuit of its own objectives by the other agency, and so provoke policy actions by that agency that disrupt the pursuit of its objectives by the first agency referred to, so that the pursuit of the objectives assigned to the agencies in fact leads away from rather than towards the attainment of the policy objectives sought. The solution to this problem, which has been provided by R. A. Mundell,[2] is the 'principle of effective market classification' – that each agency should be assigned the objective on which the policy instrument under its control has relatively the greatest influence, as contrasted with other objectives. In a fixed exchange-rate system, this means assigning external stability to monetary policy, and internal stability to fiscal policy.

The analytical essence of the assignment problem is illustrated by the two parts of Figure 7.2. For simplicity, fiscal policy is represented by the variable G, for government injections of expenditure into the

[1] For example, R. A. Mundell, 'The Appropriate Use of Monetary and Fiscal Policy for Internal and External Stability', *International Monetary Fund Staff Papers*, Vol. 9, No. 1 (March 1962), pp. 70–7.

[2] R. A. Mundell, 'The Monetary Dynamics of International Adjustment Under Fixed and Flexible Exchange Rates', *Quarterly Journal of Economics*, Vol. LXXIV, No. 2 (May 1960), pp. 227–57.

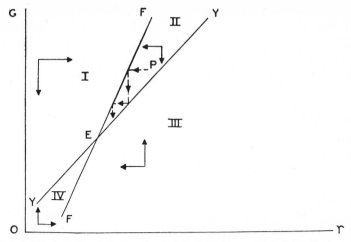

Figure 7.2. (a) Fiscal Policy for Internal Balance, Monetary Policy for External Balance.

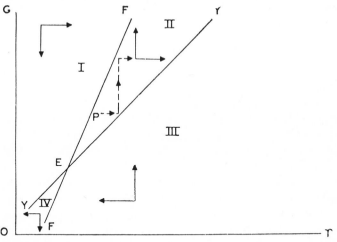

(b) Monetary Policy for Internal Balance, Fiscal Policy for External Balance.

economy, and monetary policy by the variable *r*, representing the rate of interest. In each case the *YY* curve represents the combinations of increasing fiscal laxity and monetary stringency that will preserve domestic full employment, and the *FF* curve represents the combinations of increasing fiscal laxity and monetary stringency that will preserve equilibrium between the current and capital accounts of the balance of payments. The *FF* curve must slope upwards more steeply than the *YY* curve, because a movement rightwards along the *YY* curve implies no change in the current account (since the level of output and employment is held constant) but an improvement of the capital account due to the increase in the interest rate; to offset this and keep the overall balance of payments in balance, government expenditure must be increased still more, to worsen the current account sufficiently to counteract the increased capital inflow. The intersection of the *YY* and *FF* curves at *E* shows the mix of fiscal and monetary policy required to achieve the two policy objectives of external and internal balance.

Now assume that the two objectives of economic policy are each assigned exclusively to one of the policy instruments, the controllers of the relevant instrument being instructed to operate their policy in the direction indicated by the relation between the actual state of the economy and the assigned target of full employment on external balance. Figure 7.2 depicts the two possible assignments, the internal balance to fiscal policy and external balance to monetary policy, and the converse; in each case, the horizontal arrows depict the direction in which monetary policy will be moving, and the vertical arrows the direction in which fiscal policy will be moving, for the four states of the economy into which the *YY* and *FF* curves divide the diagram. (I = deficit and over-full employment, II = surplus and over-full employment, III = surplus and deficient demand, IV = deficit and deficient demand.) For assignment (a), the arrows always point towards the policy-equilibrium point *E*, indicating that under this assignment of targets to policy variables the operations of the policy authorities will converge on equilibrium. For assignment (b) however, the arrows point away from the equilibrium in regions II and IV, indicating that equilibrium may be approached only in an oscillatory manner, or may not be reached at all, depending on the precise nature of the policy responses to disequilibrium. (A crude way of appreciating the dynamic difference between the two assignments, easily manageable in diagrammatic terms, is to assume that the fiscal- and monetary-policy authorities take turns in changing their policies, each changing its policy instrument so as to bring the economy onto the *FF* or *YY* curve, whichever corresponds to the policy objective for which it is responsible; the dynamics of adjustment in the two assignment systems are illustrated by the dotted paths starting from the disequilibrium point *P* in region II.)

The assignment problem has occupied much attention in the literature; but it should be noted that the problem is created by the assumption that administratively efficient governmental policymaking requires the assignment of one objective to each controller of a policy instrument, and that the problem could be avoided by intragovernmental co-ordination of the use of policy instruments, all being used jointly in pursuit of all policy objectives.

The welfare problem, in its most basic sense, derives from the fact that under the fixed exchange-rate system the international flow of capital, in the sense of real resources as contrasted with international security purchases and sales, is determined by the deficits (surpluses) on current account that result from the relative international competitiveness of the various countries, given their domestic price levels, employment policies and exchange rates. Determination of international capital resource flows by these factors is to be contrasted with the classical mechanism of adjustment, under which domestic price levels (or exchange rates) would adjust so as to generate current account surpluses and deficits corresponding to desired international capital movements generated by the pursuit of maximum returns on investment. The resulting pattern of international capital movements obviously need not be anything like an efficient one, since there is no reason to expect that the real return on investment in countries with current account deficits is higher than that on investment in countries with current account surpluses; it may on the contrary involve a serious distortion of the allocation of new real investment resources, and a consequent welfare loss for the countries concerned and the world economy. Analysis of these welfare losses, however, has barely begun; and, indeed, the conceptual tools for dealing with the welfare aspects of investment problems remain to be developed.[1]

---

[1] For relevant analyses, see John Hause, 'The Welfare Costs of Disequilibrium Exchange Rates', *Journal of Political Economy*, Vol. LXXIV, No. 4 (August 1966), pp. 333–52; and my 'The Welfare Costs of Exchange Rate Stabilization', *Journal of Political Economy*, Vol. LXXIV, No. 5 (October 1966), pp. 512–18. Chap. 10 Note 5 below.

Given the fact that the international monetary system governs the international movement of real capital in this fashion, there arises a problem in the welfare economics of second-best (or perhaps third-best): whether the international flow of financial capital should be accommodated to the real capital flows by the fiscal–monetary policy mix technique analysed above, or whether the accommodation should be achieved by the imposition of interest-equalization taxes or other controls on international capital movements designed (at least partially) to insulate monetary and fiscal policy from being dominated by the obligation to maintain international balance, such as the United States and the United Kingdom have been imposing in recent years.[1] In the United States, at least, international monetary experts have an instinctive preference for freedom of international capital movements, and have tended to condemn the interest-equalization tax and other interventions in international capital movements as undesirable interferences with economic efficiency and violations of the purposes of the fixed exchange-rate international monetary system.

This argument, however, is questionable on two grounds. First, it can be objected that since private international capital movements are motivated by expected net private return, and since the relation of net private return to gross social return is heavily inflenced by taxes and other governmental policies, there is no *a priori* reason for placing much confidence in the principle of freedom of private international capital movements as a guarantor of economic efficiency in the international allocation of world investment resources. Second, and more important, the argument for freedom of capital movements assume an international adjustment mechanism capable of achieving the real international transfers private individuals and enterprises want to make; in the absence of such a mechanism, with the real transfers determined by countries' relative international competitiveness, the argument is essentially that countries' monetary–fiscal policies should be adjusted so as to induce the owners of capital to want to transact just the amount of international financial transfers that matches the predetermined real transfers. This entails adjusting

---

[1] This part of the analysis draws heavily on a brilliantly-reasoned paper by Franco Modigliani: 'International Capital Movements, Fixed Parities, and Monetary and Fiscal Policies', unpubl. MS (October 1966).

each country's rates of domestic investment and saving to the level of interest rates at which financial and real transfers balance; and there is no reason to think that this procedure is superior to controlling capital movements and allowing the rates of domestic saving and investment to be determined by government policy, or by

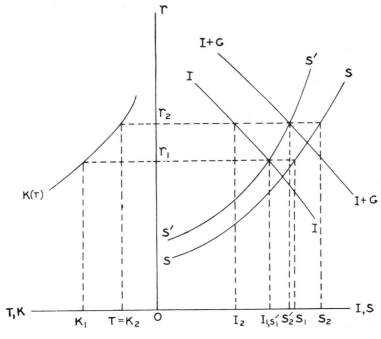

Figure 7.3

private decisions operating in the context of some agreed budgetary policy. (These alternatives allow for the two possibilities that the government may wish to implement an overall growth policy by means of its fiscal policy, or that the population is content to fix budgetary policy by some criterion not related to growth, e.g. a cyclically balanced budget, and to let the rate of growth be determined by private savings and investment decisions.)

The problem is illustrated in Figure 7.3, which is again drawn to represent the U.S. position in the early 1960s; for simplicity, it is assumed that fiscal policy is initially adjusted to some structure of taxes and expenditure considered socially optimal, and that in order to obtain the level of domestic interest rates required for international balance the policy-makers increase government expenditure, financing it by additional borrowing, at the same time contracting the money supply to the extent required to prevent the increased government expenditure from raising aggregate income above the full-employment level. On the right-hand side of the diagram, II represents the full employment investment demand curve, SS the full-employment supply curve of private real saving, and $S'S'$ the full-employment supply curve of real saving less the real capital exports provided by the current account surplus. If there were no problem of balancing the current account surplus and the capital account deficit, equilibrium would be reached at the interest rate r_1 with rates of saving and investment respectively I_1 and S_1, corresponding to the desires of savers and investors at an equilibrium interest rate r_1. But at the interest rate r_1, as shown on the left-hand side of the diagram, desired exports of financial capital, K, would exceed the current account surplus, T. In order to balance its balance of payments while maintaining freedom of capital movements, the policy-makers would have to increase government expenditure by the amount G, contracting the money supply simultaneously, to arrive at the level of interest rates r_2 at which $K_2 = T$, in the process increasing private domestic saving to S_2 while cutting domestic investment to I_2.

In the new equilibrium, domestically-invested saving exceeds domestic investment by $I_2S'_2$, this amount corresponding to purchases of government debt issued to finance increased government expenditure. This part of private domestic saving makes no contribution to increasing the future income of the economy, constituting merely the acquisition by savers of a future claim on income which has to be taxed away from the community at large; in fact, the real investment that contributes to future income has been reduced from I_1 to I_2. By providing an alternative asset (government debt) with a private yield to which there corresponds no social yield, the policy-makers have made private real saving larger and private real investment smaller than they would otherwise be.

If, on the contrary, the authorities used controls on the export of capital to restrict such exports to the level $K_2 = T$, the economy could be kept at the initial equilibrium position, without the wastage of private saving in financing government expenditure. In this situation, it would appear that the government was preventing private individuals from undertaking profitable foreign investments in the amount of $K_1 - K_2$; but since in any case they can only be allowed to undertake foreign investments in the amount of K_2, the real situation is that savers are forced to invest at home at the interest rate r_1 instead of being bribed to invest at home by the offer of government debt yielding at the rate r_2, this yield being obtained not from additional production but from additional future taxes on other income-earners, at the expense of the reduction of potential future national income consequent on the reduction in real investment induced by the increase in interest rates to r_2. The issue is therefore primarily one of redistribution between savers and taxpayers; and so far as efficiency is concerned, it is a question not of efficiency versus inefficiency in the international allocation of capital, but of inefficiency versus efficiency in the use of the domestic saving potential, the fiscal–monetary mix technique wasting that potential in additional debt-financed government expenditure, and the control technique using it for investment in increasing future national income.

It should be emphasized, however, that this is very much an issue of second-best welfare economics. The first-best solution for a country faced with this policy problem – on the crucial assumption, which has been questioned above, that private-profit-motivated international investment promotes efficient international allocation of new investment resources – would be a devaluation, to increase the current account surplus so as to permit the transfer of a large amount of foreign investment.

2. *The international economic system*

The analysis of the single country in the world economy in the first part of this section assumed that the policy-makers in the individual country can take the situation in the rest of the world, and especially the level of foreign interest rates, as given. This assumption made it possible for the country to achieve internal and external balance simultaneously by resort to an appropriate mix of domestic fiscal and monetary policy. When the analysis is extended, however, to include the interactions of national economic policies in a world economy of two or more countries, the situation becomes more complex. In the first place, it is no longer possible for a country to secure its domestic objectives of internal and external balance by use of its own policy instruments alone; it can always be frustrated by inconsistent use by other countries of their policy instruments. In the second place,

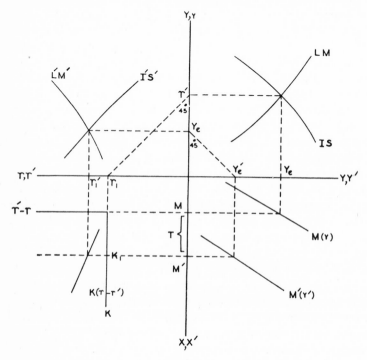

Figure 7.4

because the balances of payments of all the countries in the world economy must sum to zero ('Cournot's Law'), the external balance objective of all countries will be achieved if all but one of them achieve it. Hence, whereas in the single-country case examined previously there were two policy objectives requiring two policy instruments to implement them, in the n-country case there will be $2n-1$ objectives, requiring only $2n-1$ policy instruments; in other words, there will be one degree of freedom, or one spare policy instrument, in the system. This fact means that one country, and one country alone, can use one of its policy objectives for some other purpose; this poses the practical problem of which country will have this degree of freedom, or of how this degree of freedom can be used for some international purpose.

The problem of achieving external and internal balance in a two-country international system is illustrated in Figure 7.4; in the figure, unprimed symbols refer to country 1 (again represented so as to conform to the situation of the United States in the early 1960s) and primed symbols to country 2 (the rest of the world). Each country's imports are presumed to be a function of its national income, the IS curves being drawn to incorporate the full-employment level of imports by (exports to) the other country. The international flow of financial capital is assumed for simplicity to be a function of the interest rate differential between the two countries.

The figure represents one possible position of international economic-policy equilibrium. The monetary and fiscal policies of country 1 inherent in the locations of the IS and LM curves generate full employment in that country with the interest rate r_1, while the policies inherent in the locations of $I'S'$ and $L'M'$ generate full employment in country 2 with the interest rate r_1'. The difference between the full-employment imports of the two countries gives country 1 a current account surplus of T, while the interest-rate differential $r_1' - r_1$ generates a financial capital flow from country 1 to country 2 of K_1, just equal to the trade surplus T.

Two important propositions are evident from the construction of the figure. The first is that the achievement of international policy equilibrium is possible only if countries 1 and 2 are prepared to harmonize their economic policies, in the sense of establishing the relationship between r and r' required to balance the international financial capital flow and the real resource flow created by the difference between the full-employment imports of the two countries. To put the point another way, country 2 could always frustrate a fiscal–monetary policy mix adopted by country 1 in pursuit of internal and external balance, by adopting a laxer fiscal policy and tighter monetary policy than would produce an interest rate in that country consistent with the interest rate generated by country 1's

183

policy mix (in terms of Figure 7.4, such a policy would shift $I'S'$ and $L'M'$ to the left, maintaining their intersection at income Y'_e). Second, there is obviously an infinite number of combinations of fiscal-monetary policy mixes in the two countries that would balance the financial capital flow with the real resource transfer – because both countries could relax fiscal policy and tighten monetary policy in such a way as to preserve the required interest-rate differential, and conversely. This means that one country could peg its interest-rate level at any desired level, internal and external balance for the two countries together being preserved by an appropriate fiscal policy in that country and fiscal–monetary policy mix in the other; alternatively it could fix its fiscal policy, e.g. by insisting on maintaining a balanced budget for a fixed level of government expenditure, internal and external balance for the world economy being preserved by an appropriate fiscal policy in the other country and appropriate monetary policies in both.[1]

The presence of the degree of freedom associated with Cournot's Law gives rise to what has been termed 'the redundancy problem' (one redundant policy instrument). This problem, it should be noted, was absent from the classical gold-standard mechanism, because the basing of national money supplies on an overall fixed total of world gold reserves prevented countries from pursuing independent monetary policies – the gold constraint absorbed the degree of freedom. It arises in the present international monetary system because national monetary policies have been cut free of the gold constraint.

There are two possible solutions to the redundancy problem, each of which raises difficulties that have been reflected in acrimonious disputes between surplus and deficit countries in the early 1960s. One would be to allow one country to absorb the degree of freedom, and to govern one of its policy instruments by other objectives than external and internal balance; this was essentially the solution

[1] In a previous essay on this point, I erroneously implied that the country enjoying the degree of freedom could use it to receive a desired structure of its balance of payments, e.g. size of current account deficit and matching capital inflow: 'The Objectives of Economic Policy and the Mix of Fiscal and Monetary Policy under Fixed Exchange Rates', in W. Fellner, F. Machlup, R. Triffin and eleven others, *Maintaining and Restoring Balance in International Payments* (Princeton: Princeton University Press, 1966), Ch. 8, pp. 149 ff. This is incorrect: the balances on trade account are fixed by the relative price levels of the countries.

advocated by many Americans in the early dollar deficit years when they pressed for employment via monetary policy while tacitly assuming congressional control of fiscal policy, in fact demanding *two* degrees of freedom. The difficulty with this solution, as experience shows, is that other countries will want the freedom of policy that can by necessity only be allowed to one of them. The other solution would be to agree on an internationally desirable use of the one degree of freedom, e.g. by agreeing on an average level of world interest rates desirable from the point of view of world growth. The difficulty with this solution, as experience also shows, is essentially the same: that countries differ strongly in their views of what is desirable. Specifically, there has been a persistent disagreement between the Americans, who have favoured low rates of interest, and the Europeans, who have favoured high rates of interest. Moreover, the dispute has been thoroughly entangled in a more basic dispute over who should bear the burden of longer-run adjustment to international disequilibrium, the Europeans favouring a more deflationary system that would throw a larger share of the burden on the deficit countries, and the Americans and British favouring a more inflationary international monetary system.

The redundancy problem is inherent in the logic of the international monetary system, given the assumption that countries have the objectives of internal and external balance and control of their monetary and fiscal policies. In practice, however, the system has been struggling in part with two problems that are the converse of redundancy. In the first place, not all countries have the capacity to use fiscal and monetary policy in the required mixes: the United States only adopted the principle of using fiscal policy for control purposes with the tax cut of 1964, and its ability to use fiscal policy is considerably restricted by the constitutional division of powers; similarly, West Germany lacks the central authority to use fiscal policy in this fashion. Secondly, countries do not in fact confine themselves in their international economic policies to the objective of external balance, which all can pursue consistently. Instead, they have other balance-of-payments objectives, relating to the composition of their international accounts, which may well be inconsistent with those of other nations, and, moreover, impossible to pursue with the policy instruments they have available. As particular examples, both

Canada and the Western European countries regard their current account deficits as undesirable – which means the adoption of an objective with respect to the size of other countries' current account surpluses not necessarily consistent with those countries' objectives – and seek to correct these deficits by balance-of-payments policies (such as import substitution) which are inappropriate to the problem (since a remedy requires increasing domestic saving or reducing domestic investment) but which may nevertheless aggravate the balance-of-payments problems of the countries with current account surpluses matched by capital outflows. In addition, many countries are particularly averse to American investment within their borders, and seek to limit or prevent it by policies that are inconsistent with American policies towards foreign investment by U.S. residents and corporations.

II. PROBLEMS OF THE INTERNATIONAL MONETARY SYSTEM

1. *The instability of the gold exchange standard*

The present international monetary system is a gold exchange standard, i.e. a system in which countries maintain fixed exchange rates by means of holdings of international reserves that include a national currency – specifically the United States dollar – in substitution for the basic international reserve – gold – which is in inadequate supply. The rate of growth of the stock of gold available for holding as monetary reserves (new gold production less private hoarding and other non-monetary usage plus Russian gold sales) has in the post-war period fallen substantially short of the rate of growth of demand for international reserves by countries other than the United States, and these countries have made up the difference by accumulating reserves of dollars, which are convertible on demand into gold. These dollars, in turn, have been supplied through the medium of a sustained United States balance-of-payments deficit.

An international monetary system of this kind is inherently unstable, in the sense that the passage of time inevitably erodes the foundation of the system in confidence in the convertibility of the dollar, by steadily reducing the ratio of U.S. gold reserves to U.S. dollars held as international monetary reserves by other countries and – at least eventually – steadily reducing the absolute amount of gold reserves held by the United States. The reason is that, if other countries hold reserves of dollars and gold in a fixed ratio and their demand for reserves increases more rapidly than the supply of monetary gold, their demand for additional gold reserves can only be satisfied by allowing them to absorb a disproportionate share of the new gold supplies, and if their demand for additional gold is large enough its satisfaction will require not only the new gold supplied but also a drawing on the U.S. gold reserves. Since dollars held by other countries as reserves are increasing faster than the world stock of monetary gold, while U.S. gold reserves must be increasing less fast or actually decreasing, the ratio of U.S. gold reserves to U.S. dollar liabilities to the monetary authorities of other countries must be falling over time. That is, the international liquidity position of the United States must be steadily weakening, thereby undermining the objective basis for confidence by the rest of the world in the unlimited convertibility of their reserve dollars.

This problem, which may be termed the 'long-run confidence problem', is illustrated in Figure 7.5. The northeast quadrant shows the international reserve position of countries outside the United States (the rest of the world). Initially, these countries hold R_1 of international reserves, divided between D_r of dollars and G_r of gold according to the desired international assets ratio, r_r. The northwest quadrant shows the total world gold stock, initially G_1, divided between rest of the world holdings of G_r and U.S. gold reserves, G_a. The southwest quadrant (to which the dollars held by the rest of the world are transferred diagrammatically by means of a 45° line in the southeast quadrant) shows the international liquidity position of the United States; initially the United States holds G_a of gold reserves and has D_r of dollar liabilities outstanding, and hence has a ratio of gold reserves to dollar reserve liabilities given by the slope r_a with reference to the vertical axis.

Now suppose that, as a result of new gold production, the world monetary gold stock rises from G_1 to G_2, while as a result of world economic growth the total reserves demanded by the rest of the world rise by a greater proportion, from R_1 to R_2. If the rest of the world maintains the same ratio of gold to dollars in its reserves as previously prevailed, its dollar holdings rise to D'_r, while U.S. gold reserves fall to G'_a the U.S. ratio of gold to reserve-dollar liabilities falling to r'_a.[1] The U.S. international liquidity position would necessarily deteriorate; and it would continue to deteriorate so long as the rest of the world's demand for reserves grew faster than world gold supplies and it maintained its initial ratio of gold to dollars in international reserves.

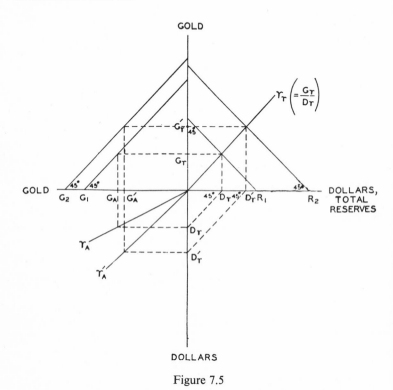

Figure 7.5

The deleterious effects of the worsening of the U.S. international liquidity position on confidence in the convertibility of the dollar,

[1] U.S. gold reserves G'_a might initially rise rather than fall by comparison with their initial level, G_a, if the rate of increase of reserves demanded by the rest of the world or the ratio of gold to dollars held by the rest of the world were sufficiently small; but ultimately, as the total reserves of the rest of the world increased relative to the world gold stock, the increase in the rest of the world's demand for gold would come to exceed the increase in world gold supplies and U.S. reserves would have to fall.

and hence on the usability of the dollar as an international reserve currency, could be avoided in two ways. First, this deterioration might be regarded as acceptable or even desirable by the rest of the world, on the grounds that the United States possessed a disproportionate share of the initial world gold stock. This was in fact the case up to about 1958. But for the rest of the world to accept a steady deterioration of the U.S. liquidity position while continuing to hold and use dollars as international reserves would amount to a deliberate decision to accept the progressive substitution of dollars for gold as the basic international reserve, since it would imply a decreasing expectation that dollars would be encashed into gold. Moreover, eventually the United States would run out of gold reserves from which to supplement the contribution of new gold supplies to the reserves of the rest of the world, and at that point the rest of the world would be forced to accommodate its gold–dollar ratio to the rate of increase of world gold supplies.

The second alternative would be for the rest of the world to progressively reduce its ratio of gold to dollar reserves held, so as to enable the United States to maintain its international liquidity position (ratio of gold reserves to dollar liabilities) intact. Since that would involve a steady reduction in the absolute level of gold reserves held by the rest of the world, it too would involve a deliberate decision to substitute dollars for gold as the basic international reserve. Moreover, eventually the United States would come to hold all the world's gold stock, and thereafter its liquidity position would deteriorate as a result of the disparity between the rates of growth of the rest of the world's demand for reserves and the world gold stock.

Thus both of the solutions to the long-run confidence problem just discussed involve the ultimate substitution of the dollar for gold as the world's international reserve money. This solution the rest of the world is not prepared to accept. The alternative, of which many variants have been proposed in the early 1960s, and towards which the monetary officials of the leading countries have been working, is to develop a credit-money substitute for gold on an international basis, in place of the national credit-money substitute, the U.S. dollar, heretofore employed for this purpose.

Figure 7.5 can also be used to illustrate another aspect of the long-run confidence problem of the international monetary system, the problem as it has appeared to U.S. policy-makers in the early 1960s, in the form of the so-called 'dilemma of the deficit'. To provide the rest of the world with its desired increase in international reserves, $R_2 - R_1$, the United States must run the requisite deficit on its balance of payments (official settlements basis) of

$$D'_r - D_r + G_a - G'_a = R_2 - R_1.$$

The apparent dilemma is that if the United States runs this deficit its international liquidity position will deteriorate and its gold reserves fall, whereas if it takes policy measures to terminate the deficit to prevent these consequences, the result will be to prevent the reserves of the rest of the world from growing as rapidly as desired and therefore probably provoke policy changes injurious to world trade and economic growth. The apparent dilemma, however, is a spurious one, since the United States can create dollars for the rest of the world to hold as reserves not only by running a deficit but by purchasing foreign currencies with dollars, a procedure that would add equally to its international liabilities and assets and hence would not weaken (in fact, would arithmetically strengthen) its international liquidity position. This solution, however, might raise new problems, since to keep the system going the United States would have to sell gold as well as dollars for foreign exchange to be held in its own reserves, and the rest of the world might not regard foreign-exchange backing of dollar reserves as being as good as gold backing; and it might distrust the power that large holdings of foreign currencies might give to the U.S. monetary authorities in the foreign-exchange markets.

The foregoing analysis has been concerned with the long-run confidence problem of the present dollar exchange standard system, on the assumption that the system is working properly, in the sense of providing additional international reserves to the rest of the world at the rate at which demand for such reserves is increasing. In principle, this outcome could be secured by the pursuit of appropriate fiscal and monetary policies by the member countries of the international monetary system, on the lines analysed in section I of this chapter, interest rates in the United States and elsewhere being so aligned that the U.S. capital outflow exceeded the U.S. current account surplus by just enough to provide the rest of the world with the desired increase in gold and dollar reserves. Such close co-ordination of national economic policies, however, would be difficult to achieve in practice; and in fact in the early 1960s the policy combinations adopted by the United States and Western Europe have resulted in an outflow of reserves from the United States larger than desired by the Western European countries. These countries have attempted to force the United States to change its policies to correct the situation, by taking a higher proportion of their reserve increments in gold rather than in dollars and so aggravating the U.S. loss of gold reserves. In essence, from the point of view of the European countries U.S. policy has been led by the pursuit of domestic full employment into generating an increase in the world supply of international reserves that is inflationary for the world economy, and the European countries have reacted by using drawings of gold from the U.S. reserves to put pressure on the United States to desist from generating world inflation.

The situation resulting from this conflict of objectives may be termed 'the short-run confidence problem', or – because the method of disciplining U.S. policy by withdrawing gold if carried too far might produce an international liquidity crisis – 'the crisis problem'. Mundell has shown in another paper[1] that the crisis problem is a particular case of the assignment problem, and that the present assignment of control over the amount of dollars outstanding to the size of U.S. gold reserves and of the objective of world price stability to the rest of the world's (specifically, Europe's) control over the size of the U.S. gold reserves entails a particularly unstable policy system, whereas the assignment of world price stability to U.S. monetary policy and of the maintenance of the proper ratio of gold reserves to dollars outstanding to the rest of the world's control over U.S. gold reserves would result in a stable world policy system.

The logic of this analysis is illustrated in Figure 7.6, where dollars outstanding are measured on the vertical axis and European (rest of the world) gold holdings are measured on the horizontal axis, a decrease in these holdings implying an equal increase in U.S. gold reserves; OR' represents the world stock of gold reserves. The curve

---

[1] R. A. Mundell, 'The Crisis Problem', in R. A. Mundell and A. K. Swoboda (eds), *Monetary Problems of the International Economy* (Chicago: University of Chicago Press, 1969), Pt 6, pp. 343–50. The diagrammatic analysis presented below is adapted from that of Mundell who originated it.

RR' represents the relation between dollars outstanding and the gold stock available to the rest of the world when the United States maintains a fixed ratio of gold reserves to dollars. The line *SS'* (with a slope of −45°) represents the fixed total of gold and dollars required to maintain world price stability; this line is to be interpreted as the sum of the domestic U.S. money supply required to

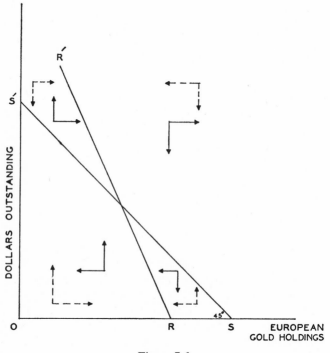

Figure 7.6

circulate the maximum U.S. income consistent with price stability, and the gold and dollar reserves required by the rest of the world to back a domestic money supply there consistent with price stability. (More generally, the total represented by the *SS'* curve can be considered the amount required as U.S. domestic money supply and rest-of-world reserves required for world price stability on the average.) The solid arrows indicate the directions of motion of the international policy system in disequilibrium situations, when the U.S. monetary authorities respond to the U.S. gold reserve in controlling the supply of dollars and the rest of the world responds to the inflationary or deflationary implications of U.S. monetary policy by withdrawing gold from or depositing it in the U.S. reserves; the arrows indicate a possibility of instability in the northeast and southwest quadrants. The dashed arrows indicate the directions of motion of the international policy system when the assignment of instruments to targets is reversed; in this case the system must be stable.

As with the assignment problem discussed in section I, however, the analysis relies on the unrealistic assumption that each policy agency (here, each national monetary authority) acts in disregard of the effects of its actions on the problem facing the other, and therefore on the other's policy actions, in spite of the fact that both economic logic and practical experience will demonstrate the interdependence of their policy problems. In this respect, the assignment problem analysis is subject to the same criticism as the literature on duopoly problems that makes use of the reaction curve concept, a literature to which in fact it bears a close analogy. In reality, the gold-reserve policies of the European countries in the recent past have been carefully designed to put pressure on the United States by threatening an international liquidity crisis without actually either bringing such a crisis about or running the danger of so doing; and there is little probability of such a crisis occurring, because it is in the interest of no country that it should.

2. *New international reserve assets*

As mentioned in the first part of this section, many critics of the dollar exchange standard system have advanced proposals to reform the system by supplementing or replacing the reserve currencies – dollars and, to a far lesser extent, sterling – by a new international reserve asset to be created by an international credit operation; and the 'Group of Ten' leading industrial countries have for some years been working out the details of a scheme of this kind.

One of the major problems raised by the proposal to create new international credit money is that of how the new money is to be distributed, and how the member countries of the international monetary system are to share in whatever benefits result from the operation. (Other, more technical problems concern the mode of coexistence of the new reserve asset with gold and the reserve currencies, and the determination of the amount and rate of increase of the new reserve asset.) This problem, which raises some fundamental issues in monetary theory, has been termed (not altogether happily) 'the seigniorage problem', by analogy with the long-standing historical practice of royal mints of using the monopoly of the coinage to extract a profit from the coinage of bullion.

To appreciate the issues involved in the seigniorage problem, it is convenient to begin with the nature of the social saving involved in the substitution of credit money for commodity money. Consider first a commodity-money system in which the monetary commodity is producible at constant cost in terms of other commodities in general. Such a system would have a stable price level; and as its output grew, it would have to devote a fraction of its real resources equal to the product of the rate of growth and the ratio of money to income to the production of commodity money. Now suppose that a monetary authority were able to substitute a non-interest-bearing paper money for the commodity money, the issue of paper money being assumed to entail negligible cost. There would be a once-over social saving equal to the real value of the existing stock of money, the resources embodied in which could be directed to more profitable uses, and a continuing social saving equal to the resources formerly used to provide the additional money required by economic growth. The once-over social saving could alternatively be represented by the flow of interest on the real resources initially embodied in the money stock; and the seigniorage accruing to the monetary authority from the use of paper rather than commodity money would at any point of time be equal to the interest on the existing money stock plus the rate of growth of that stock. The monetary authority could not, however, dispose of both these items at will. It could either use the interest on the existing money stock for its own purposes, investing the growth of the money supply in additional interest-bearing assets; or it could spend the resources put at its disposal by the issue of new money, sacrificing the growth of interest receipts on the money stock.

This analysis clarifies two aspects of the contemporary debate over the seigniorage problem. First, it is widely believed, especially among those who wish to tie international monetary reform to the provision of additional aid to the less developed countries, that the creation of a new international reserve asset involves the generation of a pool of real resources, which pool constitutes the benefit from international monetary reform that must be equitably shared. This would be true, if the alternative to international monetary reform were a commodity-money system; but the actual alternatives lie among different systems of providing international credit money (including the present dollar exchange system), so that the problem is not to dispose of a social saving generated by the substitution of credit for commodity money, but to determine the distribution of the seigniorage generated by the issue of non-interest-bearing paper money.[1] This seigniorage arises from the transfer of real resources from the holders of money to the monetary authority; and it is obvious that it would always be possible to redistribute the seigniorage to the holders of money in such a way as to exactly compensate them for the real resources they surrender. This could be done in either of two ways: by paying interest on money equal to the yield on the investment of the real resources surrendered in return for money, and by giving money as a gift to those who demand additional quantities of it (i.e. to those who desire additional money to hold as reserves, clearly not to those who would spend it).

The foregoing observation leads to the second point, that the seigniorage generated by the creation of new international reserve money could be distributed in two alternative ways: through the distribution of the interest proceeds of the investment of the new reserve asset, and through the gift of additions to the stock of the asset to members of the international monetary system. In concrete terms, the seigniorage could be distributed either by rules governing the distribution of the income derived by the authority responsible for managing the new reserve asset, or by rules governing the distribution of additions to the stock of the asset. Concretely, if it

[1] It may be noted in passing that the Hart–Kaldor–Tinbergen proposal for an international commodity reserve money entails sacrificing the social saving from the substitution of credit for commodity money, in return for the dubious gains of a price-support scheme for the producers of primary commodities. For a critique of this proposal, see my *Economic Policies Toward the Less Developed Countries* (Washington, D.C.: The Brookings Institution, 1967), Ch. 7.

were desired to channel the seigniorage to the less developed countries, this could be done either by investing the funds in commercial assets, paying no interest to holders, and distributing the income from investments as grants to less developed countries according to some income-distribution rules or by paying no interest to holders, and investing additions to the funds in non-interest-bearing perpetual loans to the less developed countries according to some loan-distribution rule; or by some mixture of the two methods. Alternatively, if it were desired not to redistribute income among the member countries, this could be achieved by investing commercially and paying interest to holders of the new reserve assets, or by distributing new assets to those countries that wished to hold them, as described above.

The method adopted for handling seigniorage, however, would make an important difference to the efficiency of international monetary reform, for a reason not yet introduced into the analysis.[1] The holding of non-interest-bearing money involves the sacrifice of the yield on real assets in which the money could alternatively be invested, with the result that at the margin money-holding must yield a service of convenience sufficient to compensate for the loss of interest, even though the additional money holdings required to reduce the convenience yield to zero could be provided at no social cost. The extraction of seigniorage by the issue of non-interest-bearing international reserve assets therefore entails an unnecessary social loss, by restricting the holding of international reserves to less than the socially optimal level. It follows that the socially optimal system of international reserve creation should either pay interest at commercial rates on holdings of international reserves, or distribute new reserves free to would-be holders of additional reserves, rather than extract seigniorage by in effect taxing the use of international reserves and distribute this seigniorage according to some ethic of international equity.

In conclusion, it may be remarked that the analysis of seigniorage and the social saving from substituting paper for commodity money

---

[1] The ensuing argument depends crucially on the assumption that new international reserves are provided at a rate just sufficient to stabilize the world price level. A rising world price level would impose a tax, and a falling world price level yield a return, on holdings of non-interest-bearing money.

presented above explains the development of the use of national currencies as international reserves. Such currencies compete with gold for the reserve role by offering an attractive interest-bearing substitute for non-interest-bearing commodity money; in so doing, they both suit the convenience of the reserve-holding countries and promote the optimization of international reserve holding. This suggests both that any attempt to return to the gold standard, as recommended by various European writers on international monetary reform, would be inevitably doomed to failure, since the incentive to find interest-bearing monetary substitutes for gold would remain; and that the creation of a new international reserve asset may not be successful in replacing dollars and sterling as international reserves, if the provisions for supplying the asset in question are too heavily dominated by the attempt to extract seigniorage.

Chapter 8

The Case for Flexible Exchange Rates, 1969*

I. INTRODUCTION

By 'flexible exchange rates' is meant rates of foreign exchange that are determined daily in the markets for foreign exchange by the forces of demand and supply, without restrictions on the extent to which rates can move imposed by governmental policy. Flexible exchange rates are, thus, to be distinguished from the present system, (the International Monetary Fund system) of international monetary organization, under which countries commit themselves to maintain the foreign values of their currencies within a narrow margin of a fixed par value by acting as residual buyers or sellers of currency in the foreign-exchange market, subject to the possibility of effecting a change in the par value itself in case of 'fundamental disequilibrium'; this system is frequently described as the 'adjustable-peg' system. Flexible exchange rates should also be distinguished from a spectral system frequently conjured up by opponents of rate flexibility: wildly fluctuating or 'unstable' exchange rates. The freedom of rates to move in response to market forces does not imply that they will in fact move significantly or erratically; they will do so only if the underlying forces governing demand and supply are them-

* The title acknowledges the indebtedness of all serious writers on this subject to Milton Friedman's modern, classic essay, 'The Case for Flexible Exchange Rates', written in 1950 and published in 1953 (M. Friedman, *Essays in Positive Economics* [Chicago: University of Chicago Press, 1953], pp. 157–203; abridged in R. E. Caves and H. G. Johnson [eds], *Readings in International Economics* [Homewood, Ill.: Richard D. Irwin, for the American Economic Association, 1968], Ch. 25, pp. 413–37). This chapter was first published in Harry G. Johnson and John E. Nash, *UK and Floating Exchanges* (London: The Institute of Economic Affairs, 1969), pp. 9–37; and subsequently in *The Federal Reserve Bank of St. Louis Review*, Vol. 51, No. 6 (June 1969), pp. 12–24; and in George N. Halm [ed.], *Approaches to Greater Flexibility of Exchange Rates* (Princeton: Princeton University Press, 1970), Ch. 8, pp. 91–111.

selves erratic, and in that case any international monetary system would be in serious difficulty. Flexible exchange rates do not necessarily imply that the national monetary authorities must refrain from any intervention in the exchange markets; whether they should intervene or not depends on whether the authorities are likely to be more, or less, intelligent and efficient speculators than the private speculators in foreign exchange, a matter on which empirical judgement is frequently inseparable from fundamental political attitudes.

The fundamental argument for flexible exchange rates is that they would allow countries autonomy with respect to their use of monetary, fiscal and other policy instruments, consistent with the maintenance of whatever degree of freedom in international transactions they chose to allow their citizens, by automatically ensuring the preservation of external equilibrium. Since, in the absence of balance-of-payments reasons for interfering in international trade and payments, and given autonomy of domestic policy, there is an overwhelmingly strong case for the maximum possible freedom of international transactions to permit exploitation of the economies of international specialization and division of labour, the argument for flexible exchange rates can be put more strongly still: flexible exchange rates are essential to the preservation of national autonomy and independence consistent with efficient organization and development of the world economy.

The case for flexible exchange rates on these grounds has been understood and propounded by economists since the work of Keynes and others on the monetary disturbances that followed the First World War. Yet that case is consistently ridiculed, if not dismissed out of hand, by 'practical' men concerned with international monetary affairs; and there is a strong revealed preference for the fixed exchange-rate system. For this, one might suggest two reasons: first, successful men of affairs are successful because they understand and can work with the intricacies of the prevalent fixed rate system, but being 'practical', they find it almost impossible to conceive how a hypothetical alternative system would, or even could, work in practice; second, the fixed exchange-rate system gives considerable prestige and, more important, political power over national governments to the central bankers entrusted with managing the system, power that they naturally credit themselves

199

with exercising more 'responsibly' than the politicans would do, and that they naturally resist surrendering. Consequently, public interest in and discussion of flexible exchange rates generally appears only when the fixed rate system is obviously under serious strain, and the capacity of the central bankers and other responsible officials to avoid a crisis is losing credibility.

The present period of the late 1960s has this character, from two points of view. On the one hand, from the point of view of the international economy, the long-sustained sterling crisis that culminated in the devaluation of November 1967, the speculative doubts about the dollar that culminated in the gold crisis of March 1968, and the franc-mark crisis that was left unresolved by the Bonn meeting of November 1968 and still hangs over the system, have all emphasized a serious defect of the present international monetary system. This is the lack of an adequate adjustment mechanism, i.e. a mechanism for adjusting international imbalances of payments towards equilibrium sufficiently rapidly as not to put intolerable strains on the willingness of the central banks to supplement existing international reserves with additional credits, while not requiring countries to deflate on inflate their economies beyond politically tolerable limits. The obviously available mechanism is greater automatic flexibility of exchange rates (as distinct from adjustments of the 'pegs'). Consequently, there has been a rapidly growing interest in techniques for achieving greater automatic flexibility, while retaining the form and assumed advantages of a fixed rate system. The chief contenders in this connection are the 'band' proposal, under which the permitted range of exchange rate variation around parity would be widened from the present 1 per cent or less to, say, 5 per cent each way, and the so-called 'crawling-peg' proposal, under which the parity for any day would be determined by an average of past rates established in the market. The actual rate each day could diverge from the parity within the present band or a widened band, and the parity would, thus, crawl in the direction in which a fully flexible rate would move more rapidly.

Either of these proposals, if adopted, would constitute a move towards a flexible rate system for the world economy as a whole. On the other hand, from the point of view of the British economy alone, there has been growing interest in the possibility of a floating rate for the pound. This interest has been prompted by the shock of devaluation, doubts about whether the devaluation was sufficient or may need to be repeated, resentment of the increasing subordination of domestic policy to international requirements since 1964, and general discontent with the policies into which the commitment to maintain a fixed exchange rate has driven successive governments: 'stop-go', higher average unemployment policies, incomes policy, and a host of other domestic and international interventions.

From both the international and the purely domestic point of view, therefore, it is apposite to re-examine the case for flexible exchange rates. That is the purpose of this chapter. Because of space limitation, the argument will be conducted at a general level of principle, with minimum attention to technical details and complexities. It is convenient to begin with the case for fixed exchange rates; this case has to be constructed, since little reasoned defence of it has been produced beyond the fact that it exists and functions after a fashion, and the contention that any change would be for the worse. Consideration of the case for fixed rates leads into the contrary case for flexible rates. Certain common objections to flexible rates are then discussed. Finally, some comments are offered on the specific questions mentioned above, of providing for greater rate flexibility in the framework of the IMF system and of floating the pound by itself.

II. THE CASE FOR FIXED EXCHANGE RATES

A reasoned case for fixed international rates of exchange must run from analogy with the case for a common national currency, since the effect of fixing the rate at which one currency can be converted into another is, subject to qualifications to be discussed later, to establish the equivalent of a single currency for those countries of the world economy adhering to fixed exchange rates. The advantages of a single currency within a nation's frontiers are, broadly, that it simplifies the profit-maximizing computations of producers and traders, facilitates competition among producers located in different parts of the country, and promotes the integration of the economy into a connected series of markets, these markets including both the markets for products and the markets for the factors of production (capital and labour). The argument for fixed exchange rates, by analogy, is that they will similarly encourage the integration of the national markets that compose the world economy into an international network of connected markets with similarly beneficial effects on economic efficiency and growth. In other words, the case for fixed rates is part of a more general argument for national economic policies conducive to international economic integration.

The argument by analogy with the domestic economy, however, is seriously defective for several reasons. In the first place, in the domestic economy the factors of production as well as goods and services are free to move throughout the market area. In the international economy the movement of labour is certainly subject to serious barriers created by national immigration policies (and in some cases restraints on emigration as well), and the freedom of movement of capital is also restricted by barriers created by national laws. The freedom of movement of goods is also restricted by tariffs and other barriers to trade. It is true that there are artificial barriers of certain kinds to the movement of goods and factors internally to a national economy (apart from natural barriers created by distance and cultural differences) created sometimes by national policy, e.g. by regional development policies, and sometimes by the existence of state or provincial governments with protective policies of their own. But these are probably negligible by comparison with the barriers to the international mobility of goods and factors of production. The existence of these barriers means that the system of fixed exchange rates does not really establish the equivalent of a single international money, in the sense of a currency whose purchasing power and usefulness tends to equality throughout the market area. A more important point, to be discussed later, is that if the fixity of exchange rates is maintained, not by appropriate adjustments of the relative purchasing power of the various national currencies, but by variations in the national barriers to trade and payments, it is in contradiction with the basic argument for fixed rates as a means of attaining the advantages internationally that are provided domestically by a single currency.

In the second place, as is well known from the prevalence of regional development policies in the various countries, acceptance of a single currency and its implications is not necessarily beneficial to particular regions within a nation. The pressures of competition in the product and factor markets facilitated by the common currency frequently result instead in prolonged regional distress, in spite of the apparent full freedom of labour and capital to migrate to more remunerative locations. On the national scale, the solution usually applied, rightly or wrongly, is to relieve regional distress by transfers from the rest of the country, effected through the central government. On the international scale, the probability of regional (that is, national in this context) distress is substantially greater because of the barriers to mobility of both factors and goods mentioned previously; yet there is no international government, nor any effective substitute through international co-operation, to compensate and assist nations or regions of nations suffering through the effects of economic change occurring in the environment of a single currency. (It should be noted that existing arrangements for financing balance-of-payments deficits by credit from the surplus countries in no sense fulfil this function, since deficits and surpluses do not necessarily reflect, respectively, distress in the relevant sense, and its absence.)

Third, the beneficent effects of a single national currency on economic integration and growth depend on the maintenance of reasonable stability of its real value; the adjective 'reasonable' is meant to allow for mild inflationary or deflationary trends of prices over time. Stability in turn is provided under contemporary institutional arrangements through centralization of control of the money supply and monetary conditions in the hands of the central bank, which is responsible for using its powers of control for this purpose. (Formerly, it was provided by the use of precious metals, the quantity of which normally changed very slowly.) The system of fixed rates of international exchange, in contrast to a single national money, provides no centralized control of the overall quantity of international money and international monetary conditions. Under the ideal old-fashioned gold standard, in theory at least, overall international monetary control was exercised automatically by the available quantity of monetary gold and its rate of growth, neither of which could be readily influenced by national governments, operating on national money supplies through the obligation incumbent on each country to maintain a gold reserve adequate to guarantee the convertibility of its currency under all circumstances at the fixed exchange rate. That system has come to be regarded as barbarous, because it required domestic employment objectives to be subordinated to the requirements of international balance; and nations have come to insist on their right to use interventions in international trade and payments, and in the last resort to devalue their currencies, rather than proceed farther than they find politically tolerable with deflationary adjustment policies.

The result is that the automatic mechanisms of overall monetary control in the international system have been abandoned, without those mechanisms being replaced by a discretionary mechanism of international control comparable to the national central bank in the domestic economic system, to the dictates of which the national central banks, as providers of the currency of the 'regions' of the international economy, are obliged to conform. Instead, what control remains is the outcome on the one hand of the jostling among surplus and deficit countries, each of which has appreciable discretion with respect to how far it will accept or evade pressures on its domestic policies mediated through pressures on its balance of payments, and, on the other hand, of the ability of the system as a system to free itself from the remnants of the constraint formerly exercised by gold as the ultimate international reserve, by using national currencies and various kinds of international credit arrangements as substitutes for gold in international reserves.

In consequence, the present international monetary system of fixed exchange rates fails to conform to the analogy with a single national currency in two important respects. First, regions of the system are able to resist the integrative pressures of the single currency by varying the barriers to international transactions and, hence, the usefulness of the local variant of that currency, and, in the last resort, by changing the terms of conversion of the local variant into other variants; moreover, they have reason to do so in the absence of an international mechanism for compensating excessively distressed regions and a mechanism for providing centralized and responsible control of overall monetary conditions. Second, in contrast to a national monetary system, there is no responsible, centralized, institutional arrangement for monetary control of the system.

This latter point can be rephrased in terms of the commonly held belief that the fixed rate system exercises 'discipline' over the nations involved in it, and prevents them from pursuing 'irresponsible' domestic policies. This belief might have been tenable with respect to the historical gold standard, under which nations were permanently committed to maintaining their exchange rates and had not yet developed the battery of interventions in trade and payments that are now commonly employed. It is a myth, however, when nations have the option of evading discipline by using interventions or devaluation. It becomes an even more pernicious myth when one recognizes that abiding by the discipline may entail hardships for the nation that the nation will not tolerate being applied to particular regions within itself, but will attempt to relieve by interregional transfer payments; and that the discipline is not discipline to conform to rational and internationally accepted principles of good behaviour, but discipline to conform to the average of what other nations are seeking to get away with. Specifically, there might be something to be said for an international monetary system that disciplined individual nations into conducting their policies so as to achieve price stability and permit liberal international economic policies. But there is little to be said for a system that either obliges nations to accept whatever rate of world price inflation or deflation emerges from the policies of the other nations in the world economy, or obliges or permits them to employ whatever policies of intervention in international trade and payments are considered by themselves and their neighbours not to infringe the letter of the rules of international liberalism.

The defenders of the present fixed rate system, if pressed, will generally accept these points but argue the need for a solution along two complementary lines: 'harmonization' of national economic policies in accordance with the requirements of a single-world-currency system; and progressive evolution towards international control of the growth of international liquidity, combined with 'surveillance' of national economic policies. The problem with both is that they demand a surrender of national sovereignty in domestic economic policy, which countries have shown themselves extremely reluctant to accept. The reasons for this have already been mentioned; the most important are that there is no international mechanism for compensating those who suffer from adhering to the rules of the single-currency game, and that the nations differ sharply in their views on priorities among policy objectives, most notably in respect of the relative undesirability of unemployment on the one hand and price inflation on the other. The main argument for flexible exchange rates at the present time is that they would make this surrender of sovereignty unnecessary, while at the same time making unnecessary the progressive extension of interventions in international trade and payments that failure to resolve this issue necessarily entails.

The case for fixed exchange rates, while seriously defective as a defence of the present system of international monetary organization, does have one important implication for the case for flexible exchange rates. One is accustomed to thinking of national moneys in terms of the currencies of the major countries, which currencies derive their usefulness from the great diversity of goods, services, and assets available in the national economy, into which they can be directly converted. But in the contemporary world there are many small and relatively narrowly specialized countries, whose national currencies lack usefulness in this sense, but instead derive their usefulness from their rigid convertibility at a fixed price into the currency of some major country with which the small country trades extensively or on which it depends for capital for investment. For such countries, the advantages of rigid convertibility in giving the currency usefulness and facilitating international trade and investment outweigh the relatively small advantages that might be derived from exchange rate flexibility. (In a banana republic, for example, the currency will be more useful if it is stable in terms of command over foreign goods than if it is stable in terms of command over bananas; and exchange rate flexibility would give little scope for autonomous domestic policy.) These countries, which probably constitute a substantial numerical majority of existing countries, would, therefore, probably choose, if given a free choice, to keep the value of their currency pegged to that of some major country or currency bloc. In other words, the case for flexible exchange rates is a case for flexibility of rates among the currencies of countries that are large enough to have a currency whose usefulness derives primarily from its domestic purchasing power, and for which significant autonomy of domestic policy is both possible and desired.

III. THE CASE FOR FLEXIBLE EXCHANGE RATES

The case for flexible exchange rates derives fundamentally from the laws of demand and supply, in particular, from the principle that, left to itself, the competitive market will establish the price that equates quantity demanded with quantity supplied and, hence, clear the market. If the price rises temporarily above the competitive level, an excess of quantity supplied over quantity demanded will drive it back downwards to the equilibrium level; conversely, if the price falls temporarily below the competitive level, an excess of quantity demanded over quantity supplied will force the price upwards towards the equilibrium level. Application of this principle to governmental efforts to control or to support particular prices indicates that, unless the price happens to be fixed at the equilibrium level – in which case governmental intervention is superfluous – such efforts will predictably generate economic problems. If the price is fixed above the equilibrium level, the government will be faced with the necessity of absorbing a surplus of production over consumption. To solve this problem, eventually it will either have to reduce its support price, or devise ways either of limiting production (through quotas, taxes, and the like) or of increasing consumption (through propaganda, or distribution of surpluses on concessionary terms). If the price is fixed below the equilibrium level, the government will be faced with the necessity of meeting the excess of consumption over production out of its own stocks. Since these must be limited in extent, it must eventually either raise its control price, or devise ways either to limit consumption by rationing, or reduce the costs of production (e.g. by subsidies to producers, or by investments in increasing productivity).

Exactly the same problems arise when the government chooses to fix the price of foreign exchange in terms of the national currency, and for one reason or another that price ceases to correspond to the equilibrium price. If that price is too high, that is, if the domestic currency is undervalued, a balance-of-payments surplus develops and the country is obliged to accumulate foreign exchange. If this accumulation is unwelcome, the government's alternatives are to restrict exports and encourage imports either by allowing or promoting domestic inflation, which in a sense subsidizes imports and taxes exports, or by imposing increased taxes or controls on exports and reducing taxes or controls on imports; or to appreciate its currency to the equilibrium level. If the price of foreign exchange is too low, the domestic currency being overvalued, a balance-of-payments deficit develops and the country is obliged to run down its stocks of foreign exchange and borrow from other countries. Since its ability to do this is necessarily limited, it ultimately has to choose among the following alternatives: imposing restrictions on imports or promoting exports (including imports and exports of assets, i.e. control of international capital movements); deflating the economy to reduce the demand for imports and increase the supply of exports; deflating the economy to restrain wages and prices or attempting to control wages and prices directly, in order to make exports more and imports less profitable; and devaluing the currency.

In either event, a deliberate choice is necessary among alternatives that are all unpleasant for various reasons. Hence, the choice is likely to be deferred until the disequilibrium has reached crisis proportions; and decisions taken under crisis conditions are both unlikely to be carefully thought out, and likely to have seriously disruptive economic effects.

All of this would be unnecessary if, instead of taking a view on what the value of the currency in terms of foreign exchange should be, and being, therefore, obliged to defend this view by its policies or in the last resort surrender it, the government were to allow the price of foreign exchange to be determined by the interplay of demand and supply in the foreign exchange market. A freely flexible exchange rate would tend to remain constant so long as underlying economic conditions (including governmental policies) remained constant; random deviations from the equilibrium level would be limited by the activities of private speculators, who would step in to buy foreign exchange when its price fell (the currency appreciated in terms of foreign currencies) and to sell it when its price rose (the currency depreciated in terms of foreign currencies). On the other hand, if economic changes or policy changes occurred that under a fixed exchange rate would produce a balance-of-payments surplus or deficit, and, ultimately, a need for policy changes, the flexible exchange rate would gradually either appreciate or depreciate as required to preserve equilibrium. The movement of the rate would be facilitated and smoothed by the action of private speculators, on the basis of their reading of current and prospective economic and policy developments. If the government regarded the trend of the exchange rate as undesirable, it could take counteractive measures in the form of inflationary or deflationary policies. It would never be forced to take such measures by a balance-of-payments crisis and the pressure of foreign opinion, contrary to its own policy objectives. The balance-of-payments rationale for interventions in international trade and capital movements, and for such substitutes for exchange rate change as changes in border-tax adjustments or the imposition of futile 'incomes policy', would disappear. If the government had reason to believe that private speculators were not performing efficiently their function of stabilizing the exchange market and smoothing the movement of the rate over time, or that their speculations were based on faulty information or prediction, it could establish its own agency for speculation, in the form of an exchange stabilization fund. This possibility, however, raises the questions of whether an official agency risking the public's money is likely to be a smarter speculator than private individuals risking their own money; whether, if the assumed superiority of official speculation rests on access to inside information, it would not be preferable to publish the information for the benefit of the public rather than use it to make profits for the agency at the expense of unnecessarily ill-informed private citizens; and whether such an agency would in fact confine itself to stabilizing speculation or would try to enforce an official view of what the exchange rate should be, that is, whether the agency would not retrogress into *de facto* restoration of the adjustable-peg system.

The adoption of flexible exchange rates would have the great advantage of freeing governments to use their instruments of domestic policy for the pursuit of domestic objectives, while, at the same time, removing the pressures to intervene in international trade and payments for balance-of-payments reasons. Both of these advantages are important in contemporary circumstances. On the one hand, a great rift exists between nations like the United Kingdom and the United States, which are anxious to maintain high levels of employment and are prepared to pay a price for it in terms of domestic inflation, and other nations, notably the West German Federal

Republic, which are strongly averse to inflation. Under the present fixed exchange-rate system, these nations are pitched against each other in a battle over the rate of inflation that is to prevail in the world economy, since the fixed rate system diffuses that rate of inflation to all the countries involved in it. Flexible rates would allow each country to pursue the mixture of unemployment and price trend objectives it prefers, consistent with international equilibrium, equilibrium being secured by appreciation of the currencies of 'price-stability' countries relative to the currencies of 'full-employment' countries. The maximum possible freedom of trade is not only desirable for the prosperity and growth of the major developed countries, but essential for the integration of the developing countries into the world economy and the promotion of efficient economic development of those countries. While the post-Second World War period has been characterized by the progressive reduction of the conventional barriers to international trade and payments – tariffs and quotas, inconvertibility and exchange controls – the recurrent balance-of-payments and international monetary crises under the fixed rate system have fostered the erection of barriers to international economic integration in new forms – aid-tying, preferential governmental procurement policies, controls on direct and portfolio international investment – that are in many ways more subtly damaging to efficiency and growth than the conventional barriers.

The removal of the balance-of-payments motive for restrictions on international trade and payments is an important positive contribution that the adoption of flexible exchange rates could make to the achievement of the liberal objective of an integrated international economy, which must be set against any additional barriers to international commerce and finance, in the form of increased uncertainty, that might follow from the adoption of flexible exchange rates. That such additional uncertainty would be so great as to reduce seriously the flows of international trade and investment is one of the objections to flexible rates to be discussed in section IV. At this point, it is sufficient to make the following observation. First, as pointed out in section II, under a flexible rate system most countries would probably peg their currencies to one or another major currency, so that much international trade and investment would in fact be conducted under fixed rate conditions, and uncertainty would attach only to changes in the exchange rates among a few major currencies or currency blocs (most probably a U.S. dollar bloc, a European bloc, and sterling, though in the event sterling might be included in one of the other blocs). For the same reason – because few blocs would imply that their economic domains would be large and diversified – the exchange rates between the flexible currencies would be likely to change rather slowly and steadily. This would mean that traders and investors normally would be able to predict the domestic value of their foreign currency proceeds without much difficulty. But, secondly, traders would be able to hedge foreign receipts or payments through the forward exchange markets, if they wished to avoid uncertainty; if there were a demand for more extensive forward market and hedging facilities than now exist, the competitive profit motive would bring them into existence. Third, for longer-range transactions, the economics of the situation would provide a substantial amount of automatic hedging, through the fact that long-run trends towards appreciation or depreciation of a currency are likely to be dominated by divergence of the trend of prices inside the currency area from the trend of prices elsewhere. For direct foreign investments, for example, any loss of value of for-eign-currency earnings in terms of domestic currency, due to depreci-ation of the foreign currency, is likely to be roughly balanced by an increase in the amount of such earnings consequent on the relative inflation associated with the depreciation. Similarly, if a particular country is undergoing steady inflation and its currency is depreciating steadily in consequence, interest rates there are likely to rise suffici-ently to compensate domestic investors for the inflation, and, hence, sufficiently to compensate foreign portfolio investors for their losses from the depreciation. Finally, it should be noted that the same sort of political and economic developments that would impose unexpected losses on traders and investors through depreciation under a flexible exchange-rate system, would equally impose losses in the form of devaluation, or the imposition of restrictions on trade and capital movements, under the present fixed rate system.

IV. THE CASE AGAINST FLEXIBLE EXCHANGE RATES

The case against flexible exchange rates, like the case for fixed ex-change rates, is rarely if ever stated in a reasoned fashion. Instead, it typically consists of a series of unfounded assertions and allegations that derive their plausibility from two fundamentally irrelevant facts. The first is that, in the modern European economic history with which most people are familiar, flexible exchange rates are associated either with the acute monetary disorders that followed the First World War, or with the collapse of the international monetary system in the 1930s; instead of being credited with their capacity to function when the fixed exchange-rate system could not, they are debited with the disorders of national economic policies that made the fixed exchange-rate system unworkable or led to its collapse. The second, and more important at this historical distance from the disastrous experiences just mentioned, is that most people are accustomed to the fixed exchange-rate system, and are prone to assume without thinking that a system of flexible rates would simply display in an exaggerated fashion the worst features of the present fixed rate system, rather than remedy them.

The historical record is too large a topic to be discussed adequately in a brief essay. Suffice it to say that the interwar European experience was clouded by the strong belief, based on pre-First World War conditions, that fixed exchange rates at historical parity values constituted a natural order of things to which governments would seek eventually to return, and that scholarly interpretation of that experience leaned excessively and unjustifiably towards endorsement of the official view that any private speculation on the exchanges based on distrust of the ability of the authorities to hold an established parity under changing circumstances was necessarily 'destabilizing' and antisocial. It should further be remarked that European interwar experience does not constitute the whole of the historical record, and that both previously (as in the case of the U.S. dollar from 1862 to 1879) and subsequently (as in the case of the Canadian dollar from 1950 to 1962) there have been cases of a major trading country's maintaining a flexible exchange rate without any of the disastrous consequences commonly forecast by the opponents of flexible rates.

The penchant for attributing to the flexible rate system the problems of the fixed rate system can be illustrated by a closer examination of some of the arguments commonly advanced against floating exchange rates, most of which allege either that flexible rates will seriously increase uncertainty in international transactions, or that they will foster inflation.

One of the common arguments under the heading of uncertainty is that flexible rates would be extremely unstable rates, jumping wildly about from day to day. This allegation ignores the crucial point that a rate that is free to move under the influence of changes in demand and supply is not forced to move erratically, but will instead move only in response to such changes in demand and supply – including changes induced by changes in governmental policies – and normally will move only slowly and fairly predictably. Abnormally rapid and erratic movements will occur only in response to sharp and unexpected changes in circumstances; such changes in a fixed exchange-rate system would produce the same or more uncertainty-creating policy changes in the form of devaluation, deflation, or the imposition of new controls on trade and payments. The fallacy of this argument lies in its assumption that exchange rate changes occur exogenously and without apparent economic reason, an assumption that reflects the mentality of the fixed rate system, in which the exchange rate is held fixed by official intervention in the face of demand and supply pressures for change, and occasionally changed arbitrarily and at one stroke by governmental decisions whose timing and magnitude is a matter of severe uncertainty.

A related argument is that uncertainty about the domestic-currency equivalent of foreign receipts or payments would seriously inhibit international transactions of all kinds. As argued in section III, trends in exchange rates should normally be fairly slow and predictable, and their causes such as to provide more or less automatic compensation to traders and investors. Moreover, traders averse to uncertainty would be able to hedge their transactions through forward exchange markets, which would, if necessary, develop in response to demand. It is commonly argued at present, by foreign-exchange dealers and others engaged in the foreign-exchange market, that hedging facilities would be completely inadequate or that the cost of forward cover would be prohibitive. Both arguments seek to deny the economic principle that a competitive system will tend to provide any goods or services demanded, at a price that yields no more than a fair profit. They derive, moreover, from the experience of recent crises under the fixed rate system. When exchange rates are rigidly fixed by official intervention, businessmen normally do not consider the cost of forward cover worth their while, but when everyone expects the currency to be devalued, everyone seeks to hedge his risks by selling it forward, the normal balancing of forward demands and supplies ceases to prevail, the forward rate drops to a heavy discount, and the cost of forward cover becomes 'prohibitive'. Under a flexible exchange-rate system, where the spot rate is also free to move, arbitrage between the spot and forward markets, as well as speculation, would ensure that the expectation of depreciation was reflected in depreciation of the spot as well as the forward rate, and, hence, tend to keep the cost of forward cover within reasonable bounds.

A further argument under the heading of uncertainty is that it will encourage 'destabilizing speculation'. The historical record provides no convincing, supporting evidence for this claim, unless 'destabilizing speculation' is erroneously defined to include any speculation against an officially pegged exchange rate, regardless of how unrealistic that rate was under the prevailing circumstances. A counter-consideration is that speculators who engage in genuinely destabilizing speculation, that is, whose speculations move the exchange rate away from rather than towards its equilibrium level, will consistently lose money, because they will consistently be buying when the rate is 'high' and selling when it is 'low' by comparison with its equilibrium value; this consideration does not, however, exclude the possibility that clever professional speculators may be able to profit by leading amateur speculators into destabilizing speculation, buying near the trough and selling near the peak, the amateur's losses being borne out of their (or their shareholders') regular income. A further counter-consideration is that under flexible rates speculation will itself move the spot rate, thus generating uncertainty in the minds of the speculators about the magnitude of prospective profits, which will depend on the relation between the spot rate and the expected future rate of exchange, neither of which will be fixed and independent of the magnitude of the speculators' transactions. By contrast, the adjustable-peg system gives the speculator a 'one-way option' in circumstances giving rise to speculation on a change in the rate, the rate can move only one way if it moves at all, and if it moves, it is certain to be changed by a significant amount – and possibly by more, the stronger is the speculation on a change. The fixed exchange-rate system courts 'destabilizing speculation', in the economically-incorrect sense of speculation against the permanence of the official parity, by providing this one-way option; in so doing it places the monetary authorities in the position of speculating on their own ability to maintain the parity. It is obviously fallacious to assume that private speculators would speculate in the same way and on the same scale under the flexible rate system, which offers them no such easy mark to speculate against.

The argument that the flexible exchange-rate system would promote inflation comes in two major versions. The first is that under the flexible rate system governments would no longer be subject to the 'discipline' against inflationary policies exerted by the fixity of the exchange rate. This argument in large part reflects circular reasoning on the part of the fixed rate exponents: discipline against inflationary policies, if necessary for international reasons, is necessary only because rates are fixed, and domestic inflation both leads to balance-of-payments problems and imposes inflation on other countries. Neither consequence would follow under the flexible exchange-rate system. Apart from its external repercussions, inflation may be regarded as undesirable for domestic reasons; but the fixed rate system imposes, not the need to maintain domestic price stability, but the obligation to conform to the average world trend of prices, which may be either inflationary or deflationary rather than stable. Moreover, under the adjustable-peg system actually existing, countries can evade the discipline against excessively rapid inflation by drawing down reserves and borrowing, by imposing restrictions on international trade and payments, and in the last resort by devaluing their currencies. The record since the First World War speaks poorly for the anti-inflationary discipline of fixed exchange rates. The reason is that the signal to governments of the need for anti-inflationary discipline comes through a loss of exchange reserves, the implications of which are understood by only a few and can be disregarded or temporized with until a crisis descends; the crisis then justifies all sorts of policy expedients other than the domestic deflation that the logic of adjustment under the fixed rate system demands. Under a flexible rate system, the consequences of inflationary governmental policies would be much more readily apparent to the general population, in the form of a declining foreign value of the currency and an upward trend in domestic prices; proper policies to correct the situation, if it were desired to correct it, could be argued about in an atmosphere free from crisis.

The second argument, to the effect that a flexible exchange rate would be 'inflationary', asserts that any random depreciation would, by raising the cost of living, provoke wage and price increases that would make the initially temporarily lower foreign value of the currency the new equilibrium exchange rate. This argument clearly derives from confusion of a flexible with a fixed exchange rate. It is under a fixed exchange rate that wages and prices are determined in the expectation of constancy of the domestic currency cost of foreign exchange, and that abrupt devaluations occur that are substantial enough in their effects on the prices of imports and of exportable goods to require compensatory revision of wage bargains and price-determination calculations. Under a flexible rate system, exchange rate adjustments would occur gradually, and would be less likely to require drastic revisions of wage- and price-setting decisions, especially as any general trend of the exchange rate and prices would tend to be taken into account in the accompanying calculations of unions and employers. Apart from this, it is erroneous to assume that increases in the cost of living inevitably produce fully compensatory wage increases: while such increases in the cost of living will be advanced as part of the workers' case for higher wages, whether they will in fact result in compensatory or in less than compensatory actual wage increases will depend on the economic climate set by the government's fiscal and monetary policies. It is conceivable that a government pledged to maintain full employment would maintain an economic climate in which any money wage increase workers chose to press for would be sanctioned by sufficient inflation of monetary demand and the money supply to prevent it from resulting in an increase in unemployment. But in that case there would be no restraint on wage increases and, hence, on wage and price inflation, unless the government somehow had arrived at an understanding with the unions and employers that only wage increases compensatory of previous cost-of-living increases (or justified by increases in productivity) would be sanctioned by easier fiscal and monetary policy. That is an improbable situation, given the difficulties that governments have encountered with establishing and implementing an 'incomes policy' under the fixed rate system; it is under the fixed rate system, not the flexible rate system, that governments have a strong incentive to insist on relating increases in money incomes to increases in productivity, and hence, are led, on grounds of equity, to make exceptions for increases in the cost of living. It should be noted in conclusion that one version of the argument under discussion, which reasons from the allegation of a persistent tendency to cost-push inflation to the prediction of a persistent tendency towards depreciation of the currency, must be fallacious: it is logically impossible for all currencies to be persistently depreciating against each other.

V. CONTEMPORARY PROPOSALS FOR GREATER FLEXIBILITY OF EXCHANGE RATES

Increased flexibility in the IMF system

The extreme difficulties encountered in recent years in achieving appropriate adjustments of the parity values of certain major currencies within the present 'adjustable-peg' system of fixed exchange rates, as exemplified particularly in the prolonged agony of sterling from 1964 to 1967 and the failure of the 'Bonn crisis' of November 1968 to induce the German and French governments to accept the revaluations of the mark and the franc agreed on as necessary by the officials and experts concerned with the international monetary system, has generated serious interest, expecially in the U.S. administration, in proposals for reforming the present IMF system so as to provide for more flexibility of exchange rates. It has been realized that under the present system, a devaluation has become a symbol of political defeat by, and revaluation (appreciation) a symbol of political surrender to, other countries, both of which the government in power will resist to the last ditch; and that this political symbolism prevents adjustments of exchange rates that otherwise would or should be accepted as necessary to the proper functioning of the international monetary system. The aim, therefore, is to reduce or remove the political element in exchange rate adjustment under the present system, by changing the system so as to allow the anonymous competitive foreign exchange market to make automatic adjustments of exchange rates within a limited range.

The two major proposals to this end are the 'wider-band' proposal and the 'crawling-peg' proposal. Under the 'wider-band' proposal, the present freedom of countries to allow the market value of their currencies to fluctuate within 1 per cent (in practice usually less) of their par values would be extended to permit variation within a much wider range (usually put at 5 per cent for argument's sake). Under the 'crawling-peg' proposal, daily fluctuations about the par value would be confined within the present or somewhat wider limits, but the parity itself would be determined by a moving average of the rates actually set in the market over some fixed period of the immediate past, and so would gradually adjust itself upwards or downwards over time to the market pressures of excess supply of or excess demand for the currency (pressures for depreciation or appreciation, rise or fall in the par value, respectively).

Both these proposals, while welcomed by advocates of the flexible exchange-rate system, to the extent that they recognize the case for flexible rates and the virtues of market determination as contracted with political determination of exchange rates, are subject to the criticism that they accept the principle of market determination of exchange rates only within politically predetermined limits, and, hence, abjure use of the prime virtue of the competitive market, its capacity to absorb and deal with unexpected economic developments. The criticism is that *either* economic developments will not be such as to make the equilibrium exchange rate fall outside the permitted range of variation, in which case the restriction on the permitted range of variation will prove unnecessary, *or* economic change will require more change in the exchange rate than the remaining restriction on exchange rate variation will permit, in which case the problems of the present system will recur (though obviously less frequently). Specifically, sooner or later the exchange rate of a major country will reach the limit of permitted variation, and the speculation-generating possibility will arise that the par value of that currency will have to be changed by a finite and substantial percentage, as a result of lack of sufficient international reserves for the monetary authorities of the country concerned to defend the par value of the currency.

In this respect, there is a crucial difference between the 'wider-band' proposal and the 'crawling-peg' proposal. The wider-band system would provide only a once-and-for-all increase in the degree of freedom of exchange rates to adjust to changing circumstances. A country that followed a more inflationary policy than other nations would find its exchange rate drifting towards the ceiling on its par value, and a country that followed a less inflationary policy than its neighbours would find its exchange rate sinking towards the floor under its par value. Once one or the other fixed limit was reached, the country would, to all intents and purposes, be back on a rigidly fixed exchange rate. The crawling-peg proposal, however, would permit a country's policy, with respect to the relative rate of inflation it preferred, to diverge permanently from that of its neighbours, but only within the limits set by the permitted range of daily variation about the daily par value and the period of averaging of past actual exchange rates specified for the determination of the par value itself. For those persuaded of the case for flexible exchange rates, the crawling peg is, thus, definitely preferable. The only question is the empirical one of whether the permitted degree of exchange rate flexibility would be adequate to eliminate the likelihood in practice of a situation which an exchange rate was so far out of equilibrium as to make it impossible for the monetary authorities to finance the period of adjustment of the rate to equilibrium by use of their international reserves and international borrowing power. This is an extremely difficult empirical question, because it involves not only the likely magnitude of disequilibrating disturbances, in relation to the permitted degree of exchange rate adjustment, but also the effects of the knowledge by government of the availability of increased possibilities of exchange rate flexibility on the speed of governmental policy response to disequilibrating developments, and the effects of the knowledge by private speculators that the effects on the exchange rate of current speculation will determine the range within which the exchange rate will be in the future, on the assumption that the crawling-peg formula continues to hold.

Evaluation of how both the wider-band and the crawling-peg proposal should work in practice requires a great deal of empirical study which, until 1969, has not been carried out on any adequate scale. In the meantime, those persuaded of the case for flexible exchange rates would probably be better advised to advocate experimentation with limited rate flexibility, in the hope that the results will dispel the fears of the supporters of the fixed rate system, than to emphasize the dangers inherent in the residual fixity of exchange rates under either of the contemporary popular proposals for increasing the flexibility of rates under the existing fixed rate systems.

A floating pound?

The argument of the preceding sections strongly suggests the advisability of a change in British exchange rate policy from a fixed exchange rate to a market-determined, flexible exchange rate. The main arguments for this change are that a flexible exchange rate would free British economic policy from the apparent necessity to pursue otherwise irrational and difficult policy objectives for the sake of improving the balance of payments, and that it would release the country from the vicious circle of 'stop-go' policies of control of aggregate demand.

A flexible exchange rate is not, of course, a panacea; it simply provides an extra degree of freedom, by removing the balance-of-payments constraints on policy formation. In so doing, it does not and cannot remove the constraint on policy imposed by the limitation of total available national resources and the consequent necessity of choice among available alternatives; it simply brings this choice, rather than the external consequences of choices made, to the forefront of the policy debate.

The British economy is at present riddled with inefficiencies consequential on, and politically justified by, decisions based on the aim of improving the balance of payments. In this connection, one can cite, from many possible examples, the heavy protection of domestic agriculture, the protection of domestic fuel resources by the taxation of imported oil, the subsidization of manufacturing as against the service trades through the Selective Employment Tax, and various other subsidies to manufacturing effected through tax credits. One can also cite the politically arduous effort to implement an incomes policy, which amounts to an effort to avoid, by political pressure on individual wage- and price-setting decisions, the need for an adjustment that would be effected automatically by a flexible exchange rate. A flexible exchange rate would make an incomes policy unnecessary. It would also permit policy towards industry, agriculture, and the service trades to concentrate on the achievement of greater economic efficiency, without the biases imparted by the basically economically-irrelevant objectives of increasing exports or substituting for imports.

The adoption of flexible exchange rates would also make unnecessary, or at least less harmful, the disruptive cycle of 'stop-go' aggregate demand policies, which has characterized British economic policy for many years. British governments are under a persistently strong incentive to try to break out of the limitations of available resources and relatively slow economic growth by policies of demand expansion. This incentive is reinforced, before elections, by the temptation to expand demand in order to win votes, in the knowledge that international reserves and international borrowing power can be drawn down to finance the purchase of votes without the electorate knowing that it is being bribed with its own money, i.e. until after the election, when the successful party is obliged to clean up the mess so created by introducing deflationary policies, with political safety if it is a returned government, and with political embarrassment if it is an opposition party newly come to power. If the country were on a flexible exchange rate, the generation of the 'political cycle' would be inhibited by the fact that the effort to buy votes by pre-election inflationary policies would soon be reflected in a depreciation of the exchange rate and a rise in the cost of living. Even if this were avoided by use of the government's control of the country's international reserves and borrowing powers to stabilize the exchange rate, a newly elected government of either complexion would not be faced with the absolute necessity of introducing deflationary economic policies to restore its international reserves. It could instead allow the exchange rate to depreciate while it made up its mind what to do. Apart from the question of winning elections, governments that believed in demand expansion as a means of promoting growth could pursue this policy *à outrance*, without being forced to reverse it by a balance-of-payments crisis, so long as they and the public were prepared to accept the consequential depreciation of the currency; governments that believed instead in other kinds of policies would have to argue for and defend them on their merits, without being able to pass them off as imposed on the country by the need to secure equilibrium in the balance of payments.

While these and other elements of the case for a floating pound have frequently been recognized and advocated, it has been much more common to argue that a flexible exchange rate for sterling is 'impossible', either because the position of sterling as an international reserve currency precludes it, or because the International Monetary Fund would not permit it. But most of the arguments for the presumed international importance of a fixed international value of sterling have been rendered irrelevant by the deterioration of sterling's international position subsequent to the 1967 devaluation, and in particular by the Basle Facility and the sterling-area agreements concluded in the autumn of 1968, which, by giving a dollar guarantee on most of the overseas sterling area holdings of sterling, have freed the British authorities to change the foreign-exchange value of sterling without fear of recrimination from its official holders. Moreover, the relative decline in the international role of sterling, and in the relative importance of Britain in world trade, finance, and investments, characteristic of the post-Second World War period, has made it both possible and necessary to think of Britain as a relatively small component of the international monetary system, more a country whose difficulties require special treatment than a lynch-pin of the system, the fixed value of whose currency must be supported by other countries in the interests of survival of the system as a whole. Under the present circumstances, adoption of a floating exchange rate for the pound would constitute, not a definitive reversal of the essential nature of the IMF system of predominantly fixed exchange rates, but recognition of and accommodation to a situation in which the chronic weakness of the pound is a major source of tension within the established system. The International Monetary Fund is commonly depicted in Britain as an ignorantly dogmatic but politically powerful opponent of sensible changes that have the drawback of conflicting with the ideology written into its Charter. But there is no reason to believe that the Fund as the dispassionate administrator of an international monetary system established nearly a quarter of a century ago to serve the needs of the international economy, is insensitive to the tensions of the contemporary situation and blindly hostile to reforms that would permit the system as a whole to survive and function more effectively.

The Panamanian Monetary System[*]

Panama is unique or virtually so among the independent nations of the world with respect to its monetary system. While a national currency standard (the Balboa) exists, and subsidiary coinage denominated in this unit is issued, the Balboa has been exactly equal in value to one U.S. dollar ever since the completion of the Panama Canal six decades ago, and all the paper currency in circulation consists of U.S. dollar currency notes, there being no locally-issued paper Balboas.

This currency system was voluntarily adopted by the 'Convention of the Republic of Panama', which exercised legislative power for the Republic, in 1904, in agreement with the U.S. Secretary of War. But in the Panamanian popular mind it is associated with much-resented treaty of 1903 between Panama and the United States that established the Canal Zone. Now that that treaty is under renegotiation in Washington, it is natural that the question of the benefits and costs of the currency system should be raised in Panama.

The Panamanian monetary system has one great advantage – absolutely guaranteed stability of the currency in terms of the U.S. dollar, the country's largest trading partner in both directions. This absolute stability is important both for the inward private foreign investment on which developing countries have had increasingly to depend for external development assistance, and for Panama's burgeoning tourist trade, most of which consists either of American tourists or of other foreigners used to making transactions in U.S. dollars. In addition, the system has undoubtedly been strategic to Panama's rapid emergence as a regional financial centre.

As against these benefits, the system has two disadvantages. The first, and primarily sentimental rather than economic, one is that

* Reprinted from *Euromoney*, Vol. 3, No. 8 (January 1972), pp. 48–52.

it is offensive to Panamanian national pride (of course in widely varying degrees) to use a foreign currency for domestic transactions. The second, and economic, one is that dollars in circulation in Panama constitute an interest-free loan to the government of the United States. The resource loss to Panama involved depends on the interest rate at which the money could otherwise be invested. This interest rate obviously depends both on the type of asset in which the money could be invested, and on the rate of inflation in the world economy in general. As regards the first point, which will be discussed in more detail below, different possible conceptions of prudent banking practice in holding reserves against currency could lead to widely different results. As regards the second, the higher the rate of inflation in the world, sooner or later the higher will be world interest rates, as asset-holders who can choose between holding fixed-interest securities and holding equities come to realize that fixed-interest securities are losing real value from the inflation and demand higher interest rates to compensate them.

Currency in circulation in Panama has been variously estimated as of the order of $25 to $50 million. Taking the higher figure for illustrative purposes, at a 6 per cent average rate of return, obtainable otherwise, this would represent a loss of real resources of $3 million a year, and $6m, at a 12 per cent average alternative rate of return, resources which could in principle be captured by the Panamanian government issuing its own currency. These figures represent roughly 1·6 per cent and 3·2 per cent of the annual Panamanian budget, though only about ·025 to 0·50 per cent of gross domestic product. These sums are certainly not negligible; but they are not magically large either. The 6 per cent assumption represents a probably high estimate of what could be gained by investing the $50 million in a fairly liquid portfolio of U.S. government securities; the 12 per cent assumption is a probably high estimate of the social value of investing it either in Panamanian enterprises or in Panamanian government debt – in the latter case on the assumption that the interest rate on such debt understates the social rate of return on Panamanian government investments in infrastructure and social-betterment projects.

It is apparently widely believed that the government of Panama could easily capture these potential gains for itself by establishing a central bank, which would issue Balboas in place of dollars. This belief, however, overlooks some important relevant considerations.

The primary problem is the loss from the interest-free loan to the United States. This loss could be largely (though not entirely) removed without establishing a central bank, by establishing instead a currency board which would issue Balboas in exchange for dollars, and invest the dollars so obtained in a range of U.S. securities. The currency board would have to keep its portfolio liquid enough to meent any demands for the conversion of circulating Balboas into dollars.

In the Panamanian context, a currency board would have the appeal of representing a logical and primarily technical extension beyond the issue of subsidiary coins to the issue of Panamanian paper money, while preserving the aforementioned advantages of guaranteed absolute fixity of the exchange rate between the Balboa and the dollar. A central bank, by contrast, carries the threat of monetary mismanagement's ending up in exchange and payments restrictions and devaluation. At a more practical level, a currency board has the great advantage over a central bank that its operations can be made fairly automatic, so that it need not require a comparable expenditure on both administrative staff and prestigious directors and a governor able and obliged to attend the annual meetings of the International Monetary Fund and make fittingly portentous speeches prepared by high-priced research staff. Nor does it require an impressive building. It should be possible to run a currency board with a small staff and one to three commissioners who need to meet only two to four times a year.

Even so, the gain would probably not be anything like the $3 million a year mentioned above, for four reasons. (1) Prudent maintenance of a liquid portfolio, including actual dollars on deposit at the Federal Reserve as well as liquid U.S. government securities, might yield an average rate of return considerably below the 6 per cent gross assumed in the preceding calculation. (2) Even if the administration were on the most modest possible scale, its total costs for staff and office accommodation might be substantial in relation to the yield achieved. (3) Once Panama began to issue Balboa currency notes it would have to bear the costs of printing and reprinting the notes; what these costs would be in relation to the interest earned would depend on the average denomination and average life of a note, and since Panama is a poor country the average denomination would be low (probably one Balboa would be the most frequently used denomination) though against this notes in circulation in rural and remote districts might remain outstanding for a period of many years. (4) Once Panama issued its own Balboas it would have to cope with the probability of forgery and the costs of preventing or controlling it.

The foregoing remarks suggest five empirical questions that should be investigated before any decision is taken on the establishment of a currency board. These are: (i) how far the Balboas would in fact be accepted instead of dollars – the replacement of course could be fostered by various government actions, but these would have some administrative cost and nuisance value; (ii) what the expected average rate of return on the portfolio of U.S. dollar assets would be; (iii) what the staff and office costs of administration would be; (iv) what the cost of printing and reprinting notes would be; (v) what costs would be involved in policing against forgery.

The proposal to establish a central bank in Panama is associated with the idea, more ambitious than that of establishing a currency board, of capturing for Panama the potential gains from being able to invest the real resources represented by the Panamanian currency circulation in domestic projects of one kind or another – essentially, given the way central banks operate, of lending these resources to the government by purchasing government debt. This would involve the same questions of returns and costs as would arise with a currency board, except that on the one hand the gross returns on the portfolio might be substantially higher, and on the other hand the directorate, staff and building costs of a central bank would undoubtedly be much higher. Further questions would arise from the fact that such a central bank, like other central banks, would most probably impose reserve requirements in terms of its notes and deposits on the commercial banks. This would capture a part of bank deposits, as well as the currency issue, for the central bank to invest, thereby increasing the resources acquired above what a currency board would command – though it should be noted that reserve requirements are essentially a special kind of tax ultimately falling on bank depositors. On the other hand, the result would likely be that the commercial banks would come to rely on the central bank to provide them with foreign currencies in case of need, rather than holding their own portfolios of foreign liquid assets; and this might involve a considerable net loss, since the central bank is likely to be a less efficient portfolio manager than the commercial banks.

The central and fundamental issue raised by the proposal for a central bank, however, is whether a central bank – and more specifically the government whose instrument it would be – could be trusted to follow investment policies that would in fact guarantee the absolute stability of the Balboa in terms of the U.S. dollar. Monetary history is full of cases where governments hungry for money that they wanted to spend on projects they considered desirable, obtained the money not by taxes but by pressing their central bank to buy more government debt than was prudent from the point of view of defending the stability of the currency. As a result in such cases, the central bank runs its international reserves and liquidity position dangerously low, and the government is driven into exchange and trade controls and eventually into currency devaluation. Both involve not only deceit and robbery of the domestic public, whose money is reduced in value by a sort of arbitrary tax imposed on it, but perhaps more important the destruction of foreign confidence in the currency and in the country and its government, which is harmful especially to foreign investment in the country's economic development. For countries short of domestic savings and dependent on foreign capital for economic development, this highly probable long-run effect is a costly price to pay for capturing the returns on the investment of the real resources represented by the domestic money supply. For Panama, there is another cogent consideration: its emerging position as a regional financial centre would probably be seriously jeopardized if it became merely another small country with its own national currency and central bank.

For these reasons, it would seem desirable for Panama at most – and still consistently with the satisfaction of national pride – to consider seriously the question of instituting a currency board, and not to involve itself in the expensive and politically dangerous business of establishing a central bank. Even the question of a currency board should be looked into very cautiously, for two reasons. First, there are the empirical questions listed above, which will determine the probable amount of net profit that might be obtained. Second, there is the possibility that even a carefully set up and limited currency board could be converted by a determined and irresponsible government into a temporary source of easy finance for its programmes.

In view of these considerations, it might be wiser for the government of Panama to retain the present monetary system of the country, but to seek compensation for the obvious inequity of interest-free lending from a poor country to a rich one in some other way. There is a fairly close parallel here with the currency-board system that used to be characteristic of the British colonies. The argument in that case was that the low-interest (not interest-free) loans implicit in the currency-board system of investing in short-term British government securities were compensated for by British development assistance and by special rights of access to the British capital market. In the case of Panama these two forms of compensation do not seem relevant. However, Panama might ask *either* for a reasonable share of the profits of the U.S. Federal Reserve System, calculated on the basis of the estimated circulation of U.S. dollars in Panama and the profits made by the Federal Reserve per dollar in circulation, *or* for a swap loan from the Federal Reserve or some similar device designed to enable Panama to cope more efficiently with the large seasonal swings in her balance of payments.

As a final remark, these notes have been concerned only with the currency circulation of Panama. Probably a much larger volume of Panama's financial transactions is conducted through deposits at banks. As already mentioned, these depositors could be taxed through the imposition of a reserve requirement in terms of central bank notes and deposits. Apart from that, and assuming that the banking system is reasonably competitive, there would be nothing to gain by persuading or forcing it to denominate its deposits and loans in Balboas instead of dollars, because presumably the Panamanian holders of dollar-denominated bank deposits receive services from the banks that represent the returns the banks get from investing those deposits minus their costs of operation. Indeed, insisting on the Balboa as the unit of bank accounting might seriously hamper Panama's development as a regional financial centre.

Chapter 9

The Monetary Approach to Balance-of-Payments Theory[*]

My purpose in this chapter is to present the main outline of a new approach to the theory of the balance of payments and of balance-of-payments adjustment (including devaluation and revaluation) that has been emerging in recent years from several sources. Concretely, this new approach is to be found on the one hand in the change in policy orientation adopted by the British government under pressure from the International Monetary Fund after the failure of the devaluation of 1967 to produce the expected improvement in the British balance of payments, the theoretical basis for the new orientation being traceable back to the work of the Dutch economist J. J. Koopmans; and on the other hand to the theoretical work of my colleagues at the University of Chicago, R. A. Mundell, and his students – though it is only fair to note that economists elsewhere have been working along similar lines. Its essence is to put at the forefront of analysis the monetary rather than the relative price aspects of international adjustment.

To put the new approach in perspective, it is helpful to go back to the origins of balance-of-payments theory in the work of David Hume, and specifically to his contribution of the analysis of the price-specie-flow mechanism. Hume was concerned to refute the concentration of the mercantilists on the objective of accumulating precious metals within the country, and their consequent recommendation of policies designed to bring about a surplus on the balance of payments. His analysis, couched in terms relevant to the emerging new approach to balance-of-payments theory, showed that

[*] A lecture delivered at the Graduate Institute of International Studies, Geneva, Switzerland (February 5, 1971); forthcoming in Michael B. Connolly and Alexander K. Swoboda, *International Economics: The Geneva Essays* (tentative title), (London: Allen & Unwin, 1972).

229

the amount of money in a country would be adjusted automatically to the demand for it, through surpluses or deficits in the balance of payments, induced by the effects on relative national money price levels of excess supplies of or excess demands for money. Hence the mercantilist desire to accumulate 'treasure' was in conflict with the basic mechanism of international monetary adjustment and could only be *ephemerally* successful.

Three points are worth noting about the price-specie-flow mechanism at this stage. First, in contemporary terminology, it assumes (in line with the stylized facts of that time) that all money is 'outside' money (precious metals); i.e. there is no commercial or central banking system capable of creating money not backed by international reserves, domestic money and international reserves being the same thing. Second, the mechanism of adjustment focuses on international transactions in goods, as distinguished from securities, a characteristic that has remained dominant in balance-of-payments theory. Third, in the detailed analysis of the mechanism there is a rather awkward compromise between the assumption of a closed and of an open economy, in which it is assumed that domestic prices can vary from purchasing-power parity under the influence of imbalances between money demand and money supply, but that such variations give rise to changes in trade flows which alter the balance of payments and hence the domestic stock of money in the longer run. As we shall see, the new approach to balance-of-payments theory, while basically Humean in spirit, places the emphasis not on relative price changes but on the direct influence of excess demand for or supply of money on the balance between income and expenditure, or more generally between total acquisition and disposal of funds whether through production and consumption or through borrowing and lending, and therefore on the overall balance of payments.

Hume's analysis ran in terms of an automatic mechanism of international adjustment motivated by money flows and consequential changes in national money price levels. The subsequent elaboration of the theory, up to and partly through the 1930s, retained the general notion of automaticity while adding in the complications required by the existence of credit money provided by commercial banks and of central banking based on partial international reserve holdings, and by the possibility of attraction or otherwise of international short-term capital movements through international interest-rate differentials. In addition, Cassel contributed the purchasing-power-parity theory of the equilibrium determination of the values of floating exchange rates.

In the 1930s, under the stimulus on the one hand of the collapse of the international regime of fixed exchange rates and the emergence of mass unemployment as a major economic problem, and on the other hand of the Keynesian revolution – which altered the basic assumptions of theory from wage and price flexibility with full employment to wage rigidity with normal mass unemployment – a new approach to balance-of-payments theory emerged, one which viewed international adjustment not as an automatic process but as a policy problem for governments. The key problem, the classic article on which is Joan Robinson's essay on the foreign exchanges, was the conditions under which a devaluation would improve a country's balance of payments. On Keynesian assumptions of wage rigidity, a devaluation would change the real prices of domestic goods relative to foreign goods in the foreign and domestic markets, thereby promoting substitutions in production and consumption. On Keynesian assumptions of mass unemployment, any repercussions of these substitutions on the demand for domestic output could be assumed to be met by variations in output and employment and repercussions of such variations onto the balance of payments regarded as secondary. Finally, on the same assumption together with the general Keynesian denigration of the influence of money on the economy and concentration on the short run, the connections between the balance of payments and the money supply, and between the money supply and aggregate demand, could be disregarded. Attention was therefore concentrated on the 'elasticity conditions' required for the impact effect of a devaluation – i.e. of the associated change in relative real prices – to be an improvement in the balance of payments. These conditions were, for a simple model with perfectly elastic supplies and initially balanced trade, that the sum of the elasticities of home and foreign demand for imports should exceed unity (the so-called 'Marshall–Lerner condition'); and for more complex models assuming independent elasticities of demands for imports and supplies of exports, a fearfully complex algebraic expression cumbersome but challenging to derive and explore. (Much of the interest in this body of work lay in the related questions of whether a devaluation that improved the balance of payments would necessarily turn a country's terms of trade against it, and increase domestic employment.)

The so-called 'elasticity approach' to devaluation proved demonstrably unsatisfactory in the immediate postwar period of full and over-full employment, owing to its implicit assumption of the existence of unemployed resources that could be mobilized to produce the additional exports and import substitutes required to satisfy a favourable impact effect. Recognition of this by the profession came in three versions. One was carping at the irrelevance of 'orthodoxy theory' (which the elasticity approach really was not), generally associated with the recommendation of exchange controls and quantitative import restrictions as an alternative to devaluation. The second was S. S. Alexander's 'absorption approach', which argued essentially that a favourable effect from devaluation alone, in a fully-employed economy, depends not on the elasticities but on the inflation resulting from the devaluation in these conditions producing a reduction in aggregate absorption relative to aggregate productive capacity. One part of the mechanism that might bring this about in Alexander's analysis is worth mentioning as foreshadowing the new approach to be discussed below; the 'real balance effect', by which the rise in prices consequent on the excess demand generated by devaluation deflates the real value of the domestic money supply and so induces a reduction in spending out of income.

The presentation of the 'absorption approach' as an alternative to the 'elasticity approach' led to considerable controversy and extensive efforts to reconcile the two. The truth lies, however, in recognition that a fully employed economy cannot use devaluation alone as a policy instrument for correcting a balance-of-payments deficit. It must use a combination of devaluation – to obtain an allocation of foreign and domestic demand among domestic and foreign output consistent with balance-of-payments equilibrium – and deflation – to match aggregate domestic demand with aggregate domestic supply. More generally, it must use a proper combination of what I have elsewhere called 'expenditure-reducing' and 'expenditure-switching' policies. This general principle is developed at length in James Meade's classic book on *The Theory of International Economic Policy: The Balance of Payments*, though it was known before. It constitutes the third, and most useful, version of recognition of the inadequacies of the 'elasticity approach' as well as providing a synthesis between that approach and the 'absorption approach', that is logically satisfactory (though not economically satisfactory from the point of view of the new monetary approach). Unfortunately, Meade presented his analysis in terms of a short-run equilibrium analysis, and on the assumption that the policy-makers understood the theory as well as he did, both of which characteristics made the book extremely inaccessible to policy-makers and may help to account for the bumbling of British demand-management policy after the devaluation of 1967. Also, following the tradition of British central banking and monetary theory, Meade identified monetary policy with the fixing of the level of interest rates, a procedure that automatically excludes consideration of the monetary consequences of devaluation by assuming them to be absorbed by the monetary authorities (this is the reason for the economic objection to the Meade synthesis mentioned above).

Subsequent to the work of Meade and others in the 1950s, the main development in conventional balance-of-payments theory has been the development of the theory of the fiscal–monetary policy mix, following the pioneering contributions of R. A. Mundell. In the general logic of the Meade system, a country has to have two policy instruments if it is simultaneously to achieve internal and external balance (full employment and balance-of-payments equilibrium). In Meade's system, the instruments are demand management by fiscal and/or monetary policy, and the exchange rate (or controls or wage–price flexibility). What if wages are rigid, and controls and exchange rate changes are ruled out by national and international political considerations? A solution can still be found, at least in principle, if capital is internationally mobile in response to interest rate differentials. Fiscal expansion and monetary expansion then have the same effects on the current account, increasing imports and possibly decreasing exports, but opposite effects on the capital account, fiscal expansion increasing domestic interest rates and attracting a capital inflow and monetary expansion having the opposite effect, so that the two policies can be 'mixed' so as to achieve a capital account surplus or deficit equal to the current account deficit or surplus at the level of full employment of the economy. This extension of the Meade approach has lent itself to almost infinite mathematical product differentiation, with little significant improvement in quality of economic product, and will not concern us further, except to note that theoretical investigation of the model led naturally into the question of what would happen if capital were perfectly mobile, and specifically the implications of this assumption for the ability of the monetary authority to control the domestic money supply.

To recapitulate, the essential structure of what may be termed the standard model of balance-of-payments theory is a Keynesian model of income determination, in which flows of consumption and invest-ment expenditure are determined by aggregate income and demand-management policy variables (taxes and expenditures, and interest-rates), and the level of exports and the division of total expenditure between domestic and foreign goods (imports) are determined by the exchange rate which fixes the relative real prices of exports relative to foreign prices and of imports relative to domestic prices. By choosing a proper mix of demand-management policies and the exchange rate, the authorities can obtain full employment consis-tently with any current account surplus or deficit. The net current account surplus (or deficit) is equal to the excess (or deficiency) of the economy's flow of production over its flow of absorption, or to the excess (or deficiency) of its exports over its imports, or to its net excess (deficiency) of the flow of savings in relation to the flow of investment. By convention, but by no means necessarily, the current account surplus or deficit is identified with the overall balance-of-payments position; it is easy enough to add in the determination of the balance on capital account by the differential between domestic and foreign interest rates, as is in fact done in the theory of the fiscal–monetary policy mix.

The basic assumption on which this system of balance-of-payments analysis rests, and which forms the point of departure of the new 'monetary' approach to balance-of-payments theory, is that the monetary consequences of balance-of-payments surpluses or deficits can be and are absorbed (sterilized) by the monetary authorities so that a surplus or deficit can be treated as a flow equilibrium. The new approach assumes – in some cases, asserts – that these monetary inflows or outflows associated with surpluses or deficits are not sterilized – or cannot be, within a period relevant to policy analysis – but instead influence the domestic money supply. And, since the demand for money is a demand for a stock and not a flow, variation of the supply of money relative to the demand for it associated with deficit or surplus must work towards an equilibrium between money demand and money supply with a corresponding equilibration of the balance of payments. Deficits and surpluses represent phases of stock adjustment in the money market and not equilibrium flows, and should not be treated within an analytical framework that treats them as equilibrium phenomena.

It should be noted, however, that this criticism applies to the use of the standard model for the analysis and policy prescription of situations involving deficits or surpluses; where the standard model is used for the analysis of the policies required to secure balance-of-payments equilibrium, it is generally not subject to this criticism because by assumption the domestic money market will be in equilibrium. But even in this case the fiscal–monetary mix version of it is open to criticism for confusing stock adjustment in the market for securities, in response to a change in interest-rate differentials between national capital markets, with a flow equilibrium.

In order to obtain flow-equilibrium deficits or surpluses on the basis of stock adjustments in the money market (and also possibly the securities market) it is necessary to construct a model in which the need for stock adjustments is being continuously re-created by economic change – in other words, to analyse an economy, or an international economy, in which economic growth is going on. This is one of the important technical differences between the new 'monetary' models of the balance of payments and the standard Keynesian model – and a potent source of difficulty in comparing the results of the two types of analysis.

A further difference between the two types of models is that the 'monetary' models almost invariably assume – in contrast to the emphasis of the standard model on the influence of relative prices on trade flows – that a country's price level is pegged to the world price level and must move rigidly in line with it. One justification for this assumption is that, at least among the advanced industrial countries, industrial competition is so pervasive that elasticities of substitution among the industrial products of the various countries approximate more closely to infinity than to the relatively low numbers implicit in the standard model. Another and more sophisticated justification is derivable from the general framework of the monetarist approach, namely that changes in relative national price levels can only be transitory concomitants of the process of stock adjustment to monetary disequilibrium and that in the longer-run analysis of balance-of-payments phenomena among growing economies attention should be focused on long-run equilibrium price relationships – which for simplicity can most easily be taken as constant.

This point has sometimes been put in terms of the positive charge that the standard model rests on 'money illusion', in the sense that it assumes that workers will accept a reduction in their real standard of living brought about by a devaluation which they would not accept in the form of a forced reduction of domestic money wages. An alternative version of this charge is that the standard model assumes that workers can be cheated out of their real marginal product by devaluation. The charge, however, is incorrect: if rectification of a balance-of-payments deficit requires that the domestic marginal product of labour in terms of foreign goods falls, because the price of domestic goods relative to foreign goods must be reduced in the foreign and home markets to induce substitution between these goods favourable to the balance of payments, it requires no money illusion but only economic realism for the workers to accept this fact. Applications of the standard model to the case of devaluation, however, do require the assumption of money illusion if the elasticities of substitution between domestic and foreign goods are in fact high (approximately infinite), and it is nevertheless assumed that wages will remain unchanged in terms of domestic currency. For in this case it is being expected that workers will be content to accept wages below the international value of their marginal product, and that employers will not be driven by competition for labour in the face of this disequilibrium to bid wages up to their marginal productivity levels. The issue therefore is not one of the standard model wrongly assuming the presence of money illusion on the part of the workers, but of its possibly wrongly assuming low elasticities of substitution between domestic and foreign goods – which is an error in empirical assumptions rather than in model construction.

One further difference between the two types of model of balance-of-payments theory is worth noting. Whereas the Keynesian model assumes that employment and output are variable at (relatively) constant prices and wages, the monetary models assume that output and employment tend to full-employment levels, with reactions to changes taking the form of price and wage adjustments. This difference mirrors a broader difference between the Keynesian and quantity theory approaches to monetary theory for the closed economy. The assumption of full employment in the monetary balance-of-payments models can be defended on the grounds that these models are concerned with the longer run, and that for this perspective the assumption of full employment is more appropriate than the assumption of general mass unemployment for the actual world economy since the end of the Second World War.

I now turn from the discussion of theoretical issues in model construction to an exposition of some monetarist models of balance-of-payments behaviour in a growing world economy. The models to be constructed are extremely simple, inasmuch as they concentrate on the overall balance of the balance of payments, i.e. on the trend of international reserve acquisition or loss, and ignore the composition of the balance of payments as between current account, capital account and overall balance, as well as the question of changes in the structure of the balance-of-payments accounts that may occur as a country passes through various stages of economic growth. Nevertheless they will, I hope, provide some interesting insights into balance-of-payments phenomena.

To begin with, it is useful to develop some general expressions relating the growth rates of economic aggregates to the growth rates of their components or of the independent variables to which they are functionally related. These can be established by elementary calculus, and are merely stated here. In the formulas, g is the growth rate per unit of time of a subscripted aggregate or variable, A and B are components of an aggregate, $f(A, B)$ is a function of A and B, and η denotes the elasticity of the aggregate defined by the function with respect to the subscripted variable. Then we have

$$g_{A+B} = \frac{A}{A+B} g_A + \frac{B}{A+B} g_B$$

$$g_{A-B} = \frac{A}{A-B} g_A - \frac{B}{A-B} g_B$$

$$g_{AB} = g_A + g_B$$

$$g_{A/B} = g_A - g_B$$

$$g_{f(A, B)} = \eta_A g_A + \eta_B g_B$$

(where η denotes an elasticity).

I begin with a discussion of monetary equilibrium in a single country, maintaining a fixed exchange rate with the rest of the world, assumed to be growing over time, and small enough and diversified enough in relation to the world economy for its price level to be the world price level, and its interest rate the world interest rate. (Differentials between domestic and foreign prices indices, or between domestic and foreign interest rates, could readily be allowed for, provided they are assumed fixed by economic conditions.) In addition, it is assumed that the supply of money is instantaneously adjusted to the demand for it, because the residents of the country can get rid of or acquire money either through the international market for commodities or through the international securities market. Which mechanism of adjustment of money supply to money demand prevails will determine the way in which monetary policy affects the composition of the balance of payments, but that is a question not pursued in the present analysis.

The consequence of these assumptions is that domestic monetary policy does not determine the domestic money supply but instead determines only the division of the backing of the money supply the public demands, between international reserves and domestic credit. Monetary policy in other words, controls the volume of domestic credit and not the money supply; and control over domestic credit controls the balance of payments and thus the behaviour of the country's international reserves.

The demand for money may be simply specified as

$$M_d = p(fy, i)$$

where M_d is the nominal quantity of domestic money demanded; y is real output; i is the interest rate or alternative opportunity cost of holding money; p is the foreign and therefore domestic price level; and multiplication of the demand for real balances, $f(y, i)$, by p assumes the standard homogeneity postulate of monetary theory. The supply of money is

$$M_s = R + D$$

where R is the international reserve and D the domestic credit or domestic assets backing of the money supply. Since by assumption M_s must be equal to M_d,

$$R = M_d - D$$

and

$$g_R = \frac{1}{R} B(t) = \frac{M_d}{R} g_{M_d} - \frac{D}{R} g_D$$

where $B(t) = dR/dt$ is the current overall balance of payments. Letting $r = R/M_s = R/M_d$, the initial international reserve ratio, and substituting for $g M_d$,

$$g_R = \frac{1}{r}(g_p + \eta_y g_y + \eta_i g_i) - \frac{1-r}{r} g_D.$$

Simplifying by assuming constant world prices and interest rates,

$$g_R = \frac{1}{r} \eta_y g_y - \frac{1-r}{r} g_D$$

i.e. reserve growth and the balance of payments are positively related to domestic economic growth and the income elasticity of demand for money, and negatively related to the rate of domestic credit expansion. Simplifying still further by assuming no domestic growth ($g_y = 0$),

$$g_R = \frac{1-r}{r} g_D$$

i.e. reserve growth and the balance of payments are inversely related to the rate of domestic credit expansion.

These results are to be contrasted with various Keynesian theories about the relation between economic growth and the balance of payments. According to one such theory derived from the multiplier analysis, economic growth must worsen the balance of payments through increasing imports relative to exports; this theory neglects the influence of demand for money on export supply and import demand and on the international flow of securities. According to another and more sophisticated theory, domestic credit expansion will tend to improve the balance of payments by stimulating investment and productivity increase and so lowering domestic prices in relation to foreign prices and improving the current account through the resulting substitutions of domestic for foreign goods in the foreign and domestic markets. This theory begs a number of questions even in naive Keynesian terms; in terms of the present approach it commits the error of attempting to deduce the consequences of domestic credit expansion from its presumed relative price effects without reference to the monetary aspect of balance-of-payments surpluses and deficits.

Henceforth the analysis will be simplified by assuming that world interest rates are constant, so that the growth of demand for real balances depends only on the growth of real output (the growth of demand for nominal money balances depends of course also on the rate of change of the price level). This assumption can be justified on the grounds that real rates of return on investment are relatively stable, and that money rates of interest in a longer-run growth context will be equal to real rates of return plus the (actual and expected) rate of world price inflation or minus the (actual and expected) rate of world price deflation.

The foregoing model was concerned with one small country in a large world economy. The next model considers monetary equilibrium in the world system as a whole. For initial simplicity it is assumed that there is a single world money, i.e. there is no national credit money supplementing international reserves. This assumption does considerable violence to reality, but it can be rationalized on the assumption that each national economy's domestic banking system can be compressed into a functional relation between its real output and its demand for real international reserves. The essential difference between this model and the preceding one is that the world price level becomes endogenous instead of exogenous, determined by the relation between the growth rates of demand for and supply of international reserves.

For the world economy, the growth rate of demand for international money, assuming the homogeneity postulate as before, is

$$g_{M_d} = \sum_i w_i \eta_{y_i} g_{y_i} + g_p$$

where the w_i are initial country shares in the world money supply. Equilibrium requires $g_{M_d} = g_{M_s}$, where g_{M_s} is the growth rate of the world money supply. This requirement determines the rate of change of world prices,

$$g_p = g_{M_s} - \sum_i w_i \eta_{y_i} g_{y_i}.$$

The growth rate of an individual country's holdings of international money (which is also its balance-of-payments surplus, or deficit if negative, as a proportion of its initial reserves) is

$$\begin{aligned}
g_{M_j} &= \eta_{y_j} g_{y_j} + g_p \\
&= \eta_{y_j} g_{y_j} + g_{M_s} - \sum_i w_i \eta_{y_i} g_{y_i} \\
&= g_{M_s} + (1 - w_j)\left(\eta_{y_j} g_{y_j} - \sum_{i \neq j} \frac{w_i}{1 - w_j} \eta_{y_i} g_{y_i}\right) \\
&= g_{M_s} + (1 - w_j)(\eta_{y_j} g_{y_j} - \overline{\eta_{y_i} g_{y_i}})
\end{aligned}$$

where the bar denotes the average product of income elasticity of demand for real balances and rate of growth of real income in the rest of the world, or

$$g_{M_j} = g_{M_s} + \eta_{y_j} g_{y_j} - \overline{\eta_y g_y}$$

when the bar denotes the average product of the two terms for the whole world economy.

A country will acquire world money (through a balance-of-payments surplus) faster or slower than the rate of world monetary expansion according as the product of its income elasticity of demand for real balances and its growth rate of output exceeds or falls short of either this average product for the rest of the world or this average product for the whole world including itself. In the latter event it may lose international reserves even though total world reserves are growing.

If for further simplification it is assumed that the growth rate of world reserves is zero, the condition just stated determines whether the country has a surplus or a deficit. If for further simplification the income elasticity of demand for real balances is assumed to be everywhere unity, the expression reduces to

$$g_{M_j} = (1 - w_j)(g_{y_j} - \overline{g_{y_i}}) = g_{y_j} - \overline{g_y}$$

the bars successively denoting the average growth rate in the rest of the world and the average growth rate of the world as a whole, and the country gains or loses reserves according as its real growth rate is greater or less than the world average.

The preceding model aggregated national monetary systems into a demand for international money derived from real output. I now turn to a model in which the world economy possesses an international reserve money, but in which the residents of the various countries demand national monies which are based partly on international money reserves and partly on domestic credit. In the model, the total money supply for the world economy is

$$M = R + \sum_i D_i$$
$$= \sum_i w_i r_i M + \sum_i w_i (1 - r_i) M$$

where R is total international reserve money; D_i is domestic credit in country i; w_i is country i's share in the total world stock of money; and r_i is country i's ratio of international reserve money to its domestic money supply.

As before, the rate of growth of world demand for money is

$$g_{M_d} = \sum_i w_i \eta_{y_i} g_{y_i} + g_p.$$

The rate of growth of the world money supply is

$$g_{M_s} = \sum_i w_i \eta_i g_R + \sum_i w_i (1 - r_i) g_{D_i}$$

These two equations determine the rate of change of world prices, through the requirement that $g_{M_d} = g_{M_s}$:

$$g_p = \sum_i w_i r_i g_R + \sum_i w_i (1 - r_i) g_{D_i} - \sum_i w_i \eta_{y_i} g_{y_i}.$$

From previous results, the growth rate of an individual country's reserves is

$$g_{r_j} = \frac{1}{r_j}(g_p + \eta_{y_j} g_{y_j}) - \frac{1 - r_j}{r_j} g_{D_j}$$

$$= \frac{1}{r_j} \sum_i w_i r_i g_R + \frac{1}{r_j} \sum_i w_i (1 - r_i) g_{D_i} + \frac{1}{r_j} \eta_{y_j} g_{y_j}$$

$$\qquad - \frac{1}{r_j} \sum_i w_i \eta_{y_i} g_{y_i} - \frac{1 - r_j}{r_j} g_{D_j}$$

$$= \frac{1}{r_j} \left\{ \sum_i w_i r_i g_R + (\eta_{y_j} g_{y_j} - \overline{\eta_y g_y}) - [(1 - r_j) g_{D_j} - \overline{(1 - r) g_D}] \right\}$$

where the bars again indicate the average product of the barred terms for the world economy.

This expression indicates that a country's reserves will grow faster the lower its initial reserve ratio, the faster the growth of total world reserves, the higher its income elasticity of demand for money and its real growth rate relative to other countries, and the lower its international reserve ratio and rate of domestic credit expansion relative to other countries.

Simplifying by assuming that income elasticities of demand for money are everywhere unity, and that international reserve ratios are also the same everywhere, we obtain

$$g_{R_j} = g_R + \frac{1}{r}(g_{y_j} - g_y) - \frac{1 - r}{r}(g_{D_j} - g_D)$$

which shows that the growth rate of a country's reserves will on these assumptions tend to be faster than the world average if its real growth rate is greater than the world average, and slower than the world average if its rate of credit expansion is greater than the world average, and vice versa.

An alternative approach in this model is to formulate the money supply for the world in terms of the ratio of international reserves to total money stock r, initial shares in international reserves s_i, and initial ratios of domestic credit to reserves d_i. (Note that $r = 1/(1+d)$, where d is the ratio of credit to reserves.) Then

$$M = \sum_i s_i R + \sum_i d_i s_i R$$

$$g_{M_d} = \sum_i s_i (1+d_i) \eta_{y_i} g_{y_i} + g_p$$

$$g_{M_s} = r(g_R + \sum_i d_i s_i g_{D_i})$$

$$g_p = r(g_R + \sum_i d_i s_i g_{D_i}) - \sum_i s_i (1+d_i) \eta_{y_i} g_y$$

$$g_{R_j} = (1+d_j)(g_p + \eta_{y_j} g_{y_j}) - d_j g_{D_j}$$
$$= (1+d_j)rg_R + [(1+d_j)\eta_{y_j} g_{y_j} - \sum_i s_i (1+d_i)\eta_{y_i} g_{y_i}]$$
$$- [d_j g_{D_j} - (1+d_j)r\sum_i d_i s_i g_{D_i}]$$
$$= (1+d_j)rg_R + [(1+d_j)\eta_{y_j} g_{y_j} - \sum_i s_i (1+d_i)\eta_{y_i} g_{y_i}]$$
$$- \left[d_j g_{D_j} - \frac{1+d_j}{1+d} \sum d_i s_i g_{D_i} \right].$$

This alternative formulation, which will not be explored further here, naturally produces the same qualitative results as the one presented above.

The next stage in making the 'monetary' model of balance-of-payments behaviour more realistic is to introduce a reserve-currency country whose currency is held as a substitute for the basic international money. The interesting problem in this case is the behaviour of the reserves of the reserve-currency country. The total world money supply is as before the sum of reserves and domestic credit created by the individual countries; but the reserve-currency role enables the reserve-currency country to induce other countries to hold its domestic money, backed by its own domestic credit, instead of or in addition to providing their own money by domestic credit creation.

As before we have

$$g_{M_s} = \sum_i w_i r_i g_R + \sum_i w_i (1-r_i) g_{D_i}$$

$$g_p = \sum_i w_i r_i g_R + \sum_i w_i (1-r_i) g_{D_i} - \sum_i w_i \eta_{y_i} g_{y_i}.$$

But now the behaviour of the reserve currency country's reserves is determined by the relation between the growth of both foreign and domestic demand for its money, and its domestic credit expansion. Assuming homogeneity in money demand still,

$$g_{R_j} = \frac{1}{r_j}[g_p + h\eta_{y_j}g_{y_j} + (1-h)g_f] - \frac{1-r_j}{r_j}g_{D_j}$$

where h is the proportion of the reserve currency country's currency held by residents and g_f is the rate of growth of foreign demand for its money as a reserve currency, in real terms.

$$g_{R_j} = \frac{1}{r_j}[(1-h)g_f + \sum_i w_i r_i g_R + (h\eta_{y_j}g_{y_j} - \overline{\eta_y g_y})] - [(1-r_j)g_{D_j} - \overline{(1-r)g_D}].$$

If the real foreign demand for the reserve country's currency is assumed to be a constant proportion of the foreign money supply, the expression simplifies to

$$g_{R_j} = \frac{1}{r_j}[\sum_i w_i r_i g_R + h(\eta_{y_j}g_{y_j} - \overline{\eta_y g_y})] - [(1-r_j)g_{D_j} - \overline{(1-r)g_D}].$$

Assuming unitary income elasticities of demand for real balances everywhere and the same initial ratios of international reserves to domestic money, it simplifies further to

$$g_{R_j} = g_R + \frac{h}{r}(g_{y_j} - \overline{g_y}) - \frac{1-r}{r}(g_{D_j} - \overline{g_D}).$$

That is, the reserve currency country will gain reserves faster than the rate of growth of total reserves if its real growth rate exceeds the world average or its rate of domestic credit expansion is below the world average, and vice versa.

An alternative formulation of the problem, using the same two assumptions for simplicity, is to ask what rate of growth of foreign holdings of the reserve currency is necessary to enable the reserve currency country's reserves to grow at the world rate. The answer is

$$g_f = \frac{1}{1-h}[(1-r)(g_{D_j} - \overline{g_D}) - (hg_{y_j} - \overline{g_y})].$$

That is, foreign demand for the reserve currency must grow faster, the faster the reserve currency country's rate of domestic credit expansion relative to the rate of credit expansion abroad and the slower its real rate of growth relative to the real world growth rate.

Finally, I apply the general class of monetary models of the balance of payments developed above to the problem of the effects of a devaluation of a currency. The application is not entirely theoretically satisfactory, since the mathematics employed relate to continuous change whereas a devaluation is a once-over affair. Still, the results are suggestive.

For this problem, retain the assumption that domestic prices must keep in line with foreign prices, but introduce an exchange rate that can be changed, representing devaluation by an instantaneous rate of change of the exchange rate. The demand for money now becomes

$$M_d = \rho \, p_f f(y, i)$$

where p_f is the foreign price level and ρ is the price of foreign currency in terms of domestic. The rate of growth of reserves then becomes

$$g_R = \frac{1}{r}(g_\rho + g_{p_f} + \eta_y g_y + \eta_i g_i) - \frac{1-r}{r} g_D.$$

(Note that this formula reintroduces the interest rate as a determinant of the demand for money; for analysis, g_i may be interpreted as an expected rate of change of the money interest rate.)

There are several points to notice about the formula, with specific reference to the British devaluation of the pound in 1967 and the initial failure of that devaluation to improve the balance of payments.

First, aside from the scale factor $(1-r)$, devaluation is equivalent to domestic credit contraction; its function is to deflate domestic real balances and thereby to cause domestic residents to attempt to restore their real balances through the international commodity and security markets.

Second, since devaluation is a one-shot affair, it can be only a transitory factor for improvement in the balance of payments. Lasting improvement can only be achieved via a decrease in the rate of domestic credit expansion.

Third, the beneficial transitory effects of devaluation on reserves and the balance of payments can be offset or neutralized by any one or more of the following developments: (i) an increase in the rate of domestic credit expansion, which the authorities may allow either unwittingly or as a consequence of efforts to hold down interest rates on government debt; (ii) a fall in the growth rate (though this requires modifying the model to allow unemployment, which may be induced by deflationary official policies or by lags in the adjustment of production to demand); (iii) a rise in interest rates inducing a fall in the demand for real balances relative to income: here interest rates have to be interpreted to include the expected money rate of return on holdings of goods, which may be expected to rise temporarily as a consequence of devaluation and the inflationary expectations generated by it.

It may be noted in passing that the equation for devaluation can be converted into an equation for the motion of a freely floating exchange rate as a function of policy variables, as follows:

$$g_\rho = rg_R + (1-r)g_D - g_{p_f} - \eta_y g_y - \eta_i g_i.$$

The monetary models of the balance of payments surveyed in this chapter are long-run models, inasmuch as they assume full employment of resources and the necessity for domestic price levels to keep in line with the world price level. The Keynesian model with which they have been contrasted applies to a shorter run in which these assumptions do not necessarily, or commonly, hold. The Keynesian model has become the basis for policy-thinking and policy formulation. The monetary models suggest that it may be very misleading to rely on the Keynesian model as a guide to policy-making over a succession of short periods within each of which the Keynesian model may appear to be a reasonable approximation to reality.

ADDENDUM

The formulas presented in the text can be applied to a number of other problems than those mentioned, simply by rearranging terms. Thus, if a small country in an open international economy wishes to maintain a certain balance-of-payments surplus (growth rate of reserves), it must control the growth rate of domestic credit according to the formula

$$g_D = \frac{1}{1-r}(g_p + \eta_y g_y + \eta_i g_i - r g_R^*)$$

where g_R^* is the desired growth rate of reserves.

Similarly, in a world economy without a reserve-currency country, if there is an international monetary authority that has control over the growth of world reserves, and it seeks to maintain world price stability, the formula it must follow (assuring stability of interest rates) is

$$g_{MS}^* = \sum_i w_i \eta_{y_i} g_{y_i}.$$

Note that this formula will not imply a constant growth rate of world reserves over time, if income elasticities of demand for money, or growth rates of real output, vary among countries.

The formula is still more complex if the fractional-reserve character of domestic money supplies is allowed for, being

$$g_R^* = \frac{\sum_i w_i \eta_{y_i} g_{y_i} - \sum_i w_i (1 - r_i) g_{D_i}}{\sum_i w_i y_i}.$$

Note that the presence of a reserve-currency country does not affect this formula; however, it affects the empirical value of it indirectly through the effects of reserve-currency status on the willingness of the reserve-currency country to expand domestic credit, and the possible desires of other countries to expand domestic credit in order to avoid accumulating excess stocks of the reserve currency.

Finally for a country on a floating exchange rate, the movement of the exchange rate over time is related to domestic credit expansion and exchange-market intervention intended to (or having the effect of) altering the country's international reserves by the formula

$$g_\rho = r g_R^* + (1 - r) g_D^* - g_{p_f} - \eta_y g_y - \eta_i g_i.$$

(The last term should probably be dropped, as a transitional factor.)
Note. Arturo Brillembourg has pointed out to me an implicit assumption in the analysis of the effects of devaluation presented above,

namely that the capital gains on the domestic value of international reserves are sterilized and have no effect on the money supply. For the longer run it would be more reasonable to assume that these gains are lent or transferred to the government and spent. In that case, $M_S = R + D$, $r = \dfrac{\rho R}{\rho R + D}$, and $g_R = \dfrac{1-r}{r}(g_p - g_D) + \dfrac{1}{r}(\eta_y g_y + \eta_j g_j + g_p)$. This formulation brings out more clearly than mine the symmetry between devaluation and domestic credit contraction, since there is no 'scale factor' as in my analysis. In this case

$$g_\rho = \frac{1}{1-r}(\eta_y g_y + \eta_j g_j + g_p) - \frac{r}{1-r}g_R - g_D,$$

in which equation the movement of the exchange rate can be thought of as determined by the authorities' desired rate of growth of reserves g_R. In a truly floating rate case, r goes to zero and $g_\rho = \eta_y g_y + \eta_j g_j + g_p - g_D$.

Chapter 10

Five Notes[1]

1. The Welfare Costs of Exchange Rate Stabilization *

This note is concerned with the welfare costs to a country, to the rest of the world, and to the world as a whole, of the stabilization of the country's exchange rate in the face of fluctuations in its domestic price level relative to the foreign price level. Such stabilization is effected by the accumulation and decumulation of exchange reserves. In real terms, a surplus in the trade balance used to finance the accumulation of reserves involves a transfer to the rest of the world; and, conversely, the use of reserves to finance the trade deficit involves receipt of a transfer from the rest of the world. If countries are assumed to maintain full employment, it must also be assumed that they follow the domestic policies required to effect such transfers. Specifically it must be assumed that the surplus country arranges to reduce domestic expenditure below the full-employment income level sufficiently to create the excess of income over expenditure

* Reprinted from the *Journal of Political Economy*, Vol. LXXIV, No. 5 (October 1966), pp. 512–18. Copyright 1966 by The University of Chicago, all rights reserved.

[1] The problem considered in this article was first posed and analysed by John Hause ('The Welfare Costs of Disequilibrium Exchange Rates', *Journal of Political Economy*, Vol. LXXIV (August 1966), pp. 333–52). Hause employs a partial-equilibrium approach, which suppresses the 'absorption' or 'transfer' aspects of international disequilibrium; the analysis presented here was worked out to remedy this deficiency.

Hause has since (in private correspondence) criticized the analysis presented here, arguing in effect for the standard differential calculus approximation

$$p = \pi = \frac{(1-m_1-m_2)t}{n_1+\eta_2-1}.$$

The purpose of the more cumbersome algebra presented below, however, is precisely to escape the limitations of differential calculus to infinitesimally small variations around an equilibrium point, since there is no means of knowing how closely the calculus approximates to changes of economically finite magnitude.

required to finance the transfer, and the deficit country arranges to increase domestic expenditures above the full-employment income level sufficiently to create the excess of expenditure over income required to dispose of the transfer.

Analytically, the problem of the welfare costs of exchange rate stabilization in the face of variations in the domestic relative to the foreign price level is equivalent to the problem of the welfare costs of deliberate destabilization of the exchange rate for the purpose of acquiring and disposing of foreign-exchange reserves when the relationship of domestic to foreign prices would otherwise be constant at the equilibrium (balanced-trade) level. This is the way the problem is formulated here.

For simplicity it is assumed that the world consists of only two countries, each of which produces a single good, the price of which is constant in terms of domestic currency. Full employment is assumed to be maintained in each by the levying of taxes or the distribution of subsidies so calculated that, whatever the exchange rate, the demand for domestic output from domestic and foreign sources just exhausts the full-employment supply; government surpluses are assumed to be invested in the currency of the other country, and deficits to be financed by the sale of foreign exchange. (It may equally well be assumed that the governments buy and sell currency through sales and purchases of gold.) The exchange rate is assumed to be fixed by the government of the country under analysis ('country 1', the rest of the world being 'country 2'). The analysis consists in contrasting two policies, assumed to prevail over a two-period sequence. The first ('policy 1') is maintenance of the exchange rate at the same equilibrium (balanced-trade) level in both periods, this level being assumed for mathematical simplicity to entail a unit price of foreign currency in terms of domestic. The second ('policy 2') is the raising of the price of foreign exchange in the first period sufficiently to achieve an accumulation of reserves of foreign exchange T (symbolizing the transfer abroad of resources worth T in terms of the foreign product) and the lowering of the rate in the second period sufficiently to decumulate the reserves accumulated in the first period.

In the analysis, p and Π, respectively, denote the proportional change of the exchange rate under policy 2 from the level that would rule under policy 1 in the first and second period, Y_1 and Y_2, the full-employment outputs and earned incomes of the two countries, and $Y_2 \pm T$ and $Y_1 - (1+p)T$ and $Y_1 + (1-\Pi)T$, the disposable incomes of the two countries in the two periods, after the governments have arranged by appropriate taxes or subsidies for the financing and disposition of the transfer implicit in the accumulation and decumulation of reserves. Changes in disposable incomes affect import demands through marginal propensities to import m_1 and m_2, while changes in the exchange rate affect import demands through price elasticities of demand for imports η_1 and η_2. In the welfare-cost analysis, it is assumed that the countries have zero social rates of time preference, so that second-period gains or losses do not need to be discounted for comparison with first-period losses or gains. It is also assumed (implicitly) that the marginal utility of income is constant.

The balance-of-payments equation for country 1, in terms of its own currency, in the first period is

$$M_2(Y_2 + T, 1+p) - (1+p)pM_1[Y_1 - (1+p)T, 1+p] = (1+p)T$$

expressing the condition that the trade surplus of country 1 must suffice to make the transfer required to accumulate foreign-exchange reserves in the amount T. The equation determining p, the increase in the price of foreign exchange associated with the transfer by comparison with the price that would rule under policy 1, is (remembering that under policy 1, $M_2 = M_1$)

$$m_2 T + (M + m_2 T)\eta_2 p + m_1(1+p)T + [M - m_1(1+p)T]\eta_1 p$$
$$- p[M - m_1(1+p)T] = T + pT.$$

(It should be noted that the relative price changes associated with the exchange-rate change are assumed to operate on the quantities of trade that would occur *after* fiscal policies in the two countries had adjusted the relationships between output and expenditure to what is required to finance and dispose of the implicit real transfer.) Rearranging terms, this equation becomes

$$[(M + m_2)T\eta_2 + (M - m_1 T)\eta_1 - (1 - m_1(T - (M - m_1 T)$$
$$- (\eta_1 - 1)m_1 pT]p = (1 - m_1 - m_2)T.$$

Neglecting the term in p^2, and writing $t = T/M$ for the ratio of the transfer to the level of exports and imports under policy 1, this yields

$$p = \frac{(1 - m_1 - m_2)t}{(\eta_1 + \eta_2 - 1) - (m_1\eta_1 - m_2\eta_2 + 1 - 2m_1)t}.$$

The numerator of this expression is the well-known criterion for whether a transfer turns the terms of trade against or in favour of the country making the transfer, on the assumption of exchange-market stability. The first expression in the denominator is the familiar criterion for exchange stability in this kind of model; the whole expression in the denominator, however, is the criterion for stability in the present case, which assumes non-infinitesimal transfers. Following convention, it is assumed in the following analysis that the exchange market is always stable and that a transfer will turn a country's terms of trade against it.

For convenience in subsequent mathematical manipulations, it is convenient to define the following compound parameters: $x = (1 - m_1 - m_2)$, the well-known transfer parameter; $y = (\eta_1 + \eta_2 - 1)$, the exchange-stability parameter; and $z = (m_1\eta_1 - m_2\eta_2 + 1 - 2m_1)$, which may be termed the 'public-finance' parameter. These definitions permit the equation determining p to be rewritten as

$$p = \frac{xt}{y - zt}.$$

For the second period, the balance of payments of country 1 in terms of its own currency is

$$M_2(Y_2 - T, 1 - \Pi) - (1 - \Pi)M_1(Y_1 + \Pi T, 1 - \Pi) = -(1 - \Pi)T.$$

From this equation is derived the equation determining Π,

$$\Pi = \frac{xt}{y + zt}.$$

It is evident that Π may be greater or less than p in absolute value, depending on whether z is negative or positive.

The exchange-stability parameter is assumed of necessity to be positive; exchange-market stability also requires that $y - tz$ and $y + tz$ be positive, i.e. that $y > |tz|$. Clearly, nothing can be assumed *a priori* about the sign of z. Nor in principle can anything be assumed about the sign of x, though by tradition x is normally assumed to be positive.

By comparison with policy 1, policy 2 entails for country 1 a welfare loss in period 1 and a welfare gain in period 2. The welfare loss in period 1 has two components: the foregoing of consumption required to finance the transfer, and the loss of welfare due to the higher cost of imports resulting from the adverse movement of the exchange rate and terms of trade resulting from the transfer. The former loss, as a proportion of the policy 1 level of imports, is $(1 + p)t$; the latter, which is approximately measured by the increase in the price of imports multiplied by the average of the volumes of imports before and after the price increase, is on the same basis

$$p[1-(1+p)m_1 t](1-\tfrac{1}{2}\eta_1 p).$$

Similarly, the welfare gain in period 2 has two components: the expansion of consumption made possible by the transfer, and the welfare gain resulting from the reduction in the relative price of imports associated with the transfer. The total welfare gain is

$$(1-\Pi)t+\Pi[1+(1-\Pi)m_1 t](1+\tfrac{1}{2}\eta_1\Pi).$$

It follows by subtraction that the net welfare cost to country 1 (which might be negative, indicating a welfare gain) is

$$C_1 = (1-m_1)t(p+\Pi)+p-\Pi-\tfrac{1}{2}\eta_1(p^2+\Pi^2)$$
$$-m_1 t(1-\tfrac{1}{2}\eta_1)(p^2-\Pi^2)+\tfrac{1}{2}\eta_1 m_1 t(p^3+\Pi^3).$$

The final term is assumed to be negligible in the following analysis.

For country 2, there are a welfare gain in period 1 and a welfare loss in period 2. These must be evaluated at country 2's relative prices, which are the reciprocals of country 1's relative prices, $1/(1+p)$ and $1/(1-\Pi)$. These may be approximated, for relatively small price changes, by $1-p$ and $1+\Pi$; however, since there is no guarantee that changes in the terms of trade between the two countries' products will be small enough to legitimize the approximation,[1] it is preferable to employ the closer approximations $1-p+p^2$ and $1+\Pi+\Pi^2$.

---

[1] The first two approximations were employed in the equations deriving p and Π; use of the second two closer approximations would make the coefficients of the

On these approximations, the welfare gain of country 2 in the first period, as a proportion of imports or exports under policy 1, is

$$t+(p-p^2)(1+m_2t)1[+\tfrac{1}{2}\eta_2(p-p^2)]$$

and its welfare loss in period 2 is

$$t+(\Pi+\Pi^2)(1-m_2t)[1-\tfrac{1}{2}\eta_2(\Pi+\Pi^2)];$$

its net gain from policy 2 (which may be negative), obtained by subtraction, and neglecting terms of third and higher orders, is

$$G_2 = p-\Pi+m_2t(p+\Pi)+(\tfrac{1}{2}\eta_2-1)[p^2+\Pi^2+m_2t(p^2-\Pi^2)].$$

This need not be positive, even if $p>\Pi$, owing to the presence of the term $(\tfrac{1}{2}\eta_2-1)$.

For both countries together, the welfare loss from policy 2 (which might be negative) is

$$\begin{aligned}
L = C_1-G_2 &= (1-m_1-m_2)t(p+\Pi)-\tfrac{1}{2}(\eta_1+\eta_2-2)(p^2+\Pi^2)\\
&\quad +\tfrac{1}{2}t(p^2-\Pi^2)(\eta_1m_1-\eta_2m_2-2m_1+2m_2)\\
&= xt(p+\Pi)-\tfrac{1}{2}(y-1)(p^2+\Pi^2)\\
&\quad +\tfrac{1}{2}t(p^2-\Pi^2)(z-1+2m_2).
\end{aligned}$$

From the equations $p = xt/(y-zt)$, $\Pi = xt/(y+zt)$, it follows that

$$p-\Pi = \frac{2t^2xz}{y^2-z^2t^2}$$

$$p+\Pi = \frac{2txy}{y^2-z^2t^2}$$

$$p^2-\Pi^2 = 4\frac{x^2t^2yzt}{(y^2-z^2t^2)^2}$$

and

$$p^2+\Pi^2 = 2\frac{x^2t^2(y^2+z^2t^2)}{(y^2-z^2t^2)^2}.$$

terms in p^2 and Π^2 equal to $\eta_1+\eta_2-1 = y$, rather than η_1-1, but these terms are in any case assumed negligible in the determination of p and Π.

These values yield the following cost and benefit expressions:

$$C_1 = \frac{t^2 x}{(y^2 - t^2 z^2)^2} \{ 2(y^2 - t^2 z^2)[z + (1 - m_1)y] - x\eta_1$$
$$(y^2 + t^2 z^2 - 2m_1 t^2 yz) - 4m_1 t^2 xyz \}$$

$$G_2 = \frac{t^2 x}{(y^2 - t^2 z^2)^2} \{ 2(y^2 - t^2 z^2)(z + m_2 y)$$
$$+ (\eta - 2)x(y^2 + t^2 z^2 + 2m_2 t^2 yz) \}$$

$$L = \frac{t^2 x^2}{(y^2 - t^2 z^2)^2} \{ (y^2 - t^2 z^2)y + y^2 + t^2 z^2 - 2yt^2 z + 4t^2 m_2 yz \}.$$

Disregarding terms in t^4 as negligible, these expressions can be approximated by

$$C_1' = \frac{t^2 x}{y^2 - 2t^2 z^2} [2z + 2(1 - m_1)y - x\eta_1]$$

$$G_2' = \frac{t^2 x}{y^2 - 2t^2 z^2} [2z + 2m_2 y + x(\eta_2 - 2)]$$

$$L' = \frac{t^2 x^2}{y^2 - 2t^2 z^2} (y + 1).$$

In terms of the original parameters, the expressions that determine the signs of the cost and benefit expressions are:

for C_1',

$$(1 + m_1 + m_2)\eta_1 + 2\eta_2(1 - m_1 - m_2) - 2m_1;$$

for G_2',

$$2(m_1 + m_2)\eta_1 + \eta_2(1 - m_1 - m_2) - 2m_1;$$

for L',

$$\eta_1 + \eta_2.$$

Thus policy 2 (the equivalent of exchange rate stabilization by the accumulation and decumulation of reserves) must involve a loss of welfare for the world as a whole as compared with policy 1 (the equivalent of a flexible exchange rate).[1] It does not, however, neces-

---

[1] This can be proved for L as well, provided t is assumed to be less than unity. The expression in square brackets can be rewritten in the following two equivalent forms:

$$y(y^2 - t^2 z^2) + (y - tz)^2 + 4t^2 m_2 zy + 2ytz(1 - t)$$

and

$$y(y^2 - t^2 z^2) + (y + tz)^2 - 2ytz[1 - tm_2 + t(1 - m_2)].$$

sarily entail a welfare cost for country 1 or a welfare gain for country 2: if the elasticities of international demand are low enough, consistently with exchange-market stability, country 1 may gain and country 2 may lose from exchange rate stabilization. A necessary condition for this result, on these approximations, is that the elasticity of country 1's demand for imports be less than unity.

In order to gain information on the possible quantitative magnitudes of the welfare effects of exchange stabilization, the values of C_1, G_2 and L (the general formulas, not the approximations) were computed for the following values of the parameters:

$m_2 = 0$;

$m_1 = 0.00, 0.10, 0.20, 0.25, 0.30, 0.40, 0.50$;

η_1 and $\varepsilon_1 (= \eta_1 - m_1$, the pure substitution elasticity of demand for imports in country 1$) = 0.25, 0.50, 0.75, 1.00, 1.25, 1.50, 1.75, 2.00, 2.50, 3.00$;

$t = 0.05, 0.10, 0.15, 0.20, 0.25$.

The single value $m_2 = 0$ was selected to represent the most typical case of a small country stabilizing its exchange rate in a large world economy, the range of values of m_1 to represent varying degrees of dependence of that country on international trade. The results revealed a large number of examples of losses to the rest of the world (G_2 negative) and a small number of examples of gains to the exchange stabilizing country (C_1 negative). In all these cases, the sum of the elasticities of international demand was low, not over 1.60 for negative G_2s and not over 1.25 for negative C_1s.

Table 10.1 shows the costs to country 1 and the gains to country 2 for a selection of combinations of the elasticities in the case in which $m_1 = m_2 = 0$. This case corresponds to analysis on Hause's lines, in which the effects of the financing of the transfers implicit in a surplus–deficit sequence on international demands are neglected. In this case, the world loss depends only on the sum total of the demand

---

For $t \leqslant 1$, the first expression must be positive if z is positive, and the second expression must be positive if z is negative; hence L must be positive regardless of the sign of z, for $t \leqslant 1$. Actually, the expression is necessarily positive for z positive and $m_2 \geqslant 0.5$, or z negative and $m_2 \leqslant 0.5$; for z positive and $m_2 \leqslant 0.5$, it is necessarily positive for $t < 1/(1-2m_2)$; and for z negative and $m_2 > 0.5$, it is necessarily positive for $t < 1/(2m_2-1)$.

Table 10.1

Individual Costs and Gains from Two-Period Transfer and Reversal, as Percentage of One-Period Trade in Absence of Transfers, Assuming $m_1 = m_2 = 0$

η_1	η_2	$C_{\frac12}$					G				
		$t=0.05$	$t=0.10$	$t=0.15$	$t=0.20$	$t=0.25$	$t=0.05$	$t=0.10$	$t=0.15$	$t=0.20$	$t=0.25$
0·50	0·75	8·16	34·47	80·86	39·51	*	2·69	5·22	−36·91	−656·80	*
0·75	0·50	7·03	27·89	50·98	−16·30	*	1·56	−1·36	−66·80	−859·30	*
0·50	1·00	2·52	10·24	23·75	43·99	72·22	0·99	3·82	7·93	11·79	11·11
0·75	0·75	2·26	9·12	20·79	37·41	58·33	0·73	2·69	4·97	5·22	2·78
1·00	0·50	2·00	7·99	17·82	30·84	44·44	0·47	1·56	2·01	1·36	−16·67
0·50	1·50	0·88	3·53	8·00	14·41	22·89	0·38	1·51	3·40	6·08	9·56
0·75	1·25	0·81	3·27	7·40	13·28	21·00	0·31	1·25	2·80	4·95	7·67
1·00	1·00	0·75	3·01	6·80	12·15	19·11	0·25	0·99	2·20	3·81	5·78
1·25	0·75	0·69	2·75	6·20	11·02	17·22	0·19	0·73	1·59	2·69	3·89
1·50	0·50	0·62	2·50	5·60	9·90	15·33	0·12	0·47	0·99	1·56	2·00
0·50	2·50	0·34	1·38	3·11	5·55	8·71	0·16	0·63	1·42	2·54	3·99
1·00	2·00	0·31	1·25	2·82	5·03	7·89	0·13	0·50	1·13	2·02	3·18
1·50	1·50	0·28	1·13	2·54	4·52	7·07	0·09	0·38	0·85	1·51	2·36
2·00	1·00	0·25	1·00	2·25	4·00	6·25	0·06	0·25	0·56	0·99	1·54
1·00	3·00	0·22	0·87	1·96	3·48	5·43	0·03	0·12	0·27	0·47	0·72
3·00	1·00	0·19	0·78	1·75	3·12	4·89	0·08	0·33	0·75	1·34	2·11
2·00	2·00	0·17	0·67	1·50	2·67	4·18	0·06	0·22	0·50	0·89	1·40
3·00	1·00	0·14	0·56	1·25	2·22	3·47	0·03	0·11	0·25	0·44	0·69
2·00	3·00	0·13	0·50	1·13	2·00	3·13	0·05	0·19	0·42	0·75	1·18
2·50	2·50	0·12	0·47	1·06	1·88	2·93	0·04	0·16	0·35	0·63	0·98
3·00	2·00	0·11	0·44	0·98	1·75	2·74	0·04	0·15	0·28	0·50	0·78
2·50	3·00	0·10	0·42	0·94	1·68	2·63	0·03	0·13	0·33	0·59	0·93
3·00	2·50	0·10	0·40	0·89	1·58	2·47	0·03	0·12	0·28	0·50	0·78
3·00	3·00	0·09	0·36	0·81	1·44	2·25	0·03	0·12	0·27	0·48	0·75

* These cases failed to fulfil the stability conditions.

258

elasticities and not on their individual values; the world loss for all elasticity combinations computed is presented in Table 10.2. Table 10.3 presents selected results chosen to illustrate both the effects of rising values of the elasticities and the effects of varying the relative weights of the marginal propensity to import and the substitution elasticity in a given elasticity of country 1's demand for imports. In reading the tables, it should be noticed that the national losses and gains and the world losses are measured as a percentage of the equilibrium trade of one period. The corresponding magnitude *per*

Table 10.2

World loss from two-period transfer and reversal, as percentage of one-period trade in absence of transfers, assuming $m_1 = m_2 = 0$

$\eta_1 + \eta_2$	$t = 0.05$	$t = 0.10$	$t = 0.15$	$t = 0.20$	$t = 0.025$
1·25	5·47	29·25	117·80	696·30	*
1·50	1·53	6·42	15·81	32·20	61·11
1·75	0·78	3·18	7·38	13·69	22·66
2·00	0·50	2·02	4·60	8·33	13·33
2·25	0·36	1·45	3·28	5·87	9·29
2·50	0·28	1·11	2·52	4·49	7·06
2·75	0·22	0·90	2·03	3·61	5·66
3·00	0·19	0·75	1·69	3·01	4·71
3·50	0·14	0·56	1·26	2·24	3·51
4·00	0·11	0·44	1·00	1·78	2·78
4·50	0·09	0·37	0·83	1·47	2·30
5·00	0·08	0·31	0·70	1·25	1·95
5·50	0·07	0·27	0·61	1·09	1·70
6·00	0·06	0·24	0·54	0·96	1·50

* This case failed to fulfil the stability conditions.

period would be half that shown. The results indicate that the losses from exchange stabilization may indeed be substantial if the elasticities of international demand are low or deficits and surpluses are a significant proportion of international trade.

In conclusion, attention should be called to the importance of the assumption that the sum of the marginal propensities to import is less than unity (the transfer parameter is positive). If this assumption happened not to be fulfilled in actuality, the results would be appreciably different from the normal cases emerging from the present

Table 10.3

Individual and total costs and gains from two-period transfer and reversal, as percentage of one-period trade in the absence of transfers, for $m_2 = 0$ and varying values of the substitution elasticity (ε_1) and marginal propensity (m_1) components of η_1

η_2	ε_1	m_1	$t = 0.05$			$t = 0.15$			$t = 0.25$		
			C_1	G_2	L	C_1	G_2	L	C_1	G_2	L
0.25	1.25	0.00	1.74	0.22	1.53	14.86	0.95	15.81	30.56	−30.56	61.11
	1.00	0.25	1.08	0.22	0.85	9.39	1.05	8.34	23.19	4.63	27.12
	0.75	0.50	0.56	0.18	0.38	4.98	1.45	3.53	13.26	2.57	10.69
0.75	0.75	0.00	2.26	0.73	1.53	20.79	4.97	15.81	58.33	−2.78	61.11
	0.50	0.25	1.17	0.32	0.85	10.56	2.50	8.06	29.05	3.96	25.09
	0.25	0.50	0.44	0.06	0.38	3.90	0.50	3.40	10.59	1.03	9.56
1.00	0.50	0.00	2.52	0.99	1.53	23.75	7.93	15.81	72.22	11.11	61.11
	0.25	0.25	1.22	0.37	0.85	11.06	3.12	7.95	31.07	7.02	24.05
	0.00	0.50	0.37	−0.00	0.37	3.34	−0.03	3.37	9.12	−0.20	9.32
0.25	1.75	0.00	0.56	0.06	0.50	4.99	0.39	4.60	13.44	0.11	13.33
	1.50	0.25	0.39	0.10	0.28	3.46	0.88	2.58	9.44	2.03	7.41
	1.25	0.50	0.23	0.11	0.13	2.11	0.97	1.14	5.84	2.58	3.26
0.75	1.25	0.00	0.69	0.19	0.50	6.20	1.59	4.60	17.22	3.89	13.33
	1.00	0.25	0.41	0.13	0.28	3.69	1.13	2.56	10.23	2.97	7.26
	0.75	0.50	0.20	0.08	0.13	1.83	0.70	1.13	5.06	1.90	3.16

1·25	0·75	0·00	0·81	0·31	0·50	7·40	2·80	4·60	21·00	7·67	13·33
	0·50	0·25	0·43	0·15	0·28	3·91	1·37	2·55	10·90	3·76	7·15
	0·25	0·50	0·17	0·05	0·13	1·54	0·42	4·12	4·27	1·16	3·11
1·50	0·50	0·00	0·88	0·38	0·50	8·00	3·40	4·60	22·89	9·56	13·33
	0·25	0·25	0·45	0·16	0·28	4·02	1·48	2·54	11·21	4·11	7·10
	0·00	0·50	0·16	0·03	0·13	1·40	0·28	1·12	3·88	0·78	3·10
0·50	2·00	0·00	0·33	0·06	0·28	2·99	0·47	2·52	8·25	1·18	7·06
	1·75	0·25	0·23	0·07	0·16	2·06	0·65	1·42	5·71	1·74	3·97
	1·50	0·50	0·14	0·07	0·07	1·25	0·62	0·63	3·49	1·72	1·77
1·00	1·50	0·00	0·39	0·11	0·28	3·51	0·99	2·52	9·76	2·69	7·06
	1·25	0·25	0·24	0·08	0·16	2·16	0·75	1·41	6·00	2·06	3·94
	1·00	0·50	0·13	0·06	0·07	1·13	0·50	0·63	3·13	1·39	1·74
1·50	1·00	0·00	0·44	0·17	0·28	4·02	1·51	2·52	11·27	4·20	7·06
	0·75	0·25	0·25	0·09	0·16	2·25	0·85	1·41	6·27	2·36	3·92
	0·50	0·50	0·11	0·04	0·07	1·00	0·38	0·62	2·77	1·04	1·73
2·00	0·50	0·00	0·50	0·22	0·28	4·54	2·02	2·52	12·78	5·71	7·06
	0·25	0·25	0·26	0·10	0·16	2·35	0·94	1·41	6·53	2·63	3·90
	0·00	0·50	0·10	0·03	0·07	0·87	0·25	0·62	2·42	0·70	1·73

261

analysis. In particular, it seems likely that country 1 would normally gain and country 2 normally lose as a result of exchange stabilization by country 1 in that case.

Chapter 10

2. Seigniorage and the Social Saving from Substituting Credit for Commodity Money*

The original meaning of seigniorage, the difference between the circulating value of a coin and the cost of the bullion and minting, involves a once-for-all gain to the issuer on the issue of money. Owing to the durability of the precious metals, especially gold, one can reasonably assume that this gain is realized only once per unit of money in existence, though, presumably, worn, clipped or sweated coins would come back eventually for melting down and reissue. If one wished to take account of that, one would regard the money supply as yielding a flow of seigniorage $(v-c)_1, (v-c)_2, \ldots, (v-c)_\infty$, which could in turn be summed into a capital value of the right to issue money:

$$\sum_{t=0}^{\infty} \frac{v-c}{(1+i)^t} = (v-c)\frac{1+i}{i}$$

where v is circulating value, c cost, and i the interest rate ruling over the period between recoinages. This expression differs from the usual formula for the capitalized value of an income flow because the first yield accrues immediately.

Seigniorage can be levied, presumably, because the public is prepared to pay a premium for the convenience of having coins of uniform size and certified as to weight and fineness of metal, greater than the cost of minting precious metal into such coins, and because the state can impose a monopoly of minting and thereby extract the difference. By taxing the conversion of metal into coins the state discourages the use of coins in payment as contrasted with the barter of precious metal for goods, and thereby imposes a welfare loss on the community. On the other hand, to the extent that the cir-

* Reprinted from Robert A. Mundell and Alexander K. Swoboda (eds), *Monetary Problems of the International Economy* (Chicago: University of Chicago Press, 1969).

culating value of coins is above their real resource cost, the levy of seigniorage reduces the real resources required to be invested in creating any given money supply, and so gives rise to a social saving. A full analysis of the welfare effects of seigniorage in a commodity-money system, however, would require an analysis of its effects on the supply of precious metals, which does not seem worthwhile pursuing here, if only because any social saving is likely to be negligible.

Now consider the replacement of a commodity money – the issue of which is assumed for simplicity not to be subject to seigniorage – by a purely paper money, assumed to be non-interest-bearing and to cost nothing to print. The replacement frees the resources embodied in the stock of commodity money for other more productive uses and yields a social saving equal to the value of these resources. This social saving accrues to the monetary authority, which is able (by assumption) to persuade (or force) the public to surrender the commodity in exchange for paper. The monetary authority can then invest the resources formerly embodied in the money stock in productive assets. The 'seigniorage' resulting from the operation can be thought of either as a capital sum – the real value of the money supply – or as a flow of income to the monetary authority equal to the real value of the money supply multiplied by the average rate of return on whatever assets the paper money (more accurately, the resources released by the substitution of paper for commodity money) has been invested in. (These may be government debt, in the case of a central bank, or public goods of some sort, if the government is assumed to appropriate the seigniorage.)

Now, retaining the assumption that money is non-interest-bearing and costless to issue, assume that the economy is growing and that additional money is issued at a rate sufficient to keep the price level stable. The issue of this money entails a social saving *by comparison with what would occur under a commodity-money system*, where real resources would have to be devoted to producing the additional money. If for simplicity the commodity-money system is assumed to be able to produce the monetary metal at constant cost, the social saving referred to is equal to the real value of the additional money issued. If, more realistically, the monetary metal is assumed to be a depletable resource, the marginal real cost of extraction of which rises as more is extracted, the price level in the commodity-money system would have to fall over time, so that some part of the increase in the money supply would be provided costlessly through appreciation of the existing stock, and the social saving from the issue of additional money instead of the production of additional commodity money would be less than the real value of the increase in the paper-money stock. In the extreme case of inability to produce additional commodity money, the additional real balances demanded as a result of economic growth would be provided by a fall in the price level, at zero social cost. This result would also occur in a paper-money system in which the money supply was held constant. (Obviously there is no difference between a paper- and a commodity-money system if the money supply [in nominal terms] is constant.) But social welfare will be higher in a paper-money system with a fixed money supply than in one in which the money supply is expanded to keep the price level constant, because in the former system the falling trend of prices provides a yield to the holders of real balances and encourages a greater use of money, which greater use increases welfare at no social cost. (This proposition is subject to the qualification that if prices fall at a percentage rate greater than the rate of return on real assets, the public will want to hold money rather than real assets and the system is likely to break down.)

The issue of additional paper money at a rate sufficient to keep the price level constant yields seigniorage to the monetary authority equal to the real value of the quantity of money multiplied by its rate of growth. It follows from the previous paragraph that this seigniorage will be equal to the social saving implicit in the use of credit money rather than commodity money, if the marginal real cost of production of the monetary commodity is constant, and otherwise will exceed that social saving, which may be zero. Furthermore, by comparison with a paper-money system in which the quantity of money is fixed (and subject to the qualification mentioned at the end of the previous paragraph), the levying of seigniorage by a monetary policy of maintaining stable prices involves a social loss, resulting from the restriction of the use of money as a consequence of its zero yield. In other words, the maintenance of a stable price level imposes an 'inflation tax' on holders of money, by comparison with a policy of keeping the money supply constant and allowing prices to fall over time (subject again to the aforementioned qualification).

Putting together the two concepts of seigniorage as the gain from the replacement of commodity by paper money, neither of which bears interest, and the gain to the monetary authority from issuing the additional paper money required to keep the price level stable while growth goes on, total seigniorage at any point of time is the sum of (i) the real growth of the money supply and (ii) the yield on the investment of the resources freed by the past substitution of the existing paper-money supply for commodity money. That is, seigniorage received by the monetary authority and available for distribution is $(i+g)M$, where i is the interest rate available on assets and g is the growth rate of demand for money at a stable price level, both defined for an appropriate time unit, and M is the existing money supply (indifferently measurable in nominal or real terms).

Now suppose that there are real costs incurred in maintaining the stock of money. In the case of currency, the notes have a production cost which includes the cost of the fine paper and intricate printing necessary to forestall forgery and the cost of maintaining security; in addition the notes wear out and have to be replaced. In the case of deposit money there are bookkeeping costs. Let these costs be at the rate c per unit of money per period of the previous analysis. Then the seigniorage on the existing stock of money becomes $(i-c)M$. As for the seigniorage on the issue of new money, such issue involves assuming the obligation of the cost stream c, the present value of which will be c/i. Hence the net seigniorage of this kind will be, not gM, but $[(1-c)/i]gM$. The formula for total seigniorage is therefore

$$\left[(i-c) + \frac{(i-c)}{i} g \right] M = (i-c)\frac{(i+g)}{i} M = \frac{(i-c)}{i}(i+g)M.$$

This formula also represents the social gain from the substitution of paper money for commodity money when the paper money is expanded so as to maintain a stable price level and when in the commodity-money system the real cost of production of the commodity money is constant so that the price level would be stable in that system also.

The foregoing formula applies at a moment of time and adds together an income flow from the existing money stock and a capital gain for the monetary authority accruing from the expansion of the stock; it therefore assumes implicitly that the capital gain on past increases of the money supply has been invested by the monetary authority at the ruling rate of interest. The flow of income from seigniorage available to the monetary authority for current utilization may be one or the other of these two elements of income, but cannot be the sum of the two. That is, by always investing the capital gain the monetary authority can secure an income stream $(i-c)M_t$ where M_t is the stock of money at time t; alternatively, by always consuming the capital gain the monetary authority can secure an income stream

$$(i-c) M_0 + \frac{(i-c)}{i} g M_t$$

where M_0 is the money stock existent at the time the policy of consuming capital gains commenced and will be zero if that policy has always been followed.

In the preceding formulas, c has been defined as a real cost stream associated with the operation of a unit of the money supply. Alternatively, c may be conceived as an interest charge paid to the holders of money to induce them to hold it. Such a charge represents, not a social cost, but a transfer of seigniorage (and of social benefit from a paper-money as compared with a constant-cost commodity-money system) from the monetary authority to the holders of money. If the provision of money were competitive, as for example it would be in an unregulated deposit-banking system, c would be equal to i and there would be no seigniorage, no income flow for the monetary authorities either from earnings on the stock of money or from capital gains. Such a system would obviously require some means of limiting the rate of increase of the money supply to what would be consistent with a stable price level; alternatively, the monetary authority might deliberately forgo seigniorage and pay interest on money equal to what it earned on the assets backing the money supply. The payment of interest on money would eliminate the social loss due to the restriction of the use of money by the extraction of seigniorage.

This analysis has some obvious implications for current discussion of the problem of international monetary reform and the analysis of reform proposals. To elucidate these, it is convenient to assume that credit money is costless to operate, and that in the alternative commodity-money system the real cost of production of the monetary commodity is constant.

In the first place, a number of proposals for the reform of the international monetary system, such as the first Stamp Plan and the report of the UNCTAD expert group, have seized on the notion of a flow of social saving implicit in the expansion of international credit reserves rather than gold reserves and argued that this saving should be placed at the disposal of the less developed countries. This means in effect retaining a commodity-money system, so far as new credit reserve-holdings by the developed countries are concerned. (The Hart–Kaldor–Tinbergen proposal goes further, seeking to establish a full commodity-reserve-money system at the international level and in so doing to eliminate the social saving accruing to the world from the use of credit rather than commodity reserves, in order to achieve the extremely doubtful benefits of stable nominal – not real – prices of primary products.) The fact that there is a social saving implicit in the use of credit rather than commodity money, however, does not – contrary to the tenor of some of the arguments employed – mean that allocation of this social saving to the less developed countries would entail no real sacrifice by or loss to the developed countries that accumulate additional reserves. This would be true if the only choice available in international monetary reform lay between a commodity-reserve system and a credit-reserve system in which the social saving had to be distributed to the less developed countries; but in fact the choice lies among credit-reserve systems with differing distributional consequences. Furthermore, it is possible to define a credit-reserve system that would be distributionally neutral: distributional neutrality requires merely that each country that contributes to the social saving by holding additional reserves receives back the amount of its contribution in the form of command over the real resources saved. Such a distributionally neutral system for expanding international liquidity could be established by means of a composite reserve-unit scheme in which countries' participations corresponded to their shares in the expansion of the demand for reserves.

In the second place, the foregoing analysis indicates that, if the distributional question about alternative liquidity schemes is formulated in terms of the levying and distribution of seigniorage –

which assumes that no interest is paid on holdings of credit reserves (or, more generally, that interest is paid at a rate below the rate of returns on the assets held against such reserves) – the distribution problem may arise in either or both of two forms. That is, the scheme could pay no interest on its liabilities (credit reserves held by the various countries) and charge a commercial rate of interest on its loans, thereby collecting seigniorage in the form of an annual income which would have to be distributed according to some agreed principle. At the other extreme, it could realize the seigniorage as a flow of capital gains from the expansion of holdings of non-interest-bearing international reserves, distributing these as cash grants according to some agreed distribution principle. As a middle course it could charge interest on its loans at a rate below the rate of return on, or alternative opportunity cost of, the real investments financed by those loans, receiving seigniorage partly as an explicit income flow to be distributed by an income-allocation rule and partly as an implicit flow of capital gains distributed by a loan-allocation rule. To the extent that it paid interest on holdings of international reserves, part of the seigniorage potentially collectable would be redistributed automatically according to the distribution of owner-ship of the international reserves that constitute its liabilities. Finally in this connection, it should be noted that to the extent that seigniorage is realized as an income flow not subject to a distribution rule, the distribution problem is left to determination by the manage-ment of the scheme – which may, of course, appropriate it to itself in the form of operating outlays (salaries, opulent office facilities) or spend it on the provision of public goods (such as research on international monetary problems).

In the third place, an important conclusion of the foregoing analysis is that any international liquidity plan that invokes the explicit or implicit collection and redistribution of seigniorage is necessarily inefficient and involves a social waste, inasmuch as seigniorage is derived from paying a rate of interest on reserve liabilities less than the alternative opportunity cost of holding them, and thereby restricts the holding of reserves and the realization of the full potential social saving from the use of credit money. An optimal system would pay a rate of return on reserve money equal to the rate of return available on investments made on commercial terms. Such a system would involve foregoing seigniorage, and the associated power to redistribute the social saving implicit in the expansion of reserve holdings; instead, this saving would be distributed automatically to the countries that held the additional money. (A distributionally neutral scheme for allocating seigniorage in proportion to additional credit reserves held would achieve the same result if countries rationally took account of the seigniorage earned on their reserve-holdings.)

The foregoing analysis rests on the theoretical abstraction of assuming a single world rate of return on real investment. In the real world of imperfect international mobility of capital, the rate of return on real investment and correspondingly the alternative opportunity cost of holding reserves vary internationally. If, nevertheless, it is required of a liquidity plan that it pay a uniform rate of interest on its liabilities and charge a uniform rate of interest on its loans, there will necessarily be implicit seigniorage in the form of a capital gain to borrowing countries whose rate of return on real investment exceeds the plan's lending rate, and most probably also explicit seigniorage in the form of income accruing from a difference between the plan's deposit and lending rates; and therefore there will necessarily be a problem of determining the distribution of the seigniorage. If no explicit rules are laid down, the problem will be solved by the discretionary control of the management of the plan over the rationing of loans and the disposition of the plan's operating income. The alternative of adjusting deposit and loan rates to the circumstances of individual countries, suggested by the criteria of distributional neutrality and optimal supply of reserves, would obviously encounter difficulties when reserves were used to finance deficits and surpluses. This is a problem that others might be interested in pursuing.

3. Efficiency in International Money
Supply *

In the analysis of efficiency in the domestic money supply, it is empirically reasonable and theoretically convenient to regard the use of currency by the public and in the reserves of commercial banks as a rather minor facet of the monetary system, and the problems of efficiency associated with the non-payment of interest on currency as secondary to the problem of efficiency in the supply and use of deposit money created by banks. In the international monetary system, however, the 'currency' – monetary gold reserves – bulks large by comparison with the 'deposits' – the reserve currencies of sterling and the dollar and drawing rights of countries in the International Monetary Fund. (IMF drawing rights are of course not strictly speaking deposits, but they can be more readily assimilated to deposits than to currency, since their creation requires the use of credit.)

The use of gold as the ultimate reserve base of the international monetary system entails three types of inefficiency. First, and in practice most important, the supply of gold for monetary purposes is not controlled with the achievement of any such social objective as world price stability in view. Instead, as Robert Triffin especially has emphasized for many years, the supply of new monetary gold is dependent on the vagaries of new gold production, Russian gold sales, and private industrial and hoarding demands. In the classical system of international monetary theory, the basing of the inter-

* This section is to be read in conjunction with Ch. 3 above, since it is a development of the first part of that chapter. The two were in fact combined in a lecture on 'Efficiency in Domestic and International Money Supply' delivered at the University of Surrey at the invitation of Ruth Troeller on February 7, 1968; see *International Economics*, No. 3 (Guildford: University of Surrey, March 1970), pp. 3–16. They were subsequently used as the basis for the Frank D. Graham Lecture at Princeton University in May 1969.

national monetary system on a producible commodity money was considered to be desirable, since variations in the general price level in relation to a fixed price for gold would produce automatically stabilizing inverse variations in the rate of new gold production. Given the high ratio of stocks to new production, the time-span of such automatic self-stabilization is, however, too long to be relevant to contemporary policy concerns, even if the world were otherwise prepared to abide by the gold-standard philosophy. Moreover, the occurrence from time to time of new gold discoveries and improvements in the technology of gold production and reclamation, together with the depletability of the world's gold resources, make it certain that stabilization of the monetary price of gold would ensure instability rather than stability of the money price level of goods in general. A major problem of efficiency in the international monetary system, therefore, is to replace the gold standard by a more rational system of providing for the expansion of international reserves, or to correct for its defects by a supplementary system of international reserve creation that would achieve the same effect.

Second, gold is a commodity and its production requires the use of real resources. Dependence on it therefore involves refusal to exploit the possibility of creating money at zero social cost, which in the domestic economy is achieved through the use of fiat currency and deposit money, on the basis of the credit of the government and central bank on the one hand and of the commercial banking system on the other. Efficiency in the use of world productive resources would require the substitution of an international credit money for gold reserves, and the diversion of monetary gold to directly productive uses.

Third, gold is non-interest-bearing. There is therefore an incentive to the holder of reserves in the form of gold to hold a socially suboptimal quantity of it, and also to substitute for it interest-bearing deposits in the specific form of reserve currencies. In itself, such substitution accomplishes a social saving from the world point of view, inasmuch as it economizes on the use of real resources to produce gold for monetary purposes. But insofar as the reserve currencies are inferior as monetary substitutes for an international reserve as reliable as gold, there is some social loss on this account; and insofar as the freedom to convert international reserve currencies into gold at will generates international monetary instability, there is a social loss. Further, it should be noted that, contrary to the case of currency in domestic circulation, which passes fairly rapidly from hand to hand among many small economic units, gold held as international reserves generally changes hands relatively slowly from one large transactor to another, so that there would be little practical difficulty in paying interest on holdings of an international reserve asset that might be substituted for it.

The conclusion that emerges from consideration of these three defects of gold as an international reserve money is that gold should be replaced by some sort of international credit-reserve asset, created at approximately zero social cost, which should in principle bear interest so as to encourage countries to hold as near as possible to the satiety level of demand for it, and the quantity of which should be increased by international arrangement at a rate conducive to stability of the world price level.

This general principle already disposes of a number of suggestions for the reform of the international monetary system that have been advanced in recent years, notably the Rueff recommendation of a return to the pure gold standard and the Hart–Kaldor–Tinbergen recommendation to establish an international commodity-reserve money. Both of these would be subject to the same criticisms on efficiency grounds as those listed above, with the differences that the Hart–Kaldor–Tinbergen scheme might be better than the gold standard inasmuch as it would average out the problems of uneven incidence of technical progress in production as between the monetary commodity and other goods over a wide range of monetary commodities, but worse, that it would impose the equivalent of a negative interest rate on the reserve asset in the form of storage and deterioration costs for the commodities included in the reserve basket. The principle also casts doubt on the efficiency and probable effectiveness of schemes for international monetary reform that call for the replacement or supplementation of holdings of reserve currencies by holdings of non-interest-bearing reserve assets, either holdings of revalued gold as under the Rueff plan or holdings of non-interest-bearing (or low-interest-bearing) new international reserve assets as under some alternative plans. An extreme case of the latter alternative is the Roosa plan, under which countries would actually be required to pay interest on their holdings of new international reserves created by an international credit operation.

The general principle stated above appears to point to the desirability of a new international institution (or a reorganization of the International Monetary Fund into an institution) that would issue interest-bearing liabilities which it would put into circulation by the purchase of interest-bearing assets in the world's financial markets, the interest earned paying the cost of the interest disbursed, operating costs being deducted, and the quantity of its liabilities being increased each year in accordance with the requirements of world price stability with a growing volume of world trade and production. If the world capital market functioned reasonably efficiently, it would not matter where the world central bank – for that is what it would be – acquired its assets; but under present conditions of world capital-market imperfection, it would be necessary for the allocation of acquisitions among national capital markets to be regulated according to some principle of equity.

Two objections can, however, be raised to the proposal to provide new international reserves on world central banking lines. The first, which has been argued most forcefully by Fritz Machlup, is that the banking concept of liabilities having to be backed by assets is fallacious when applied to the provision of international reserves, and should not be perpetuated in this context: the use of any money depends ultimately on its acceptability in settlements, and while for other moneys this quality may require convertibility into some better (more widely acceptable) form of money, e.g. convertibility of a national into international money, the ultimate international money must be inconvertible into any other better money and dependent for its use purely on its acceptability for the settlement of transactions. This argument is correct; but taken at its face value it implies the provision of a non-interest-bearing international reserve money (since without interest-bearing assets where is the money to come from to pay interest on the monetary liabilities?), which on the preceding argument would involve inefficiency. The second objection is that the use of the banking format involves the appearance of an ability to create real resources for lending out of nothing, and would give rise to international squabbling over rights to borrow the resulting real resources. Such squabbling has already been manifest in the demands of the less developed countries that new international reserves should be given to them in the first instance and earned back by the developed countries.

In fact, however, the principle of payment of interest on international reserves required by international efficiency considerations can be served, without the need for explicit interest payments on the monetary liabilities, and the associated necessity of a banking apparatus of liabilities backed by interest-yielding assets, if new international reserves are created by an international credit operation ensuring acceptability of the newly-created assets in settlement of international deficits and surpluses, and the participants in the scheme are either obliged to pay interest or entitled to receive interest at a rate approximating the return available on real investment of funds, on deviations of their actual holdings from their initial participations in the new reserves. In effect, under such a scheme countries are simultaneously lending to and borrowing from the scheme at zero interest on the lesser of their initial participation in and their actual holdings of such reserves, and receiving or paying interest only on their net lending or borrowing with reference to their initial position. They are in the same position as an individual domestic customer of a bank that charges competitive interest on overdrafts and pays competitive interest on deposits.[1] The only question of efficiency that would arise under such a system of international reserve creation would be whether the lending and borrowing rates approximated the alternative opportunity cost of capital. If they did, the initial participation shares in the scheme would be a matter of indifference to the participating countries. If they did not, the participation shares would involve net advantages or disadvantages to the participating countries. In consequence, depending on the balance of bargaining power among the participants, the total of new international reserves provided might be either too large or too small for world price stability. Such a situation would, however, be corrected by inflation or deflation. With the resulting distribution of reserves, total reserves would be sub-optimal if the lending and

---

[1] Note that the same situation would not be achieved by the establishment of a world central bank that paid no interest on its liabilities, and distributed profits on its assets either to its depositors according to a fixed distribution rule, or in the form of concessionary low interest rates on its loans.

borrowing rates – which represent the yield implicitly derived from holding international reserves and the alternative opportunity cost of international illiquidity – were below the rate of return on real investment.

In this context, the Special Drawing Rights plan approved at the Rio meetings of the International Monetary Fund and World Bank in September 1967 is on balance an important and in some ways revolutionary improvement in the present system of providing international reserve assets. It accepts the principle that new international reserves should be provided on the scale required to meet the growth of demand for international liquidity. It recognizes that new international reserves can be provided without satisfying the banking philosophy's insistence on the need for assets to back the new international monetary liabilities. And its form meets the requirements of efficiency in international monetary organization, in the general sense of conforming with the principle that interest should be paid on reserves. The two questions it raises are: first, whether the combination of participation shares and interest rates it envisages are or are not a close approximation to the efficiency requirements; and second, whether in fact it will become an existing and effective supplement to the present gold-based international monetary system. As to the first question, there is an unfortunate propensity among the designers of international monetary arrangements to believe that interest rates for international reserve-borrowing and reserve-lending transactions should be kept low, in relation to comparable commercial interest rates, thereby creating incentives for countries to hold reserves smaller than would be socially optimal; this propensity is reflected in the Special Drawing Rights scheme, as well as in other reform plans recently propounded (the Roosa plan being as mentioned an extreme case) and in the structure of the International Monetary Fund itself. As to the second question, time alone will tell.

Chapter 10

4. Border Taxes, Border Tax Adjustments, Comparative Advantage, and the Balance of Payments*

(with Mel Krauss)

'Border tax adjustments', often referred to briefly and misleadingly as 'border taxes', have been the subject of international discussion recently in two contexts. On the one hand, U.S. public opinion has been very critical of the decision of certain Common Market and other European countries to move to a system of value-added taxes on the destination principle, which change has been seen as harmful to the U.S. balance-of-payments position.[1] On the other hand, the German decision of November 1968 to compensate for Germany's refusal to revalue the deutschmark by reducing her rates of tax remission on exports and tax imposition on imports was widely regarded as a constructive step towards the restoration of international monetary equilibrium, and official opinion has since occasionally favoured variation of border tax adjustments as a means of promoting international monetary equilibrium.

The purpose of this note is to demonstrate, by means of a general-equilibrium analysis of the border tax adjustment problem that in both cases cited, the analytical treatment of the effects of changes in border tax adjustments rests on adopting a short-run approach to such adjustments in which domestic prices and exchange rates are assumed to be fixed and no account is taken of the mechanism of international adjustment; and that in a longer-run context in which the international adjustment mechanism is assumed to be functioning, changes in border tax adjustments should make no difference to international trade, provided that the taxes to which the

---

* Reprinted from *Canadian Journal of Economics*, Vol. III, No. 4 (November 1970), pp. 595–602.

[1] For ten years, France was the only member of the European Economic Community to employ the value-added method of taxation. Subsequently, the rest of the Six have followed suit.

277

adjustments apply are truly general. In this connection it is remarked that there is an essential distinction to be drawn between *border tax adjustments*, whose purpose is to equalize the conditions of competition between domestic and foreign producers and so permit comparative cost to govern trade patterns; and *border taxes*, which properly understood are taxes on the crossing by trade of international frontiers (e.g. a tariff) and hence restrict trade volumes below what would be indicated as desirable by the principle of comparative advantage. The real problem with border tax adjustments, it is contended, arises when the taxes to which the adjustments relate are not truly general, and/or when the adjustment has to be made by an approximation of the average effect of such taxes on the competitive position of domestic *vis-à-vis* foreign producers.

I

A border tax, properly interpreted, is a tax imposed when goods cross an international border, and as such must be inimical to international trade and therefore to the achievement of the economic benefits of international specialization and division of labour. A border tax *adjustment*, on the other hand, is an adjustment of the taxes imposed on a producer when the goods he produces cross an international border. Such an adjustment may involve an addition to or a subtraction from the taxes he has already paid; and if the adjustment in question implies either equal rates of taxation of imports and subsidization of exports, or equal rates of subsidization of imports and taxation of exports, the effect of the adjustment is to leave the relative competitive positions of exporting and import-competing industries in the domestic market unchanged. This is merely an application of the well-known principle that taxation of imports and subsidization of exports is equivalent to a devaluation of the currency, and that under long-run full-employment and price-flexibility conditions a devaluation will be offset by an equal inflation of domestic prices.

However, only in the long run when the exchange rate or factor prices has adjusted to preserve external balance will it be a matter of indifference which type of border tax adjustment is applied. In the short run, with both domestic factor prices and the exchange rates fixed, taxation of imports and subsidization of exports will give a monetary competitive advantage to domestic goods over foreign goods in both the domestic and the foreign market, tending to improve the country's balance of payments, while the converse will apply when exports are taxed and imports subsidized.

The function of the border tax adjustment, in the long run, and in contrast to the border tax *per se*, is to equalize the conditions of competition between domestic and foreign producers. Border tax adjustments may be based on either of two principles: the origin principle and the destination principle. Under the origin principle, a tax is imposed on the domestic production of goods, whether exported or not, and under the destination principle, the same tax is imposed on imported goods as on domestically-produced goods destined for consumption by domestic consumers, while domestically-produced goods destined for consumption by foreigners enjoy a rebate of the tax. The origin principle involves no visible border tax adjustment, while the destination principle involves a border tax adjustment to the full extent of the tax. But the long-run effect of either principle of border tax adjustment is the same.[1]

This point is best understood by considering initially a closed economy. In such an economy, a government imposing a flat-rate tax on spending power could choose to impose it either as a proportional tax on factor incomes, or as a proportional tax on total expenditure. In the former case it would appear as a tax on production (the use of factors), in the latter case as a tax on consumption and investment (the expenditure of factor incomes). But in either case its real effect would be exactly the same. Its monetary effect, i.e. its effect on either raising domestic commodity prices with factor prices unchanged or lowering factor prices with commodity prices unchanged, would depend on the monetary policy of the government,

---

[1] This point has been known since the publication of the so-called 'Tinbergen Report' (European Coal and Steel Community, High Authority, *Report on the Problems raised by the Different Turnover Tax Systems applied within the Common Market* [March 1953]). Actually, as recorded elsewhere by one of the present authors (in Harry G. Johnson, Paul Wonnacott and Hirofumi Shibata, *Harmonization of National Economic Policies Under Free Trade* [Toronto, 1968]), it was largely the contribution of W. B. Reddaway, a member of the Tinbergen Committee (see W. B. Reddaway, 'The Implications of a Free Trade Area for British Taxation', *British Tax Review* [March 1958], pp. 71–9).

the latter effect resulting if the money supply were kept constant (or increased at the normal rate) and the former if the money supply were increased (above normal) in proportion to the tax rate.

Now suppose the same country existing in an international economy, and suppose that a general tax is imposed. Whether the form of the tax in a closed economy is initially a consumption tax or a production tax, its form or apparent incidence in the open economy will depend on the border tax adjustment principle employed. Specifically, if the origin principle is employed, with no tax rebate on exports or taxation of imports, domestic factor prices must fall in money terms so as to absorb the burden of the tax, so that domestic products can remain competitive with foreign products in the foreign and domestic markets, and the country's trade remain balanced. Conversely, if the destination principle is employed, domestic factor prices will not be affected, since the tax rebate frees exporters from the burden of the tax, and the compensatory tax imposed on imports equalizes conditions of competition between domestic producers of import substitutes and foreign exporters to the domestic market, and domestic prices must rise to the extent of the tax. Under the origin principle, the tax appears as a tax on production while under the destination principle it appears as a tax on consumption; but in either case it remains a proportional tax on domestic spending power. Under the origin principle, since domestic commodity prices are unchanged, there is no need for monetary policy to change the domestic money supply; under the destination principle, the rise in the domestic price level requires an increase in the domestic money supply which may be provided either through domestic monetary expansion or through a transitory balance-of-payments surplus.

It follows that it makes no difference to the exploitation of comparative advantage through trade which principle of border tax adjustment is applied, provided again that the tax is a truly general tax. (It should be noted, however, that this is an important proviso, given the importance of trade in invisibles, which generally escape destination-principle adjustment.) Similarly, in the long run a decision by a country or trading group to change from one principle of border tax adjustment to another should make no difference to its international competitive position.

This, however, is not the light in which businessmen and governments see the matter. For this there are two reasons, one fallacious and one valid in content. The first is that practical people tend to look at the form of the border tax adjustment, without appreciating its consequential effects on domestic factor and commodity price levels – i.e. to see the tax adjustment or its absence, but not its general equilibrium repercussions. Consequently, the use of the origin principle is typically regarded by the domestic exporter as imposing an unfair competitive disadvantage on him, insofar as he has to pay domestic production taxes higher than those paid by his foreign competitiors, while the use of the destination principle also tends to be regarded by domestic exporters as imposing an unfair competitive disadvantage on them, insofar as consumption taxes imposed in foreign countries with destination principle adjustments are at higher rates than domestic consumption taxes, so that the foreign exporter to a country pays a border tax adjustment lower than that paid by the domestic exporter.[1] Both propositions, by ignoring the consequential adjustments of commodity or factor prices to the principle of border tax adjustment, wrongly identify a principle which does not discriminate between foreign and domestic producers with such discrimination. This fallacy is encouraged by the common practice of referring to 'border tax adjustments' as 'border taxes', a practice which implies that explicit adjustments (under the destination principle) or implicit adjustments (under the origin principle) constitute a tax on international as distinct from domestic trade. The fallacy is exemplified by the long-standing belief in the United States that, since the U.S. tax system relies primarily on corporation and personal income tax, to which the origin principle applies, while European tax systems rely more on consumption taxes to which the destination principle applies, U.S. producers are placed at an unfair disadvantage in international competition, which should be corrected by some policy change; and also the U.S. contention that the decision of the E.E.C. countries to move towards

---

[1] Note that in the first case the alleged unfairness consists in the domestic producer's having to pay more taxes on production than the foreign producer; in the second case, it consists in the domestic producer's having to pay a higher price of admission to foreign markets than the foreigner has to pay for admission to the domestic market.

a value-added tax with destination-principle border adjustments represents increased trade discrimination against the United States.[1]

The second and rather more justifiable reason for business and governmental concern about border tax adjustments is that, in the short run in which exchange rates and domestic money factor prices are fixed, a change from one system of border tax adjustment to another can indeed affect a country's international competitive position and balance of payments. Specifically, a change from the origin principle to the destination principle will give a subsidy to exports and impose a tax on imports, and hence tend to improve the balance of payments, so long as factor prices remain unchanged; and conversely for a change in the opposite direction. These changes are in fact equivalent respectively to a devaluation and an appreciation of the currency, with respect to commodity trade. Hence, from the short-run balance-of-payments viewpoint, the United States could snatch some advantage from introducing border tax adjustments for corporation profits taxes, or replacing such taxes by a value-added tax with destination-principle border adjustments; and it will be placed at a disadvantage by the European move towards such a value-added tax, though only to the extent that that tax does not merely replace previously existing taxes unaccompanied by a border tax adjustment. For the same reason, the reduction in German border tax adjustment rates of 1968 (which amounted to a partial movement from the destination to the origin principle) should have contributed to decreasing the German surplus; the reduction was in fact commonly recognized as equivalent to an appreciation of the mark for

[1] See, for example, the paper read by Stanley S. Surrey, former Assistant Secretary of the Treasury of the United States, before the 73rd Annual Congress of American Industry of the National Association of Manufacturers, New York City (Washington, D.C., 1968). The DISC proposal recently adopted by the U.S. intends to counter the alleged European tax discrimination against U.S. exporters by granting them a postponement of the corporation income tax due on export profits, so long as such profits are reinvested in export related activities. In effect, this proposal is equivalent to an export subsidy without an import charge of equal rate, and thus, unlike the destination-principle border tax adjustments it pretends to counter, is inimical to an efficient allocation of resources. The maximum subsidy per unit of exports is equal to the profits tax rate times the proportion of profits in the export price. This assumes that reinvestment earns the same rate of return as any other dollar the company could obtain; if not, the subsidy is less because it is tied to reinvestment.

the purposes of commodity trade.[1] In either case, however, the change of border tax adjustment principle, through its effects on trade and the balance of payments, will set in motion pressures on factor prices which in the long run will eliminate the short-run balance-of-payments gain or loss. In the long run, the behaviour of countries' balances of payments will depend on other factors than border tax adjustments, specifically, on their overall demand-management policies.

The foregoing analysis has made no explicit reference to tariffs, which interact with the border tax adjustments in determining the commercially profitable trade. Generally speaking, tariffs will simply offset the pattern of comparative advantage, and the resulting effects on trade will generally make the level of domestic factor prices and commodity prices higher than it would be under free trade, as a consequence of the effects of the tariff in drawing factors of production out of exporting into import-competing industries.

The foregoing analysis of the long-run irrelevance of the choice of principle in border tax adjustments has an important application to a recent debate concerned with tax harmonization in common markets, in which it has been contended by several writers that 'mixed systems' of border tax adjustments, i.e. systems that use one type of adjustment for trade with other members and the other type for trade with outsiders, are incompatible with allocative efficiency.[2] This is

---

[1] For an analysis of this equivalency, see Gottfried Haberler, 'Import Taxes and Export Subsidies, A Substitute for the Realignment of Exchange Rates?', *Kyklos*, Vol. XX (1967).

[2] This view was first put forward in the Tinbergen Report (pp. 25, 37) and later implied by the conclusion of the so-called 'Neumark Report' (*Report of the Fiscal and Financial Committee of the European Economic Community*, unofficial translation by Dr H. Thurston, International Bureau of Fiscal Documentation [Amsterdam, 1963]), which advocated equalization of internal, indirect tax rates to avoid allocative distortions, and has been accepted rather uncritically in the literature. A rationale of it was attempted by one of the present authors (in Melvyn Krauss, 'Tax Harmonization and Allocative Efficiency in Economic Unions', *Public Finance*, vol. 3 [1968], pp. 367–71), and accepted by Douglas Dosser ('A Comment on Tax Harmonization and Allocative Efficiency in Economic Unions, by Melvyn Krauss', *Public Finance*, Vol. 3 (1968) pp. 376–7); it was also accepted by the other author in a passing reference (see p. 19 of Johnson, Wonnacott and Shibata, *op. cit.*); and also by Paul Wonnacott (*op. cit.*), who makes the error several times—on pp. 48 and 51, and in fn. 17 on p. 49. The authors apologize to the readers of this note for their earlier (independent) failures to think the problem through to its logical conclusion. In extenuation,

untrue, as shown by the following argument. Consider first the analogy between a common market and a closed economy consisting of states among which factors of production are immobile but goods are free to move without interference from border taxes. Each state in such an economy can choose whatever system of border tax adjustment it prefers, without affecting the efficiency of the allocation of resources in the economy; all that the choice will affect will be whether its commodity price level is above, or its factor price level below, those of states using the alternative principle. Now consider such an economy to be trading with other countries, again under free-trade conditions. Whatever it does in its internal trade, its choice between applying the destination and the origin principles to its external trade should make no real difference, providing that if it uses the destination principle the rates of border tax adjustment are common for all member states. If it applies the origin principle, its internal price level will be equal to the world price level; if it applies the destination principle, its internal price level will be above the world price level to an extent determined by the rate of border tax adjustment. This follows from the equivalence of border tax adjustments with currency devaluation.[1] If now the economy imposes a common tariff against the outside world, internal factor prices and commodity prices must rise to maintain general equilibrium. But any distortions of trade must be the consequence of the tariff, and not of the system of border tax adjustment employed.

II

It has long been recognized that, where consumption or production taxes are not perfectly general (i.e. are non-proportional as between

they would plead that, in a common market, the usual assumption of factor immobility—on which the analysis of this note is based—no longer holds, so that differences in rates of taxation on production may lead to distortions of factor allocation. (The analysis of the influence of differences in tax systems when factors are mobile requires taking account of both taxes paid to and benefits derived from the national government; on this point see Johnson in Johnson, Wonnacott, and Shibata, *op. cit.*, pp. 17–24, and Krauss, 'The Tax Harmonization Problem in Free Trade Areas and Common Markets', *The Manchester School of Economic and Social Studies*, Vol. 37, No. 2 [June 1971], pp. 71–8.)

[1] Of course, if the rate of rebate on exports is less (greater) than the rate of compensating tax on imports, the effect is to impose a net tax (subsidy) on international trade, with corresponding effects on the relation of the domestic to the foreign price level.

goods), the principle of border tax adjustment does make a difference to allocative efficiency. For example, a country that imposes a specially heavy tax on production of a particular commodity because it wishes to discourage consumption will worsen the efficiency of world resource allocation unless it applies the destination principle; conversely, if the tax is imposed because production of the commodity has social disadvantages, resource allocation will be worsened unless it applies the origin principle. Such cases are well known and require no further discussion, though they are important in practice.

Less well-known, however, are the trade effects of indirect taxes that are not truly general. Ordinarily, a consumption tax restricts consumption of the taxed good, the external reflection of which is either a reduction of imports of substitute products manufactured in foreign countries or an expansion of exports of the taxed commodity or both; conversely, a production tax restricts production of the taxed goods, contracts exports and increases imports of substitute products. The net trade effect of either tax, however, is not clear since the balance-of-payments adjustments required for external equilibrium induce trade movements opposite to those stemming from the tax's direct trade effect. All that can be said in the way of general principle is that consumption taxes are likely to increase trade should they fall exclusively on exportables and decrease trade should importables bear their essential burden, while production taxes normally will increase trade when levied exclusively on importables and decrease trade in the reverse instance.

Of further interest is the case when taxation is not general and, contrary to what has been assumed previously, the rebates to exporters and compensating taxes imposed on importers under the destination principle are not exactly adjusted to the taxes paid on consumption of domestically-produced goods (or on production of goods for the domestic market). In this case the effect will be to tax international trade if the export rebate is too small or the import border tax adjustment too large, and to subsidize international trade if the export rebate is too large or the import adjustment is too small, for the relevant good.

These possibilities are particularly relevant when it is a question of a shift from one type of tax to another, each with destination-principle border tax adjustments; for such a shift may have the net result either of subsidizing or of taxing international trade, by comparison with the initial position. A case in point is the decision of the European Economic Community to shift from the gross-turnover tax to the value-added tax. Under the former tax the border tax adjustments were necessarily crude, based on rough averages, since the tax burden on industry imposed by the tax depended on the degree of vertical integration in the industry. Under the latter tax, exact adjustments are more feasible, because the tax borne by an individual domestically-produced-and-sold good is more easily identified.[1] Hence the change-over is probably desirable from a global point of view, insofar as it removes distortions of comparative advantage other than those deliberately established by tariff policy. From the point of view of the United States, however, not only might the effect be unfavourable from the short-run balance-of-payments point of view, but it might be unfavourable from the long-run point of view of increasing U.S. gains from international trade. Moreover, the short-run and long-run self interests of the United States in the change might conflict. In the short run, with fixed exchange rates and factor prices, the net effect of the change would be to worsen or improve the U.S. balance of payments, according to whether its net effect was to subsidize European exports and tax European imports or vice versa. In the long run, the United States would gain from European subsidization of international trade, i.e. of both exports and imports, and lose from European taxation of international trade, whether of exports or of imports. Thus a change from one tax to another with destination-principle adjustments that would improve the U.S. balance of payments in the short run might worsen the U.S. terms of trade in the long run.

[1] For an analysis of the problems associated with exact border tax adjustments with the value-added tax, see Mel Krauss and Peter O'Brian, 'Some International Implications of Value Added Taxation', *National Tax Journal*, Vol. 23, No. 4 (December 1970), pp. 435–40; also Mel Krauss and Richard M. Bird, 'The Value-Added Tax: Critique of a Review', *Journal of Economic Literature*, Vol. 9, No. 4 (December 1971), pp. 1167–73.

Chapter 10

5. Are You Worth Your Weight in Gold?*

When a person is extraordinarily effective in performing his responsibilities, so much so that he appears indispensable to the organization that employs him, he is frequently said to be 'worth his weight in gold'. The implication is that he is extremely valuable to the organization, far more valuable than any remuneration he may receive. But inflation has been gradually eroding the real value (purchasing power) of gold, while rising educational levels and technical progress have been gradually increasing the value of human beings. In consequence, a significant number of people in our society have become worth far more than their weight in gold. For these people, to say that they are worth their weight in gold is not to praise them but to belittle them, since it implies that they are grossly overpaid.

Gold is currently priced at $35·00 an ounce. This, however, is a Troy ounce, not the avoirdupois ounce used in weighing people. It takes 14·58333 Troy ounces to make a pound avoirdupois. Hence a pound of gold, in terms of the system of measurement of human weight, is worth $510·41⅔; an ounce of gold, in terms of the same measurement system, is worth $31·90; and a hundredweight of gold is worth $51,041·66⅔. Hence a person who weighed 125 pounds would have to be worth $63,802·08, a person who weighed 150 pounds would have to be worth $76,562·50, a person who weighed 175 pounds would have to be worth $89,322·92, and a 200 pounder would have to be worth $102,083·33, to be worth his weight in gold.

People's weights vary with their age, height, and sex, and it is these variations that are of interest to insurance companies, public health authorities, and others interested in compiling statistics of average weights. Hence it is difficult to find average figures for the

* Reprinted from the *Journal of Political Economy*, Vol. 75, No. 2 (April 1967), pp. 205–7. Copyright 1967 by The University of Chicago Press, all rights reserved.

typical American male or female adult: Margaret Reid has, however, provided me with the following figures:[1] the average American adult male weighs 168·5 pounds, the average American adult female weighs 139·1 pounds, and the average American adult weighs 153·5 pounds. To be worth their weight in gold, therefore, the average American male adult would have to be worth $86,000, the average American female adult $71,000, and the average American adult $78,300 (all figures rounded to the nearest $100).

How much is a person worth? Colloquially, this question refers to the value of a person's holdings of property, that is, to his wealth. The notion of a person's being 'worth his weight in gold', however, is usually taken to refer to his value on the job, rather than to his wealth. For the purpose of assessing the value of a person in this sense, economists have invented the concept of 'human capital'; i.e. they look at the worker or salaried employee as a kind of capital equipment, which contributes a stream of productive services to the economic system and receives in exchange an income that represents the return on the human capital. Like other capital equipment, human capital can be valued in two different ways, useful for different purposes. One way is by the cost of producing it; this is most useful for assessing the value of people who have just completed some stage of their formal education. The other way is by the present value of the stream of income that a particular item of human capital will yield over its probable remaining future lifetime; this is most useful for assessing the value of people already established in a career.

Some estimates of the average investments in human-capital formation involved in the formal education system have been furnished me by Herbert G. Grubel and Anthony D. Scott. According to their figures (which relate to 1956 and include both education costs and foregone earnings) it takes an investment of $2,240 to complete eight years of elementary school, $7,926 to complete four years of high school, $18,722 to complete four years of college (the B.A.), $26,336 to complete two years of graduate school (the M.A.), and $33,950 to complete four years of graduate school (the Ph.D.); all figures relate to total cost cumulated from the beginning of

---

[1] Weights are for adults aged 20–59; the average for males and females is based on the 1960 population (Agricultural Research Service, 1960).

elementary school. These figures, however, seriously understate the amounts of the investments involved, because they make no allowance for the accumulation of interest on the investments between the time they are made and the time of graduation.

A rough calculation of the true value of the investments involved in the various levels of educational attainment, assuming a 5 per cent rate of interest, indicates the following capital values of people at the point of graduation:[1] eight years of elementary school, $2,745; four years of high school, $9,621; four years of college, $23,628; two years of graduate school, $34,046; four years of graduate school, $45,553. To these figures should properly be added whatever values people would have if they had no education whatever; but this can probably safely be regarded as negligible. On the basis of these figures, it appears that – contrary to the expressed belief of some eminent educators – the products of the education system are not worth their weight in gold, except for students who have completed four years of graduate school and weigh 89·2 pounds or less.[2]

The alternative method of estimating the capital value of a person is to calculate the present value of his expected future earnings. Burton Weisbrod (1961) has used this method to estimate the values of American males by age ranges from 0–4 to 70–74 years of age. At a 4 per cent discount rate, he finds that a male aged 0–4 is worth $27,124 – which makes boy babies worth considerably more than their weight in gold – and that the value of a male rises rapidly with age to

[1] The calculation assumes that the costs are the same per year within each stage of the educational system and are incurred at the middle of the year.

[2] The use of a higher interest rate would of course increase the capital values and make many more graduates appear to be worth their weight in gold. Using the 8 per cent rate corresponding to the average rate of return on business investment, the values would be as follows: elementary school, $3,095; high school, $10,869; college, $27,425; two years of graduate school, $41,225; four years of graduate school, $57,321. On the basis of these figures, a person who had finished two years of graduate work would be worth his weight in gold if he weighed less than 80·8 pounds, and a person who had completed four years of graduate work would be worth his weight in gold if he weighed less than 112·1 pounds. The 8 per cent rate probably results in a serious overstatement, however, because the educational costs relate to the single year 1956, whereas the costs of educating a person would have been incurred in previous years and would have been lower due the fact that foregone earnings and education costs increase steadily over time. The 5 per cent rate used in the text can be considered as equivalent to the 8 per cent return on business investment, less a factor of 3 per cent for the secular increase in education costs.

a peak of $57,494 at ages 25–29, declining thereafter to $241 in the age group 70–74. In the age group 20–34, the average value is $55,836, so that on the average any male in this age group who weighs less than 109·4 pounds is worth more than his weight in gold. Since men in this age group weigh considerably less than older men, it is probable that a significant proportion of them are worth more than their weight in gold.

Weisbrod's figures relate to the average of all males. Gary S. Becker (1964) has produced more detailed estimates of the average age wealth profiles of male graduates of various levels of education in the year 1939, i.e. of the capital values of the future earnings of these men at different ages.[1] According to his estimates, wealth (i.e. capital value) peaks at 39 at which age the graduate of seven or eight years of schooling (elementary school) is worth about $34,000, the graduate of twelve years of schooling (high school) is worth about $49,000, and the graduate of sixteen or more years of schooling (college, or college plus graduate school) is worth about $71,000. Using the typical weight of 168·5 pounds previously selected (value $86,000), it appears that the average elementary-school graduate is never worth more than about two-fifths of his weight in gold and a high-school graduate never worth more than seven-twelfths of his weight in gold, whereas at his maximum a college graduate is worth about 82·5 per cent of his weight in gold. In fact, the average college graduate of this weight is worth at least 80 per cent of his weight in gold between the ages of 37 and 41.

Are you worth your weight in gold? To find out, you must first determine the value of your weight in gold, using the figures previously given of $510·42 per pound and $31·90 per ounce. Then you must determine the present (capital) value of your future earnings.

As a very rough estimate indeed, you might start with the amount of your life insurance, since this is a capital sum, and its magnitude is related to the premiums you can afford to pay, which in turn is related to your income. To compensate for the probability that your

---

[1] See especially Becker's (1964) Chart 3, p. 146, and subsequently. The estimates allow for the secular upward trend of earnings with increasing productivity and employ an 8 per cent discount factor corresponding to the average rate of return on business investment.

insurance underestimates your value, you should probably reckon your value at double the face value of your insurance. Alternatively, you might reckon your value at four times the value of your house, since mortgage lenders generally follow the principle that you should spend no more than a quarter of your income on housing, so that the value of your house will represent approximately a quarter or less of the capitalized value of your income.

Both of these methods, however, are appropriate only for younger people (say, 39 and under), since for older people insurance and house values reflect past income rather than the capitalized value of future income. If you want to be really accurate, you will have to estimate your future earnings year by year and determine their

Table 10.4

Total no. of earning years	Present-value multiplier
5	4·5
10	8·1
15	10·9
20	13·1
25	14·8
30	16·1
35	17·2
40	18·2
45	18·7

present value; and this will require an intricate actuarial calculation. A reasonable rough approximation, however, can be obtained by starting with your present annual earnings, estimating the number of years you expect to be an earner, and multiplying your annual earnings by the present-value multipliers contained in Table 10.4. (These multipliers assume a 5 per cent discount rate for future earnings; for numbers of years between those shown, use an average of the two nearest multipliers.)

To illustrate the use of the table, a man earning $10,000 a year and expecting to work ten years altogether would be worth $81,000 – more than his weight in gold provided he weighs less than 158·7 pounds. Similarly, a man earning $5,000 a year and expecting to earn it for twenty years altogether would be worth $65,000 – and worth his weight in gold provided he weighed no more than a shade under 127·4 pounds.

Try the calculation youself. You will probably be surprised to find that you are worth your weight in gold. If you are not, you may be able to derive some consolation from the thought that if you went on a diet and lost a few pounds you might quite easily make it.

REFERENCES

Agricultural Research Service, *Home Economics Research Report*, No. 10 (1960).

Gary S. Becker, *Human Capital: A Theoretical and Empirical Analysis with Special Reference to Education* (New York: Columbia University Press, 1964).

Burton Weisbrod, 'The Valuation of Human Capital', *Journal of Political Economy*, Vol. LXIX, No. 5 (October 1961), pp. 425–36.

Part III

THE INTERNATIONAL
MONETARY CRISIS

Chapter 11

The International Monetary Crisis, 1969*

Among the academic experts who specialize in the study of the international monetary system, it has been known for over a decade that that system was approaching a liquidity crisis; that it could not long survive in its existing form. The officials concerned with the actual operation of the system came tardily to accept the judgement, and to work out plans for the necessary reform of the system. But their progress was too slow to keep pace with the economic dynamics of international monetary crisis. Almost immediately after agreement had been reached on a plan for the reform of the system – in August–September 1967 – the expected crisis broke. Triggered by the devaluation of sterling in November 1967, successive waves of speculation on a devaluation of the dollar in terms of gold led to massive outflows of gold from official reserves into private hands, with the result that in March 1968 the world's monetary authorities decided to sever the link between the official and the private gold markets. That decision put an end to the international monetary system of the post-Second World War period – the gold exchange standard based on the dollar as reserve currency – while leaving open the question of the direction in which the system would evolve thenceforward. That question involves the roles to be played in future by gold, dollars, and the newly invented international reserve asset called 'Special Drawing Rights'. Subsequently, a chain of developments associated basically with the undervaluation of the German mark, but sparked by the 'events' of May 1968 in France and leading through the 'Bonn crisis' of November 1968 – in which the

* Presented as the *Third Monash Economics Lecture* (September 8, 1969); reprinted from I. A. Macdougall and R. H. Snape (eds), *Studies in International Economics: Monash Conference Papers* (Amsterdam: North-Holland, 1970), Ch. 7, pp. 105–20.

Germans refused to appreciate and the French to devalue – to the speculation on an appreciation of the mark in May and to the actual devaluation of the franc in August 1969, have called expert attention to another major problem of the postwar international monetary system, the absence of sufficient flexibility of exchange rates.

My purpose in this chapter is to explain what has gone wrong with the international monetary system, in terms of general theoretical principles, and to discuss the alternative solutions that have been proposed for its problems. As a preliminary, I shall comment briefly on the nature of the present international monetary system, and the requirements that it must meet if its functioning is to promote rather than frustrate the achievement of desirable objectives in the world economy.

The present international monetary system is a system of fixed rates of exchange among national currencies. Such a system, ideally at least, provides for the world economy the same advantages as the establishment of a single national currency provides for the individual national economy – very broadly, the facilitation of transactions across local or regional boundaries. For this reason, the fixed exchange-rate system is generally regarded as conducive to the maintenance of a liberal international economic order and the promotion of world economic welfare and economic growth. But it can only serve these objectives if the maintenance of fixed exchange rates is possible, consistently with the maintenance of liberal national economic policies with respect to international trade and payments. If instead fixed rates can be maintained only by widespread interventions in international transactions, the appearance of world economic integration is bought at the expense of the reality. Thus, to serve its intended functions a fixed rate system must meet further requirements which will permit the preservation of liberal international economic policies. Specifically, a fixed rate system must provide adequate international liquidity, include an effective mechanism of international adjustment, and command confidence in the stability of the international values of the major currencies.

A nation which adheres to the fixed exchange-rate system obliges itself to stabilize the value of its currency in the foreign-exchange market by offsetting private excess supplies of or demand for its currency in the market by purchases or sales of its currency. For this to be possible, there must exist some kind of international money that it can use to purchase excess supplies of its own currency from foreigners, and that it will accept in exchange for sales of its own currency to foreigners. Each nation will wish to carry a normal stock of this international money in its international monetary reserves, against the risk of fluctuations in its balance of payments. Moreover, this desired stock of international reserves will grow over time as the national economy and its international transactions grow. The international monetary system must provide a global level of internationally acceptable and usable money, and/or credit convertible into money – 'international liquidity' – to satisfy the demands of the nations in the system at any time, and a rate of growth of international liquidity over time sufficient to meet the growth of demand resulting from world economic expansion. If it fails to do so, there will be deflationary pressures on world prices and money incomes, as nations compete for the scarce global stock of reserves and the increments to it. In the contemporary world, nations will seek to avoid deflationary pressures by resorting to interventions in international trade and payments to avert losses of international reserves.

No finite amount of international reserves in a country's possession however, will enable a country indefinitely to spend internationally more than it takes in, i.e. to run a continuing balance-of-payments deficit. Nor will any finite stock of reserves held by other countries permit one country to run an indefinitely sustained balance-of-payments surplus. Consequently, if countries are not to be driven into attempting to remedy balance-of-payments disequilibria by interventions in international trade and payments, there must exist some mechanism for adjusting such disequilibria, i.e. for restoring payments balance for the initially deficit and surplus countries. This involves both the adjustment of a country's aggregate demand for real resources to its productive capacity, and the adjustment of its domestic price level relative to the world price level so that its purchases from abroad are balanced by its sales abroad.

Within certain limits, liquidity and adjustment are clearly substitutable requirements of a well-functioning international monetary system. More liquidity is a substitute for more effective and speedy adjustment; and more rapid growth of liquidity is a substitute for more rapid improvement of the efficiency of the adjustment mechanism. (This consideration has to be qualified, however, by recognition that it relates to liquidity in real terms, and that more liquidity in nominal terms may be dissipated by world price inflation.)

The third requirement, confidence in the stability of the international values of the major currencies, clearly is something that cannot be fully controlled by international monetary arrangements, since confidence may be strongly affected by national political developments. However, this requirement would be largely fulfilled, or at least failures of confidence could be readily contained, if the system provided an adequate combination of liquidity provision and adjustment mechanism. Conversely, inadequacies of the system with respect to liquidity and adjustment are certain to provoke crises of confidence in individual currencies.

These are the three requirements of a well-functioning international monetary system of the fixed exchange-rate type. As already mentioned, the post-Second World War system has been progressively failing to meet them. It has increasingly manifested problems under all three heads: the technical literature has pretty well agreed on a classification of the problems of the system as 'the liquidity problem', 'the adjustment problem' and 'the confidence problem'.

That the system has come to manifest these problems increasingly in the 1960s is a paradox of modern economic history, and an ironic reflection on man's ambitions for economic and social engineering through planned institutional reform. For these very problems were responsible for the collapse of the interwar gold exchange standard, reconstructed after the First World War in imitation of the nineteenth century gold standard; and it was the deliberate intention of the designers of the International Monetary Fund, the centrepiece of the post-Second World War international monetary system, to establish a system that would be proof against the fatal flaws of the interwar system.

The international monetary collapse of the interwar system in the 1930s involved a liquidity problem – a growing shortage of gold, the basic reserve of the system, and the use of the pound sterling, a chronically weak currency, as a substitute for gold; an unsolved and basic adjustment problem, resulting from the overvaluation of the pound sterling and the undervaluation of the French franc at the parities adopted for these currencies, and the inability of Britain in particular to adjust by the classical method of deflation; and a confidence problem manifested in the massive international flows of 'hot money' that attacked one major currency after another.

Under the IMF system, the liquidity problem was to be solved by supplementing national gold reserves by a pool of national currencies on which nations could draw for additional financing of deficits in exchange for their own currencies; in addition, provision was made for a general increase in the monetary price of gold, if this was agreed to be desirable. The adjustment problem was to be eased by permitting nations in 'fundamental disequilibrium' to alter the international values of their currencies by international agreement; a 'scarce-currency clause' – never in fact invoked – also permitted trade discrimination against chronic surplus countries. The confidence problem was to be dealt with by allowing nations to impose controls on international short-term capital movements; this provision has, however, been ineffective, because the significant disturbing short-term capital movements in recent years have taken the form of swings in normal commercial credits, not flights of idle balances.

Despite these well-thought-out provisions to avoid a recurrence of the problems of the interwar period, the same problems have re-emerged, although in an environment of general prosperity rather than deep depression. The only major difference, which parallels the conjunctural change, has been that whereas in the 1930s the United States was regarded as a threat to the system as a result of its chronic surplus position, in the 1960s the United States has come to be regarded, at least in Europe, as a threat because of its chronic deficit position. Why have the old problems re-emerged?

The main reason is to be found in the inadequacy of the provision through the International Monetary Fund to supplement gold with international credit facilities, and especially to provide for growth of international liquidity at a rate adequate to meet the needs of the expanding world economy. IMF drawing rights, as a form of international credit available only on conditions, are inferior in quality as international reserves to gold and to owned reserves in general. The initial quantity of them was fixed on a very cautious scale, and the real value of both gold reserves and initial drawing rights was more than halved by the postwar inflation of world prices; and subsequent increases in IMF quotas of drawing rights have failed to keep pace with the rapid postwar growth of international trade and payments.

Instead of being met by increases in international credit reserves provided through the International Monetary Fund, the needs of an expanding world economy for growing international reserves were met by a growth of holdings of particular national currencies (the 'reserve currencies') as substitutes for and supplements to gold reserves. Initially, British methods of war finance incidentally provided a stock of reserve currency in the form of the sterling balances. This was a one-shot contribution to international liquidity, since the problems of the British economy inhibited accumulation of further sterling balances, and in fact after the 1967 devaluation these balances started to be run down at a rate serious enough to require special international arrangements to consolidate the position. Far more important was the rapid growth in holdings of U.S. dollars by foreign central banks, which during the 1950s was a natural concomitant of the emergence of the United States as the dominant Western power in international economic and political relations. The emergence of the dollar as an international reserve currency, increasingly important in relation to gold, meant the re-establishment of the gold exchange standard that had developed in the 1920s and foundered in the 1930s; it was consequently not surprising that the same problems reappeared. There was, however, one fundamental difference that both accounts for the failure of the gloomier predictions of another international monetary collapse to come true, and has created options for the contemporary world that did not exist in the interwar period: the shift from the pound to the dollar as the reserve currency meant a shift from a declining to a dominating power, both industrially and in terms of importance in international economic and political affairs.

Consider first the problem of confidence. Any system of fixed exchange rates is vulnerable to crises of confidence in a particular currency, if there exists any possibility that the exchange rate of that currency may be changed. (In this connection, the IMF provision for changes in exchange rates in cases of 'fundamental disequilibrium' has greatly aggravated the confidence problem that it was intended to help to control.) It is important here to distinguish between crises of private confidence, and crises of central bank confidence, in the currency. Private speculation can produce a massive outflow of funds from a country; but the resulting reserve loss and need for crisis action can be avoided if foreign central banks are willing to 'recycle' the funds they receive into credits to the country in difficulty. This they were not willing to do in the 1930s; but in the course of the past decade, central bank co-operation has developed to the point where the confidence problem, insofar as particular national currencies other than the reserve currency are concerned, can probably be regarded as being under fairly secure control. Special problems arise under a gold exchange standard, however, with respect to confidence in the reserve currency.

In the first place, if private individuals can obtain gold directly or indirectly from the international monetary authorities at the fixed official price, any loss of confidence on their part in the ability of the reserve currency country to maintain its exchange rate will lead to speculation on a rise in the price of gold. This speculation will tend to drain gold from international monetary reserves, and this in turn may further disturb both private and official confidence in the reserve currency. Under the 'gold-pool' arrangements adopted after the gold flurry of autumn 1960, private speculators could buy official gold indirectly through the private gold markets; and it was the drain of official gold into private speculators's hands that precipitated the gold crisis of March 1968 and the termination of the 'gold pool'. Secondly, while the central banks of the non-reserve-currency countries may be willing enough, especially under pressure from the reserve-currency countries, to co-operate in 'bailing out' one of their number hit by a speculative private capital outflow, co-operation in the case of a run on the reserve currency itself is likely to be strained by jealousy of the world influence apparently conveyed on a country by the reserve-currency role, and by resentment of the apparent ability of the reserve-currency country to continue to run deficits with impunity. These strains are exacerbated by the recognition – which distinguishes the contemporary situation from the 1930s – that the rest cannot in the last resort afford a collapse of the reserve currency; all they can do is to make life difficult for the reserve-currency country.

The special problems of confidence with respect to the reserve currency derive their thrust from the fact that, by virtue of its own inherent dynamics, the gold exchange standard must inevitably approach a liquidity crisis. For this there are two reasons, analytically independent but in practice intertwined: the dynamics of gold supply and demand, and the dynamics of the reserve-currency role.

As regards gold, the gold exchange standard is a means of economizing on gold and permitting total international reserves, and the international transactions they support, to grow faster than the total gold stock. The increasing use of dollars as reserves in the postwar period has permitted an unprecedented period of world economic growth and trade liberalization, buoyed up by a mild inflationary trend of world prices. But general world growth implies growing private demands for gold for industrial, artistic, and 'traditional hoarding' purposes, while inflation makes gold both cheaper to use and less profitable to produce. Hence the non-monetary demand will creep up on the new production, and the process in its later stages will be accelerated by speculation that the monetary authorities will react by raising the price of gold. The trend and the speculation will cause a reversal in the position of the monetary authorities in relation to gold. From being net buyers they will become net sellers, a position actually reached in 1965. They then face a dilemma: either to sell while their stocks last, which means deliberately abandoning gold as the ultimate reserve of the system and necessitates the development of a credit substitute, or to restore the *status quo ante* by raising the price of gold sufficiently to generate a continuing net inflow of gold into official monetary reserves. When the crunch came in March 1968, the United States induced the other major countries to adopt a compromise solution – neither to sell nor to buy gold in the private market – that left the future resolution of the role of gold open and in doubt.

As regards the role of the reserve currency, it is an arithmetical truism that if international reserves are to grow faster than gold reserves, holdings of the reserve currency must grow faster than total reserves and *pro tanto* than gold reserves. Further, unless the non-reserve-currency countries are prepared actually to reduce their gold holdings over time, the gold reserves of the reserve-currency country must fall relative to its liabilities, with the liabilities ultimately and progressively exceeding the gold reserves backing them. This deterioration of the international liquidity position of the reserve-currency country must ultimately raise questions of confidence in its ability to maintain its exchange rate, and induce increasing reluctance on the part of the non-reserve-currency countries to accumulate further holdings of the reserve currency. Again the system arrives at a dilemma – actually a trilemma, of which two alternatives are versions of one horn of the gold dilemma, resort to international credit money instead of a rise in the price of gold. The alternatives in this case are to raise the price of gold sufficiently for new monetary gold to supply the need for expanding international liquidity; to accept the reserve currency as the international monetary standard in place of gold, deliberately easing gold out of the system; and to devise a new international credit money to substitute for, supplement, and gradually replace both gold and the reserve currency. The choice, in short, is between gold, dollars, and a new international credit money as the basis of the system.

American policy has been adamantly opposed to any suggestion that the price of gold should be raised; the Europeans have been increasingly restive under the obligations to accept and hold U.S. dollars, especially since the Vietnam War induced inflation in the United States beginning in 1965. The third alternative, creation of a new genuinely international reserve asset, was agreed on as necessary as long ago as 1963. But negotiations were long protracted by disagreement between the Americans and the Europeans over whether the new asset should be created immediately, or only after the U.S. deficit had been eliminated. On the theory just outlined, the continuation of the U.S. deficit was the necessary counterpart of the growth of demand for international reserves in the face of inadequate additions to monetary gold stocks, and could not be eliminated without the creation of an alternative asset to dollars as a substitute for gold, so that the Europeans' insistence on ending the deficit before creating the new asset was self-contradictory. Be that as it may, agreement on creation of a new asset was not reached until 1967, by which point it was too late for the new asset to be introduced in an orderly fashion without a crisis-induced change in the system.

The Special Drawing Rights plan is extremely complicated in detail, reflecting the tortuous process of negotiation that led up to it.

But in principle it is fairly simple. Essentially, the nations will create and distribute among themselves IOUs which they are pledged to accept from each other in settlement of balance-of-payments deficits, subject to a 'reconstitution' or repayment provision. In principle the plan is an enormous step forwards in rationality, since it is based on the recognition that at the international monetary level what matters is the acceptability of the asset as international money, and that international money does not require sound commercial assets behind it as do the deposits of an ordinary commercial bank. But as a solution to the international liquidity problem, the SDRs raise some difficult problems. First, when the scheme was initially agreed many experts feared that SDRs would not be created in sufficient quantity to be of real help; that fear has been largely allayed by the fact that the subsequently agreed initial scale of creation of SDRs will be rather generous. Second, the SDRs have been designed with the intention of their being as good as gold but not as attractive as dollars; this raises the so-called 'problem of coexistence', i.e. of the continued survival of all three reserve assets as desirable forms of international reserves. Third, the SDRs carry a gold guarantee, which keeps open the possibility of a rise in the price of gold and raises the question of whether SDRs will not become frozen into countries' reserve holdings because countries other than the United States will prefer to finance deficits with dollars (or possibly even gold).

Because of these prospective problems, most academic experts regard the SDR plan as inadequate to the solution of the international liquidity problem. As the next step, they recommend various plans the common feature of which is to consolidate the three international reserve assets into a single international credit money, the quantity of which would be internationally controlled. The logical end of this line of reasoning would be the equivalent of the establishment of a world central bank, a central bank of central banks, which would provide for the growth of the international money supply in the same way as a national central bank provides for the growth of the national money supply.

The problem with this solution is that it goes very far beyond the degree of international collaboration that national monetary authorities have so far been able to achieve in the operation of the international monetary system. The issues that would have to be resolved – especially the balancing of the objectives of high employment and price stability against each other – are precisely those on which nations have been most divided in the recent past. There is the further problem that the International Monetary Fund has been tarred with the brush of undue subservience to U.S. objectives, and that a nominally international monetary authority with greater powers would be subject to similar suspicion.

This implies that the other two alternatives – a rise in the monetary price of gold, and the adoption of the U.S. dollar standard – cannot as yet be ruled beyond the bounds of possibility.

As regards a rise in the price of gold, the strongest arguments for it concern on the one hand the advantages of the 'anonymity' of gold and the freedom of action that an adequate gold reserve gives to its possessor, and on the other hand, the strains that have arisen in international economic relations under the pressure to co-operate to preserve the system in recent years. In particular, the use of a national currency as an international reserve gives the reserve-currency country considerable powers of blackmail over the holders of that currency, while an international credit money raises the problem for the small countries of domination of the system by the large countries and by the struggle for power among them. Further, it should be remarked that the economic arguments against raising the price of gold turn out on inspection to be rather weak: the associated 'gift' to Russia would be a trivial side effect, while it is debatable whether the parallel 'gift' to South Africa would benefit more the white or the black South Africans; the alleged inflationary effects could be contained by appropriate sterilization policies; and the opposition of the U.S. Congress to an increase in the dollar price of gold could probably be out-manoeuvred by an adroit president.

The other alternative is explicit adoption of the U.S. dollar as the international monetary standard. While this would be anathema, at least intellectually, in many parts of the world, the severance of the official from the private gold markets in March 1968 has in fact put the Western world on a *de facto* U.S. dollar standard; and every month that passes – and especially every international monetary crisis that passes in which the private gold market does not play a significant part – helps to consolidate the *de facto* position. Moreover, as C. P. Kindleberger in particular has been arguing recently, the dollar has the advantage over both gold and SDRs of being a real and privately convenient and familiar international money. Further, the 'profit' allegedly gained by the United States from the international use of the dollar is largely illusory; it tends to be eroded by interest-rate competition among U.S. banks for foreign deposits, and also by the competition of Eurodollars (dollar-denominated deposits in non-U.S.-resident banks) with dollars provided by the U.S. banking system. Finally, the March 1968 gold crisis has put the United States in the position of being able to assert the primacy of the dollar if it so desires, and to force the rest of the world to make the uncomfortable decision between pegging to the dollar and adopting a flexible exchange rate *vis-à-vis* the dollar: for all the United States has to do is to declare the dollar inconvertible into gold at $35.00 an ounce for official foreign holders of dollars, since it is already inconvertible at that price for private holders of dollars.

To sum up the argument so far, there are still three directions in which the international monetary system could possibly evolve: international credit money, the dollar standard, and a rise in the price of gold. Of the three, a rise in the price of gold seems at present the least likely, because since March 1968 the private market in gold has ceased to exercise a significant influence on the international monetary system, and SDRs will soon provide a slightly superior asset to gold for those countries that continue to hanker after gold. Whether SDRs, and more elaborate forms of international credit money yet to be invented, will replace the dollar, or merely serve as a subsidiary asset for the nervous few, is the more interesting question about the near future of the international monetary system.

My analysis up to this point has been concerned with the liquidity problem of the fixed exchange-rate system, and the alternative ways of solving it. There has, however, always been an academically influential school of thought in favour of the contrary system of flexible exchange rates. For the most part, this school has been dismissed as hopelessly impractical by financial and commercial men of affairs. It has, however, recently been gaining a hearing, in consequence of concern about the second major problem of the international monetary system – the adjustment problem.

Under a regime of rigidly fixed exchange rates, such as the theoretical gold standard, countries have no choice but to keep their levels of aggregate demand in line with their productive capacities and their price levels competitive with the world price level. As is well-known, this implies deflation in deficit countries, and inflation in surplus countries. Countries are usually, however, averse to both marked deflation and marked inflation, and as a result of both experience and theoretical developments since the 1930s, they have learned both how to control these problems and how to stave off the balance-of-payments consequences of avoiding the discipline of the fixed rate system, for significant periods of time. Consequently, the traditional mechanism of adjustment through deficit-country deflation and surplus-country inflation has become seriously impaired. It has become a 'mechanism of reluctant adjustment'.

The IMF system was intended to provide an escape from such conflicts between internal and external stability, and to give primacy to internal stability, by allowing agreed exchange rate changes in cases of 'fundamental disequilibrium'. But, for reasons which have their roots in the circumstances of the 1949 devaluations, countries have become extremely reluctant to resort to this solution, largely for political reasons. The exchange value of the currency has become a political symbol, devaluation a stigma of national disgrace and defeat, and appreciation a symbol of surrender to pressure from other countries. In the case of the dollar (and for a period for sterling), the assumed obligations to foreign holders of the reserve currency, and the possibility of widespread foreign retaliation against devaluation, provided extra arguments against devaluation. The key position of the dollar in the system has meant that the dollar cannot be devalued; other currencies must do the adjusting in relation to the dollar, a necessity which is more acceptable to the Americans than to others. The disturbance caused by political reluctance to change exchange rates has become obvious in recent years with the long delay in the devaluation of sterling, the delay in the French devaluation made inevitable by the events of May 1968, and the persistent refusal of the Germans to appreciate the mark despite its evident undervaluation, dramatized by the abortive Bonn crisis of November 1968. In consequence, the experts have become interested in the possibility of modifying the political element in exchange rate change by introducing more automaticity of exchange rate adjustment in the fixed rate system.

Before discussing these proposals, it is appropriate to comment on the methods to which countries have resorted in the attempt to achieve balance-of-payments adjustment, as a result of their reluctance to use either the classical deflation–inflation mechanism or the IMF exchange-rate change mechanism. These methods include the subsidization of exports through tax reliefs and the restriction of imports through various subtle means; measures to restrict private foreign investment by residents and encourage inward investment by foreigners; the tying of foreign aid and discrimination in favour of domestic suppliers in government procurement; and special inter-governmental financial transactions designed to provide statistical camouflage for basic deficits and surpluses. Some of these measures are more accurately describable as 'financing' measures rather than 'adjustment' measures, since they do little or nothing to change the real situation of the economy. Others can only be regarded as adjustment policies in the context of a naive partial-equilibrium approach, or even merely arithmetical approach, to the problem of balance-of-payments adjustment. Consider, for example, export subsidies, which on the face of the matter should help to improve the balance of payments; if nothing is done to restrain aggregate demand, resources drawn into export production are likely to be replaced directly or indirectly by additional imports, with negligible overall effect on the balance of payments, the subsidies being vitiated by a general rise in domestic factor prices. Other apparently effective methods are likely in the same way simply to shift the manifestation of the underlying deficit from one item to another in the balance-of-payments accounts.

The fundamental objection to these methods of so-called balance-of-payments adjustment is that they ignore what may be termed the monetary implications of balance-of-payments disequilibrium. This is why, to the continued surprise of their proponents, these methods are rarely if ever successful in achieving balance-of-payments adjustment. Balance-of-payments disequilibrium has two monetary aspects, according to whether one is considering the position of a relatively small country in the system, or the system as a whole.

From the viewpoint of an individual country, a deficit (on a monetary interpretation) represents an attempt by residents to dispose of unwanted domestic money by spending it. To cure the deficit it is necessary to restrict the domestic money supply to the point where residents are attempting to acquire additional money by increasing export sales or reducing import purchases. Failure to appreciate this point is probably an important factor in the explanation of the long-delayed impact of the 1967 sterling devaluation. Under pressure from the International Monetary Fund, the British are now adopting a 'monetarist' approach to balance-of-payments policy.

From the viewpoint of the system as a whole, the analysis of the liquidity problem presented earlier in this chapter suggests that, so long as there is no international source – be it gold production or an international credit institution – providing regularly increasing international liquidity in accordance with the requirements of world economic growth, some country or countries will have to run deficits to accommodate the liquidity demands of the others. Specifically, the system itself has demanded a U.S. deficit during the 1960s to provide the rest of the world with reserves. Viewed in this context, U.S. balance-of-payments policies have been a fruitless endeavour, and moreover one with deleterious effects on the integration and efficient growth of the world economy. The choice is either to accept the deficits and the dollar standard, or to provide additional reserves through a different tap – the gold price, or international credit money.

These points have an important bearing on the proposals recently advanced for attaining more automatic flexibility of exchange rates. First, for the individual country more flexibility would only provide more elbow-room; short of a move to a fully floating exchange rate, a country would still be obliged to be disciplined in its domestic policy by the requirements of adherence to the system. Second, for the system as a whole, the usefulness of additional flexibility is conditional on the solution of the liquidity problem; otherwise, exchange rates are likely to be rapidly pushed to and thereafter kept at the limits of whatever additional flexibility is allowed.

Turning to the specific proposals, there are two chief contenders: the 'wider-band' proposal and the 'crawling-peg' proposal. At present, while currencies have par values fixed in terms of gold, market exchange rates can move within a narrow band (1 per cent maximum, in practice less) on each side of the parity. Within this band, rates are freely flexible. The band proposal is to widen the band to, say, 5 per cent (most advocates actually favour a smaller percentage) on each side of the currency's value in dollars, thus permitting a maximum of automatic appreciation or depreciation *vis-à-vis* the dollar of 10 per cent and *vis-à-vis* other currencies of 20 per cent. Under the 'crawling-peg' proposal, the band might or might not be widened; the essential change would be to allow the parity itself to be adjusted gradually over time, in response to experience of the relation of the parity to the actual or market rate. This could be accomplished either by giving countries the right to change their par values by discretion, subject to a maximum percentage change per year, or by fixing the par value each day or week as an average of the actual market rates prevailing over some past period, in which case the parity would automatically drift up or down in response to the currency's strength or weakness in the market.

These two proposals are aimed at rather different problems. The wider-band proposal is designed to give more flexibility in face of short-run disturbances such as speculative runs on a currency that may be expected to reverse themselves. The crawling-peg proposal is designed to accommodate persistent – but not very large – discrepancies among national rates of price inflation produced by differences in national balancing of the employment and price-stability objectives of economic policy. Since the working of the system has been characterized by both types of problem, a combination of wider band and crawling peg suggests itself as the optimum solution. Even so, as long as the amount of exchange rate change that could occur in a given period is constrained, the system would still be exposed to the risk of situations arising in which a country's par value will have to be changed by a substantial amount, and the associated problems of confidence and speculation.

While the experience of the mid 1960s suggests the desirability of greater automaticity of exchange rate adjustment, there remains a question of whether such a change would be beneficial in the longer run. On the one hand it can be argued that the successful devaluation of the franc in August 1969, and in certain respects the devaluation of sterling in November 1967, show that the present IMF system is less troublesomely rigid than it appears to be, and that the problem is one of political will and of sophistication rather than of institutional rigidity. On the other hand, it can be argued that the present system, with all its faults and shortcomings, is more conducive to the preservation and extension of an integrated world economy than would be a system that allowed more national autonomy with respect to exchange rates. It has been also argued by some that greater exchange rate flexibility would be self-defeating in the long run, because it would simply encourage the already spreading use of the dollar as the international unit of account and transactions currency.

To summarize, I have attempted in this chapter to explain the major problems of the international monetary system – liquidity, adjustment, and confidence – and to discuss the alternatives that now confront the system. These are various paths forwards out of the current crisis; which ones will be ultimately adopted remains to be determined. In this area, the tools of rational economic analysis can only illuminate the issues; ultimately, politics has to resolve them.

Chapter 12

Problems of European
Monetary Union*

The rapid development of the commitment of the six members of the European Economic Community to the establishment of a common currency as the next essential step in the evolution towards European economic and political integration is in some ways surprising, given the recent troubles of the economic communities. But it is understandable, and can indeed be viewed as virtually inevitable, in the light of the political dynamics of relations within the Community and between the Community and the United States.

Within the Community, the disruption of previously agreed arrangements by the events leading up to and including the devaluation of the franc and the appreciation of the mark in 1969, obviously required a major effort at patching up the community and trying to arrange matters so that the events of 1969 could not be repeated. Apart from this holding operation, the strategy of the proponents of European political union has always been to try to persuade the governments to accept a seemingly rather innocuous economic objective, symbolic of unity, in the hope that acceptance of the commitment would force them to take the ancillary steps towards economic unification, and especially harmonization of economic policies, that would pave the way for political unification. Before the events of 1968–69, it was widely asserted by the Europeans that the adoption of the Common Agricultural Policy ruled out forever any change in the rates of exchange among the European currencies. This assertion assumed that the European governments would be forced, by commitment to the Common Agricultural Policy, to follow domestic policies consistent with the maintenance of rigid

* Reprinted from *Euromoney*, Vol. 2, No. 11 (April 1971), pp. 39–43.

exchange rates. In fact, persistent German efforts to curb inflation on the one hand, and General de Gaulle's concession of wage rises inconsistent with the maintenance of the value of the franc as a result of the events of May 1968 on the other, made changes in the exchange values of the franc and the mark, in the long run, inevitable. When the chips were down, it was the Common Agricultural Policy and not the members' autonomy in domestic policy that had to give way. Having failed once, the Europeans were naturally inclined, not to question their concept of effective strategy, but to try the same strategy again on an altogether more ambitious scale. If the commitment to the Common Agricultural Policy was not enough to ensure a commitment to fixed exchange rates and, therefore, to the policy harmonization required to maintain fixed exchange rates, the members had to be committed directly and explicitly to the maintenance of fixed exchange rates, to induce them to accept the need for policy harmonization and therefore for the economic prerequisites to political unification. As before, the strategy rests on the belief that the sacrifice of an autonomous economic policy can be forced by a sufficiently strong political commitment to achieving an ideological symbol of political unity.

The other political dynamics concerns the relation between Europe and the United States in the international monetary system. Until 1965, the Six had been gradually accepting the idea that the United States had a special central position in the international monetary system, which obliged it to move cautiously in its efforts to correct its balance-of-payments deficit. The escalation of the war in Vietnam, without the necessary steps to finance it by increased domestic taxation, meant inflation in the United States that would inevitably spread to the rest of the fixed exchange rate world via enlarged U.S. balance-of-payments deficits, and face Europe, in particular, with the choice between accepting the inflation and protecting itself against it by appreciating its currencies against the dollar. In addition, there was the growing private use of the U.S. dollar in international trade and finance, and European fears of dollar imperialism or dollar domination, expressed in complaints about the restriction of national monetary autonomy by the growth of the Eurodollar market, and about Americans buying us out with our own money. There has been little recognition in Europe that the Common Market tariff itself encourages American firms to establish production facilities in Europe rather than export to the European market from the United States, or that the efforts of European central banks to preserve monetary autonomy, by imposing restrictions on the freedom of their banks to engage in international transactions, has itself encouraged efforts by those banks to circumvent national restrictions in the search for the profits of financial business on a Europe-wide scale through the development of the Eurodollar and Eurobond markets. In any case, it has been obvious that the main obstacle to European monetary independence in relation to the dollar has been the unwillingness or inability of individual European countries to take independent action, owing to their interdependence. The obvious answer, at least to those who think in political terms, would be to establish a single European currency that could rival the dollar as an instrument of private international trade and payments, and whose exchange value in relation to the dollar could be changed by central decisions which would not raise the issues of individual national costs and benefits, especially in relation to other European countries, that now inhibit European resistance to inflationary pressures emanating from the United States.

These two motivations towards the establishment of a common European currency, however, are in sharp inconsistency with one another. The strategy of inducing acceptance of the symbolic goal of a common currency as a means of forcing policy harmonization and eventually the preconditions of political union, assumes that the necessary preconditions for unified political decisions have not yet been established, but need to be secured by a species of political chicanery. The desire to confront the dollar with a rival currency of comparable power assumes that political agreement on both this objective and the means of achieving it already exist, and needs only to be suitably organized through supra-national institutions.

The danger in this conflict of assumptions is that Europe will stall somewhere on the way to monetary union, and so pave the way for the international dominance of the U.S. dollar. This would be a result ironic in the extreme, for since the pound, franc and mark crises of 1967–69 the United States and other leading countries have come to recognize the problems resulting from excessive rigidity of exchange rates in the present international monetary system, and have been discussing greater flexibility of exchange rates as a means of avoiding these problems. This has involved a willingness of the United States to abnegate the power in the system which the unwillingness of other countries to change their exchange rates now gives it. And the commitment of the European countries to greater rigidity in the form of the establishment of a common currency threatens to forestall that development without putting anything in its place.

The history of the evolution of the common-currency objective may be briefly described as follows. It began with the Barre Plan of February 1969, proposed by the Commission to the member states, and concerned with the co-ordination of members' economic policies and with monetary co-operation. Its starting point was the difficulties posed for the Common Agricultural Policy in particular, and trade relations among members in general, by the measures taken by Germany and France in 1968 to avoid exchange rate changes. Its main recommendations were that members should work out possible inconsistencies among their medium-term objectives with respect to growth and inflation, co-ordinate their current economic and financial policies to forestall short-term external imbalances, consult with one another prior to the final adoption of economic policy measures, and establish facilities for short-term and medium-term monetary assistance within the E.E.C. As a result of the Hague Summit Conference of December 1969, the meeting of the Council of Ministers of January 1970, and the meeting of E.E.C. Finance Ministers of February 1970, substantial parts of the Barre Plan were approved. The Council of Ministers accepted the need for increased monetary co-operation and policy consultation; and the Community's central banks set up arrangements to provide $2 billion of credit facilities for the assistance of members in balance-of-payments deficit.

In addition, the Werner Committee was set up to pursue the subject further. Its interim report of May 1970 led to agreement by members not to widen the exchange margins among their currencies – a decision which in effect blocked further progress towards increased exchange flexibility in the international monetary system as a whole. Its final report, on October 8, 1970, presented a plan for complete monetary union, and with it economic union, to be established by the end of the 1970s. The first stage of the Werner Plan, to be completed in three years, called for the establishment of free convertibility among the six currencies; rigid and irrevocable fixation of the parties of the currencies with one another; establishment if possible of a single Community currency – if national currencies were retained, their existence should have no economic significance; centralization of budgetary and monetary policy at the Community level; the adoption of a common external monetary policy; complete integration of members' capital markets by appropriate fiscal and institutional changes; and the establishment of regional policies determined at the Community level. This programme would require the establishment of two new supra-national institutions: a centre of decision for economic policy – a Community Ministry for Economic Policy, responsible to the European Parliament – and a Community system for central banks, involving co-ordination of exchange-market interventions, the pooling of international reserves, the adoption of a common representative unit, and the narrowing to zero of the margins of market exchange rate variations around the official parities.

This plan was not, however, unanimously accepted. At the Council of Ministers' meeting in December 1970, Germany and Holland argued that it was pointless to narrow the bands for exchange rate variation unless at the same time common institutions were established, whereas France refused to surrender the economic sovereignty such common institutions would demand. Nevertheless, the Werner Plan is by now firmly established in the thinking of the Community, most importantly as regards the terms on which new members may join the group.

This chapter discusses three subjects: the basic economics of fixed exchange rates among the members of a free-trade arrangement, of which the extreme case is a common currency in an economic union; the implications of such a common currency for the economic policy autonomy of the member countries; and the implications of the effort to establish a common European currency for the evolution of the international monetary system.

The basic economics involve the long-standing controversy over fixed versus flexible exchange rates, and the more recent formulation of that issue in terms of the economics of optimum currency areas.

Put very briefly, the basic argument for fixed exchange rates is the advantage of the equivalent of a common currency in promoting international competition and promoting international economic integration. The basic argument for flexible exchange rates, on the other hand, is to give countries an extra degree of freedom of domestic economic policy relative to other countries, and so reduce the pressures to intervene in international trade and payments that are likely to arise in a fixed rate system as a consequence of divergent domestic developments or policies. The issue is essentially empirical: will the advantages of fixed rates outweigh the disadvantages of loss of autonomy in economic policy, or not, in any particular case? The theory of optimum currency areas poses this question in terms of the economic characteristics of the regions of a country, or the members of a fixed exchange-rate area, that will enable a common currency to function smoothly. Analysis of the required characteristics has focused on two rather different criteria, according to whether freedom of trade or autonomy of member policies has been the starting point of the analysis. Freedom of trade focuses attention on structural characteristics that make adjustment to economic change in the face of a commitment to a fixed exchange rate difficult or easy, and suggests that mobility of factors of production among the regions of the currency area or diversity of economic activity within each region or both is conducive to beneficial participation in a common-currency area. Autonomy of national economic policies focuses attention on the harmoniousness or otherwise of national economic policy objectives, and suggests that a common-currency area requires homogeneity of attitudes in particular towards the trade-off between unemployment and inflation.

In the context of the European economic communities, the question is whether the objective of economic integration is best served by the adoption of a common currency. The advocates of a European currency assume that there is only one possible answer to that question; but their argument rests on analogy with existing national states rather than on economic analysis of the problem. That problem is whether the economic advantages of the free movement of goods and factors of production within an economic union are most likely to be secured by this or by another of the alternative

317

exchange rate arrangements available. There are three main alternatives that might be employed.

The first is a system of floating exchange rates among member currencies. This alternative was recommended over a decade ago, in connection with the European Free Trade Area proposal, by James Meade. This is the proper policy if member countries want the advantages of freedom of trade but have divergent policy objectives with respect to inflation, unemployment and economic growth, because by ensuring automatic balance-of-payments equilibrium it enables the members to pursue those objectives without obliging them to choose between sacrificing one or more of the objectives and imposing restrictions on their international trade and payments. The objections to floating exchange rates are founded either on misunderstanding of the economic logic or on misinterpretation of the facts of experience; but this is not a subject that can be elaborated on here.

The second alternative is the present international monetary system, under which exchange rates are normally fixed but the parities can be changed in cases of fundamental disequilibrium. This system is appropriate if members are in broad harmony on policy objectives, but occasionally domestic or international developments or errors of domestic policy make an existing exchange rate inappropriate. The events of May 1968 in France are an example of the kind of development for which this system is appropriate; the difference between France and Germany in the determination of their political resistance to inflation would be coped with more effectively by a floating rate system.

The chief European objection to this system stems from the Common Agricultural Policy, the argument is that changes in exchange rates among members confer a competitive advantage or impose a competitive disadvantage on one nation's farmers in competition with the farmers of other nations. This argument, however, is fallacious. If inflation is proceeding more rapidly in one member than in another, its farmers are being put at a steadily increasing competitive disadvantage by rising costs in conjunction with fixed product prices, and exchange rate adjustment simply restores the lost initial equality of competitive conditions. Objection should be made, not to exchange rate adjustment *per se*, but to making exchange rate adjustments by large and infrequent changes, which allows the loss of initial competitive parity to proceed gradually and virtually imperceptibly, and then corrects for it by arbitrary and substantial changes in relative competitive position. A floating exchange rate system would cope with this problem far more readily and satisfactorily.

The third alternative is completely rigid exchange rates among member currencies, or a common currency. This assumes both that members can agree on a common policy with respect to inflation, unemployment and growth, and that they will live with the consequences of any adverse economic developments or errors in economic-policy formation. This the members of the Community, on the evidence of experience in the past few years, have not been willing to do. Instead, they have shown themselves willing to intervene in freedom of trade and payments within the Community in order to protect their domestic-policy autonomy – notably in the measures taken by France and Germany to stave off devaluation and revaluation respectively. The Werner Report places its faith in the proposition that, with sufficient political determination, a common currency can be established; the evidence is that the political determination is to preserve and not subordinate domestic-policy autonomy.

The central point is that an economic union can obtain the benefits of free trade and factor movements under a variety of exchange rate arrangements, and that which one is appropriate depends on the circumstances and objectives of the membership. A common money is an outward symbol of, but not a prerequisite for, effective economic integration. If it could be established, it would undoubtedly promote economic integration by making commercial calculations easier throughout the market area; but the advantage of this would depend on prior effective agreement to harmonize monetary and fiscal policies. The symbol is not the reality. If the prior agreement did not exist, or existed subject to reservations in case of conflict between national and community interests, the commitment to a common currency would create tensions among the members, and encourage resort to policies employing interventions in the freedom of trade and factor movements among the members.

As already mentioned, the hope of the Europeans is that, by securing prior commitment to the objective of establishing a common currency – which has the twin appeals of symbolizing European unity and permitting resistance to the domination of the American dollar – they will be able to persuade or cajole the members of the Community into the adoption of central co-ordination of monetary and financial policies and hence bring them to a stage of economic integration at which political union will seem a small further step to take. The difficulty is that at some stage the member countries must definitely and irrevocably give up their domestic-policy autonomy in the fiscal and monetary fields. They must make an all-or-nothing choice. But the need for this choice can be disguised by the making of successive gestures towards it that involve little real cost or can be revoked if they come to do so. Thus little real sacrifice is involved in agreements to narrow the bands of exchange rate variation about parity, or to consult and communicate about national fiscal- and monetary-policy decisions. And commitments can be accepted in fair weather in the knowledge that a government always has the last-resort option of repudiating them in foul weather – as the fate of the Common Agricultural Policy testifies. One can flirt interminably with the idea of marriage, without ever actually sacrificing one's technical virginity.

To turn to the implications of a common European currency for the member countries, the main implication is the surrender of autonomy in monetary policy. There are two aspects of this. The first is that the institutional changes required to create a common monetary area and capital market will require individual countries to give up their present reliance on specific controls over their commercial banking systems to implement their monetary policies; competitive pressures and the need for policy co-ordination in a Community-wide financial system will force the gradual adoption of a homogeneous system of central bank monetary management. This will be a desirable development: there is an eccentric difference in European thinking between the production of goods, where competition is deemed to be beneficial, and the production of financial services, where competition is deemed to be antisocial and regulation desirable. The second aspect is the need to align national monetary policies with the requirements of a centralized Community policy. It is questionable how much sacrifice of autonomy this will entail:

the present degree of integration of world financial markets imposes severe constraints on the freedom of individual countries to pursue really independent monetary policies, and the different measures of detailed intervention favoured by the different national central banks appear more as means of preserving the symbolism of autonomous choice than as instruments of real independence. Whatever the truth may be, however, the individual national central banks will have to surrender whatever trappings and substance of autonomy they still possess, and become mere delegates to a central policy-making conference. This will be hard for the proud tradition of national central banking, with its ingrained belief in the superior wisdom of central bankers as compared with mere politically-selected and transient ministers of finance, to swallow.

A second implication, made much of in European thinking and in the Werner Report, is the need to subordinate fiscal autonomy to central control of national budgets. This emphasis seems overdrawn, and probably counter-productive in terms of achieving the objective of European monetary and eeonomic union, in the light of the observed roles of state and provincial governments in federal countries. In such countries, the regional governments have autonomy of fiscal policy; but that autonomy is constrained by the fact that the financing of deficits has to be obtained by borrowing in the national or international capital market on competitive terms, and cannot be provided by the creation of money. With a common European currency, the money supply would be centrally controlled and no national government could create money in its own favour; hence there would seem to be no need for central co-ordination of national fiscal policies. The perceived need for such co-ordination presumably stems from the assumption that the Community, like existing national governments, will, in fact, still have the option of resorting to inflationary finance. On that assumption, there will obviously be a need to apportion fair shares of the proceeds among the members of the group.

In the longer run, there are more fundamental implications of the adoption of a common European currency, implications derived from the theory of optimum currency areas. The centrally co-ordinated policies of the Community will have to be devised to serve the average or majority interests of the members; and this will involve conflicts of interest. As is well known from the experience of national states, a policy designed to serve the overall national interest is not necessarily beneficial to, and, indeed, may bear cruelly on, the residents of the constituent regions of the nation. Similarly, a Community economic policy could bear severely on the welfare of an individual member nation. There is likely to be a national analogue to the existing regional problem within nations, in a Community currency area. Maintenance of overall balance in the Community's balance of payments with the outside world, or (with adequate flexibility of the exchange rate against the outside world) implementation of the monetary and fiscal policies required to achieve the desired Community trade-off between inflation and unemployment, may well mean that some member nations prosper while others suffer from chronic stagnation. If nothing is done in compensation, there will be pressure for emigration of labour and capital from the stagnant to the prospering regions (nations). Within existing nations, compensation is offered in the form of regional development policies but these policies have been of very questionable success. It is even more questionable whether Community-level policies would be capable of resisting the competitive pressures for the concentration of resources in the more prosperous nations and regions of nations.

This, incidentally, is the basis for one of the major fears of the opponents of British entry into the E.E.C., as represented particularly in the recent writings of Nicholas Kaldor. The fear is that, instead of the hoped-for stimulus to British economic growth, the result will be economic stagnation, consequent on the British tendency to inflationary wage increase and the peripheral position Britain will occupy in relation to the major industrial centres of the Continent; and that the results of stagnation will be large-scale emigration of British labour and entrepreneurship to the Continent. This would pose a serious problem for the British politicians who favour entry, though they do not seem to be aware of it. Their aspiration is to take over the political leadership of Europe, on the basis of Britain's assumed technological leadership and their own assumed superior capacity for leading others. But political leadership rests on economic strength; and it would be ironical if British politicians sacrificed their economic power base futilely in the quest for new political fields to conquer. The possibility of loss of industrial strength as a consequence of membership in a European monetary union is, of course, ignored or denied by the financial experts of the City of London, who see entry into a common-currency area, probably quite rightly, as offering them the prospect of financial leadership in the Community.

Finally, let us consider the implications of the adoption of the objective of establishing a common European currency for the international monetary system. As a result of the exchange rate crises of 1967–69, the international monetary authorities came to the view that more flexibility of exchange rates was desirable and should be introduced by institutional changes in the IMF system. This change of view entailed, most notably, recognition by the U.S. authorities of the special position of the U.S. dollar as the lynch-pin of the system and the burdens that rigidity of rates against the dollar imposed on the other countries, in terms particularly of having to accept the rate of inflation set by domestic American policy. Specifically, it involved the United States becoming willing to allow other countries an escape valve from U.S. dominance of the system. The European movement to establish a common currency has effectively blocked further progress towards implementation of these ideas; the question is what the implications are for the world system.

The idea of the proponents of a common European currency is to establish a currency able to rival the dollar as a private international money, and whose exchange value can be manipulated to counter the dominance of the dollar. This, it should be noted, constitutes a reversal of the previous reluctance of the major European countries (in contrast to the British policy with respect to the pound) to allow their currencies to become international monies. There is a grain of sense in this objective inasmuch as the close trading relationships among the European countries have made them individually reluctant to make use of the international monetary autonomy the present system allows them. It would clearly be easier if the exchange values of the European currencies could be changed uniformly in relation to the dollar, by central decision, rather than individual countries' having to decide whether or not, and if so by how much, to change their parities, on the basis of informed guesses about how their European partners would react. But this observation presupposes the existence of a central decision-taking process capable of taking such a decision about the exchange value of the European currency in terms of the American, or of deciding to let the European currency float. To establish such a central monetary authority would require the prior establishment of the machinery of policy harmonization discussed above; and, as pointed out, this will involve a once-for-all decision, the approach to which can be indefinitely delayed by agreement on the making of apparently meaningful but substantially empty gestures. The danger is that the European countries will procrastinate indefinitely, in order to avoid actually reaching the chasm that has to be crossed at the end, and that in so doing they will deprive themselves of the possibility of individual exchange rate action that they enjoy under the present system, without arriving at any effective possibility of collective exchange rate action, as envisaged in the plan for a common currency. The result would be that control of the international monetary system would pass to the Board of Governors of the Federal Reserve System, whose domestically-oriented policy decisions would determine the world rate of inflation. Moreover, in the absence of an existing European international money, with a monetary domain extending unrestrictedly over the European economy, the dollar would continue to expand in its present role as the international money used in private international transactions.

In short, the difficulties involved in the process of establishing a common European currency may mean that the Europeans will achieve precisely the reverse of what they want – namely a world economy dominated still more than at present by the U.S. dollar.

Chapter 13

Inflation: A 'Monetarist' View *

Inflation is most conveniently (and neutrally) defined as a sustained
rising trend in the general price level, or – what is virtually the same
thing – a rate of expansion of money income greater than the rate of
growth of real output. Other definitions abound but they typically
attempt to insert into the definition of the observed phenomenon
either some elements of a theory of causation (e.g. 'inflation results
from excess demand') or an implicit policy recommendation (e.g.
'inflation results from excess money creation' or 'inflation occurs
when money wages rise faster than labour productivity'). Some are
essentially meaningless, like the famous *Economist* catch-phrase of
the immediate post-Second World War period, 'too much money
chasing too few goods', still others involve the economic fallacy of
assigning 'real' or 'micro-economic' causes to a 'monetary' or 'macro-
economic' phenomenon, notably the popular views that inflation is
caused by the monopoly power of trade unions on the one hand or
large oligopolistic companies on the other – the point being that
efficient exploitation of monopoly power involves fixing the most
profitable price for the labour or product in question relative to the
wages of other labour or prices of other products, the money wage
or price required for this purpose being geared to the general levels
of wages and prices.

The definition employed here concentrates on the objective
phenomenon to be explained by analysis and dealt with by policy.
It does, however, entail two difficulties. The first, which constitutes
a trap for the unwary, is that not all price increases are 'inflationary'
in the sense of contributing to the inflationary process: increases in
interest rates or purchase taxes increase business costs or consumer

* *Discussion Paper* No. 1, Rowe, Rudd & Co., London, 1972.

prices at the time of introduction, though their purpose is to counter-act inflationary pressures. The second is that the rate of price in-crease deemed to constitute an inflationary problem is not a scientific question but a political question determined by public opinion; and public opinion vacillates on the issue.

According to a long-standing and historically well-documented theory of monetary phenomena – the quantity theory of money, currently frequently described as the 'monetarist view' – inflation is associated with and ultimately causally dependent on a rate of increase of the money supply significantly in excess of the rate of growth of real output – the difference between the two rates being the rate of inflation. The theory, it should be noted, does not assert that inflation is attributable to monetary ignorance or mismanage-ment; monetary expansion and the consequential inflation is a method of taxing the holders of money to which governments may well be driven by political circumstances, in full knowledge of what they are doing. The theory rests on the proposition that there is a stable relation between real income and the amount of real purchasing power the public wants to hold in monetary form; that this money–income relationship is inversely related to the expected rate of inflation, the erosion of the purchasing power of money through inflation constituting an important element of the cost of holding money; and that in the long run people will come to expect the rate of inflation induced by the authorities through their policy with respect to monetary expansion.

The assumption that the public forms expectations about inflation, adjusts them in the light of experience, and acts on these expectations in its behaviour, is a crucial difference between the quantity-theory approach to inflation and the currently-dominant Keynesian ap-proach. It has some important implications for the assessment of the social costs of inflation. One is that, if inflation proceeds for long enough at a steady rate (and the evidence of recent history is that long is not very long), interest rates on securities fixed in money terms will adjust to include an allowance for the expected rate of inflation. This implies, contrary to popular belief, that it does not necessarily redistribute income from lenders to borrowers on fixed-interest securities (from 'rentiers' to 'entrepreneurs') or impair the efficiency of the capital markets. The main redistribution is from the holders to the issuers of non-interest-bearing money and of money-like assets with conventionally fixed yields; and this causes a social loss through the efforts of holders of money and money-like assets to avoid the inflation tax imposed on them by economizing on the use of money. In parallel fashion, one would expect the political process that fixes the money receipts of so many public-sector employees, pensioners and other social-security beneficiaries in the modern world to re-contract these payments in the light of realized or anticipated inflation, so that in the long run there would be no significant redistribution of income among social groups resulting from inflation on this account.

A second and related implication is that the major social and economic problems associated with inflation stem from changes in the actual (and consequently the expected) rate of inflation *in either direction*. Such changes falsify the expectations on which past decisions have been based, leading to both economic waste and arbitrary redistributions of income and wealth among sections of the population. Such distortions are exacerbated, when inflation accelerates, by governmental efforts to suppress its manifestations by imposing restraints on increases in the wages and prices over which the government happens to have direct or indirect control or influence. Apart from the arbitrary redistributions already mentioned, a change in the rate of inflation imposes considerable social strains in the process of adjustment of wage- and price-determination processes to the new circumstances and expectations.

The quantity-theory approach to inflation and other monetary problems fell into disrepute and virtual oblivion for two decades following the intellectual revolution in the 1930s generated by Keynes's *General Theory of Employment, Interest and Money* – a book which was really about the economic stagnation of Britain in the 1920s, but was received as a fundamental advance in understanding of the capitalist system. The *General Theory* was concerned with the economics of depression but its basic theoretical model – or at least the standard analytical model drawn from it by the leading Keynesian theorists – lent itself readily to theorizing about inflation on lines alternative to the quantity theory. In fact, most contemporary thought about inflation (apart from the monetarist view) can be related to two basic elements of the Keynesian model: the

327

assumption that in the short run relevant to policy the money wage rate can be taken as given, and the conclusion based on this assumption that the levels of output and employment will be determined by aggregate demand for output (private consumption and investment and government demand). The latter conclusion suggests the obvious proposition that inflation will occur when aggregate demand exceeds the economy's aggregate productive capacity at current levels of wages and prices – a situation usually referred to as 'demand-pull' inflation – and the equally obvious policy recommendation that the government should remedy inflation by using fiscal and monetary policy to deflate aggregate demand to the measure of the country's productive resources.

The assumption of short-run fixity of wages, transformed to a dynamic context of increasing productivity, suggests that if inflation is occurring despite the absence of evidently excessive aggregate demand, the reason is that wages, and therefore production costs, are – quite irrationally – rising more rapidly than productivity – a situation commonly described as 'cost-push' inflation; and that the proper remedy is to introduce an income policy or wage–price freeze to replace the presumed irrationality of wage-fixing behaviour. The simple but superficial logic of this policy is that, since real income in the aggregate can rise only at the rate of productivity increase, everyone should be willing to co-operate in an agreement to settle for an increase in money income that will give him his fair share in increased aggregate real income consistently with stability of the overall price level. The superficiality lies in the assumption that, in a large and diversified economy in which myriads of economic decisions are taken in the light of information on demand and supply pressures in particular commodity and labour markets, and integrated by the use of money as the common unit of account, entrepreneurs and workers can be persuaded both to accept a centralized determination of where individual wage and price decisions ought to come out in real terms, in place of their own judgements of relevant sectoral demand and supply conditions, and to accept substitution for the familiar monetary unit of account of a 'real' unit of account to which monetary calculations have to be adjusted. It may be obvious to the economists inside and outside government that on the average real incomes can rise by, say, only 3 per cent a year; but this statistical fact should not and will not persuade employers and workers in individual industries and firms that a 3 per cent increase in money wages will give the worker the increase in real income he is entitled to and the employer the labour supply he wants. Both will try to find a way around the centrally-imposed constraint in their freedom of negotiation; and there are many ways of doing so, without breaking the letter of the law.

These two strands of Keynesian theory on the subject of inflation have been integrated, since 1958, in the concept of the 'Phillips curve', named after its inventor, Professor A. W. Phillips, then of the London School of Economics. The 'Phillips curve' is essentially an inverse statistical relationship between the rate of increase of money wage rates and an index of the balance between demand and supply in the labour market, usually but not necessarily identified with the percentage rate of unemployment. By subtracting the rate of increase of productivity from the rate of increase of money wages (a procedure which involves a rather simple theory of prices and production) one obtains an inverse relationship between the rate of unemployment and the rate of inflation. Analytically, the rate of inflation corresponding to the unemployment rate associated with some conventionally-determined concept of 'full employment' can be taken as an index of the 'cost-pushfulness' of the economy, and the relation of the actual unemployment rate to the 'full-employment' rate of unemployment as an index of the presence or otherwise and the magnitude of the 'demand-pull' factor. For purposes of policy analysis, the 'Phillips curve' represents the menu of choices open to the policy-makers – the so-called 'trade-off relationship' between inflation and unemployment – under given circumstances, but also a constraint that might be made less binding by improvements in the efficiency of the labour market (which would tend to equalize demand-pressure disparities between individual sectors of that market) or altered or eliminated by an incomes policy.

The statistical data until 1970 or so appeared to lend fairly substantial support to the reality of the 'Phillips curve' for a number of countries, and therefore to the analytical and policy theories based on it – though the same kind of evidence cast considerable doubt on the efficacy of incomes policy, which apparently had little statistical effect in shifting the 'Phillips curve' in a direction favourable to the policy-makers. The theoretical foundations of the 'Phillips curve' were, however, frontally challenged by the 'neo-quantity-theory' or 'monetarist' school, led by Professor Milton Friedman of the University of Chicago, who argued that the wage-determination process will be influenced on both sides by the rate of inflation expected, so that a 'Phillips curve' can be drawn only for a given state of inflationary expectations, and will break down if the authorities attempt to use it to secure a different combination of inflation and unemployment rates than the expected inflation rate and the corresponding unemployment rate shown on the curve. More generally, Friedman argued that in the long run there is a 'natural' unemployment rate, which balances real demand and supply factors in the labour market, and which cannot be altered by fiscal and monetary demand-management policies. The trade-off is not between the average rate of unemployment and the average rate of inflation, but between less or more unemployment now and more or less inflation later. In the long run, the authorities cannot choose the rate of unemployment they want; all they can choose is the rate of inflation that will accompany the 'natural' rate of unemployment.

This attack on the fundamental assumptions of the 'Phillips curve' naturally led to attempts to test the Friedman argument by introducing the expected rate of inflation (hypothesized to be based on past actual rates of inflation) into the statistical estimation of the curve. The results showed that the rate of money wage increase did depend on the expected rate of inflation, but not to the extent required to invalidate the existence of a 'trade-off' relationship. The estimated long-run Phillips curve was considerably steeper than the short-run curve – making inflation a substantially less attractive policy for reducing unemployment – but not vertical – implying no long-run leverage for inflation with respect to the rate of unemployment. These findings, however, left some theoretical loose ends: notably, they implied that in the long run inflation would redistribute income from labour to capital, which does not fit the facts of experience. Further, the fact that the 'Phillips curve' relationship for both Britain and the United States has recently broken down, in the sense that the rate of wage increase in 1971 or so has been unprecedentedly high at unprecedentedly high rates of unemployment for the postwar period, precisely in a period of exceptionally strong (and well-publicized) inflation, suggests that the expectational factors to which

INFLATION: A 'MONETARIST' VIEW

Friedman has called attention are more important than even the more sophisticated recent 'Phillips curve' analysis has allowed for.

The alternative theories of inflation reviewed in the preceding paragraphs have one fundamental element in common: the assumption that inflationary developments in a national economy can be explained by factors endogenous to that economy, whether those factors are conceived to be excessive monetary expansion, permission of excessive aggregate demand, or the wilful wrong-headedness of the wage-determination process. This assumption may be completely arbitrary; just because a political nation exists, with its own national economic institutions and a government charged with responsibility for striking an acceptable balance between unemployment and inflation through the exercise of the policy instruments it controls, is not sufficient to ensure that economic developments are endogenously and not exogenously determined and that the government actually has the power to control those developments by use of the instruments it commands.

In fact, the major nations at least of the Western world are linked together in a world economy by the maintenance of a system of fixed exchange rates, just as the regions of a single country are linked together in a single monetary domain by the use of a common currency. Within a nation, the different regions generally experience more or less the same rate of inflation, as a consequence of the common currency in conjunction with the freedom of movement of goods, capital and labour among them – and it should be noted that this occurs in spite of substantial differences in unemployment percentages among the regions. The assumption that nations linked by the equivalent of a common currency into an integrated world economy still have significant independence with respect to both the causation and the remedification of inflation depends heavily on the assumption that the barriers to freedom of international movement of goods, labour and capital – including money itself – are both high enough and variable enough by national economic policies to provide the requisite insulation for national economies against the impact of general influences emanating from the world economy. In the short run, the existence of barriers provides some insulation; in the longer run, variability of barriers is necessary, since the limits of the insulation provided by given barriers will be exhausted.

One such insulator could be the freedom to change the exchange rate against foreign currencies provided constitutionally by the IMF system. But this freedom is severely restricted by the conventions of that system as they have developed over the postwar period. Moreover, as will be discussed in more detail later, the freedom of manœuvre that a country obtains through the ability to change its exchange rate according to the IMF rules – i.e. from one parity to another, in contrast to letting its exchange rate float on the market – is dependent on the degree of 'openness' of its economy, which determines how rapidly a change in its exchange rate is neutralized by offsetting movements of domestic wages and prices.

Given adherence to a fixed exchange rate as the normal rule, reliance has to be placed on the influence of market imperfections, tariffs, and barriers to international capital movements in fragmenting the international economy and so insulating and providing significant policy autonomy for the constituent national economies. But since the Second World War freedom of competition in international trade has been greatly increased both by successive negotiations of tariff reductions under the General Agreement on Tariffs and Trade, culminating in the successful conclusion of the Kennedy Round in 1967, and by the formation of the European Common Market and the European Free Trade Association; and, as the experience of Britain's introduction of tariff surcharges in 1964 demonstrated, the accepted rules of international trade make it extremely difficult to increase barriers to international trade to counter a balance-of-payments deficit (i.e. to insulate the economy from international competitive pressures). National economies are, to a good first approximation, now linked together in a single world market for manufactures and primary commodities (though not for agricultural products, where national protective policies have a free rein, with chaotic results for international agricultural trade).

Further, since the restoration of currency convertibility at the end of 1958, the national capital markets of the major countries have become increasingly linked in a single international capital market. This has occurred not so much through liberalization of access to national capital markets – there have been marked tendencies in the opposite direction in some countries, notably the United States – as through the development of new institutions in the form of the Eurocurrency and Eurobond markets, which constitute an international money- and capital-market alternative to and impose competitive pressures on the national capital markets. The rules of the international economic policy game permit national governments to intervene in international capital movements by methods and to an extent that would not be condoned if applied to industrial trade; but it is doubtful how effective these interventions are in insulating national capital markets from international tendencies. Again, to a good first approximation, national capital markets can be regarded as linked together in a single international capital market.

On the two approximative assumptions of an integrated world market for industrial products and primary materials and an integrated world capital market, it makes sense to consider inflation as a world phenomenon and problem, rather than as a collection of individual national phenomena and problems. This view has several important implications. One is that discussions of the reasons for inflation, and particularly of accelerated inflation, in particular countries that concentrate on the detailed development of wages and prices – and especially 'wage explosion' – as causal factors are largely beside the point: they assign causality to the mechanisms by which more fundamental causes operate to diffuse the world inflationary process. A second is that national policies such as deflation or an incomes policy will not be effective in stopping inflation in one country if inflation is rampant elsewhere in the world economy. Deflation will create unemployment without stopping inflation; while an incomes policy to the extent that it is successful will simply distort resource allocation and produce unwanted balance-of-payments surpluses. The only effective method by which a country can avoid sharing in a world inflation is to combine anti-inflationary domestic policies with a floating (upward) exchange rate, as Canada has been doing since the beginning of June 1970. A third is that if inflation is considered a serious problem, it must be tackled at the world level by co-ordinated national, or by international, economic policies.

As is well-documented in a recent Report by the Secretary-General of the Organisation for Economic Cooperation and Development (*Inflation: The Current Problem* [December 1970]), the rate of inflation in the member countries (which includes all the major non-communist industrial nations) has been significantly higher since 1965 than it was before, and has been accelerating recently. In accordance with the well-known institutional bias of the OECD towards regarding each country as a special case, the Report tends to explain this by special factors operating in each country, and particularly the development of inflation in the United States, which bulks large in the aggregate; but it does recognize (though it does not explore) the possibility of common causation. To cope with the problem, it reiterates at length its long-recommended policy solution, the adoption of incomes policies by the various national governments.

It is possible, on the basis of the evidence of the OECD Report, to interpret the increase in the average rate of inflation since 1965 on Keynesian lines, in terms of a 'world Phillips curve', since on the average countries appear to have been maintaining a higher rate of productive-capacity utilization than in the preceding period. Such an explanation would call into question the OECD's recommendation of universal incomes policies, and suggest that to moderate world inflation countries would have to agree to increase their average rates of unemployment permanently – which would appear a formidable problem for international negotiation.

This Keynesian explanation leaves unanswered, however, the question of why countries committed to fixed exchange rates should have felt free to allow higher levels of activity and employment at the risk of more inflation and – more important – balance-of-payments difficulties. The answer lies in the position of the dollar as an international reserve currency, and the freedom this has given the United States to run balance-of-payments deficits and hence to allow domestic inflation. In brief, the United States has had no external reason for trying to avoid inflation, because any consequential deficit would be financed by accumulations of dollars in the rest of the world; and because a U.S. deficit implies a surplus for the rest of the world, the rest of the world as a whole has had no external reason for trying to avoid inflation either. In fact, their policy-makers have been faced with the awkward dilemma that, the more they try to resist inflation for domestic reasons, the more dollars they accumulate in financing the U.S. deficits – and without being very successful in resisting inflation.

334

INFLATION: A 'MONETARIST' VIEW

This brings us to the 'monetarist' view of the reasons for the acceleration of inflation since 1965: that it has been the ultimate consequence of an increase in the rate of world monetary expansion, an increase attributable primarily to the excessively expansionary monetary policy pursued by the United States in recent years, and diffused to the rest of the world through the U.S. payments deficit.

The 'monetarist' interpretation has been strongly disputed, on a variety of grounds that recall older debates about the international application of the quantity theory of money, and which boil down to the difficulty of finding statistical evidence of changes in monetary and trade flows large enough to appear capable of accounting for the international transmission of inflation. Objections of this kind, however, appear to depend on a rather naive interpretation of the relevant theory. In the first place, if, as suggested above as a useful first approximation, the world market for manufactures and primary materials is assumed to be integrated, prices and wages in individual countries will tend to adjust directly to world market levels for prices and comparative-efficiency levels for wages, without the need for either excess demand generated through a current account surplus (on a Keynesian theory of inflation) or prior movements of international reserves and domestic money supplies to bring about these adjustments (on a quantity-theory view of inflation). In the short run, depending on the domestic monetary policy followed, this adjustment may involve an increase in unemployment; in the longer run, on the second approximation of an integrated capital market, the extra money supply required to support higher domestic wages and prices can be obtained through the capital account of the balance of payments (international borrowing) as well as through the current account (an excess of production over expenditure being used to buy money in the commodity markets). But – and this is the second important point – the extra money required does not have to be obtained through a balance-of-payments surplus. It may instead be created by domestic credit expansion; and it will be so created if the authorities do not wish to accumulate large additional foreign exchange reserves. In short, adjustment of domestic prices and wages to world inflation does not require a prior export surplus or monetary inflow; and the monetary flows that actually occur will be determined by domestic credit policy, rather than being an independent causal factor.

The 'monetarist' view of world inflation has two important implications for policy. The first is that the new Special Drawing Rights at the International Monetary Fund, created in response to an assumed prospective shortage of international liquidity, may in fact provide fuel for further world inflation rather than facilitate the reduction of barriers to world trade and payments as intended. The second is that, if the rest of the world seriously desires to moderate or halt inflation, it must either float its exchange rates against the dollar, on the Canadian model – which might seriously disrupt the whole fabric of world trade and payments – or persuade the United States to alter its monetary policy to a less expansionary one consistent with price stability in the United States and therefore in the world economy. This latter alternative poses a serious problem for international diplomacy, since many American experts are convinced that monetary expansion (and inflation) are essential to the maintenance of high employment. The 'monetarist' position on the other hand suggests that this is not so, though 'monetarism' in the United States has recently gone into decline owing to the fact that monetary restraint has involved a high cost in unemployment in return for a low benefit in terms of slowing inflation. The most recent, and as yet highly controversial, 'monetarist' theorizing on the subject, by Professor R. A. Mundell of the University of Chicago, argues that monetary policy governs only the rate of inflation, and that fiscal policy governs the level of unemployment. On this theory, a swing of U.S. policy from fiscal tightness and monetary ease to the converse would serve both U.S. and world interests.

In conclusion, it may interest British readers to provide a few comments on the bearing of the foregoing essay on recent British inflation. First, the 'monetarist' view suggests that Britain was bound sooner or later, after the devaluation of 1967, to have an inflation sufficient both to offset the devaluation itself and to catch up with the world inflation. 'Cost-pushfulness' by the unions is a description of the mechanism, but not an explanation of the causation, of recent inflation; and an 'incomes policy' is, on abundant past evidence, not an answer but an irrelevance. Second, there is a serious danger that governmental efforts to combat inflation by imposing restraints on wages and prices within the government's control will distort the allocation of resources to no long-run useful purpose in slowing inflation. Third, with respect to the social desirability of slowing or stopping inflation, there is no hope of doing this, except marginally and transitorily, so long as the country maintains a fixed rate of exchange with other countries in a world dominated by inflation in the United States. The problem rather is to prevent overshooting in the adjustment of British wages and prices to the world inflation – a far more difficult problem than that of maintaining price stability in a closed economy. Finally, in the same connection, market processes of wage and price determination, and political processes for adjusting governmentally-determined salaries and social-security benefits, will provide a certain degree of rough justice in protecting the public against the impact of inflation in the longer run. Again, the main danger is that government will introduce serious distortions by attempting to suppress inflation through its control over or influence on certain kinds of incomes.

Chapter 14

Problems of Stabilization Policy in an Integrated World Economy*

This chapter is concerned with three subjects: the basic theory of the balance of payments in terms of which stabilization theory is conducted in the contemporary world; the problem of stabilization in a monetary union; and the problem of stabilization in the world economy as a whole. These subjects are related, but are treated in separate sections.

I. THE THEORY OF THE BALANCE OF PAYMENTS

The theory of the balance of payments that has come to be widely accepted by both economic theorists and practical policy-makers derives from the Keynesian revolution and the empirical conditions of the 1930s and owes much to Joan Robinson's classic essay on foreign exchange and subsequently to Volume I of James Meade's *The Theory of International Economic Policy*, on *The Balance of Payments*. According to one contemporary version of the theory, a country has two policy targets – internal and external balance, or full employment with a stable price level and a balanced balance of payments – and needs two instruments to achieve these targets – respectively demand management through fiscal and/or monetary policy, and control over the division of domestic and foreign expenditure between domestic and foreign goods through the choice of the exchange rate and/or the use of controls of various kinds on items in the current and the capital accounts.

It is clear from recent experience that this model is an extremely defective guide for policy-making in the contemporary world, which

* Prepared for the conference on 'Demand Management – Illusion or Reality?', Bergedorf, West Germany (June 20–1, 1971); published in Herbert Giersch (ed.), *Demand Management – Globalsteverung* (Tubingen: J. C. B. Mohr, 1972).

is characterized by a high degree of economic integration, and especially by a high degree of freedom of commodity trade enforced by restrictions on the freedom of countries to intervene in trade and capital movements, by a high degree of rigidity of exchange rates, and by a high degree of international mobility of capital – and is also characterized by high degrees of diversification of economic structure and of international competitiveness among the industrial products of the major countries. In these conditions, certain assumptions of the conventional model stand out as particularly apt to be misleading.

Two major assumptions of the conventional model are particularly worthy of note, both stemming from the historical and intellectual origins of the theory, and specifically from the general unemployment of the 1930s and from the static assumptions of Keynesian theory, especially the assumed 'stickiness' of wages and prices. The first is the assumption of stability of both domestic and foreign prices, in the relevant currencies, up to the full-employment level. This assumption to begin with begs the question of whether the political definition of 'full employment' is consistent with price stability, both at home and abroad; on the contrary, contemporary experience is that both the home and the foreign countries tend to define full employment as a level of unemployment that generates inflationary pressure for themselves and for the world system. Moreover, contemporary work on the dynamics of inflation suggests that there are appreciable lags involved in both the generation and the suppression of inflationary expectations, so that a given current level of unemployment may be consistent with price stability at one point of time and with raging inflation at another. And finally on this point, the theory assumes that the politicians who determine policy agree on the economists' definition of the policy objectives, whereas the politicians are fully aware that demand expansion generates more employment and hence more votes in the near-term future, and inflation and balance-of-payments difficulties only in the longer-term future, and in using this fact generate what has come to be known as 'the political cycle' in economic activity.

The assumption of stable domestic and foreign prices is associated with a particular view of the nature of industrial competition and of the role of exchange rate policy in achieving policy targets, a view that may be termed the 'monopolistic-competition' view of industrial competition among the advanced countries. According to that view, different countries' products are imperfectly competitive, and the conjuncture of domestic-currency wage and price levels and the exchange rate determine the volumes of domestic sales in the foreign market and of foreign sales in the domestic market. Hence exchange rate changes, allied with appropriate demand management, can influence the balance of payments on current account. Moreover, because sales are a function of relative prices, relative price reductions induced by exchange rate devaluations will not (by implication) set up domestic price-and-wage-inflationary pressures unless the quantitative effects on sales of exports and import substitutes give rise to excess aggregate demand – a possibility that can be avoided by appropriate demand management.

The contrasting view is that the industrial products of the major countries are highly competitive – the elasticities of substitution approach infinity – and that devaluation of a currency will in due course produce a matching inflation of domestic prices. On this view, devaluation works, not by altering permanently the relation between the world prices of domestic and foreign goods, but by transitorily deflating the purchasing power of domestic money and so leading the public to try to export more and import less in order to accumulate real money balances. Devaluation, in other words, is merely a substitute for monetary restraint, made necessary by the failure to exercise sufficient monetary restraint at an earlier stage.

The second key assumption of the conventional models is that the international mobility of capital is either entirely absent, or sufficiently inelastic to permit countries to have independence in their monetary policies, and hence a choice between monetary and fiscal policies as instruments of demand management. The contrary view is that the international mobility of capital is now so great that national efforts to use monetary policy either for restraint or for expansion will quickly produce balance-of-payments effects through the capital account that will defeat the policy. The one exception is the United States, which as the source of the rest of the world's reserve currency does not have to worry about its balance of payments – and hence has the freedom to impose on the rest of the world whatever degree of deflation or inflation it chooses for domestic-policy reasons.

These defects of the conventional models of balance-of-payments theory have led in the past few years to the development of a new, 'monetarist', approach to balance-of-payments theory. Unfortunately – as is true in the wider field of monetary economics – there is an unoccupied and debatable middle ground between the extremes of simplicity of the theoretical models produced by Keynesians on the one hand and monetarists on the other, and the reality of experience with which the practical policy-maker has to deal. In each case, the middle ground concerns the division of the effects of changes in aggregate demand between changes in prices and changes in quantities, with the Keynesians tending to assume that, short of 'full' employment, quantities and not prices should respond, and the monetarists tending to assume that prices rather than quantities are the variable that responds to demand management.

To fix ideas, let us assume a fully-integrated world in which both goods and capital are perfectly mobile. Such a world would have a rate of inflation determined by the relation between its rate of real growth and its rate of overall monetary expansion, at least in the long run. In the short run, unwarranted expectations of price stability or of inflation would permit actual rates of inflation to vary downwards or upwards from the rate of inflation theoretically consistent with the relation between aggregate real growth and aggregate monetary expansion. But in the long run, all members of the system would experience the same rate of inflation – so long as they maintained fixed exchange rates with the rest of the world. If they devalued they would temporarily have more inflation, if they revalued they would temporarily have less. But they could only have a sustainedly different rate of inflation from the rest of the world if they cut themselves off from it by having a floating exchange rate – the only arrangement that would permit them to pursue an independent monetary policy and therefore an independent policy with respect to domestic prices.

There are three implications of this model that are relevant to the current problem of stabilization. The first is that the necessity of a common rate of inflation does not necessarily imply equal rates of increase of measured price indexes. Specifically, given the existence of 'sheltered sectors' that both produce non-tradeable goods and services and do not enjoy the same rate of increase of productivity in the non-tradeable as in the tradeable sector, one would expect to observe a faster rate of 'inflation' according to an overall price index such as consumer prices or the GNP deflator in the countries where productivity in tradeable goods is growing faster. A related point is that one would not expect to be able to determine whether a currency was overvalued or undervalued by observing and comparing its export price index with the indexes of other countries. The second implication is that a country in the system has no control over its domestic money supply. Since money can be imported (or exported) through the balance of payments, what a country controls by monetary policy is not the money supply but the proportion of the money supply that is backed by domestic credit. This means that a country in which real output and therefore the demand for money is growing rapidly, and/or in which the growth of domestic credit is being tightly constrained by policy, will tend to have a large persistent balance-of-payments surplus, and vice versa. It also means that the debate over rules versus authorities, and especially the recommendation of a rule to govern the rate of expansion of the domestic money supply, is completely irrelevant for an economy on a fixed exchange rate. Such an economy will have to have the world rate of inflation, regardless of what it tries to do with its monetary policy. A rule for monetary expansion can only make sense for a country on a floating exchange rate; and even in this case, there will be a problem concerning the proportion of the domestic money supply that foreigners choose to hold.

The third, and perhaps most important, implication of the model is that in a fixed exchange-rate system there is no hope – at least for most nations – of pursuing an independent domestic price level policy. If the authorities aim at controlling prices, and specifically at achieving a lower rate of inflation than the world level, they must wind up in one of two uncomfortable and unsustainable situations: either they will have the same rate of inflation as everyone else, combined with either a lot of unemployment or a current account surplus that impoverishes their producers for the benefit of foreigners; or they will have domestic inflationary pressure and a capital account inflow that eventually they will be unable to handle. In the first case they will eventually be obliged to adopt an inflationary monetary policy; in the second they will have to revalue or go to a floating (i.e. appreciating) exchange rate.

As already mentioned, the pure model of an integrated world economy just presented is not very realistic. In its purest form, all countries have full employment (according to their empirical labour-market conditions) and the same rate of inflation of traded-goods prices, and monetary policy affects only the balance of payments. By the same token, fiscal policy does not affect the balance of payments – since by assumption fiscal deficits are financed by capital inflows – and either influence the level of employment or do not do so, according to one's theory of fiscal policy, and specifically whether fiscal policy can influence the level of employment relative to what it would be in a competitive international market. This raises two theoretical (and empirical) questions about fiscal policy: whether fiscal policy can increase the level of employment in the non-tradeable sectors above what it would otherwise be, and whether fiscal policy can increase the proportion of the labour force seeking work that would accept employment at any given level of real wages. And it raises one major question about monetary policy: whether monetary policy can influence the level of employment. Contrary to the pure theory, the evidence is that monetary policy can influence the level of employment – and this implies most obviously that there is imperfect competition between domestic and foreign sources of capital, so that domestic monetary restraint can bite into the financing and therefore the level of domestic economic activity.

A more realistic and empirically relevant model, in my view, would involve two assumptions. The first would be incompletely perfect substitutability between domestic and foreign tradeables, on the one hand, and between domestic tradeables and domestic non-tradeables on the other, so that a relatively inflationary policy in one country could lead to a shift of resources from tradeables into non-tradeables, creating a balance-of-payments problem whose solution would require a devaluation, which devaluation would create unemployment in the non-tradeable sector. Conversely, a relatively deflationary policy would create inflationary pressure in the economy, combined with a balance-of-payments surplus, and a revaluation would create unemployment in the tradeable sector.

The other assumption would be imperfect substitutability between domestic and foreign credit, so that monetary restraint could create unemployment by making it difficult or impossible to finance domestic activity – at least subject to a search time-lag. These assumptions, nevertheless, while explaining fluctuations in employment levels and also price level movements in the short term, by comparison with the implications of the pure monetary model, would leave the longer-run implications of the monetary model intact. In the longer run, the economy would have to share in the world rate of inflation, and could not combat it by either fiscal or monetary policy, unless these were applied with steadily increasing severity. Moreover, demand management would be confronted by all the problems associated with the formation and implementation of inflationary expectations.

II. PROBLEMS OF STABILIZATION IN A MONETARY UNION

A monetary union among a group of countries may be advocated either for the direct economic advantages which currency unification may confer, or as a means of securing some ulterior objectives which a common currency symbolizes. In either case, it needs emphasizing that monetary unification is a major and novel exercise in socio-economic innovation. The currencies of supranational domain in the past have established their positions as a result of imperial conquest and expansion (including colonization of new territories) or as a result of a slow process of 'monetization' of profitable trade and exchange on the basis of use of the currency of the most powerful trading partner. Even the establishment of a single national currency has typically been a long-drawn-out and fault-fraught affair. The only examples of deliberate innovations to create a common currency in modern times have been concerned with the creation of credit money for use in transactions among central banks, not among the public – Drawing Rights at the International Monetary Fund, and recently Special Drawing Rights, as yet relatively untested. And the rise of the dollar to dominance in a world monetary system intended to be based on gold and IMF liabilities indicates the difficulty of effective innovation in the international monetary field.

The plan to establish a common European currency derives its appeal from a self-contradictory mixture of the two motives mentioned above. On the one hand, the intent is to cajole or cozen the European countries into a degree of economic integration and policy co-ordination extending far beyond anything they have hitherto been willing to tolerate, by securing their commitment to an outward symbol of integration. On the other hand, if Europe did have a common currency and the policy harmonization and central decision-taking apparatus required to control and use it, Europe could pursue stabilization policies independent of the United States – though to do so it would have to be willing either to float its currency against the dollar, or to change the exchange rate on the dollar frequently and with equanimity – and thus many of the tensions of the contemporary international monetary system could be resolved. The self-contradiction inheres in the fact that the appeal of the notion of a common currency rests on having already achieved the centralized policy-making that pursuit of the objective is hoped to force members to accept. And the danger for Europe is that the initial steps towards unification will immobilize national freedom of action against the dollar without erecting a supra-national decision-taking monetary authority, thereby accentuating still further the dominance of U.S. monetary policy over the world system.

The establishment of a common currency among a group of countries involves the sacrifice of one of the most vital elements of economic sovereignty – the ability of governments to resort to monetary expansion either to stimulate economic activity or to finance their expenditures at preferential interest rates, and if the gamble affects the balance of payments too seriously adversely, to correct the situation by devaluation instead of deflation. Agreement on the establishment of a common currency entails agreement to forgo this highly convenient privilege and to live with the implications of so doing. This would involve three major problems.

The first, which would not arise if one country were so naturally dominant that its monetary leadership was unquestionably accepted, concerns the sharing of what may rather inaccurately be called the 'seigniorage rights' of money creation. These rights as already mentioned give a privileged position to government debt in the money market; and governments will obviously have difficulty in agreeing on how the enhanced potential privileges of a supra-national money-creating authority should be shared.

The second problem is that national governments will be reduced, so far as stabilization policy is concerned, to the position of regions or provinces within present nation-states – some of which chronically prosper, and others of which chronically stagnate. Within nation-states governments have attempted to deal with the resulting problem by regional policies, but without notable success. A common currency in Europe would probably only be tolerable if accompanied by the adoption of serious commitments to differentiate the regional effects of centrally-determined policies and to equalize the regional distribution of economic activity and economic growth. There is nothing in economic history to suggest that such a commitment can be implemented – and nothing in economic theory to suggest that it should be undertaken.

The third problem is that, if a common European currency were established, it would inevitably become a reserve currency. Europe is now, and will be even more so if enlarged, the largest single unit in world trade; and it has great potential as an exporter of capital for other countries' development. The historical experience first of Britain and then of the United States suggests the inevitability of reserve-currency status. But the management of a reserve currency is something that European countries have probably wisely so far refused to contemplate. And it would involve vast changes in financial organization even if Europe trusted the City of London with the main part of the responsibility.

Assuming that a common currency could be established, controlled by a central decision-taking authority, the prime question would be how that currency should be managed. Ignoring the complications of the reserve-currency role, theoretical developments of the past decade or so suggest that the probably most effective approach to stabilization consists in adopting a floating exchange rate and expanding the overall money supply at a rate geared to the growth of demand for money at stable prices. But to make this policy effective would require both persuading individual governments to accept the implications for their domestic levels of activity and rates of growth, and containing the competition with the new Eurocurrency presented by the Eurodollar and the Eurobond markets. This competition has served a useful function in the absence of European monetary integration, albeit an uncomfortable one for the European central banks. But monetary control is only control if the monetary authority controls a relevant monetary variable; and in national central banking this has frequently entailed the suppression of substitute money and credit.

Centralized control of the money supply, whatever the principle of management on which it is based – discretion or a monetary rule – there must be if a common currency is to mean anything. But, contrary to widely held opinion, it is an open question whether there needs to be co-ordination of national fiscal policies. The asserted need for co-ordination seems to derive from the ability of governments at present to support their fiscal policies by monetary expansion if necessary. If governments had to borrow to finance deficits in an open European capital market, they could conceivably be left to govern their behaviour in accordance with the market's monetary discipline, and not be expected or required to co-ordinate policy explicitly. Certainly federal countries like Canada and the United States have not found it necessary to co-ordinate provincial or state fiscal policies. On the other hand, these subordinate units of government have never had the seigniorage privilege of money creation; and the demand for fiscal co-ordination under a common European currency may be an indirect way of ensuring fair shares in the profits of seigniorage.

III. PROBLEMS OF INTERNATIONAL STABILIZATION POLICY

As stated in section II, one of the major motivations of the proposal for a common European currency is to permit the European countries to conduct stabilization policies – particularly with regard to price stability – with the freedom from inflationary pressure (and possibly in future deflationary pressure) emanating from the United States that could be afforded by a common exchange rate floating (or possibly revalued frequently) against the U.S. dollar. At present the European countries are greatly hampered in their stabilization policies by the fact that independent adjustments of national exchange rates with the dollar have a major impact on the adjusting country's intra-European trade. Yet the establishment of a common currency, which would avoid these problems, is fraught with difficulties, as argued in section II.

An alternative approach would be to reform the international monetary system so as to eliminate the current inflationary pressure emanating from the United States, and more generally to permit the pursuit of a stabilization policy on a global basis.

As a prelude to discussion of this problem, it is perhaps necessary to defend the view that inflation is in fact a global (or at least 'Western world') phenomenon and not, as most economic commentators including the Organization for Economic Cooperation and Development seem to believe, a series of problems of individual nations attributable to particular national developments of a sociological character (specifically, outbreaks of cost-pushfulness by trade unions) that have just happened to coincide at least roughly in the past few years. 'National sociological reasons' are always appealing to politicians and to those who believe that all problems can be solved by the exercise of wise national policy-making. But very few indeed would accept a precisely analogous explanation of inflation within a nation as the result of coincidental inflationary sociological developments within the various regions of the nation. And, as a result of a great variety of developments including the lowering of trade barriers through the General Agreement on Tariffs and Trade, the return to exchange convertibility at normally fixed parities within the IMF system, the growth of an integrated international capital market in the form of the Eurocurrency and Eurobond markets, and the growth of international competition in industrial trade and investment resulting from the economic recovery and growth of Europe and the activities of the multinational corporations, the contemporary economic world has become far more similar to a single international economy like a domestic national economy than to a fragmented and only loosely and imperfectly integrated system of largely autonomous nation-states. For such an integrated world economy it makes sense to think of inflation in the various constituent countries as the result of a common cause – in 'monetarist' terms, excessive monetary expansion, sparked by monetary expansion in the United States and diffused through the world economy as a natural consequence of world economic integration.

This proposition has been disputed on the grounds that international monetary flows, national current account surpluses, etc. have not been large enough to provide a plausible explanation of inflation as a global rather than an individual national phenomenon. The contrary contention, however – apart altogether from the very dubious scientific value of its alternative *ad hoc* explanations in terms of exogenous but somehow coincident 'sociological shocks' – disregards both the direct inflation-diffusing effects of international arbitrage in traded goods and the tendency of international competition to produce a single world market price level for manufactures, and the fact that countries' monetary authorities have a choice between allowing the increase in the money supply necessary to support inflation to be provided by importation of international reserves, and providing the increased money supply themselves by domestic credit creation. In other words, inflationary monetary expansion outside the United States can be the result both of an inflow of dollars and of the adoption of policies designed to stave off an inflow of dollars.

The proposition, moreover, need not be put in 'monetarist' terms of excessive world monetary expansion. One could explain, or at least describe, the higher rate of inflation in the world since 1965 and especially in the past three years as the result of an average movement towards lower unemployment levels acting with some lag on a 'world Phillips curve'. Or one could explain it in terms of a universal decline in the importance attached by policy-makers to the balance-of-payments constraint on full-employment policies and therefore on the ability and willingness of governments to allow inflation to occur, for whatever reason it is held to tend to occur. On the one hand, particularly since the 'gold crisis' of 1968 and the establishment of the two-tier gold market, the United States has both in reality and in its own policy-thinking been relieved of any balance-of-payments constraint on domestic policies entailing inflation, owing to the international reserve-currency role of the dollar. On the other hand, the other advanced industrial countries as a group (not of course each separately) have been relieved by chronic U.S. deficits (surpluses for the rest of the world) of balance-of-payments pressures to control inflation; on the contrary, they have faced the dilemma that success in controlling domestic inflation will involve mounting contrary pressures, coming through improvement of the current and capital accounts and resulting international reserve inflows, eventually requiring exchange rate appreciation.

Assuming that stabilization is desired as a common policy objective among the advanced countries, and that stabilization for the foreseeable future means preventing or restraining price inflation (rather than avoiding a world recession of production and employment as was the problem of the 1930s), the question is what international arrangements might be capable of achieving it.

One answer, which has been parroted with increasing sophistication of description but without serious thought about the political and economic implications by the Organisation for Economic Cooperation and Development, is the adoption of national incomes policies and their co-ordination at the international level. There is no theoretical reason to expect an incomes policy however defined (short of complete centralized price and wage determination) to be effective in controlling inflation, and no empirical evidence apart possibly from one or two small countries with special political circumstances that it has ever been more than marginally and temporarily effective in reducing the rate of inflation. And there is much theoretical reason and empirical evidence to support the proposition that incomes policy may seriously distort the allocation of resources. And co-ordination of national incomes policies to achieve world price stability on some standard – which might well involve some countries' having to adopt an inflationary incomes policy – would be a still more difficult task for international economic diplomacy.

It is crystal clear from both basic monetary theory – whether Keynesian or quantity-theory – and from an overwhelming mass of empirical evidence that if inflation in the world economy is to be restrained or halted the growth of the world money supply must be confined to a rate consistent with the degree of price stability desired internationally, in conjunction with the trend rate of growth of world output.

One possibility that has been canvassed from time to time would be to persuade the United States to act 'responsibly' in its domestic monetary policy, the idea being that under the present dollar-reserve-based international monetary system price stability in the United States would force the other major countries to pursue domestic monetary and other policies that would assure stability of their price levels as well, by virtue of the balance-of-payments constraint. Charles Kindleberger has argued in the past that to achieve this, other countries should be given representation on the Board of Governors of the Federal Reserve System. That specific proposal is of course highly improbable of acceptance; and it is very unlikely that the United States would voluntarily and irrevocably commit itself to the maintenance of domestic price stability for international reasons, regardless of the cost this might entail in terms of either domestic employment or the Administration's fiscal requirements and spending programmes. The only faint hope on the horizon may be that the U.S. public will come to be convinced by recent and prospective experience that apart from the short run excessive monetary expansion affects prices but not activity and employment, i.e. that there is no lasting 'Phillips curve' trade-off between inflation and unemployment. But this is still a subject of hot dispute between 'Keynesians' and 'monetarists' in the United States, with the Keynesians so far enjoying empirical support from the econometric evidence in the Phillips curve. Moreover, another period of price stability would re-create conditions under which unemployment could be reduced for a significant period by monetary expansion. (The argument against the Phillips curve is that actual inflation becomes expected and therefore built into money interest rates and wage and price determination so that the economy returns to its 'natural' level of unemployment and capacity utilization, so that inflation can only increase activity in the period before it becomes fully anticipated.)

The other possibility is to reconstruct the international monetary system in two major respects. The first would be to eliminate the reserve-currency role of the dollar and hence subject the United States to the same international reserve and balance-of-payments discipline as confines the inflationary potential of other countries: in other words, to replace the dollar (and much less significantly, the pound sterling) by an international reserve asset used by all countries in common. The second would be to establish international control of the growth of this international reserve asset and to use this control to confine the rate of expansion of its quantity to that consistent with an internationally agreed standard of price stability. This phrasing perhaps is too strongly suggestive of the need for a 'world rule of monetary expansion'. Those who prefer discretion to rules in domestic monetary management may prefer simply to charge the wise men placed in charge of controlling the quantity of the international reserve asset to use their powers to achieve world price stability, and leave it to them to define the concept and implement it.

This alternative amounts to the establishment in effect of a world central bank.

The new Special Drawing Rights of the International Monetary Fund were intended to achieve these two changes in the course of time: to provide a substitute for gold and dollars as international reserves, and to govern the expansion of this new type of international reserves in accordance with the growth of the need for international liquidity, a need that can only be defined by reference to some assumption or objective concerning the trend of world prices. But it has always been a question whether control of the rate of expansion of a new and as yet largely untested asset that would constitute only a minor fraction of the total of world reserves or international liquidity, the larger U.S. dollar component being potentially highly variable, would tend to decrease or to increase the stability of the international monetary system. In the current and prospective circumstance of the world economy, with the dollar dominant and U.S. policy continuing inflationary, the influence of the creation of SDRs must be to accentuate world inflationary pressures and so aggravate the problems of international economic stabilization.

Failing the establishment of an effective world central banking arrangement, and given the difficulties of either persuading the U.S. monetary authority to behave responsibly or forming a common European currency that would float against the dollar, it would seem strongly advisable for countries to take up again the study initiated in 1969 after the French devaluation and German revaluation but shelved in light of the proposal for a common European currency in 1970, of the possible methods by which more exchange rate flexibility could be introduced into the present international system. The flotation of the Canadian dollar in June 1970 and of the German mark in April 1971 have demonstrated both the practical necessity of such flexibility and the desirability of institutional arrangements to legitimize resort to floating rates in appropriate circumstances and also and perhaps more important to provide alternative types of flexibility that might be more useful to a nation and less disruptive to the system under various possible circumstances.

Chapter 15

The International Monetary Crisis of 1971*

I. SEPTEMBER 1971

In a fundamental sense, the international monetary crisis precipitated by President Nixon's announcement of his 'new economic policy' on August 15, 1971 has been on the cards for at least as long as since 1958, when Professor Robert Triffin of Yale began to warn his academic and official colleagues of the dangerous instability of the IMF system of organizing international currency relationships. But the focal point for a potential crisis has changed over the intervening period, with the evolution of techniques for and the practice of international monetary co-operation among the leading countries. Moreover, while the focal point of the current crisis – the relative exchange values of other major currencies against the dollar – was predictable for at least five years in advance, most harbingers of gloom, including myself, predicted that the crisis would be precipitated by other countries exasperated with the behaviour of the dollar rather than by a U.S. Administration exasperated with the behaviour of other countries. Further, those in the United States, again including myself, who had been advocating for approximately a decade that the United States should take the action on the international monetary front that President Nixon has in fact taken – i.e. demonetization of gold in the United States, or more accurately 'de-dollarization' of gold – never intended that action to be accompanied by threats, coercive measures, and a major retreat into protectionism.

In broad formal outline, the international monetary system as it existed up until August 15, 1971 was a regime of fixed exchange rates among the major currencies, an individual country's rate

* Reprinted from *Money Management* (November/December 1971), pp. 16–18; prepared while I was Visiting Professor at the Institute for Advanced Studies, Vienna.

being alterable by international agreement in case of 'fundamental disequilibrium', based on the use of gold as the fundamental international reserve money, the rigours of gold's discipline being eased by the provision and gradual expansion of credit facilities in the form of Drawing Rights at the International Monetary Fund. In actual practice as it evolved over the postwar period, the system diverged increasingly from its formal structure, in two crucial respects. First, countries became less and less willing to alter their exchange rates either up or down – 'down' became a confession of economic mismanagement, and 'up' a condonation of mismanagement by others, as well as a blow to vocal export groups. Second, owing to world inflation, the gradual drying up of new supplies of monetary gold, niggardliness in increasing IMF Drawing Rights and above all the post-Second World War dominance of the United States in the world economy, the U.S. dollar came to be the dominant form and source of basic international monetary reserves.

The resulting international monetary system, the experts had agreed by the early 1960s, involved three serious problems, which came to be known as 'the confidence problem', 'the liquidity problem' and 'the adjustment problem'. The order of listing corresponds to the historical order in which they have troubled the system.

The confidence problem had two facets: speculation against any major currency, which might prove contagious and bring down the system, and speculation against the reserve currency, which might wipe out these international reserves by encashment for gold held by the reserve-currency country. Early concern about this problem reflected memories of the collapse of the gold exchange standard in the early 1930s. In fact, the development of central bank co-operation in the form of quick and abundant credit for countries under speculative attack narrowed that danger; the process was facilitated greatly by growing recognition that, in contrast to the pound in 1931, the dollar in the 1960s was too important for other countries to permit it to collapse. The symbol of the passing of the confidence problem was the 1967 devaluation of the pound, which had heretofore been supported by the Americans for fear of a sterling-devaluation-induced run on the dollar. While the expected run on the dollar did occur, it was frustrated by the decision to adopt the two-tier gold price system.

The liquidity problem resulted from the fact that expanding use of the U.S. dollar as a reserve substitute for gold implied both a growing U.S. deficit and an accelerating deterioration in the ratio of U.S. dollar liabilities to foreign official holders to U.S. gold reserves, neither of which could go on for long without raising increasing doubts about the stability of the value of the dollar. The obvious solution was a new international reserve asset whose growth would take over from both gold and the dollar the task of providing expanding international liquidity; and while recognition of the need for this solution was for long delayed by U.S. pride in the dollar and European refusal to admit the reserve-demand element in the chronic U.S. balance-of-payments deficit, it was eventually accomplished in the 1967 agreement to institute Special Drawing Rights at the International Monetary Fund.

The adjustment problem, like the confidence problem, had two facets. First, for countries other than the United States, unwillingness to change exchange rates up or down meant the development of cumulative disequilibria that could only be resolved by exchange rate changes undertaken under the pressure of national and international political and financial crisis. The severity of the international strains involved in obtaining the franc and mark devaluations of 1969 made the community of international monetary officials acutely aware of this problem in that year, and an IMF study of methods for achieving greater exchange rate flexibility was instituted. But the natural conservatism of central banks and IMF officials prevented it from producing any significant proposals for radical change. And meanwhile the decision of the Common Market countries to work towards a common European currency threw a roadblock in the way of progress towards greater exchange rate flexibility.

Second, given the role of the U.S. dollar as the basic reserve asset of the system, the U.S. monetary authorities did not possess the power of other countries' authorities to change the exchange rate of their currency against world currencies as a whole. (This fact is frequently, but in my view erroneously, ascribed to the technical detail that the United States maintained its par value by standing ready to buy or sell gold while other countries maintained theirs by buying or selling dollars in the market.) Any decrease in the U.S. par value (the value of the dollar in terms of gold) could be offset by changes in the par values of other currencies. Hence any adjustment of the exchange value of the dollar in terms of other currencies would not be achieved by U.S. action with respect to the price of gold; it would have to be implemented by opposite changes in the par values of other currencies.

This was the basic institutional and economic fact behind the August 1971 crisis. As already mentioned, American economists who understood the system had for many years recommended that the United States cut the link between the dollar and gold, and let the other countries choose whether to adjust their exchange rates or live with the dollar standard and the U.S. deficit, the intention being to free U.S. domestic and foreign policy from the pretence that the dollar was like all other currencies and subject to the same balance-of-payments discipline. But successive Administrations preferred the mouth-music, and the policy methods, of equalitarian hypocrisy.

This international policy stance made some international political sense up to 1965, since U.S. domestic economic policy was producing a fair degree of price stability and the U.S. government could hope that inflation elsewhere would gradually solve the adjustment problem, while it was tactful not to rub other countries' noses in the dominance of the dollar. But then came the escalation of the war in Vietnam, the failure to finance it by tax increases or cuts in other government expenditure, and the great (by U.S. standards) inflation. The United States was stuck with a deteriorating basic balance, and the other countries with the choice between accepting U.S. inflation and appreciating their currencies against the dollar.

Given European dislike of both inflation and the war in Vietnam on the one hand, and the tougher and less diplomatic line on international economic policy of the Nixon Administration on the other, it seemed reasonable to expect that the Europeans would be the first to crack under the strain of an overvalued and inflationary dollar, and that they would be driven into defensive currency appreciation; the same logic seemed to apply to Japan. But a combination of inertia, fear of change, and in Europe political animosity towards the United States prevented this. Instead, it was the United States that lost its patience.

For this, the domestic situation in the United States was responsible. On the one hand, the President had had to reverse his anti-inflationary domestic policy for the sake of winning the 1972 election; this in turn implied a sharp worsening of the balance of payments. On the other hand, protectionist sentiment had been mounting rapidly, in important part as the consequence of the implications for exporting and domestic-market industries of an overvalued currency. The United States has in addition an image of itself as a country producing a large export surplus by virtue of its technological supremacy, a surplus which finances both private investment and government expenditure abroad. When the balance-of-payments statistics showed a dramatic worsening of the balance of payments in the first half of 1971, especially in the merchandise trade accounts, what more natural reaction could there be than to blame it on the perverse refusal of the foreigners to adjust their exchange rates – and, in American fashion, to seek a policy overkill by not only cutting the link between the dollar and gold but imposing the tariff surcharge to tell the Europeans how they should react, or else?

This somewhat infantile policy package, combining a choice and a threat, has most unfortunately provoked an equally infantile reaction from Europe – a determination that the Americans must be humbled into continuing the pretence that the dollar is no different from other currencies by forcing them to accept a token rise in the price of gold as part of the sought-for realignment of currency values. This the U.S. Administration cannot do by itself (unless some dodge can be found for devaluing the dollar against SDRs without abeying the official gold price which is not subject to congressional approval); and the Congress is invariably far more irascible about foreign-imposed constraints on U.S. policy freedom than the Administration, as well as understanding better than most Europeans the irrelevance of the price of gold in the present international monetary system.

The great danger of the current situation is that European pique over the Nixon Administration's blunt reminder of the realities of the international monetary system will divert European attention to the trivial issue of the gold price and away from the far more important point that the surcharge represents a dangerous step towards general trade warfare. Here the crucial point is that the surcharge involved a shock use of a nominally non-discriminatory trade-restrictive measure to force differential international exchange rate realignment. As such, its only advantage was that it was pseudo-legitimated by its previous use by Canada and Britain, and legally available to the U.S. Administration without congressional approval. Its main disadvantages are that it is extremely difficult to see how the promise to remove it can be used to secure differential adjustments in specific exchange rates, and that very rapidly as time has passed it has come to be considered by the Commerce Department as a general trade-negotiation weapon and not as a specific monetary bargaining counter. In addition, domestic vested interests are likely to become increasingly vocal in demanding continuation of its initially incidental protective effects. Europe must avoid the temptation to try to fiddle with the gold price while the protectionists in the United States are burning up the liberal international trade and payments system that international monetary arrangements are intended to promote.

II. JANUARY 1972

Fortunately for the world economy, though the world was kept waiting on tenterhooks for an unconscionably long time, through a period of what came to be termed 'dirty floating' of exchange rates, the international monetary crisis of 1971 was resolved before the end of the year by an international agreement to realign exchange rates against the dollar, the American surcharge on imports being abandoned in return for an agreement by the European countries to undertake negotiations in the near future on a broad range of trade-policy questions respecting which European practices were regarded as 'unfair' by the American Administration. The resolution of the 1971 crisis may well, however, exact a future price in the form of another international monetary crisis in 1972 or 1973.

The agreement on exchange rate realignment involved an increase in the dollar price of gold by 8·5 per cent. This could be interpreted as a retrogressive concession to the European attachment to gold as the putative basis of the system, and a concession to the European monetary gold lobby it certainly was; but it was a point whose concession is more reasonably interpreted as reflecting American realization that the price of gold is now so unimportant to the international monetary system that any relatively small change in it was well worth any loss of face involved for the sake of obtaining a devaluation of the dollar in relation to the other major currencies. (A doubling or tripling of the gold price, of course, would have represented a major retrogression of principle.) Indeed, the change in the dollar price of gold, combined with changes in other currency prices of gold that leave the purchasing power of gold over national currencies on average virtually unchanged, should help to accelerate the movement towards establishment of an international monetary system based on SDRs. (One should note that the purchasing power of gold has been and is continuing to be steadily eroded by world inflation, and that the resolution of the crisis has done nothing to increase the attractiveness of gold as a store of real purchasing power, in contrast to the last major realignment of currency values under the IMF system, the round of European currency devaluations of 1949.)

The main problem created by the resolution of the 1971 crisis concerns the question of whether the new set of exchange rates can hold for any substantial period of time. There is some reason to suspect that, for the sake of reaching a speedy agreement, the Americans accepted smaller magnitudes of revaluation against the dollar than were necessary to cure their balance-of-payments deficit, and that the dollar will tend to remain a sick currency.

A more important point is that the period of 'dirty floating' has provided a batch of new pseudo-arguments against exchange rate flexibility – though clearly a period in which central banks are expecting a quick return to an internationally-agreed set of fixed exchange rates, and are intervening in the market in order to establish as favourable a bargaining position and eventually agreed exchange rate as possible, provides no test whatsoever of the benefits or otherwise to international trade and payments of an established regime of freely flexible exchange rates. Instead, it gives private traders the worst of all possible worlds, one in which rates are nominally flexible but actually managed for inscrutable purposes, and in which all the uncertainties of recent experience surrounding the expectation of changes in pegged rates to new pegged levels abound and are complicated by the fact that the current rate is only partially pegged but the future rate will be completely so (at least, so long as it lasts).

The one bright spot in the resolution of the crisis, so far as the international monetary system is concerned, was the decision of the International Monetary Fund to sanction fluctuations of market exchange rates within 2·25 per cent each side of par values for the time being, in place of the previous 'band' of a maximum of 1 per cent each side of par. This can be interpreted as evidence of the ability of the Fund to learn from experience and exercise imaginative vision, contrary to the impression it has frequently given in the past. But the wider band may be short-lived, since IMF members may choose both not to use it themselves and to put pressures on others not to do so; in particular, the European countries may well want to revert to their previous programme of pursuing the establishment of a common currency through the initial phase of gradually eliminating variations in their currencies' values relative to one another. Also, as mentioned in earlier chapters, the economic function of the wider band is to transfer some of the burden of stabilizing speculation from the central bank to private banks and commercial enterprises, and further to enable the central bank to penalize so-called 'destabilizing speculation' by those who believe that the official par value of a currency cannot be held by its authorities. The wider band can do little if anything to solve the major problem of the system revealed by the experience of the past seven years or so, the necessity of adjusting par values to divergent price trends in the member countries of the system. Since there is no reason to believe, on the basis of the process by which the 1971 crisis was resolved, that nations have become any more willing than before either to harmonize their domestic economic policies or to make appropriate exchange rate changes with appropriate speed, the prospect of repeated international monetary crisis still looms before us.

International monetary crises, however, should not be identified with international economic collapse – as should be evident both from the past quarter-century of international monetary history and from the crisis of 1971 itself. So long as governments and their publics remain cognizant of the central lesson of the Keynesian revolution, that mass unemployment is an unnecessary and policy-avoidable evil, international monetary crisis will not be allowed to produce the kind of world economic disaster that the world's central bankers allowed it to produce in the early 1930s. For that boon, perhaps, public enlightenment about economic policy may be less responsible than the recognition in other countries, evident in the course of the 1971 crisis, that the United States is too big a factor in world production, demand and employment for anyone really to want to try to force its Administration, even if this were possible, to the classical gold-standard remedy for a balance-of-payments deficit, namely mass deflation of demand and consequent mass unemployment.

The international monetary system itself aside, there remains the problem that, despite the agreement by the Europeans to negotiate with the Americans on the broad issues of trade policy that have increasingly been irking the latter, the crisis and the temporary import surcharge gave a fillip to protectionism in the United States that may well have produced a permanent change in U.S. attitudes towards the world economy and its system of organization. In this connection, European irresponsibility towards the international monetary system in 1970–71 may impose a heavy future cost on the less developed part of the world, which has gained greatly from the generally liberal pattern of world trade and monetary arrangements in the past twenty-five years and stands to lose most from any significant retreat into protectionism and regionalism.

Author Index

Subject Index